I0892878

KINDRED
VOICES

KINDRED VOICES

A LITERARY HISTORY OF MEDIEVAL ANATOLIA

Michael Pifer

Yale
UNIVERSITY PRESS
New Haven & London

Published with assistance from the foundation established in memory of Calvin Chapin of the Class of 1788, Yale College.

Copyright © 2021 by Michael Pifer.
All rights reserved.
This book may not be reproduced, in whole or in part, including illustrations, in any form (beyond that copying permitted by Sections 107 and 108 of the U.S. Copyright Law and except by reviewers for the public press), without written permission from the publishers.

Yale University Press books may be purchased in quantity for educational, business, or promotional use. For information, please email sales.press@yale.edu (U.S. office) or sales@yaleup.co.uk (U.K. office).

Set in MT Baskerville and MT Bulmer types by Newgen North America.
Printed in the United States of America.

Library of Congress Control Number: 2020951728
ISBN 978-0-300-25039-8 (hardcover : alk. paper)

A catalogue record for this book is available from the British Library.

This paper meets the requirements of ANSI/NISO Z39.48-1992 (Permanence of Paper).

10 9 8 7 6 5 4 3 2 1

For Knar

Though it is wingless, featherless,

It goes faster than the swallow.

It roams aimlessly from country to country,

It returns, it comes, bringing many guests.

—Nersēs Shnorhali (fl. twelfth century)

O Solomon, tune the strings of that ḳopuz,

That we may learn this language of the birds.

—Gülşehrī (fl. early fourteenth century)

CONTENTS

MAP 1. Anatolia and neighboring regions, c. 1280.

A NOTE ON TRANSLITERATION AND CITATION

Medieval Anatolia was awash with many languages and scripts, as well as with authors and audiences with multiple cultural affiliations. To keep things as simple as possible for the reader, this book generally follows the transliteration system of the *International Journal of Middle East Studies* for Arabic, Persian, and Turkish. For Classical and Middle Armenian, it uses the Library of Congress's romanization system, which is perhaps the most readable for nonspecialists and therefore preferred here. For Greek, it uses the transliteration system of the *Journal of Modern Greek Studies.* Words that frequently appear in English (Qur'an, Sufi, etc.) and place-names that are still in use today preserve their common English spellings. Other proper names from the medieval period appear with diacritical marks.

For those who care to wade deeper into the weeds: many words, particularly names and titles, appear in more than one linguistic context and could thus potentially be transliterated in different ways. The name of the Sufi order founded by Rūmī's followers after his death might be rendered as Mawlawiyya (reflecting a transliteration from Arabic), Mawlaviyya (from Persian), or Mevleviye (from Turkish, which also gives us the Mevlevi order in common English usage). In such cases, transliteration adheres to the linguistic context most relevant to the discussion at hand (Persian in this example). The same is true for the titles of works and names of individuals: the poet Gülşehrī composed verse in Persian and Turkish but is better known for his Turkish poetry (and, presumably, for being Turkish). And so he appears here as Gülşehrī and not as Gulshahrī (reflecting a transliteration from Persian).

Another caveat: Middle Armenian is rich with sundry loanwords of Arabic, Persian, and Turkish origin. In cases where I transliterate those loanwords directly from the Armenian script, my transliteration follows the Armenian spelling unless otherwise noted. It is therefore worth observing that true consistency in spelling, imposed by a single transliteration system, remains elusive when we speak of medieval Anatolia. On occasion, such uniformity would also be historically misleading in light of the complex linguistic and cultural heterogeneity of the period. My aim, then, is simply to be clear without erasing difference.

Last but not least, all citations of Rūmī's *Maṣnavī* in the notes give the book number, then the line number(s) after a colon.

INTRODUCTION

A Measured Hospitality

“The day was Saturday, on the cusp of Sunday, / and I was descending from the monastery on high,” says a certain Hovhannēs of Erzincan in a late medieval Armenian poem. He could not know, as he swung his censer and read aloud from the Psalms, that a stranger was about to change his life:

> For a time I was coming, for a time reading,
> That I might go and arrive by the midday hour.
> I came, and was engulfed in such flame.
> I did not write. I did not read.
>
> Someone rode a gray stallion,
> She came and passed by, daring as a Mongol,
> She had eyes that would conquer Tabriz,
> Her eyebrows bore away my mind.
>
> She dropped an apple. I paid no heed.
> She dropped another. I stooped and picked it up.
> “*Sēn miwsiwrman, Mōlla ghĕzi,*
> *Bēn Hovhannēs, kʿēshish oghli.*
> What does your apple have to do with me?”[1]

When Hovhannēs addresses Asha, the woman who would become his beloved, he does so in her language. “You are a Muslim, daughter of a *mullā*,” he explains simply in Turkish. “I am Hovhannēs, son of a priest.” And then he switches back to Middle Armenian—“What does your apple have to do with me?”

The poem is brimming with oppositions of many kinds: between the monk and Asha; between his superiors and her father the *mullā*; between Hovhannēs and his kin, who urge him not to associate with infidels; between Asha and her kin, who desire his conversion to Islam; between their respective Muslim and Christian communities, whose fault lines run deepest at the moment when convergence seems possible. In the end, Hovhannēs and Asha marry, binding their families together in a new—albeit contentious—network of kindred relations. Yet Asha’s conversion to Christianity, which occurs abruptly in the final stanza, would hardly resolve the manifold tensions that simmer between our protagonists and their societies. The multifaceted relationship between Hovhannēs and Asha, far from having little import, would seem to stir up lasting consequences for the city of Erzincan (or Erznka, as it is called in Armenian), touching the lives of *mullā*s, monks, and everyone in between.

Herein lies a great irony. Hovhannēs’s question—“What does your apple have to do with me?”—is meant to keep Asha at arm’s length. The effect, however, is the opposite. His question draws her into a multilingual dialogue that informs the structure, if not represents the primary theme, of the poem. Strikingly, by speaking in Asha’s language, Hovhannēs establishes a manner of communicating that is comprehensible to Armenian and Turk alike. What’s more, his knowledge of Turkish advances an implicit claim: he is already part of her world, even before her intrusion into his. This relationship, moreover, cuts both ways. Asha also calls to him, in her enticing voice, in both Turkish and Middle Armenian:

—Եօրու, եօրու, կեաւուր օղլի,
Կեօթուր պիզտէն մուհալ սօզի,
Սէն Յովհաննէս, քէշիշ օղլի,
Պէն միւսիւրման[,] մօլլա ղըզի,
Զիրար սիրենք խօշ կու լինի։

Rendering of Armeno-Turkish in the modern Turkish script:

—Yörü, yörü, gâvur oğli,
Götür bizden muhal sözi,
Sen Hovhannēs, keşiş oğli,
Ben müsürman[,] molla ğızi,
Zirar sirenkʿ khōsh ku lini.

Translation from Turkish to English:

—Come along, come along, infidel's son,
Drop the absurd talk with us!
You are Hovhannēs, son of a priest,
I am Muslim, daughter of a *mullā.*
Zirar sirenkʿ khōsh ku lini.[2]

"Let us love each other," Asha proposes at the end, speaking directly in Hovhannēs's mother tongue. "*Khōsh ku lini,*" she reassures him. *It will be sweet.*[3] Her voice serves as a foil to his own, mirroring his code switching even as she puts forth a counterproposal. Asha teases a union that seems unthinkable yet in some ways has already arrived.

The story of Hovhannēs and Asha belongs to a polyvocal and multireligious world, made both legible and audible by these dialogic verses. In fact, this poem is littered with sundry poetic techniques, unhomed from any single language. An octosyllabic meter, common to both Armenian and Turkish poetry, runs through our lovers' dialogue, uniting their languages within the same rhythmic pattern.[4] Most stanzas end in blocks of the same end rhyme (*aaaa, bbbb*), a literary technique reminiscent of monorhyme in Arabic poetry, which Armenians had adapted several centuries prior.[5] In contrast to Asha, who converts irrevocably to Christianity by the poem's end, the language of the poem wanders freely across multiple cultural terrains, picking up loanwords of Arabic, Persian, and Turkish origin along the way.

Through this encounter, we are invited to consider—as medieval audiences were invited to consider—the knotty problem of negotiating competing claims for one's affiliation. As this poem makes clear, different axes of belonging—religion, language, community, even poetics—were not bundled together uniformly but instead could engage premodern audiences in different ways, and to different ends, at the same time. This poem, in other words, is highly performative. It depicts the union between a Christian and Muslim, but it also showcases an evolving set of relationships, borne across a dizzying array of languages and peoples, that had recently given rise to new expressions of literary culture even beyond Erznka. How, then, might we begin to parse this convergence in literary systems or account for the heterogeneous communities that produced and read poems like this one? How did premodern poets and audiences, from diverse ethnic and religious affiliations, navigate these shared languages, and intersecting ways of living and being, through literature? And how might a closer attentiveness to this poetic mode, in which the voices of disparate peoples mixed together in oppositional and transformative ways, provoke a more integrative mapping of Anatolian literary history?

Kindred Voices tells the story of a seismic shift in the literary production of medieval Anatolia, from roughly 1250 to 1340, by shedding light on chimeric couplings of many kinds: those unexpected unions thematized within, and enacted by, the composition of poems such as *Hovhannēs and Asha*. As we shall see, the commingling of diverse peoples and languages shaped the literary landscape here in significant ways, binding together Muslim and Christian poets in analogous modes of composing poetry and policing the confessional boundaries of their audiences. Sundry unions—between peoples, religious cultures, even aesthetic systems—furthermore played important roles in the development of nascent literary cultures, such as Anatolian Turkish and Middle Armenian, and in the subtle transformation of preexisting ones in Anatolia, including New Persian and, in some cases, medieval Greek. At its core, this book offers a new understanding of poetry and of poetic composition in medieval Anatolia, charting the ways in which its literary cultures came to be networked together, across a host of heterogeneous societies, in complex and asymmetrical ways.

During this period, the land of Rūm ("Rome," or the formerly Byzantine territories) was in a state of political instability and demographic flux. Anatolia had long been a predominantly Christian region, populated mainly by Greeks and Armenians, and to a lesser extent by Georgians and Syrians. However, after the collapse of the Bagratuni and Artsruni Armenian kingdoms in the mid-eleventh century, and following the victory of the Seljuk Turks over the Byzantines in 1071, Armenians migrated southward and westward in large numbers.[6] Armenian sources of the thirteenth century assert an expansive Hayastan (Armenia) that included territory from Sis in Cilicia to Gandzak in Azerbaijan, despite the fact that Armenians had, for the most part, lost sovereignty over much of this space.[7] Cilicia, the last Armenian kingdom, on the northeastern shores of the Mediterranean Sea, was settled by the descendants of migrant Armenian nobles and their families on the fringes of this sizable territory.

Of course, in this period, many if not most boundaries in Anatolia were fuzzy—both territorially and culturally—even though they did not, at the same time, cease to exist. In this book, the term "Anatolia," a Latinization of the Greek *anatolē* ("east," or where the sun "rises up"), is used in the modern sense to demarcate a peninsula whose hazy eastern frontier runs roughly along a diagonal line from the eastern region of the Taurus Mountains to Trebizond (now Trabzon). This book thus employs "Anatolia," as well as its closest premodern analogue, "Rūm," to discuss a geographic region that drew together actors from different principalities, empires, and intercultural zones, even as it does so without erasing the specific peoples and pasts that populated this contested space.[8]

It is therefore important to observe that this age of migration and displacement did not extend to Armenians alone. For entirely different reasons, itinerant Persian scholars, looking for patronage and new audiences, traveled westward from Khorasan at this time, bringing many landmark literary and theological works with them.[9] So too did Turkic peoples from Central Asia settle throughout the lands of Rūm, a region which Arabs, Jews, and Kurds also called home. This influx of Turkic peoples would begin gradually in the eleventh and continue in the thirteenth century, when the Mongol incursions would overturn the regional balance of power once more. These waves of migrations and invasions would also have a profound effect on cultural production in Rūm, tilting its center of gravity eastward, away from Byzantium and toward the Persianate world. The interior of Anatolia, where this story largely takes place, would be gradually drawn into the cultural currents that swept through Central Asia, the Iranian plateau, and much of the Middle East.[10]

As this story begins, Byzantine power is on the wane. Soon Rūm, now ruled by the Seljuks, a Turkic dynasty that had come to occupy a large swath of central Anatolia, will be effectively reduced to a protectorate of the Mongols, in 1248.[11] Multiple *beyliks*, small principalities run by Türkmen rulers (*beys*), will shortly begin to be carved out across Rūm, further fragmenting its kaleidoscopic political landscape. The Ottomans, who shall govern a beylik just southwest of Byzantium, will eventually sweep away their rivals—along with the Byzantines—in the ascendant name of ʿOs̱mān (fl. early fourteenth century).[12] It is no wonder, then, that local governors and religious authorities began to face a similar set of problems during this era: How to strengthen community bonds at a time of widespread migration? How to stabilize a region where power changed hands so rapidly? And how to communicate—even with a single people—across a sea of seemingly irreducible difference?

Poets, the main protagonists of this story, grappled with such questions as well, in part because they sought to bring new audiences together, gradually transforming outsiders into intimates and strangers into kinfolk. These figures came to practice a measured hospitality, selectively accommodating some—but not all—forms of linguistic and cultural alterity within their literary production. Many are still celebrated as foundational or pivotal figures within their own literary traditions, such as Jalāl al-Dīn Rūmī in Persian, Yūnus Emre in Turkish, and Frik and Kostandin Erznkatsʿi in Armenian. Others have fallen into relative obscurity, despite the significance of their works during their lifetimes, such as Sulṭān Valad and ʿĀşıḳ Paşa, who both composed verse in Arabic, Persian, and Turkish. These poets were not attached to any court and certainly did not receive patronage for the composition of rhymed verse. Yet over the course of three generations, this cohort of wordsmiths collectively helped to usher in a new era of Anatolian literary history.

Too often, modern scholarship has treated these poets in relative isolation from one another, fracturing the literary field along rigid lines of ethnic difference. When read alongside each other, however, these figures reveal a more tessellated literary landscape of premodern Anatolia, provoking a reevaluation of the boundaries that are often drawn around their respective poetic cultures. For example, Sulṭān Valad, Rūmī's son and eventual successor, composed many early lines of colloquial Greek poetry, drawing upon a Christian symbolic vocabulary to impart an Islamic message. ʿĀşıḳ Paşa, who composed an early book of Turkish poetry in Anatolia, penned a Middle Armenian couplet in this same work, performatively asserting that all languages could participate in divine revelation. Similarly, the Armenian poet Frik quoted linguistically Persian verses in his devotional poetry even as he instructed his audience to read those verses through Christian eyes.

A kind of strategic multilingualism is at play here, in which similar voices asserted dissimilar visions for the future of Rūm. Many other interlocutors joined in this dialogue, weaving a patchwork of literal and symbolic languages, at once interconnected and pulled taut by incongruous desires. Theirs is the invitation of Asha: an address both familiar and foreign, sonorous and seductive, provoking encounter and demanding response. Of course, as Hovhannēs reminds us, convergences in the literary landscape were also fraught terrains. Here forms of cultural and linguistic reciprocity came to mark the front lines of a fervent competition, waged over the many orientations and affiliations of Rūm's diverse audiences. This is the story of that competition, of Asha's invitation and Hovhannēs's response, and the ways in which a century of cross-cultural exchange would radically transform literary production across medieval Anatolia.

So: what does your apple have to do with me?

From Literary Trees to Polyvocal Communities

"The History of Ottoman Literature has yet to be written," remarked the visionary Orientalist E. J. W. Gibb in 1900.[13] One might suppose that this sentence, which inaugurates his six-volume *A History of Ottoman Poetry,* would ring false by the time his monumental study reached its conclusion. But Gibb, with typical modesty, acknowledged that his work would never be comprehensive. Indeed, his predecessor, the Austrian scholar Joseph von Hammer-Purgstall, had already produced a thorough compendium of the lives of Ottoman poets some sixty years prior.[14] Whereas Hammer-Purgstall's history loosely resembles the premodern genre of the *tazkira,* a collection of vignettes culled from the lives and works of poets, Gibb's landmark literary history follows a different trajectory. His intention was ultimately "to trace the successive phases through which Ottoman poetry has passed, to discover the influences which have brought these about, and in this way to present as it were a panorama of the rise and progress of this poetry."[15] The result, a meticulous work of scholarship, was the first attempt to spin out the entire scope of Ottoman literary history on a continuous narrative thread.

Of course, with "Ottoman," Gibb had something particular in mind. He was not occupied with most, or even many, of the literatures produced within the Ottoman Empire, which at its height wrapped halfway around the Mediterranean basin and was home to a wide array of peoples and tongues. Nor did he wish to focus exclusively on poetry composed for the court, where Ottoman sovereigns conducted their affairs. Instead, because Arabic and Persian literary cultures were already known in the West, he wished to correct a general impression among his compatriots that "Turks have no literature."[16] *A History of Ottoman Poetry* therefore endeavors, with a few detours, to tell a story about Anatolian Turkish peoples: their singular labor, upon a single literary tradition, throughout the ages unto the present day. Gibb's innovation, in other words, was to narrate the "progress" of a literature in a manner reminiscent of how one might narrate the history of a nation.

At the dawn of the twentieth century, the intersection between literary history and national history looked quite broad. Two years after Gibb's first volume saw the light of day, his friend Edward G. Browne produced the first installment of *A Literary History of Persia,* another magisterial work based upon a similar organizing principle. Tellingly, Browne, the erudite son of a shipbuilding magnate, took his inspiration not from literary studies but rather from the popular national histories of his day.[17] In the same vein, he likewise set out to explain "the national genius" of the Persians themselves. "For it was the intellectual history of the Persians which I desired to write," he explains to his readers, "and not merely the history of the poets and authors who expressed their thoughts through the medium of the Persian language."[18] Just eight years later, in 1910, Vrtʿanēs Pʿapʿazean broke similar ground with the revised publication of his panoramic *History of Armenian Literature* (*Patmutʿiwn hayotsʿ grakanutʿean*), tracing the development of Armenian literary production from just before its dawn, when poems and songs were transmitted orally and the Armenian alphabet did not yet exist, until his present day.[19] This too is the story of a literature, oral and written, only insofar as it was first the story of a people whose existence necessarily anticipated it.[20]

We need not look far to encounter similar histories from adjacent literary cultures. A popular literary history of the Greeks, which claims that their literature sprang from the soil "without marked traces of foreign admixture," was published in English in 1890, for instance.[21] Four years later, a literary history that surveys Syriac authors, half-heartedly praised as "apt enough pupils of the Greeks," likewise saw the light of day.[22] And in New York City, the publishing house Charles Scribner's Sons ran an entire series in the same spirit. By the time Browne's *Literary History of Persia* graced its presses, so too had monographs on the literatures of India, Ireland, and America; soon, new volumes on the literatures of Jews, Arabs, Scots, Russians, and the French would join their ranks. Generally speaking, these literary histories aim to render disparate artifacts of cultural production meaningful insofar as they bear the indelible fingerprints of a single ethnic group.[23] The enduring masterpieces of a people, read along monolingual and monoethnic pathways of transmission, were now capable of furnishing nations with comprehensive cultural genealogies of how they came to be.[24]

We might call this the etic approach to literary history, which projects modern categories of analysis, reverse-engineered from the nation form, backward onto our premodern subjects. Were we to visualize the shape of such history, it would undoubtedly assume the form of an insular family tree, rarely deviating from its essentially racial or ethnic roots. Although each tree's branches might intertwine with those of other trees, their trunks ascend in a continuous manner, remaining indisputably legible as "Turkish," "Persian," "Armenian," "Greek," "Syriac," or "Georgian." We can graph these national literary histories as an unbroken series of linear and parallel lines, each branching independently along a similarly historical and morphological axis, each essentially rooted upon an incongruently national or ethnic soil.[25] In other words, the conceptual shape of etic literary history does more than arrange its narrative in a chronological fashion. Namely, the arboreal model arguably produces many of literary history's analytic categories, including the notion that each "nation" must have its own correspondent literary "tradition," as well as an overinflated binary between what is indigenous and what is exogenous to a particular cultural set. In this conception, outside influences upon a literary tradition are symptoms of a more pernicious disease: the dilution of a people's genuine national character by foreign elements, if not by foreigners themselves.[26]

This close correlation of nationalism and literary history, in which "the importance of linguistic barriers was quite unduly magnified," has long been observed.[27] But while our understanding of such barriers—linguistic, cultural, religious—has necessarily changed over the past century, literary histories that concern medieval Anatolia have not always kept pace. Much of the scholarship produced on Anatolian literary history over the twentieth century continued to cleave to various iterations of this arboreal model. Hence we find a proliferation of studies on Turkish *or* Persian *or* Armenian *or* Greek literature, many of which employ a largely monoethnic or monolingual framework even without necessarily falling back on essentialized notions of race or language. There is, of course, a sharp difference between premodern literary histories based on the nation form and those that simply skew toward a single ethnic or linguistic case study. Still, the arboreal model enjoys a precedence that rarely merits the justification, or sometimes even the acknowledgment, of its practitioners.

In fact, the earliest challenges to the arboreal model have come from beyond literary studies. This is in part because Mehmet Fuat Köprülü, a towering scholar who helped to inaugurate the modern era of Turkish studies, employed the phylogenetic tree to such persuasive effect that it took root in a variety of disciplines. Köprülü was particularly occupied by—what seemed to him—a difficult truth to swallow: the earliest poets of Anatolian Turkish unabashedly drew inspiration from Persian literature. What, then, was so Turkish about the origins of Anatolian Turkish poetry? For Köprülü and his many followers, the predominate solution was to bifurcate Turkic literary culture along high and low expressions of religiosity, positing that urban poets fell under Persian influence but rural poets retained their authentic folk traditions.[28] Only in recent decades have scholars, such as Cemal Kafadar, Ahmet T. Karamustafa, Tijana Krstić, and Ethel Sara Wolper, begun to problematize these binaries. Others, including Seta B. Dadoyan, Antony Eastmond, Rachel Goshgarian, Dimitri Korobeinikov, Sergio La Porta, Nicolas Trépanier, and Sara Nur Yıldız, have unsettled a host of anachronistically national and religious categories of analysis, within not only Islamicate but also Christian case studies.[29] This growing cohort of historians, rather than positioning Muslims and Christians as pugilistic antagonists or as premodern forerunners of multiculturalism and tolerance, has brought needed attention to intense forms of cross- and intracultural negotiation by the peoples of Rūm.[30]

To conceive of Anatolian literary history as more than a grove of independent trees, we must also consider how cross- and intracultural negotiations informed the composition of poetry. As a number of studies on shared poetic genres and forms in medieval Anatolia attest, it is now well known that the boundaries between cultures were more porous than initially envisioned at the dawn of the twentieth century.[31] Most recently, for instance, A. C. S. Peacock has shed light on the Islamization in Rūm from the joint perspective of Arabic, Persian, and Turkish literary texts, demonstrating that each played different roles in this process during Mongol rule.[32] Likewise, it is equally well known that the differences and conflicts between peoples did not resolve into some kind of frictionless, multicultural utopia.[33] The salient question now facing the field, then, is not to what extent literary production might refract cross-cultural porousness from a different historical perspective but rather in what ways the literary landscape is itself due for a reassessment on a more holistic level. This book therefore insists on the ways in which both Muslims and Christians negotiated the heterogeneity of their communities in a manner *specific* to literary production. In other words, it asks what the composition and performance of poetry might reveal about, and what ends they might serve within, the contested space of a multilingual and multireligious society.

Such questions recast the literary landscape in dialogic and responsive terms: less a grove of vertical family trees and more a horizontal series of pathways, spanning multiple languages and communities, that developed and shifted in relation to one another. As we shall see, far from eschewing the "foreign" and spurning what was "nonnative," poets in medieval Anatolia selectively welcomed the literary conventions of others into their compositions, if not actual others into their communities. This strategic accommodation of difference would fulfill a variety of functions that, in concert, would help to produce a social and religious sea change in medieval Anatolia. During this time, poetry provided a kind of social infrastructure, bringing together smaller communities within multifarious societies and imparting pointed forms of religious instruction or discipline. In fact, as this book shows, literary production helped the peoples of Rūm to navigate the complexity of their societies in many ways. Poetry prompted audiences to adopt specific cultural and literary affiliations; it trained readers to make meaning out of scriptural texts, preexisting literary works, and social contexts in similar manners; and it even redrew—but never totally erased—the subtle lines of inclusion and exclusion that bound some groups together and kept others apart. Above all, poetry conditioned a form of vision: a way of looking at the world, and of probing the cultural, linguistic, and religious boundaries that structured urban life.

In this light, it is not just that poets in Anatolia wrote verse against a diverse social and cultural backdrop. What matters, I contend, is that these poets explicitly and implicitly engaged with such diversity—and with one another—in discerning manners, striving to corral the unruly and heterogeneous world of medieval Anatolia into a coherent worldview. Moreover, they taught their audiences to do the same. "I know that every man cannot learn from scripture," writes Hovhannēs Erznkatsʿi, an Armenian poet whom we shall meet in chapters 1 and 7, in one poem. "That is why I wrote this," he concludes, "so you may hear it from me."[34] In the city of Konya, not so far from Erznka, the Persian poet Rūmī expressed a complementary sentiment. His poetic masterpiece, the *Maṣnavī,* was not a commentary on the Qur'an, he insisted. Rather, it *was* the Qur'an, insofar as it drew from the same divine wellspring of meaning, but revealed these secrets in a different way.[35] These poets, like so many others, used cosmopolitan literary conventions to compose poetry that was scripturally *adjacent,* seeking to incubate knowledge of Christianity or Islam in ways that scripture did not or could not. Significantly, they often did so by displaying a keen awareness of literary production in other linguistic and cultural contexts, and even by responding directly or indirectly to those contexts in their compositions.

Within the polyvocal societies of premodern Anatolia, in which different poets and poems often competed for the attention of similar (or even the same) audiences, the narrative threads of "national" literary history become inexorably tangled. These societies therefore share something with Hovhannēs and Asha, whose dialogic voices suggest a parable for literary production writ large. As we recall, Asha extends an invitation to Hovhannēs in his mother tongue; he answers her in kind, mirroring the rhythm and meter of her address. They speak, however, at cross-purposes: one interlocutor uses this language to urge conversion to Islam, just as the other employs it to reassert a Christian orientation. At the same time, a reciprocal poetics serves as the medium for the unfolding of this heated negotiation even as it unsettles the supposed absolutism of either position. It is in this sustained responsiveness—between Christians and Muslims, Armenians and Turks, languages and aesthetic systems—that a dialogic and integrative history of literary production in Anatolia begins to emerge. Of course, this history, like the poetics that preserves it, becomes legible only when we allow "Armenian" and "Turk" to inhabit the same stage: to react with and against one another; to accept some overtures and reject others; in a word, to *speak* to each other. And, on a much vaster scale, the same is true about the expansive dialogue that unfolds within, and across, the many poetic cultures of Rūm.

The Adaptive Act

Kindred Voices restores this dialogism to our understanding of the Anatolian literary landscape, shedding light on the relationships that premodern poets crafted for themselves—and their communities—laterally across multiple linguistic and cultural contexts. Certainly, all utterances are dialogic, as Mikhail Bakhtin reminds us, since all speech anticipates a response from others (whether those others were originally intended as addressees or not).[36] However, in medieval Anatolia, this responsiveness was also filtered through a particular historical dynamic. Composition, in this world, was a social activity. After all, to compose for an audience is essentially to engage with an audience; it is simultaneously to respond to the expectations of a community and to elicit certain responses in return. It is therefore not surprising that the composition of poetry reflected the mixed demographic character of Rūm.

Over the arc of this book, we shall observe as authors and audiences respond to one another, and to the diverse literary cultures that developed in Anatolia, through a variety of literary techniques. Here it is common to find Muslims marshaling the imagery, and even the theological language, of Christianity to teach an audience about Islam. So too is it common to come across Christians who rewrote the poetics of Islamicate or Persianate literature to instruct an audience in Christianity. Sometimes poets responded to a poem in one language by composing a new work in a different language, preserving the meter and style but altering the narrative content. At other times, audiences asked poets to engage with the literary field in a selective manner, ushering a single discourse, trope, or narrative into a new linguistic orbit of meaning making. The sheer variety of this activity can be somewhat arresting and therefore difficult to pin down with a critical vocabulary specific to any single language, either modern or premodern.

To the extent that these different acts are related, however, it is still through an easily recognizable gesture: a set of practices by which authors and audiences reached across the putative borders of their own literary traditions, first to admit and then to alter the poetics of adjacent literatures. Such carefully hospitable gestures lie at the heart of our story. A primary argument of *Kindred Voices* is that a broad portfolio of compositional techniques—gloss and commentary, citation and quotation, emulation and adaptation, translation and transposition, response and rejoinder, paraphrase and pastiche—played a crucial role in shaping a fundamentally integrative literary landscape in medieval Anatolia. This landscape was integrative to the extent that poets and audiences were broadly cognizant of poetic trends and texts produced in nearby communities and often drew upon this knowledge to provisionally re-create, in different tongues, the literary cultures of their neighbors.[37]

Most simply, these practices helped to facilitate the migration of what Sheldon Pollock calls "a prevailing set of norms" or cosmopolitan literary "codes," including "everything from lexicon and metric to rhetoric, genre, and aesthetic," across multiple linguistic systems and religious communities.[38] It is important to note, however, that these practices not only produced cross-cultural convergence in the literary field but also served as sorting mechanisms after convergences had already taken place. Hence, they often attempted to make convergences legible and meaningful—but in the "right" way. By imposing new meanings upon literary codes that had ceased to belong to any single people or language, poets in Anatolia often reasserted certain religious or confessional boundaries, at a time when differences were not always clear in the aesthetic, literary, or musical realm. To put this differently, the literary landscape of Rūm may have been drawn together by affinitive literary forms and styles shared across its many poetic cultures, but it was also drawn apart by disparities that could not be so easily absorbed.

Let us begin this journey, then, by examining an act of adaptation that would inform literary production for centuries to come. In 1045, a powerful Armenian named Grigor Magistros, who held the Byzantine office of *dux Mesopotamiae*, entered into a heated debate with a Muslim, whom he simply names "Manazi," in Constantinople.[39] This figure, identified by Abraham Terian as Abū Naṣr al-Manāzī, a vizier to the ʿAbbasids, reportedly put forth a bold claim: the Qur'an was superior to the Bible not only theologically but also aesthetically, as its language soared to sublime heights that the New Testament could not hope to reach.[40] Al-Manāzī rested this argument on one point in particular. "While it is not difficult for poets to theologize in a new way and on their own," he claimed, "such expression, however, flows with difficulty from the outset." In contrast, as he asserted, the Prophet was "endowed with the Spirit" and therefore could recite the spiritual verses of the Qur'an in "identical rhyme" without effort.[41] The argument, at its heart, is a simple one. The labor of poets is not equivalent to the grace of the "Spirit."

Grigor, surprisingly, conceded this point. He therefore proposed, with the help of the Holy Spirit, to rewrite the Bible as a long-form poem in Classical Armenian. Moreover, he proposed to do so by employing monorhyme, a poetic technique common in Arabic literature, in which each line terminates with the same sound. This had not previously been attempted in Armenian poetry. Yet, so emboldened, Grigor threw down the gauntlet:

> Then, placing my hope in the Holy Spirit, in the Lord, the Creator and Sustainer, I began to say, "It is neither through prophetic vision nor through signs, nor through skill, but that the poetry of the Arabs, as in the course of ordinary speech, tends to end the lines with rhyme, which you call *qāfiya*. Since you deem it a prophetic revelation, that which took your Muḥammad forty years to write, I could put it in lines for you in four days, beginning from Adam until the second coming of his Creator. Moreover, I could write it for you in lines ending with that magnificent rhyme of the letter *nūn* which you were praising." And [al-Manāzī] kept betting, many a time, "You couldn't do it."[42]

Obviously, there is more at work here than a willingness to experiment in rhyme. In effect, Grigor sought to demonstrate that the Holy Spirit guided the aesthetics of Christian poetry in a way that would be legible, even audible, to his Muslim counterpart. Hence, if it took the Prophet forty years to recite the Qur'an, it would take Grigor only four days, so long as the Holy Spirit aided him.

True to his word, Grigor set about composing a versified adaptation of the Bible, preserving a singular rhyme scheme (ending in the sound *een*) throughout. Four days later, he appeared before al-Manāzī again and began to read his finished poem. In his performing voice, the Bible acquired a strange new sound, previously unheard in Armenian literature. In short, it used a rhyme scheme common to Arabic poetry, even as it co-opted this rhyme to subvert the Qur'an. Reportedly, al-Manāzī was dumbstruck, although not exactly by Grigor or his Bible:

> He was astounded, greatly amazed, and choking with stutter, he asked, "By what skill were you able to write this book so expertly and quickly?" In my truthfulness I said, "When we Christians resort to prayer, the Holy Spirit comes to our aid and teaches us the whole truth." And he confessed with astonishment that the God of the Christians is great.[43]

This (highly dubious) response strikes at the heart of Grigor's adaptation. What his versified Bible really amounts to, as I have argued elsewhere, is a defense of Christianity via an astonishing show of poetic equivalency—a demonstration that Armenian poetry can do what Arabic poetry can do, and, most important, that it can do so with divine sanction.[44] Grigor's composition and positionality as a poet therefore serve as proof texts, sites in which Armenian Christians and Arab Muslims might see an uncanny commingling of poetic systems, supposedly prompting even a learned Muslim scholar to proclaim the soundness of the Christian faith. Yet it is significant that Grigor does not appeal to a theological or overtly polemical argument to achieve this miraculous outcome. He appeals, instead, to a manner of composing poetry that is familiar to both parties, one in which authorship hangs upon divine providence. The salient question, which we shall revisit throughout this book, is why a poet might feel compelled to undertake this adaptive labor in the first place. Whom is this poem really for?

After all, there is no indication that al-Manāzī understood a great deal of Classical Armenian (though perhaps we should not sell this polymath short). Nor is it entirely believable that this "Manazi," stunned by Grigor's virtuosic performance, confessed the truth of Christianity. The dialogue between Grigor and "Manazi," then, likely seeks to engage with a different kind of audience, one that lingers just beyond the frame of this encounter. In short, this poem and its supplementary account of creation would seem to be intended for the consumption of other Armenians. As S. Peter Cowe has observed in his important article on Islamicate and Armenian poetics, diverse Armenian poets began to employ monorhyme in their compositions in the centuries following Grigor's adaptation, apparently using the versified Bible as their model. This in turn facilitated a subtle epistemic shift in Armenian literary production, as monorhymed poetry came to serve as a suitable vehicle for conveying scientific and philosophical thought, which previously was the domain of prose.[45]

In other words, there really is a conversion at the heart of this story, but it is not the conversion of "Manazi." Instead, what becomes "Christian" is the *poetics* of a "Manazi"—the alluring sound that (re)produces a different kind of Bible, and different forms of knowledge, for a Christian audience familiar (to whatever degree) with Arabic poetry. Grigor, through a praxis of adaptation and a story that frames this praxis, thus provides his audience with a manner of theorizing their own literary production, should they choose to compose in monorhyme and partake of the gifts of the Spirit for themselves. Hence, formal innovations in Armenian literary culture were not only aesthetic exercises but also bore lasting consequences for how audiences considered what literature is and, more important, what literature can *do*. Grigor and Manazi are not the only figures that matter in this story, and the adoption of monorhyme is a cogent example of this.

Of course, Grigor still borrows from al-Manāzī, and not the other way around. This is perhaps what has made scholars like Köprülü so uncomfortable with the Turkish adoption of Persianate poetics: from a formal perspective, the putatively active literary culture imprints itself, so it would seem, upon its passive counterpart. Hence Köprülü—and many others—framed this kind of adaptive labor as a choice (in fact, a dreadfully wrong choice) by the "influenced" poet, who mimics the works of foreigners without pausing to count the cost.[46] Particularly in the early twentieth century, when modern notions of "originality" and "authenticity" were valued above all, formalist mappings of literary exchange ironically seemed to reinforce the marginal status of certain literatures upon the global literary stage. Thus, as we have seen, classical Greek literature was considered autochthonous and self-reflexive, a sign system that ultimately indexed the ancient Greeks themselves. But lesser-studied literatures, such as Syriac, were relevant only insofar as they too pointed back toward the Greeks.

Vestigial traces of this problem still linger today. One does not necessarily need to know about Grigor to study Arabic literary production. However, scholars must grapple with the presence of al-Manāzī to understand the production of Armenian poetry in eleventh-century Constantinople. It is a simple yet unfortunate truth that adaptations such as Grigor's Bible have not spurred a broader reevaluation of how literary production worked, on the ground, within Islamicate literatures—such as Arabic, Persian, and Turkish—which are increasingly grouped together as a comparative set based on a shared religious culture.

Poets like Grigor challenge us to expand this set, in part because they allow us to consider how the intersections between premodern literary cultures could extend beyond doctrinal commonalities, just as they also generally transcended modern anxieties about influence. From Grigor's point of view, the versified Bible was successful because it *preserved* a gesture backward toward Arabic poetics while still opening a space of difference between Classical Armenian and Islamicate literature. His explicit focus on the circumstances in which he composed poetry thus allows us to envision medieval literary composition in more emic terms—that is, in ways closely aligned with how premodern authors conceived of their own poetic compositions and the kindred ties they forged with other literary cultures, both in theory and in praxis. Moreover, when we peer at the literary landscape "from the inside out," to borrow Pollock's phrasing,[47] we find that this modality of composition regularly comes to the fore: a set of practices by which poets drew upon preexisting literary models and strategically recombined diverse literary codes in the service of new contexts and audiences. From this vantage point, it becomes clear that the constituent elements that cohere in any literary code are far more mobile, and far more fungible, than arboreal models of literary history have long suggested.

A View of Composition from Above

Here it is instructive to broaden our view of premodern composition beyond the Anatolian Peninsula. Throughout this book, I shall trace literary production along two general axes. The first is one of linguistic orientation, perhaps best defined by the Persianate sphere: that is, those literatures which drew aesthetic cues—large or small portions of their literary codes—from New Persian literature. By the thirteenth century, New Persian had begun to loom large in the Islamicate world, rivaling Arabic in prestige and even making inroads into Central Asia, the Caucasus, and China. At the outset of our story, Persianate literary culture had already begun to set down roots in Anatolia, where it would interface with Middle Armenian and Anatolian Turkish in different ways.[48]

The second axis, however, was never so linguistically tethered. Instead, it comprised a set of adaptive techniques of composition that was common throughout the premodern world. In recent decades, scholars such as Paul E. Losensky, Walter G. Andrews, Saliha Paker, Franklin D. Lewis, and Murat Umut Inan have shown that equivalent practices have played a central role in the development of many literatures, particularly during the early modern period (c. 1500–1800). In Renaissance Italy, for instance, authors fashioned a new vernacular literary culture partly through the studied emulation of literary models from earlier historical eras, a practice known as *imitatio*. Another form of literary emulation, known in Persian as *istiqbāl* ("welcoming" or "reception"), shaped the development of Safavid literature, allowing a new generation of poets to engage with, and subtly rewrite, the poetry of their predecessors. So too did early modern Turkish poets compose verse in like ways, in particular by writing *naẓīre* (Persian: *naẓīra*), parallel poems, in response to individual works created by their Persian counterparts.[49]

This book establishes that analogous praxes of composition have a longer history, and indeed a more culturally, linguistically, and religiously entangled legacy, than is often realized. A more expansive view of these praxes, alongside an attendant metastory *about* composition, also teases a more integrative mapping of the foundational literary works that were produced in the medieval period, helping to recalibrate modern, post-romanticist conceptions of literary "adaptation" from a series of premodern and emic perspectives.

In fact, a constellation of adaptive practices played crucial roles in the (re)formation of multiple literary cultures from al-Andalus to the Levant, Anatolia to the Iranian Plateau. For instance, to the southeast of Anatolia, John bar Maʿdanī (d. 1263), the Christian patriarch of Antioch, wrote

Syriac poetry as a counterpoint to Arabic literature, even crafting a direct literary response to Ibn Sīnā's *al-Qaṣīda al-ʿayniyya* (*Ode on the Soul*).[50] Other Syriac poets in the thirteenth century, such as Khāmīs bar Qardāḥē, employed literary tropes and genres common in Arabic poetry during this period, contributing to what some have called a renaissance of their tradition. Akin to their Armenian counterparts, these Syriac Christians infused their own literary codes with new modes of expression, yet they did so by engaging in oppositional dialogue with the Islamicate world.[51]

To the northeast of Rūm, Georgians likewise repopulated Persian literary models with their own concerns, characters, and settings. Shotʿa Rustʿaveli (fl. late twelfth to early thirteenth century), the author of the *Vepʿkhistqaosani* (*The Man in the Panther's Skin*), a seminal Georgian romance, writes quite matter-of-factly about his source of inspiration. "This Persian tale, now done into Georgian, has hitherto been like an orphan pearl, cast in play from hand to hand," he famously declares. "Now I have found it and mounted it in a setting of verse."[52] In premodern Europe, memory was generally prized above imagination and "creativity," as Mary Carruthers has shown; medieval authorship often relied less on a process of composition ex nihilo than on the skillful internalization, collation, and recombination of preexisting texts in one's mental storehouse.[53] In the Caucasus, a roughly analogous understanding of composition seems to have taken root. Rustʿaveli frames his authorship as the labors of a treasure seeker and stone setter, both of which demand specialized knowledge and, indeed, distinct kinds of artistry. His is a creative labor *because* and not despite the fact that it works by means of rediscovery, reclamation, and recontextualization.[54]

This kind of analogy and this mode of writing were by no means unique. Indeed, similar praxes of composition seem to have multiplied in the eleventh and twelfth centuries, when new literary vernaculars developed from Europe to South Asia, in turn facilitating the spread of shared literary codes across an astonishing array of languages. In al-Andalus, for example, Jewish authors had employed the themes and vocabulary of Islamicate literature since at least the tenth century. These poets even developed a prosody that "lent Hebrew verse the rhythms of Arabic," imitating not only the content but also the very sonic qualities of Islamicate poetry, much as Armenians did on the other side of the Mediterranean basin.[55]

One product of this world, the twelfth-century author Petrus Alfonsi, a Jewish convert to Christianity, composed a frame tale in Latin, titled *Disciplina Clericalis* (*Discipline of the Clerics*), precisely in this manner. As Alfonsi reports, he sought to fashion didactic and moralizing stories by adapting "partly from the sayings of wise men and their advice, partly from Arab proverbs, counsels, fables and poems, and partly from bird and animal similes."[56] Most likely, as John Tolan has noted, this adaptation of "Arab proverbs, counsels, fables and poems" stems more from a particular tradition than from a single text.[57] Alfonsi probably had in mind the Arabic translation of the *Kalīla and Dimna,* which nests multiple stories within a single overarching narrative.[58] His adaptation of this tradition, made possible through the Latinate adoption of frame-tale technology, would prove immensely popular in Europe, in part clearing the way for subsequent frame tales, such as those in *The Decameron* by Giovanni Boccaccio (d. 1375) and *The Canterbury Tales* by Geoffrey Chaucer (d. 1400), in the following centuries.[59]

It is entirely fitting, then, that many masterworks of (retroactively) national literatures make overt gestures to their adaptive origins. This is true even when we visit locales that are removed from the Mediterranean world. For instance, in *The Canterbury Tales,* one of a group of pilgrims makes a strange request of the Clerk on the long road to Jerusalem. "Telle us som mery thing of aventures," the Host begs his erudite companion:

> Youre termes, youre colours, and youre figures,
> Kepe hem in stoor til so be ye endyte
> Heigh style, as whan that men to kinges wryte,
> Speketh so pleyn at this time, we yow preye,
> That we may understonde what ye seye.[60]

The clerk not only grants this request but also informs his audience that he has audaciously lifted his tale from the pen of Petrarch (d. 1374). In fact, Petrarch had adapted the same tale, about a maiden named Griselda, from Boccaccio, who in turn claimed to have fashioned it out of an oral variant.[61] However, we should recall that, in Chaucer's telling, the Host does not ask the Clerk merely to rehearse a popular tale for the benefit of a new audience. Rather, his request is highly particular: he desires the performance of a *type* of story ("som mery thing of aventures"), potentially adapted across linguistic boundaries, but not the transference of a certain rhetorical and poetic style ("youre termes, youre colours, and youre figures"), which the clerk is to keep in store. The clerk, however, weaves a crafty thread between these two desires: he makes selective alterations to Petrarch's Latin tale, whose content he denigrates as "impertinent," even as he still patterns his words in a rhetorically erudite style, in the ostensible trappings of a "heigh" literary culture.[62] In his performative retelling of this tale, the clerk thus offers an implicit reflection on the characteristics that encode English poetry *as* poetry, balancing the expectations of his local audience against the looming backdrop of the Latinate world.

Contemporary Muslim poets took part in an equivalent labor. In fact, Turkish literary history after the coming of Islam begins with a similar act. In the late eleventh century, Yūsuf Khāṣṣ Ḥājib helped to usher in the dawn of Turkish letters by composing the *Ḳutadgu bilig* (*Wisdom of Royal Glory*), the first Turkish mirror for princes, in the service of the Karakhanid court. Far east of Grigor's Constantinople, Yūsuf likewise made recourse to a poetic argument in which theory and praxis are impossible to untangle. "I found Turkish speech to be a wild mustang," he writes. "Grasping her gently, I drew her near. I caressed her and won her love."[63] In pragmatic terms, Yūsuf seems to have domesticated the "wild mustang" of Turkish speech by patterning the *Ḳutadgu bilig* in the *mutaqārib* meter, thus composing the earliest known Turkish work to employ *ʿarūż* (Arabic: *ʿarūḍ*), the metrical system that was previously the domain of Arabic and Persian literature.[64] In other words, his adaptive act configured the Turkish language as literary according to preexisting Arabic and Persian metrical forms even as it aimed to privilege Turkic understandings of sovereignty within the Islamicate world. Another irony, if only from the national vantage point: the domestication of Turkish as a literary language was demonstrated primarily by writing in the meters, genres, and literary styles of non-Turkic peoples.[65]

From our lofty vantage point, we can see that asymmetrical encounters among multiple literary cultures shaped each of these acts of composition. Likewise, each reflects the attempt by individuals (or by interpretive communities) to parse colliding literary orbits, on a macro scale, in highly minute and granular ways: on the level of style, narrative, genre, or meter. At the same time, each of these literary works is also quite different. So different, in fact, that to group them together on formal grounds would make little sense. Perhaps this is the reason why these works are rarely—if ever—discussed within the same comparative frame. The adaptive acts that shaped these masterworks provide a more robust basis for comparison, not because these acts are the same—for they each rest on a whole constellation of dissimilar historical, linguistic, and geographic contingencies—but because they allow us to envision how seemingly isolated acts of adapting other literatures were in fact quite commonplace, and indeed even foregrounded, through metaphor or narrative, in many of the major literary works produced in this period. To read such practices independently of one another, as though they were merely flukes in the grander scheme of literary history, is to miss a story so expansive that it seems to have vanished from our field of vision altogether: a particular process by which premodern literature is composed at the juncture of two or more languages, alongside the transference of a narrative from one tongue to another known as translation.

This broadened perspective helps to fine-tune the ways in which we measure poetic innovation during the medieval era, in terms of both those authors who emulated other authors and those poetic cultures that acquired parts of their literary "codes" from other languages. As this brief examination of composition suggests, across great swaths of the premodern world, artful composition had little to do with modern notions of "originality." Instead, new compositions were generally measured by their ability to introduce subtle permutations of meaning into preexisting literary models.[66] Perhaps counterintuitively, the development of cosmopolitan literary codes across multiple languages thus provided a baseline for poetic *differentiation* to occur, as diverse authors folded heterogeneity back into widely circulating literary genres, styles, and forms. This is especially true in the case of medieval Anatolia, where new forms of cross-cultural reciprocity and similar compositional techniques provided the grounds for poets to reassert difference from other literary systems in their works.

Arguably, even the Armenian adoption of Arabic literary conventions looks different when we consider that Muslim poets, in geographically adjacent cities, often composed texts by responding to other poetic cultures in an analogous manner. Armenian poets help to decenter the assumption that cross-cultural literary exchange occurred simply because all the participants were part of the Islamicate world, or that "minor" literatures were simply "influenced" by literary cultures attached to imperial powers or favored at court. Simply put, these adaptive modalities of composition were hallmarks of premodern literary production; they usher us into a world in which composition hung, as a rule, upon the circumspect response to other literary texts and codes. And, in this sense, literary production in the premodern world was quintessentially dialogic in nature, as it was guided by a responsiveness that others inspired. Yet this fuller picture emerges only once we expand our view to encompass more than a single encounter between lone Armenian and Arab poets.

In fact, there is reason to believe that Grigor would not have considered the flows of influence to be so unidirectional after all. "We must honestly admit," he notes, "that [al-Manāzī] was distinguished and highly esteemed for composing encomia and works in Homeric and Platonic meter and verse."[67] In practical and immediate terms, this meant that al-Manāzī could debate the merits of multiple literary systems, including Arabic and Greek, in a manner that was familiar to his Armenian interlocutor. Grigor's adaptation demonstrates an analogous aesthetic fluency, in both Armenian literary production and Armenian poets, by design. This is the entire subtext of the exchange: not just that Armenian poetry can do what Arabic does, or that Arabic poetry can do what Greek does, but that Grigor can do what al-Manāzī does. And, as he implicitly assures his readers, you might do it too.

A Road Map to Rūm

By enlisting modes of cross-cultural composition as our guides to medieval Rūm, we can map the connections between literary cultures as forms of labor and, indeed, as continually renegotiated relationships. In medieval Anatolia, both authors and audiences exercised a subtle agency in this labor, as did other interlocutors, seen and unseen, from other communities. So too did poetic texts (and literary codes) participate in this dialogue, suggesting the possibility of their own transformation, through new compositions, in other tongues.

Hovhannēs and Asha remind us that the stakes of engaging in this conversation, and of successfully navigating convergences in the literary landscape, were quite high. Because poetry aimed to produce a form of knowledge about living and being in medieval Anatolia, it would come to exert a unique force on the tides of Islamization and ensuing waves of counter-Islamization that swept through the region. From the mid-thirteenth through the mid-fourteenth century, adaptive praxes of composition there often had a dual function specific to Anatolia: they sought, simultaneously, to infuse fresh meaning into preexisting literary codes—even those produced by other peoples—and to offer religious instruction in a resonant manner. Hence, for many authors in premodern Anatolia, the composition of poetry and the assertion of confessional or communal boundaries were intimately entwined. To rewrite and reinterpret poetic works and literary cultures, then, was often to subtly redraw where those boundaries lay. Most simply, it was to offer a competing vision for belonging and meaning making in medieval Rūm.

This was the project of Jalāl al-Dīn Rūmī, a giant of Persian letters, whom we shall meet in chapters 1 and 2. When Rūmī left his home in Khorasan as a boy and migrated westward to Anatolia, he encountered a world in which it was customary to welcome strangers with song, dance, and forms of religious devotion. Chapter 1 paints a detailed picture of these encounters, reconstructing how medieval Anatolia encouraged Rūmī's poetic sensibilities. It particularly examines a metaphor employed by Rūmī—*dar āmīkhtan,* "to mix"—that both describes his own hospitable "mixing" with the peoples of Rūm and illuminates his adaptive practice of "mixing" together disparate literary styles, themes, tropes, and sources in the creation of a new literary work. Rūmī's masterpiece, the six-book collection of poetry known as the *Maṣnavī-yi maʿnavī* (*Rhymed Couplets of Spiritual Meaning*), is the very product of such mixing, as it recombines the style and meter of translocal Persian poets at the request of Rūmī's local followers.

From this beginning, chapter 2 offers a succinct close reading of the first story of the *Maṣnavī,* which ushers its audience into the hermeneutics of the entire work. Notably, this story depicts a dialogue between Rūmī and his foremost student, Ḥusām al-Dīn Chalabī, a native of Anatolia who was perhaps of Kurdish descent. Rūmī may have dictated the *Maṣnavī,* but it was Ḥusām al-Dīn who wrote it down, recited it back to his master in a strong voice, and taught others to read his manuscript aloud. I argue that the *Maṣnavī* is shaped by a form of dialogism, not only between

Rūmī and Ḥusām al-Dīn but also between the text and its audience, who performatively partake in the dynamics of its opening story: a strange encounter between a king in need of spiritual instruction and a visitor from another realm. When we read the *Maṣnavī*, we are also reading a miniature of Rūm, the product of a literary field shaped by authors and audiences in different ways. This chapter therefore establishes a pattern of omnivorous adaptation—and of generative dialogue—that we shall revisit throughout the book.

Chapter 3 examines what happened to this mode of composition, and the diverse interpretive communities in Konya, after Rūmī's death. There is a widespread assumption that Rūmī's son Sulṭān Valad felt an unbearable agony at the thought of succeeding his father. Whereas Rūmī's *Maṣnavī* is seen as generative and productive, Sulṭān Valad's poetry has long been viewed as reductive and less vital. In many ways, this assumption extends to the earliest literary works composed in Anatolian Turkish, which Sulṭān Valad helped to inaugurate as a literary language according to prevailing standards within the Persianate world. Stunningly, he composed his *Rabāb-nāma* (*Book of the Rebec*) in Arabic, Persian, Turkish, and Greek, encoding each language in the lyrical style and hermeneutical project of his father's masterwork. Although the concept of imitation was multifaceted in premodern Anatolia, this chapter shows that Sulṭān Valad did not conceive of literary emulation as a reductive, anxiety-riddled act. Instead, by "following" in the style of his father, he constructed a new literary genealogy for himself and his audiences—a genealogy that encompassed works of not only Persian poetry but also Greek and Turkish, now seen as fit to make meaning Islamically. I contend that such genealogies—of both the biological and the fictive variety—provide important sites for theorizing the kindred relationships among multiple literary cultures from a medieval point of view.

Chapter 4 broadens the geographic, textual, and generic scope of this story. Leaving behind the city of Konya, we follow Sulṭān Valad's representatives as they spread throughout Rūm. This allows us to envision how the intersecting literary landscapes of Anatolia might sound and resound as different kinds of performers recited Greek, Turkish, and Armenian poetry aloud. Warrior-minstrels cross our path from the Greek romance

Digenēs Akritēs, the Turkish *Book of Dede Ḳorḳut,* and the Armenian romance *The History of the Youth Farman,* singing songs that are strangely reminiscent of one another.

This journey culminates in an encounter with Yūnus Emre, whom Cemal Kafadar calls "*the* classical poet" of Anatolian Turkish.[68] In the Köprülü paradigm, Yūnus Emre has come to stand for all that is authentically Turkic about Turkish literary culture, separate and distinct from the urban centers where Persianate influence abounded. However, Yūnus Emre's representation of himself as a peripatetic poet, wandering in isolation from town to town, belies a more complicated story. In fact, as we shall see, he drew on converging poetic and symbolic languages that were common to Anatolia and its adjacent regions. This chapter therefore reevaluates the ways in which we conceptualize what is native and what is foreign, indigenous and exogenous, to each of these intersecting literary cultures. It also suggests that the literary cultures of Anatolia had agency of their own, teasing their reinvention in other linguistic contexts.

Chapter 5 turns to the city of Kırşehir, where Sulṭān Valad's followers attempted to spread the teachings of their master. Here we meet Gülşehrī and ʿĀşıḳ Paşa, two of the earliest authors of Anatolian Turkish poetry, who each riffed on the verses of Rūmī for different ends. Gülşehrī, for instance, claimed to encounter Rūmī and Sulṭān Valad in a vision, along with four other poets. As he reports, these "world-conquering" poets commanded him to join their ranks by composing a work equivalent to their own. Gülşehrī accomplished this by writing first a Persian *maṡnavī* known as the *Falak-nāma* (*Book of the Celestial Sphere*) and later a Turkish adaptation of the *Manṭiq al-ṭayr* (*Speech of the Birds*) by ʿAṭṭār (d. 1221). Much as Rūmī had drawn upon the meter of the *Manṭiq al-ṭayr* to write his *Maṡnavī,* Gülşehrī's adaptation enabled him to blend literary styles and stories together in an enticing manner, in part to offer relevant instruction to audiences in Kırşehir. So too did ʿĀşıḳ Paşa engage in this kind of labor, as he modeled his massive *Garīb-nāme* (*The Book of the Stranger*), one of the earliest long-form Anatolian Turkish poems, on the *maṡnavī* genre. As this chapter argues, the earliest poets of Anatolian Turkish sought to accommodate certain types of difference—linguistic, ethnic, devotional—within an Islamic hermeneutic frame even while championing Turkish as a literary language according to prevailing standards across the Islamicate world. Hence, while Gülşehrī crafted a fictive poetic kinship between himself and six masters of Persian poetry, ʿĀşıḳ Paşa shaped a similar kind of genealogy between the Turkish literary language and its Persian and Arabic antecedents.

Muslim poets were not alone in accommodating linguistic and cultural heterogeneity in their compositions. Chapter 6 examines how Armenian poets in and around medieval Cilicia, the last Armenian kingdom, adapted vocabulary, genres, themes, tropes, and styles from Islamicate literature. As it shows, such poets generally instructed their audiences to read their compositions within a distinctly Christian interpretive frame. In fact, nearly all of the earliest poets who composed in "vernacular" Armenian (also known as Middle Armenian) took part in this enterprise, in which adaptation and hermeneutics were tightly braided together. For example, Saint Nersēs Shnorhali (d. 1173), the great-grandson of Grigor Magistros, rewrote the Bible as a series of interlocking riddles, training his audience to read scripture in a particular manner through the lens of poetry. The celebrated poet Frik not only quoted Persian poetry—in the original language!—in his compositions but also directed his audience to interpret these verses as a commentary on the Christian afterlife. As this chapter shows, so too did Frik guide readers to understand familiar Persianate literary tropes and themes in a Christian light. By bringing these and other poets into dialogue, this chapter rereads Armenian vernacular poetry through the literary practices that shaped it, such as gloss and quotation in particular. As we shall see, it is precisely the ways in which these poets did *not* translate wholesale texts that enabled them to recast different literary cultures within an Armenian Christian idiom.

Chapter 7 brings this story to a close in the early fourteenth century, on the cusp of Ottoman expansion. Here we return to a city that Rūmī's family passed by on their migration through Anatolia: Erznka (or Erzincan), which Rūmī's father once complained was full of many "bad people."[69] Despite the reluctance of Rūmī's family to enter this metropolis, Armenian audiences there offer an inverted look at many of the same problems, and approaches to composing poetry, that could be found in Konya. Much as Rūmī's disciple Ḥusām al-Dīn requested that he compose the *Maṣnavī* in the meter of ʿAṭṭār and the style of Sanāʾī (d. 1131), Christian audiences made strikingly similar demands of Armenian poets. Kostandin Erznkatsʿi (fl. late thirteenth to early fourteenth century), an Armenian poet who was trained in a nearby monastery at least until he was a teenager, shall be our literary guide to this city. Famously, as Kostandin tells us, his audience desired him to compose an adaptation of the Persian poet Firdawsī's *Shāh-nāma* (*Book of Kings*). He obliged, enigmatically instructing his audience to recite his work in the "voice" of the Iranian epic history of kings, now rendered in a Middle Armenian idiom.[70]

This book explores instructions like Kostandin's in both a literal and a figurative manner: what might composing poetry in the literary "voices" of others have meant, and what might it have accomplished, for medieval audiences? The city of Erznka allows us to ask this question from a different vantage point, circling back around to the complex dynamic between author and audience from which we began. This reciprocal relationship, which produced a literary field, represents an ongoing dialogue that transcends the creation of any individual poem. It was therefore not enough to fashion a new literary culture: the poets of thirteenth- and fourteenth-century Anatolia also attempted to form a listening public and an interpretive mode that would generate new meanings long after composition came to an end. In a very real manner, literary works and the audiences who consumed them served to produce one another.

Armenian poets during this period forged a new poetic culture whose cultivation was driven less by literary translation than by an attempt to reach, and communicate with, different kinds of audiences, as well as to teach them how to understand the meanings of non- or extra-Christian literary works. Middle Armenian literary culture is therefore evocative of what Muhsin J. al-Musawi terms "the medieval Islamic republic of letters" while paradoxically existing within and apart from it. For al-Musawi, this "republic" was less a geographic space than a historical condition that enabled cross-cultural exchange between Muslims across the expansive Islamicate world. In medieval Anatolia, however, the presence of Christian authors offers an alternative way of considering how and why various practices of adaptation, emulation, and response facilitated poetic exchange across languages. As I show, this process was driven as much by religious difference—that is, by the need to differentiate confessional boundaries and to teach audiences to participate in a process of making meaning differently—as by a shared fluency in any single religious culture. And in this difference, Armenian literary culture offers Persian and Turkish literatures a vital counterpoint, demonstrating that a widespread theory and praxis of poetic composition had taken root in Rūm, extending far beyond any single linguistic or religious community.

Kindred Voices tells, through a series of selective vignettes about composition and performance, a particular story about this formative moment in Anatolian literary history. It is far from the only story. Still, this book aims to produce a new image, and a dialogic understanding, of literary production in medieval Rūm while also raising questions about literary composition, adaptation, emulation, and hermeneutics that have broader relevance across the premodern world. The mixing of diverse peoples in this region gave rise to affinitive literary cultures, articulated by kindred voices—modes of composing literature that remained hospitable to difference and strikingly cognizant of others. Despite nineteenth-century projects of nationalization that disarticulated these literary cultures as distinctly "Persian," "Turkish," "Greek," and "Armenian," their development cannot be understood within the isolating frame of monolingualism. These voices come to us from an other Anatolia, out of the mouths of others, and they unsettle boundaries of many kinds, both medieval and modern.

CHAPTER ONE

STRANGER ENCOUNTERS

Two Accounts of Creation

Sometime during the 1330s, while the traveler Ibn Baṭṭūṭa (d. 1369) was passing through the lands of Rūm, he stayed for a short period in Konya. He marveled at the city's fine architecture, wide streets, abundant apricot trees, gardens, and orderly bazaar. He was perhaps most intrigued by the mausoleum of the Persian poet and "pious Imam" Jalāl al-Dīn Rūmī (d. 1273), known in his day simply as Mawlānā—"our master."[1]

Ibn Baṭṭūṭa visited the nearby hospice, where Rūmī's followers offered shelter to strangers, long enough to hear a tale about their master. The story went like this: Rūmī had been a distinguished Muslim preacher and theologian, earning wide renown throughout Anatolia. One day while Rūmī was giving a lecture, a man wandered by selling sweetmeats. Rūmī paused and asked for a morsel, but when he brought the sweetmeat to his lips, he immediately abandoned his lecture, followed the sweet seller outside, and wandered off into the country. Years passed; life went on. But then, one day, a disheveled Rūmī appeared in Konya again. To the astonishment of all, he could speak only in the *masnavī* form—rhymed couplets of Persian poetry! Although his followers didn't understand this odd speech, they ran after their master and scribbled down his every word. Eventually, these disciples compiled his poems into a work called the *Masnavī-yi ma'navī* (*Rhymed Couplets of Spiritual Meaning*), comprising six books and a staggering twenty-five-thousand-plus couplets. It was a work, Ibn Baṭṭūṭa noted, that the inhabitants of Konya still meditated upon, taught, and recited aloud in their hospices on Thursday nights.[2] Although he couldn't have guessed this at the time, it would become one of the most widely read and celebrated works in all of Persian literature.

Ibn Baṭṭūṭa's story may reflect an imperfect acquaintance with Konya's history—he did, after all, spend only a short time there—but it still captures the essence of what many regard as Rūmī's defining moment. This was, of course, his meeting with Shams al-Dīn Tabrīzī, a peripatetic mystic who became Rūmī's spiritual guide and transformed his practice of Islam. By Ibn Baṭṭūṭa's time, hagiographers were portraying the meeting between these men as an epochal event, producing a kind of spiritual shock wave that would reverberate across Anatolia for centuries. One account even claims that Rūmī immediately lost consciousness when he first engaged Shams in dialogue.[3] Historically and hagiographically speaking, there can be no doubt that Shams altered Rūmī's practice of Islam, inspiring him to follow a less legalistic and more esoteric path. But there's also a troubling logic that underpins Ibn Baṭṭūṭa's report: in line with this reasoning, Rūmī's composition of the *Masnavī* had everything to do with Shams—and perhaps more generally, everything to do with Persian culture, with Islamic mysticism, with the art of poetry—and nothing to do with Konya itself. Like the Qur'an handed down from heaven, the *Masnavī* miraculously appears in Anatolia, but has little to say about it.

This manner of thinking about literary production in premodern Anatolia still has a foothold today, largely in popular English translations of Rūmī's poetry but also in otherwise nuanced scholarly works. According to most accounts, after Shams al-Dīn mysteriously disappeared from Konya, Rūmī began to write poetry for the first time, composing the *Dīvān-i Shams-i Tabrīzī*, a massive collection of poems, many of which predate the long-form *Masnavī*. It has long been thought that Rūmī simply had no choice but to write these poems, as Shams al-Dīn's absence whipped him into a lyrical frenzy. A. J. Arberry offers us a characteristic example of this view: "The intense excitement of these adventures [searching in vain for Shams al-Dīn] transformed Jalāl al-Dīn from the sober divine into an ecstatic wholly incapable of controlling the torrent of poetry which now poured forth from him."[4] Arberry is hardly alone in this assertion. Afzal Iqbal, for instance, presents the claim in highly similar terms:

> Rumi was thirty-seven when Shams entered his life. For thirty-seven years there is no evidence of his inclination towards poetry. The Muse suddenly appears in the form of Shams and the earliest poems which have been traced belong to the period when Shams left him for the first time, probably in the year 1245. How is it, then, that the man who was destined to be one of the greatest figures in the literature of Persia did not write even a single verse for the best part of his life? The answer is simple. Rumi did not belong to the school of conventional poets who wrote because it was fashionable or useful to do so. There came a stage in his life—an exploding and explosive stage—when he could no longer help being a poet.[5]

It is clear from Rūmī's own testimony that Shams al-Dīn played a pivotal role in encouraging his composition of poetry. It also is likely, especially given his ecstatic *ghazal*s and quatrains, that Rūmī enjoyed a gift for spontaneous composition. Still, there is something troubling about depicting him as completely devoid of agency in the turbulent wake of Shams al-Dīn's absence, as though he simply could not help composing poetry after this singular moment in his life. This view falls generally in line with nineteenth- and twentieth-century assumptions of what "lyric" poetry is—namely, the unmediated, extemporaneous utterance of the poet's true affective state, addressed to no one. Such conceptions of the lyric in particular—as something "*over*heard," to borrow John Stuart Mill's famous definition of poetry—are generally uninterested in questions of audience or reception, as Anne Janowitz and Virginia Jackson have observed.[6] Yet Anatolia was far more than a fungible staging ground for the magnificent encounter between Rūmī and Shams. Instead, this region shaped the person of Rūmī and his proclivity toward poetic composition in tangible ways.[7]

Ibn Baṭṭūṭa stayed in Konya for only a short time before moving on. We ought to linger here a little longer, allowing a more socially dynamic account of Rūmī's poetry, and of the reading and listening public that shaped it, to emerge. This account comes to us from Shams al-Dīn Aḥmad Aflākī (d. 1360), who was a devotee of Rūmī's grandson ʿĀrif Chalabī (d. 1320) and lived in Konya when Ibn Baṭṭūṭa visited.[8] It is conceivable that Aflākī and Ibn Baṭṭūṭa even listened to the *Maṣnavī*'s recitation together, in the same captive audience, one evening at the hospice near Rūmī's tomb. Aflākī offers us a counterweight to the spontaneous outpouring of Rūmī's lyric poetry, long after Shams was out of the picture. In its place, he narrates a different account of poetic composition—not about Rūmī's *ghazals* or "lyric" poetry but rather about Rūmī's masterwork, the monumental *Maṣnavī*. Aflākī's hagiography is important to this story—despite its liberal depiction of miraculous events—because it allows us to examine how Rūmī's community theorized his literary production, in emic terms. Crucially, Aflākī's understanding of composition also helps us to understand how audiences in Konya engaged with Rūmī's poetry, how they made it meaningful in their own lives and experiences, and how they fashioned a history, and a peculiar genealogy, to explain its shadowy genesis.

Aflākī's *Maṣnavī* origin story begins on a night sometime around 1260, when Ḥusām al-Dīn Chalabī (d. 1284), Rūmī's foremost student, went out looking for his teacher. Ḥusām al-Dīn was troubled. He had recently learned that his companions, also followers of Rūmī, had been utterly dazzled by three challenging works of Persian poetry: the *Ilāhī-nāma* of Sanāʾī (d. 1131) and the *Manṭiq al-ṭayr* and *Muṣībat-nāma* of ʿAṭṭār (d. 1221).[9] He had been spellbound as well, reflecting on the abundance of strange (*gharīb*) meanings in these books, though he could not grasp their inner secrets. Knowing that opportunities pass like clouds, Ḥusām al-Dīn met with Rūmī in private and, lowering his head, made a striking request: if Rūmī would compose a new book "in the style of the *Ilāhī-nāma* of Ḥakīm [Sanāʾī] but in the meter of the *Manṭiq al-ṭayr*," he could render these "strange meanings" clear for the benefit of all humankind. It would be, Ḥusām al-Dīn concluded, a work of major compassion and aid.[10]

Rūmī, never one to miss a beat, immediately removed a piece from the top of his turban and placed it in Ḥusām al-Dīn's outstretched palm. There in the flickering lamplight, Ḥusām al-Dīn made out several couplets of poetry inscribed on the strip, beginning with the famous lines

> Listen to this reed, how it laments,
> It tells a story of separations—[11]

The strip, Aflākī would later report, was a commentary on "the secrets of universals and particulars" that Ḥusām al-Dīn's autodidact companions had not understood.[12] What Ḥusām al-Dīn found there were the first couplets of Rūmī's eventual masterpiece, the *Masnavī,* itself generative of many more strange meanings.

In stark contrast to Ibn Baṭṭūṭa's report, Aflākī depicts composition and meaning making as communal activities—sites where author and audience engage with each other, make and respond to requests, and even adapt the styles of other authors to serve new contexts. Such engagements produced the text of the *Masnavī,* which Rūmī composed aloud. For years, as Aflākī went on to explain, Ḥusām al-Dīn took up his pen, dipped it in the small ink pot by his lap, and committed the stirring words of his master to paper. When he was done, he recited the words back to Rūmī "in a good and raised voice," affording his master an opportunity to reflect on these newly composed lines of poetry. Sometimes this activity followed these men to unusual places. Whether on the road or in the bathhouse, sitting or in motion, Rūmī would recite new lines of the *Masnavī,* presumably leaving Ḥusām al-Dīn to commit them to memory before they returned home.[13] Rūmī composed the *Masnavī,* but Ḥusām al-Dīn embodied it, preserved it with his hand on paper, and communicated it back to Rūmī in his own voice.

As is well known, Ḥusām al-Dīn was more than a scribe; he was Rūmī's student, companion, and first successor in what would become the Mawlaviyya order, the community that developed around Rūmī's teachings.[14] Without Ḥusām al-Dīn's persistence, it is reasonable to think that the *Masnavī* would not exist—at least not in its present form. For instance, Rūmī notes at the beginning of the second book that his work "was delayed for a time," alluding to the death of Ḥusām al-Dīn's wife.[15] The bereaved Ḥusām al-Dīn had abstained from transcribing Rūmī's poetry for a few years. It was only when he was ready to remarry that he approached his master again. Aflākī tells us that Ḥusām al-Dīn wept and pleaded with Rūmī to continue his work, and after much begging, Rūmī finally acquiesced.[16] We find this pattern woven throughout the *Masnavī.* At the opening of book 5, for instance, Rūmī simply notes: "The King Ḥusām al-Dīn, who is the light of the stars / craves for the fifth book to begin."[17] Elsewhere, perhaps anticipating the very kind of story that Ibn Baṭṭūṭa would later report, Rūmī implicitly rebukes those who would minimize Ḥusām al-Dīn's role. "It is you," he tells Ḥusām al-Dīn, "by your light, that the *Masnavī* has outshone the moon,

Your sublime ambition, O expected one,
Guides this [*Maṡnavī*]—God knows where.

You have tied the neck of this *Maṡnavī*,
You guide it in that direction you know.

The *Maṡnavī* runs after. The guide is concealed!
Concealed from the ignorant, lacking in sight.

Because you have been the source of the *Maṡnavī*,
If it has increased, you have made it grow.

Because you so desire it, God so desires it;
God grants the faithful what gives them delight.[18]

Or, as Rūmī declares elsewhere, the title of the *Maṡnavī* might as well be the *Ḥusām-nāma*—the *Book of Ḥusām*. "From the allure of a scholar like you," Rūmī says to his transcribing companion, "the *Book of Ḥusām* has wound through the world."[19] Rūmī composed the *Maṡnavī*; Ḥusām al-Dīn guided its composition in "unseen" ways. The agencies of both men shaped the production of Rūmī's masterwork, but differently. It is impossible to tell a story about the *Maṡnavī*'s composition, therefore, without some attempt to parse this relationship and the historical currents that shaped it.

In this sense, the *Maṡnavī* is the product of an encounter not only between different men but also between different worlds. Rūmī was born into a Persian-speaking family more than fifteen hundred miles to the east, likely in the town of Vakhsh, sometime around 1207. The town was small—so small, in fact, that Rūmī's companions claimed their master was from the more recognizable, and culturally prominent, city of Balkh. Along with many Persians of his generation, Rūmī's father decided to secure a more lasting form of patronage and prominence in the west. As we will see, this desire eventually brought him to a region that encompassed the formerly Byzantine territories of Rūm (Rome), where the Seljuk Turks courted the cultural and religious prestige of Persian scholars. Rūmī was an adolescent when his family made the long journey westward. He came of age in a foreign land.

Ḥusām al-Dīn, on the other hand, was a native of Rūm, born and raised in the city of Konya. His father, Akhī Turk, had likewise immigrated west, but from the region of Urmia, in northwestern Iran, where many different peoples lived. It seems, as Rūmī believed, that Ḥusām al-Dīn's family was of Kurdish descent.[20] Akhī Turk led a local *akhī* group, an urban confraternity modeled on the Islamicate *futuwwa* movement, that offered spiritual instruction to young men in the city. When he died, his followers apparently tried to persuade Ḥusām al-Dīn to assume leadership of this brotherhood. But Ḥusām al-Dīn turned them down. Instead, he labored to turn his servants and companions into followers of Rūmī, even at great personal cost to himself.[21] It may have been that these brothers initially preferred what was already familiar, the community of the confraternity over the preacher from Khorasan. Ḥusām al-Dīn, it seems, did not. As we will see throughout this book, this kind of preference would shape the literary and religious cultures of Anatolia in remarkable ways.

The epochal meeting between Shams al-Dīn and Rūmī was certainly life changing. Still, we should have something more to say about the far less dramatic, much more mundane, but quietly transformative encounter between Rūmī and Ḥusām al-Dīn, whose subsequent relationship led to the production of the *Maṡnavī*. What this and the following chapter propose is not simply to locate the *Maṡnavī* within a historical context but rather to examine what its composition might have to tell us about the literary and cultural milieu in which it was produced (and vice versa). In stark contrast to Ibn Baṭṭūṭa's report, the figure of Ḥusām al-Dīn offers us a valuable starting point for considering a more reciprocal and dynamic relationship between poets and their communities in medieval Anatolia, whereby the agencies of both authors and audience(s) shaped the literary field, in different ways. How then might we read the *Maṡnavī* as a product of this very particular history—as an encounter and form of engagement between the peoples of Rūm and Jalāl al-Dīn (before he became Rūmī)? What would it look like to read the *Maṡnavī*—a towering work of Persian literature—as something else, something more locally rooted and dialogically inclined? How might we read the *Book of Ḥusām*?

The Journey West

Let's return for a moment to Ḥusām al-Dīn, a strip from Rūmī's turban in his hands, as he laid eyes on the first lines of the *Maṡnavī*:

Listen to this reed, how it laments,
It tells a story of separations—

"Since I was cut from the reed bed,
Man and woman have wept in my wailing.

I desire a breast lacerated by separation,
So that I may express the pain of ardent longing.

Whoever has fallen far from their source
Seeks a return to the days of being together."[22]

From the first line of the *Maṡnavī*—*Listen!*—we enter into a world of dialogue and sound, performance and audition, inaugurated by the lonely reed itself. The reed complains for a simple reason: it has been plucked from the serene marshes where it grew. Far from its source, the reed (*nay*) has become the pen (*qalam*), its tip cut into a pointed nib. In this light, its "story of separations" amounts to the text of the *Maṡnavī,* which contains a series of interlocking tales that guide the listener toward unity with God. The reed serves as both the organizing symbol of Rūmī's masterpiece and the instrument that produces it.

However, this is only part of the story. There is also a nontextual component of the reed's "discourse," which would have been apparent to Ḥusām al-Dīn on that fateful night. *Nay* is also the word for "reed flute"—a simple musical instrument, made of a hard stalk and pierced with six holes, that produced a sweet and sorrowful sound. No one would have had to explain to Ḥusām al-Dīn why the reed laments. Along with the *nay*, Rūmī's followers played a variety of musical instruments, including the kettledrum; the *rabāb* (rebec), an instrument akin to the bowed lute; the *ṭanbūr,* a long-necked plucked lute; and cymbals. In fact, both the performance of music and the recitation of poetry were key to the practice of *samāʿ* (audition), a form of religious devotion that brought about ecstatic states in its listeners.[23] As Ḥusām al-Dīn understood, music and sound work in concert with Rūmī's words, allowing an experienced listener to contemplate their separation from God through a variety of mediums, including the rising and falling human voice reciting the *Maṡnavī* aloud.

If the reed's music served as a performative analogue for the text, the reed itself was arguably an analogue for its author and (by extension) its readers: those who would lament with and through the reed flute.[24] Like the reed, its audience would develop a feeling of being out of place, far from their source, that is central to the project of the *Maṡnavī*. However, to understand what this out-of-place mood might have been like, as well as how the historical place of Anatolia contributed to it, a different story of separation must be told. This one, like the story of the *nay*, is also characterized by moods of estrangement, by dislocation and hospitality, and by voice and song. It is the story of Rūmī's migration west, to the lands of Rūm, where he encountered diverse forms of cultural production that would subtly inform his development as a poet. The cumulative experiences of this journey would, moreover, eventually suggest a different path forward than the one tread by his father.

Rūmī's father, Bahā' al-Dīn Valad (d. 1231), was already some sixty years old when he decided to relocate his family to Anatolia. He seems to have grown increasingly frustrated, as a lifelong jurisconsult and preacher, by his inability to secure greater patronage in his home country; he therefore decided to seek his fortune elsewhere. In a final sermon before departing for Anatolia, Bahā' al-Dīn condemned his perceived competitors and peers, likening himself and his teachings to a stranger (*gharīb*) in a country of devils.[25] His timing was fortuitous, as the Mongols would conquer the region of Khorasan by 1221. To the Valad family, this conquest seemed like divine retribution for the worst slight of all: Bahā' al-Dīn's estrangement in his own land.

We possess only a shadowy glimpse of the Valad family's journey to Anatolia.[26] However, even from Aflākī's hagiographic reports, a somewhat austere and cautious picture of Bahā' al-Dīn begins to emerge. For instance, when the Valad family stopped in Baghdad, the eminent Sufi intellectual 'Umar al-Suhrawardī (d. 1234) is reported to have welcomed them personally. Despite this overture of hospitality, Bahā' al-Dīn refused to stay at the local *khānaqāh*, or Sufi hospice, retorting that "a madrasa is more suitable for imams!" Later, he even rebuked the representatives of the caliph, who had come to him laden with gifts: "[The caliph's] riches are unlawful and dubious," he declared. "It's improper to favor or reside in the dwelling of someone who's a habitual wine drinker and who listens to the songs of stringed instruments and the fife [*mizmār*]."[27] It is worth observing that Aflākī's report likely hyperbolizes these encounters, in part to emphasize

Bahā' al-Dīn's importance. There is also good reason to suppose that Bahā' al-Dīn's view of music was not so rigid either, as he seems to have found it acceptable to listen to musical performances in certain contexts, but he did not consider them necessary to spiritual development.[28] Still, since Bahā' al-Dīn's descendants would later center both woodwind and stringed instruments in their devotional practices and lives, it seems odd that Aflākī would emphasize his distaste for musical performance were there not some truth behind this depiction.[29]

If Bahā' al-Dīn had truly wished to avoid such customs, he was headed in the wrong direction. From Baghdad he took his family on a pilgrimage to Mecca, whence they traveled to Anatolia (see map 2). It was there, in the formerly Byzantine territories, where Bahā' al-Dīn perhaps felt overwhelmed by the diversity of institutions that had emerged to house strangers, guests, and travelers. He appears to have tried to avoid most of them. "A madrasa is suitable for imams," he argued again before reaching Rūm, "a *khānaqāh* for shaykhs, a palace for princes, an inn [*khān*] for merchants, convents [*zavāyā*] for rogues [*runūd*], and a stone bench [*maṣṭaba*] for strangers [*ghurabā*]."[30] This taxonomy of hospitable institutions reflects a broad need in Anatolia, on almost every level of society, to organize people

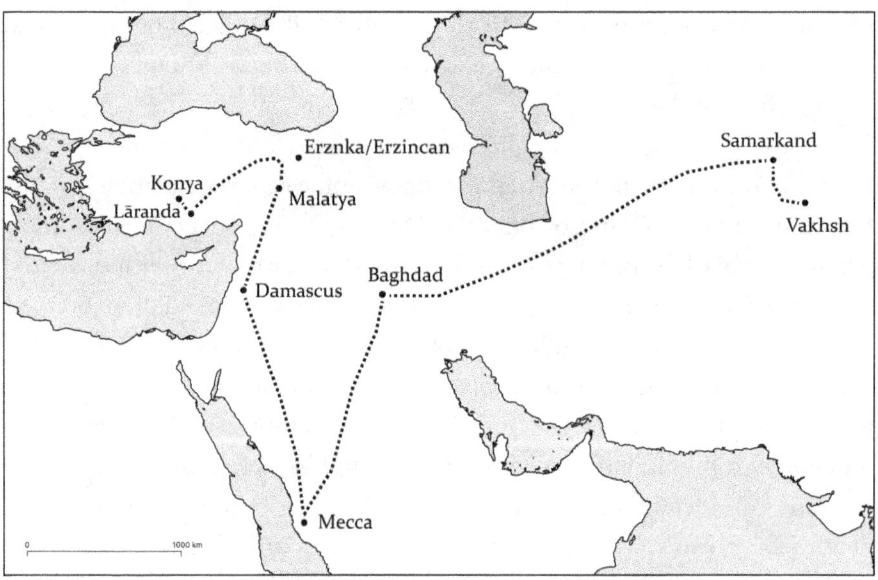

MAP 2. The Valad family's journey west.

from elsewhere around a new, and sometimes volatile, political order.[31] Beginning around the late twelfth century, the Seljuks had even implemented a massive program of constructing caravansaries, which housed travelers and allowed the royal court to move seasonally throughout Rūm.[32] These caravansaries, which were flanked by imposing walls and often featured ornate marble gates and spacious courtyards, punctuated the region's sloping green landscapes with rigidly geometric expressions of Seljuk power; they would have immediately captured a traveler's eye and imagination.

Urban hospitality would likewise undergo a sea change during Rūmī's time in Anatolia. A great deal of cross-cultural contact occurred around the institution of the *khānaqāh,* which functioned as a communal center for prayer and religious discussion, provided a space for engaging with visitors and strangers, and offered lodging for travelers and food for the poor. An increasing number of Sufi hospices were founded from the latter half of the thirteenth century in Anatolia, transforming urban spaces with their stability and providing spiritual centers of gravity at a time of mass immigration and political uncertainty.[33] Demographic upheaval increased after the Mongol incursions reduced the Seljuks' territory to an Ilkhanid protectorate in the mid-thirteenth century, in some ways rendering such institutions, as well as the lodges of urban confraternities, even more vital to preserving social order. Besides Muslims, Christians and Jews were likewise drawn into the spiritual and social lives of these organizations. Sufi dervishes even acquired Greek and Armenian adherents, occasionally adapting the symbolic languages and devotional practices of Christianity in the process, as Ethel Sara Wolper has observed.[34]

What would it have been like for the young Rūmī to travel through Anatolia at this pivotal moment in history? Although our sources emphasize that Bahā' al-Dīn desired to stay only at the comparatively austere religious schools of law, that may have been difficult. Traveling one century later, Ibn Baṭṭūṭa marveled at the degree of hospitality he experienced in Rūm:

> This country called *Bilād al-Rūm* is one of the finest regions in the world; in it God has brought together the good things dispersed through other lands. Its inhabitants are the comeliest of men in form, the cleanest in dress, the most delicious in food, and the kindliest of God's creatures. This is why the saying goes "Blessing in Syria and kindliness [*al-shafaqa*] in al-Rūm," since what

> is meant by the phrase is the people of this land. Wherever we stopped in this land, whether at hospice [*zāwiya*] or private house, our neighbors both men and women (who do not veil themselves) came to ask after our needs. When we left them to continue our journey, they bade us farewell as though they were our relatives and our own kin, and you would see the women weeping out of grief at our departure.[35]

Middle Eastern cultures of hospitality have old roots, but such customs likely acquired a new institutional dimension in Anatolia during Bahā᾽ al-Dīn's lifetime. One century later, in nearly every city that Ibn Baṭṭūṭa visited, men from urban confraternities would insist he spend the night under their roof. In the city of Lādhiq, near the present-day Denizli, two brotherhoods nearly came to blows over the right to host Ibn Baṭṭūṭa. In the end, the two parties drew lots, and Ibn Baṭṭūṭa stayed with the winners on the first night, enjoying a sumptuous banquet that was followed by a recitation of the Qur'an, singing, and dancing. He stayed with the other brotherhood on the next night. The *samāʿ* and dancing (*raqṣ*), he observed, were even better on the second evening.[36]

Ibn Baṭṭūṭa's experience reflects a pattern in Anatolia that was prevalent by the fourteenth century. In city after city, representatives of different *akhī* groups—the same kind of organization that Ḥusām al-Dīn's father had led a century prior—would seek out travelers like Ibn Baṭṭūṭa as part of their daily activities. They would bring these travelers back to their spacious headquarters, which were usually endowed buildings, with cool and dark interiors arrayed with colorful rugs and silver candlesticks. At night, these "brothers" would offer their guests fruit and sweetmeats on opulent trays, or even present visitors with precious gifts.[37] These confraternities also seem to have followed a familiar after-dinner ritual. Following a recitation of the Qur'an, their members would sing and dance—or practice *samāʿ*, which was one of their defining activities. In Konya, for instance, Ibn Baṭṭūṭa reports that "the entertainment with which this *qāḍī* [judge] honored us, and his hospitality to us, was even greater and more handsome than the entertainment of his predecessors."[38] In Bursa, the "*samāʿ* and dance" made "a sublime night" for the traveler.[39] The musical cultures of Rūm, which went hand in hand with a practice of hospitality, were not always consigned to private courtyards or buildings. In Lādhiq, *akhī* members took to the streets with colorful flags, trumpets (*būqāt*), drums (*ṭubūl*), and pipes (*anfār*) to celebrate the end of Ramadan, "all aiming to outdo one another in magnificence." The poor also joined in this celebration of fast breaking, songs and sounds lingering brightly in their ears as they ate.[40]

Music and hospitality, strangers and separation, devotion and rivalry. In thirteenth-century Anatolia, these things were beginning to shape communities—perhaps in ways that Bahā' al-Dīn wished his son to avoid. For instance, when passing by Erznka (contemporary Erzincan), Bahā' al-Dīn refused to enter the city. "Bad people abound in that place," he dismissively told his companions.[41] What kind of reputation would have kept Bahā' al-Dīn away? For one, as many have suggested, the city was largely populated by Christian Armenians, who drank wine and ate meats forbidden by Islam. However, lest we paint too stark a divide between Christians and Muslims in Rūm, it should be noted that some of these Armenians hewed closely to their Muslim neighbors in devotional practice and even poetic taste. For instance, Hovhannēs Erznkatsʻi (d. 1293), a learned Armenian theologian, later helped to found an Armenian confraternity in Erznka which he modeled on the Islamic *futuwwa* and *akhī* movement.[42] His brotherhood encouraged its members to abstain from drinking wine, just as Muslims did. Armenians in Erznka also valorized practices of hospitality analogous to those of their Muslim counterparts, both within and beyond the institution of the *akhī* lodge.

Armenian hospitality perhaps involved a poetic and musical component as well. Hovhannēs, for instance, composed an early poem on strangers in vernacular or Middle Armenian—a language whose nascent literary culture was replete with Arabic and Persian loanwords and loan concepts. It is therefore not surprising that he employed a Persian and Arabic term for "stranger," *gharīb,* to extol the importance of welcoming others:

> Let him who speaks badly of the stranger [*ōtar*] become a *gharīb* himself.[43]
> May he go to a foreign land, may he know the worth of a *gharīb;*
> Even if gold should rain down upon him,
> Separated from his loved ones, that gold is not worth ashes.[44]

This is the same term used by Bahā' al-Dīn, who felt mistreated as a *gharīb* in his native land—a slight that, in the eyes of the Valad family, led to the Mongol invasion as a divine form of retribution. There was clearly an awareness, as part of the age's episteme, that one must treat guests and strangers well. As we shall see, in Anatolia this awareness was often expressed through a widespread poetic and musical culture, grounded in an equally common vocabulary for describing who strangers are and what hosts owe them. Hovhannēs's poem might therefore offer a glimpse into the city that Bahā' al-Dīn sought to avoid. This is underscored by the poem's form, the *kafa,* a quatrain with a fixed number of syllables ending in monorhyme. In Armenian, *kafa*s were often recited or sung aloud, sometimes accompanied by a stringed instrument known as the *sāz,* which Persians and Turks in Rūm also played. It is not so difficult to imagine that performers could have chanted this poem to the very strangers they sought to host and console.[45]

Hence, across a variety of institutions in Anatolia, caring for strangers meant more than putting a roof over their heads or a meal on a platter: it meant exposing them to particular forms of religious devotion, it meant playing music, and it sometimes meant reciting or singing poetry—even if guests could not understand the language or came from a different background. "If a *vardapet* [teacher of the church] comes from another country, let the leaders of the brothers go to see and honor him," Hovhannēs instructed his brothers. They were also to offer, like their Muslim counterparts, hospitality to all visiting monks and hermits. But the instruction goes even further, as Hovhannēs moreover commands them "to speak lovingly and listen to all tribes of people, so that [the brothers] might grow wise from every nation."[46] Perhaps ironically, this was the very attitude that Rūmī would later adopt, as he sought out not only Muslims or Persian speakers but also Greeks and Armenians in the city of Konya. Thus, instead of viewing this Christian city as separate from the gradually more Turkic and Muslim world around it, we might consider Erznka as having represented part of a broader culture that Bahā' al-Dīn wished to keep at arm's length: one in which the lines between Christian and Islamic devotional practices were not always so demarcated, one in which the fife and stringed instruments were not only heard but valorized, one in which strangers were drawn into a world of song, poetry, and dance.

It is plausible that Bahā' al-Dīn was able to hold some of this culture of hospitality and audition at bay. But it is unlikely, given his family's decade-long migration through Anatolia, that they would have been able to separate themselves from these cultures altogether. It is in this milieu that Rūmī came of age. According to Aflākī, Bahā' al-Dīn settled in Āqshahr, close to Erznka, and taught in a madrasa there for four years.[47] The Valad family later resettled to the east, in Lāranda (Karaman), where the teenage Rūmī, then seventeen years old, married his first wife in 1224. By the time that the Seljuk sultan 'Alā' al-Dīn Kay-Qubād (d. 1237) invited Bahā' al-Dīn to teach in nearby Konya, Rūmī already had two sons, who knew Anatolia as their native home.

Bahā' al-Dīn would have been almost eighty years old when his family arrived in Konya, located today in south central Turkey. He lived only a few more years and therefore did not witness the transformation in his son that arguably began to germinate long before Shams al-Dīn appeared on the scene.[48] This transformation might have made Rūmī seem somewhat strange to his father—perhaps as strange as the culturally interstitial Christians in Erznka could appear to a travel-weary preacher from Khorasan. Whereas Bahā' al-Dīn scorned the *mizmār*, Rūmī would choose the displaced *nay* as the central metaphor of his *Maṡnavī*. Whereas Bahā' al-Dīn supposedly condemned stringed instruments, Rūmī would become adept at playing the *rabāb,* which, as some of his more conservative contemporaries lamented, had grown popular in the region at the time.[49] In a kind of gleeful hazing of these critics, Rūmī would even openly refer to the *rabāb*'s sound as an alternative form of the afternoon prayer.[50] Finally, whereas Bahā' al-Dīn sought to avoid "bad" Christians, Rūmī would willingly stroll through the city's Christian neighborhoods. He did not limit himself to interactions with only a certain kind of (devout Muslim) person.

Years later, Shams al-Dīn would encourage Rūmī to put away the teachings of his father in order to explore other forms of religious devotion, including the controversial practice of *samā'*. It is therefore telling that after Shams al-Dīn's mysterious disappearance from Konya, Rūmī's first acts were to commission a six-cornered *rabāb* in honor of his absent companion and to begin more openly practicing *samā'*, both of which would gradually become hallmarks of his followers over the next century.[51] But although Shams may have inspired a new appreciation of the commingled sounds of fife and *rabāb,* poetry and song, it is not as if he brought this culture to Anatolia: it was part of a broader vernacular in which the heterogeneous peoples of Rūm were already becoming fluent, regardless of their linguistic or religious affiliation. After all, across Rūm, one way of caring for strangers, of welcoming outsiders into the social fabric of one's community, was expressed through the performance of poetry and music. As Rūmī once explained before singing a *ghazal* about separation, which he accompanied with the *rabāb*, "Caring for *gharīb*s [*gharīb-navāzī*] is the work of men of religion."[52]

Simply put, it would be difficult to avoid this ubiquitous hospitable and audible culture. After all, sounds are unruly, transgressing boundaries in ways that corporeal objects cannot. In certain modern (often Western) cultures of audition, listening to music has more and more become a private and exclusionary affair, much like contemporary habits of reading. But in premodern Anatolia, the soundscape of the city resounded with proclamations, with marketplace banter, with sermons, with prayer, with music, and with poetry. Perhaps to the chagrin of figures like Bahā' al-Dīn—at least as he is represented in Aflākī's account—one could not always control where or how this sonic culture would make itself heard, no matter how many madrasas one stayed at.

A simple anecdote illustrates how performances—even performances that were intended to be private—facilitated encounters between different peoples in Konya. One evening, Rūmī was wandering the streets of Konya and stopped dead in his tracks. His ears had seized upon someone playing the *rabāb* at a nearby wine tavern in the Christian part of the city. Caught in the delight of spontaneous listening, Rūmī began to practice *samā'* in the street, shouting and dancing for hours. Armenians gradually emerged from doorways to observe him as the night slowly gave way to dawn. The next day, some Armenians were so moved that they reportedly converted to Islam.[53] This story, much like the originary moment of composition between Rūmī and Ḥusām al-Dīn, suggests that performance and audition occurred in a milieu where the *meaning* of sound was produced communally. In this anecdote, the lines between performer and audience are blurred, as Rūmī—a coincidental member of the audience—guided these Christians to experience their music through an explicitly Islamic mode of audition. The ambiguous nature of this audition allowed Christian and Muslim, musician and audience to commingle in different ways, adopting different roles that shifted with the revolutions of the melody.

Rūmī did not necessarily seek out this music—he encountered it, as one would, in the streets and the shops, as part and parcel of everyday life in Konya. This culture bound him to the peoples of Konya in mutually generative ways. It was the voice of Rūm, and it called to him.

Mixing with Others

Despite being the seat of Seljuk power in Rūm, the city of Konya occupied a liminal position in many ways. For one, it was home to a wide array of peoples, including Persians, Jews, Turks, Arabs, Kurds, and a sizable population of Armenians and Greeks. Cilicia, an Armenian kingdom, lay about one hundred miles to the southeast. Meanwhile, the Hellenic world of the Byzantine Empire was only a short distance to the west. And the political landscape changed again with the incursion of the Mongols, who roundly defeated the Seljuks at the battle of Köse Dağ in 1243.

If we were to tell a political or religious history of Rūm rather than a literary history, a very different story would begin to unfold—one of shifting political alliances, one of the rise and fall of sultanates and principalities, one of foreign invaders and militaristic conquest. In a biography of Anatolia, these events would constitute the main beats of our character's life. But in some ways, the concepts of hospitality, of treating strangers well, of adapting the poetry and musical cultures of others, and of strengthening communal ties were also connective tissues of Rūm. They wound through its body, giving it a recognizable shape, enveloping its nervous system—in this case, the highly educated elites of Anatolia—and binding its peoples together in ways that religious and political cultures might not.

In other words, to conceive of Anatolia as a character in this story, it is necessary to move beyond the political events that happened in this region and begin to excavate something more intangible but no less real: how the disparate elements of its body made it "who" it was—sometimes despite the ways in which its elites and sovereigns conducted themselves, or the manner in which various principalities rose and then fell to the ascendant Ottomans. That widespread musical and poetic cultures, by no means monolithic or utopian, undergirded these visible features of life in Rūm is not immediately apparent, especially if we limit our frame of reference to a single linguistic, literary, or religious tradition. It is necessary to adopt a more expansively comparative approach for the fullness of an integrated, connective literary history to emerge. Still, the shadowy contours of this tissue might be glimpsed below the skin's surface, so to speak, even upon Rūmī's early establishment in Konya, after he returned from completing his education abroad in Damascus following the death of his father.

In fact, one does not have to speculate whether Rūmī would have composed something like the *Masnavī* had he remained in Khorasan. In a sermon found in his *Fīhi mā fīh* (*In It What's in It*), he emphatically claims that were it not for the peoples of Rūm, he would not have composed poetry at all:

> I'm so enamored that when these friends [*yārān*] approach me, out of dread lest they grow bored, I recite poetry so they might occupy themselves with that. Otherwise, what's poetry to me? By God, I loathe poetry. In my presence, there's nothing worse than it. It's the same as when someone who has thrust his hand into tripe washes it for the sake of a guest's appetite. Since the guest hungers for tripe, [this work] has become obligatory for me. Or [it's like when] a man notices what goods are needed by the people in such and such a city, and which commodities are desired by customers; these he also buys and sells, although the commodities are quite inferior.

If the journey westward left any impression on Rūmī, it was presumably that the people of Rūm embraced a variety of poetic and musical cultures in a different way than did the people of Khorasan—perhaps even differently than Rūmī himself, who was still his father's son, after all. "In our country and among our people, there was not a more shameful kind of work than the art of poetry," he claims. "If we had remained in that country, we would have lived in accordance with their nature. We would have exercised what they required, such as giving lectures, composing books, chastising, preaching, cultivating asceticism, and performing outward deeds."[54]

Rūmī's companions seem to have accepted this pretense for composing poetry: Farīdūn ibn Aḥmad Sipahsālār paraphrases this sermon in his hagiography of the Valad family, for instance.[55] Scholars, however, have interpreted this oft-cited declaration in different ways. Arberry, for instance, contrasts these sober words against Rūmī's ecstatic relationship with Shams al-Dīn, implying that without Shams in particular, "nothing seems less likely than that [Rūmī] would turn poet."[56] Franklin D. Lewis understands the passage as an indication of "the anxiety of the professional preacher and juridically-trained scholar" who had to justify his composition of poetry to his more conservative colleagues.[57] Finally, Annemarie Schimmel has cautioned against taking these words at face value, especially since Rūmī felt such an urgent desire to compose a collection, or *dīvān,* of poetry while mourning his absent spiritual guide, Shams al-Dīn.[58] Clearly, he enjoyed more than a perfunctory relationship with the poetic arts.

Still, it would be productive to shift our focus somewhat. Regardless of how Rūmī claimed to *feel* about composing poetry, it is significant that he dressed his justification for it not in terms of his relationship with Shams al-Dīn but rather in two broad metaphors of social engagement, one rooted in the economics of supply and demand and the other in a practice of hospitality. Figuratively, it is clear that Rūmī is both the merchant—someone who needed to peddle goods and services in a particular city—and the host, duty bound to ensure the entertainment of his guests. In Rūm, as we have already seen, part of that duty entailed welcoming and engaging others with a performance of music and poetry. Rūmī's fear of boring his initiated audience of "friends," a fear alleviated by reciting poetry, suggests that he internalized this culture of welcoming others in a manner that was congruent with the cultural and social mores of his milieu.

Significantly, in both metaphors, Rūmī frames his drive to compose poetry as a manner of engaging with his companions in Konya, above and beyond any other motivating concern. He apparently came to equate poetic composition with a form of social engagement quite early on. One afternoon, in the midst of explicating higher secrets to his followers, Rūmī began to reflect on what had drawn his family to Anatolia in the first place. "[God] brought us from the domain of Khorasan to the country of Rūm and provided a refuge for our descendants in this pure country, that we might sprinkle our divine elixir upon the copper of [the people of Rūm's] existence," he explained. This encounter between the Valad family and the local population would produce a lasting metamorphosis. The peoples of Rūm "would be completely turned into the philosopher's stone," he continued, "and they would become confidants [*maḥram*] of the world of hidden knowledge and intimates [*hamdam*] of the holy sages of the world."

Finally, Rūmī then recited—or at least, Aflākī chose to quote—a couplet about this strange alchemy:

> You brought me from Khorasan to be among Greeks,
> To mix with them, and a pleasing religious path to seek.[59]

What might it mean to "mix" among the Greeks, and more broadly, the peoples of Rūm? The salient verb in this couplet, *dar āmīkhtan,* hints at a variety of cross-cultural entanglements, reflected in both Rūmī's literary production and his social activity. In the *Maṣnavī,* for instance, Rūmī's depiction of the annunciation of Jesus "could be easily taken to be a piece of Christian devotional literature," defying expectations of what Islamic poetry adopts as its subject matter, as Schimmel has observed.[60] Similarly, in his *Dīvān* we find a handful of short poems that literally mix together both Persian and Turkish couplets, or Persian and Greek couplets.[61]

Such mixing also took place in the public sphere. Christians reportedly wept when listening to Rūmī's sermons in public, despite the complaints of his followers that even Muslims had difficulty understanding the nuances of his teachings, let alone nonbelievers.[62] These reactions, however, did not impede Rūmī. Though he clearly championed Islam, he also asserted that those who were "fearful" (*tarsā,* also meaning "Christian") and unable to take the religion of Muḥammad should still cling to Jesus and learn to renounce the world.[63] In other words, Rūmī may have wanted to shape "a pleasing religious path" for the peoples of Rūm, and he was willing to do so by engaging with them, to a certain degree, on their own terms and in accessible ways.

Sometimes this meant charging preexisting literary works with new meaning. Once, Rūmī's disciples overheard him reciting a bawdy poem that was popular among "female prostitutes in Arab lands."[64] The poem seemed unbecoming to a Muslim preacher: it concerned the purchase of sexual favors and passion swiftly sated in medieval Damascus. Puzzled, his disciples demanded an explanation. Rūmī replied that the literal dimension of the words was not important. Instead, he argued that the poem had a hidden meaning: when understood in the proper light, it became a secret meditation on the cost of spiritual poverty.[65] His interpretation might seem to take liberties that no modern critic would dare. But to Rūmī, this kind of reading allowed the modeling of an explicitly Islamic hermeneutics, one in which it became possible to understand even scandalous or extrareligious source material within a semiotics of mysticism.

It seemed to Rūmī that higher spiritual meanings could be excavated anywhere. The more unlikely the source, the better. The marketplace, buzzing with economic activity, therefore offered another setting for mixing with the diverse inhabitants of Konya—sometimes to the chagrin of his followers. They came across their master bowing to a simple Armenian butcher, telling Jews that their religion was superior to Islam, and even performing *samāʿ* there.[66] These encounters also allowed Rūmī to practice his hermeneutics in public. He would stroll through the bazaar, letting strange sounds fill his ears. One day he overheard a Turkish seller of fox (*dilku*) skins crying, "Dilku, dilku!" to passersby. In Persian, *dil kū* homophonically means "where is the heart?" Rūmī wandered home, repeating "Dil kū" as he contemplated the inner spiritual (Persian) meaning of a Turkish word.[67] In another famous account, he began to perform *samāʿ* to the resounding beat of a goldsmith's hammer.[68] In essence, he incorporated the soundscape of the bazaar into his devotional practices, thereby demonstrating how one might uncover higher secrets and spiritual meanings in quotidian spheres.

At other times, Rūmī pushed the boundaries of what could and could not be adapted to reveal hidden secrets. It was one thing to transform the meaning of bawdy poetry or the soundscape of the bazaar but something else entirely to rewrite Islamic scripture. Yet Rūmī similarly reinterpreted the Qur'an by adapting, recombining, and elaborating upon its narratives in the *Maṡnavī*. One way he achieved this was through a particularly intensive practice of scriptural citation. In fact, the *Maṡnavī* quotes and cites the Qur'an more extensively than do most didactic poems, including works by Sanāʾī and ʿAṭṭār.[69] So frequent are the scriptural references in Rūmī's poetry that the famous poet ʿAbd al-Raḥmān Jāmī (d. 1492) is reported to have proclaimed the *Maṡnavī* "the Qur'an in Persian."[70]

It is telling, then, that this practice stirred up trouble in Konya. The poet Qāniʿī (fl. thirteenth century), who served at the Seljuk court, once challenged Rūmī by declaring, "I never liked Sanāʾī, for he was not a Muslim!"[71] When Rūmī asked in what sense Sanāʾī was not a Muslim, Qāniʿī replied: "Because he has incorporated [*tażmīn;* Arabic: *taḍmīn*] verses from the sacred Qur'an into his poetry and made them into rhymes." It is worth noting that Qāniʿī did not take issue with the content of Sanāʾī's *Ḥadīqat al-ḥaqīqa* as much as with its adaptive engagement with the Qur'an, which is considered the direct speech of God and therefore not translatable, let alone open to revision through Persian poetry.[72] Rūmī responded with a characteristically fierce rebuke, noting that because Qāniʿī was content (*qāniʿī*) with external appearances, he did not realize that Sanāʾī had actually composed a commentary on "the secrets of the Qur'an," insofar as he drew from the sea (*baḥr*) of the Qur'an and poured it into the meter (*baḥr*) of poetry. Qāniʿī reportedly repented on the spot and became a devoted follower of Rūmī.

To adapt heterogeneous texts, to recombine sources and sounds across linguistic fields, was thus implicitly to vie over what things were allowed to mean, who was allowed to determine meaning, and which things were allowed to be "*meaningful in terms of Islam,*" to use Shahab Ahmed's phrasing.[73] The charge that Qāniʿī leveled was not that Sanāʾī was a bad poet—it is that he did not seem like a particularly *Muslim* poet. Rūmī, on the other hand, defended the practice of *taẓmīn* as an essentially Islamic activity, seemingly more difficult to master and more important than traditional forms of exegesis.[74] To read the *Masnavī* as the *Book of Ḥusām*—as a form of "mixing" with the peoples of Rūm—we therefore need to see this practice of adaptation through Rūmī's eyes: a means of drawing both texts and communities into a particular interpretive framework at the same time. Rūmī's practice aimed to recombine—to mix—sources, literary styles, elements from popular culture(s), and even audiences to deliver a transformative, alluring Islamic message. To adapt so omnivorously in this manner was to remain open to the possibility that nearly anything and anyone had the potential to reveal "higher meanings" in Islam, both equally and differently. It was to speak in a poetic voice that was at once foreign and familiar, unveiling strange meanings in inviting ways.

Rūmī perhaps had something like this in mind as he reflected on his family's journey to Anatolia. Certainly, God had wanted him to "mix" among the Greeks and to produce a good religious doctrine. But the latter had proved difficult and might have been impossible had he taken the more withdrawn, insular path of his father. At some point Rūmī decided to do things differently. "And when we observed [that the people of Rūm] were not drawn toward God in any way," he finally explained, "and that they remained deprived of divine secrets, we provided them with those [spiritual] meanings in a way suitable to them—through the elegance of *samāʿ* and rhythmical poetry, which is agreeable to the temperament of people."[75]

As Lewis has noted, Rūmī was never a professional poet.[76] He was not formally trained in the poetic or musical arts, and he certainly did not receive patronage from the Seljuks, or later the Ilkhanids, to compose lines of limpid verse.[77] His value to these sovereigns was not directly in his literary production but rather in his ability to bolster their spiritual and cultural authority at an uncertain time. However, as Rūmī soon realized, "the people of Rūm are musicians and given to beauty in expression."[78] To shape his community on its own terms, to participate within that community, he would gradually become a poet-musician himself. This particular drive to "mix" with the inhabitants of Konya, expressed through the production of poetry and music, evokes another meaning of *āmīkhtan,* from which *dar āmīkhtan* is derived: to compile or to compose.[79] Rūmī's couplet "You brought me from Khorasan to be among Greeks, / To mix with them, and a pleasing religious path to seek," immediately followed by a discussion of poetry, invited his audience to contemplate the multivalent ways that their master "mixed" with his city. Consequently, to understand how the composition of poetry and the cultivation of an audience went hand in hand, we might consider "mixing" as a metaphor for *authorship*—a manner of composing by divine sanction that explicitly sought to transpose, to recombine, and to blend.

In fact, numerous scholars have shown that premodern Arabic and Persian literary theory contains a wide array of terms to describe such literary mixing.[80] This vocabulary contributes to a premodern theory of literary adaptation, or the mixing of disparate sources to produce something new. For example, the practice of *tażmīn*, which includes both the citation of scripture and the wholesale quotation of verse by another poet, enables one to respond to words from a preexisting text in a surgically precise manner. The technique of *muʿāraża* (Arabic: *muʿāraḍa*), on the other hand, allows poets to engage with another's poem in a more holistic fashion, in part by adopting the same meter and rhyme scheme.[81] As many have pointed out, analogous practices came to be known by a variety of terms by the fifteenth century, such as *istiqbāl,* which means to "welcome" a previous literary work into a new one; *tatabbuʿ*, to write in the same meter by "following behind" a previous work; and *javāb-gūʾī* or *naẓīra-gūʾī*, meaning roughly to "answer" or "respond" to a previous work.[82] Paul E. Losensky distinguishes these intentional responses to previous literary works, whereby poets "willingly and publicly acknowledge the voice of the other," from more conventional forms of borrowing typified by *sariqāt*, which express the relationship between "the author and the conventional corpus of poetic themes and topoi."[83] Hence, for Losensky, in adaptive practices like *istiqbāl* and *javāb-gūʾī*, poets "interpret and evaluate the subtext and its world of meaning in terms of their communicative act and the semiotic matrix of their time," whereas *sariqāt* are necessary for composition within the "rule-governed, classical tradition," wherein particular themes and topoi are generally considered the property of all poets.[84]

Certainly, Rūmī acknowledged his debt to other poets. Yet although he welcomed a staggering number of voices into the resonant chambers of his poetry, other factors shaped his literary output as well. If we allow ourselves to step further back from Western notions of influence, which frequently describe an anxious, unidirectional relationship between a dominant author (the one who acts) and a more passive author (the one who is acted upon), we can observe a different kind of agency, which shaped literary production in Rūm. This agency not only was authorial but also partly belonged to Konya itself: to the diverse Persians and Turks, Armenians and Greeks, Jews and Kurds who populated its homes and streets. As the philosopher and sociologist Bruno Latour has noted, one does not need to be an agent, in a classical sense, to have agency—even inanimate objects have agency. In Latour's example, a puppeteer may control her marionette, but the marionette's fluid mobility may suggest new possibilities, movements, and gestures to the puppeteer.[85] What seems quite clear, from Rūmī's testimony, is that the musical and poetic cultures prevalent in Konya suggested possibilities of engagement that had previously not occurred to him, or to his father.

Quite obviously, however, the people of Rūm *were* agents. They may not have all been literate, or literate in the same way, but they still performed, reflected on, or simply listened to a variety of musical and poetic works that were circulating throughout the region. In fact, just as Rūmī openly acknowledged that other works of poetry shaped the *Maṡnavī,* he also described how his audiences informed his approach as an author. After noting that the people of Rūm had a penchant for poetry and music, he directly equated this aptitude with his drive to compose literature. It would not be enough to merely deliver the Friday sermon or preach in the streets—a subtler hand was needed. In his words, his relationship with his community resembled that of a physician with a sick child. As he explained,

> When the child grows ill and is disgusted by the physician's sherbet [*sharbat-i ṭabīb*], necessarily desiring beer [instead], the ingenious physician [*ṭabīb-i ḥāẕiq*] employs a ruse: having poured medicine into a beer pitcher, he gives it to her so that she mistakes it for beer; then she drinks the sherbet with relish. Cleansed from the causes of the disease, she dresses in a cloak of health, and her crooked constitution becomes straight.

In a performative flourish, Rūmī then recited (or at least Aflākī quotes) a few couplets from the *Masnavī*. And, as if to demonstrate his point, these couplets quite literally mix Arabic from the Qur'an into the different form of Persian poetry:

> Come for [relief from] the malady without cure,
> We [are] the remedies for the infirm, one for each.
> We are the physicians and the disciples of God.
> The Red Sea gazed at us; [in Arabic] *so it parted!*[86]

Verses like these offer a succinct encapsulation of the "mixing" that Rūmī describes. In this case, such mixing entailed the adaptation of preexisting literary and musical forms—even if they originated elsewhere—to express an explicitly Islamic message. This message sought to be recognizable in its poetic form and sound and, at the same time, to introduce translocal religious discourses to emerging audiences in Rūm.

As this book will demonstrate, the musical and poetic cultures of the region—regardless of where they developed originally—had a particular way of migrating across religious, linguistic, and cultural spheres. Moreover, the hospitality of these peoples extended not only to strangers but also to the musical and poetic cultures of "others," which individual poets so often invited into their own compositions. This atmosphere created a kind of aural reciprocity, one in which Rūmī might break into *samāʿ*

while listening to Armenian musicians playing the *rabāb* in a tavern and Armenians might hear something resonant in Rūmī's own musical performances. Thus, Aflākī reports that a drunken Christian once burst upon a session of *samā*ʿ, forgetting where he was, after hearing the inviting sound of the *rabāb* from the street outside.[87] Rūmī's teachings, the proper "medicine" that Anatolia needed, would have to acquire a similarly inviting flavor, mixed into the beer pitcher of Persian poetry and the musical cultures of Konya, to achieve that kind of resonance. Rūmī may have been, on some level, a stranger in Rūm, but he also wanted to become its physician.

This idea to mix seems not to have occurred to Bahā' al-Dīn. However, to a native of Konya, like Ḥusām al-Dīn Chalabī, it could have seemed rather obvious—perhaps not even worth mentioning. This helps to explain why, according to Aflākī's report, Ḥusām al-Dīn desired a new poetic work in the style and meter of two existing Persian poems. It was not merely because he liked their sound or style but rather because he wanted the *Maṣnavī* to illuminate their innermost meanings. As we have seen here, the mechanism for illumination was not exegesis alone: it was the very practice of adaptation, this hospitable manner of charging familiar sounds, stories, and imagery with fresh meanings, that local audiences craved. Adaptation as a fundamental mode of meaning making was so familiar to Ḥusām al-Dīn and to Rūmī that neither man felt the need to explain why an adaptation of Sanā'ī and ʿAṭṭār, and not an exegesis, was desired in the first place.[88] Just as tellingly, Rūmī had reportedly already begun this undertaking, not because he necessarily anticipated Ḥusām al-Dīn's request but in part because adaptive composition was simply one of the engines that drove literary production in the greater region—a region in which poetic works had a form of agency, as they overtly suggested the possibilities of new compositions to their audiences.

Rūmī had learned that much like a silkworm's thread, sticky in the groves near Konya, the meanings of sounds and stories were highly malleable, binding disparate branches together into an elastic whole, a web of signification that gently enveloped the peoples of Rūm. Poetry and music, those twin pillars that had welcomed him to this region, now became indispensable means for engaging with his community. These were, after all, mediums that the peoples of Rūm already used to draw others into their own religious and communal spheres—why couldn't the reverse be true?

CHAPTER TWO
THE MACROCOSMIC *MAṢNAVĪ*

The Heuristic of Others

Ḥusām al-Dīn copied down the sinewy inscription from his master's turban—the opening of the *nay*'s lament. Then, likely seated by his master with pen in hand, he must have waited in anticipation for Rūmī to begin composing poetry aloud. What might have crossed Ḥusām al-Dīn's mind as he listened, elated, to the very first story of the *Maṣnavī*—a tale that would make good upon the "story of separations" that the *nay* had promised?

"Listen, O friends, to this story," Rūmī began, promising to reveal the truth of his audience's spiritual condition.[1] Ḥusām al-Dīn perhaps felt he was on the verge of unlocking a great mystery, as though a veil were slipping from the summit of higher meanings, that sublime abode of Sanāʾī and ʿAṭṭār. But Rūmī's words might have struck him as uncanny for another reason: no dry theological treatise, the *Maṣnavī* is a masterwork of literary adaptation. As the eminent Iranian scholar Badīʿ al-Zamān Furūzānfar has discovered, Rūmī rewrote the overwhelming majority of stories listed in the *Maṣnavī*'s headings from preexisting source material.[2] The *Maṣnavī* deconstructs notions of "high" and "low" culture, presenting a sophisticated theology couched in the language of popular stories and delivered in a coherent poetic form. At times it shifts from tales of copulation to citations of the Qur'an without losing a beat (so scandalizing Reynold Nicholson, its famous English translator and erudite interpreter, that he would render erotic sections of the poem in a fussy, buttoned-up Latin). Elsewhere it appears to remix selections from the poetry of Sanāʾī and ʿAṭṭār, the *Iḥyāʾ ʿulūm al-dīn* (*Revival of the Religious Sciences*) by the theologian al-Ghazālī (d. 1111), commentaries on the Qur'an, stories about the lives of the prophets, and popular works such as the *Kalīla and Dimna,* a well-traveled frame tale. In sum, these adaptations bring together a cacophony of literary and theological voices.

Certainly, there is no single way to interpret a work as overtly polyvocal and polysemous as the *Mas̱navī.* However, I argue that to read the *Mas̱navī* as the *Book of Ḥusām,* we should approach it as a work that itself "mixes" across different social and literary realms. This chapter therefore offers a reading of the *Mas̱navī* as a miniature, a microcosmic fractal, of a certain historical experience in thirteenth-century Konya—that is, as part of the historical relationship between Rūmī and Ḥusām al-Dīn, but also as part of an analogous and dialogic relationship between the *Mas̱navī* and its audience. As we shall see, the first tale of the *Mas̱navī,* which serves as an extended introduction to the entire work, draws the audience into this relationship in a highly performative manner. It also replicates and refracts, albeit in a highly discursive mode, the historical experience of Rūmī's own reception in Rūm. It does not reduce that experience to one of autobiography but rather elevates it to one of analogue, allowing the historical agents who performed and reflected upon the *Mas̱navī* to gain insight into their own spiritual conditions through the fungible stories of "others."

To read the *Book of Ḥusām,* we'll need to change our focus and dig deeply into the *Mas̱navī*'s first tale, as well as some of its labyrinthine sources, for ourselves. Even on that day with Rūmī, Ḥusām al-Dīn might have realized that the first story of the *Mas̱navī* mixes diverse sources into something new.[3] Perhaps he even recognized that one originally sprang from the pen of a twelfth-century Persian author, Niẓāmī ʿArūẓī (Niẓāmī the Prosodist).[4] In Niẓāmī ʿArūẓī's telling, the Shah of Gorgan invited Ibn Sīnā—Avicenna, as he's known in English—who had traveled westward from his home in Khwarazm, to diagnose an infirm youth. Avicenna inspected the pallid young man by taking his pulse and reciting the names of different districts and streets, waiting to feel a flutter in the youth's veins. When he uttered the name of a particular district, he received his sign: the young man's heart began to pound wildly. After some questioning, Avicenna learned that the youth had fallen in love with a woman who lived on a certain street in that district. Lovers must be united, Avicenna declared, as separation causes affliction. The story concludes in the comic tradition—with a joyous wedding.[5]

Rūmī's adaptation, on the other hand, transforms this simple tale into a performative dialogue on how to engage with, and even interpret, the *Maṣnavī*.[6] His version begins not with the wise physician but with a shah who had fallen madly in love with a poor handmaiden. The Shah, consumed with passion, purchased the lowly handmaiden, uprooted her from her life, and whisked her away to his palace. However, once parted from her loved ones, she lost the will to live, growing thin and white as a strand of hair. Still, the Shah could not bring himself to release her. He soon fell ill himself. The fates of the handmaiden and the Shah were now bound, and it seemed neither would live long. Even the royal physicians, who in their arrogance forgot to utter "If God wills it," were unable to obtain a cure.

At his wit's end, the Shah raced to a nearby mosque, where he fell asleep, soaked in tears. Suddenly, in the realm between sleeping and waking, an old man appeared to him in a dream. The man commanded him not to be afraid, for he bore good tidings:

> He said: "O Shah, good news: your hopes are answered.
> If a stranger [*gharībī*] comes to you tomorrow, he is from Us.
>
> When he comes, he is an ingenious physician [*ḥakīm-i ḥāẕiq*],
> Know his truthfulness, that he is honest and loyal.
>
> Behold total enchantment in his treatment,
> Behold God's endowment in his temperament!"[7]

Taking heart, the Shah rose from his dream and spent the next day overlooking his realm, waiting for the *gharīb,* the one who would reveal secrets. Suddenly, the stranger appeared in the distance, dignified like "a sun among shadow."[8] The Shah was so plainly overwhelmed that he ran to greet the otherworldly stranger on the road, embracing his guest as an intimate companion.[9] Rūmī cloaks this encounter in the traditional language of hospitality: the Shah kissed the guest's brow and hand; he welcomed him profusely and inquired about the road. Their meeting of souls is a joyous affair, bounteous as a convivial gathering (*majlis*) and open table (*khwān-i karam*).[10] "Welcome, O chosen and accepted one!" the Shah effused, eventually steering his beloved guest toward the ailing handmaid.[11]

Much like Avicenna, this strange physician immediately began to monitor the handmaid's pulse, inquiring about her hometown and the streets in her neighborhood. Through this method, he surmised her inner secret: she had fallen in love with a goldsmith who lived in another city, and their separation was killing her. Straightaway, the physician summoned this goldsmith to the Shah's palace, luring him with the promise of wealth and honor. Ḥusām al-Dīn, still seated on the floor next to his master, perhaps expected a happy ending to follow. Instead, the story took a dark turn: rather than marrying off the handmaiden and the goldsmith, the divine physician mixed poison into a sweet-tasting sherbet (*sharbat*), which he offered his guest.[12] Gradually, as the poison did its work, the goldsmith's beauty faded. Soon the handmaid was freed of her attachment. In the end, the goldsmith died from ingesting this poisonous brew, and the Shah and the handmaid were restored to full health.

It was a stunning reversal of the original tale's conclusion. Perhaps sensing his audience's potential confusion, Rūmī concludes the story on a cautionary note. The stranger, he argues, was certainly not wicked but instead was like Khiḍr, commonly identified as the unnamed "green" saint of the Qur'an.[13] It is worth fleshing out this comparison for a moment to appreciate the purpose of Rūmī's adaptation. In the Qur'an (18:65–82), God sends a servant and "friend," Khiḍr in the Sufi reading, to instruct Moses. Although Moses pledges to submit to Khiḍr's will, he finds it difficult to comprehend his teacher's alien conduct. In the course of their travels together, Khiḍr destroys a perfectly fine ship, murders a young man, and repairs a wall near a city of inhospitable people. In disbelief, Moses demands an explanation. Khiḍr replies that a hidden reason lay behind each action: the boat would have fallen into malicious hands; the young man would have dishonored his parents; in repairing the wall, the saint ensured that the inhospitable people would never find a treasure buried in their town.

In a common Sufi interpretation of this account, Moses lacks the ability to discern good from evil without a spiritual guide (Persian: *pīr;* Arabic:

shaykh). In Rūmī's version, the implication is that the *audience* is likewise unprepared to grasp the *Maṣnavī*'s method of instruction. As we've seen, this method mixes together other stories—in this case, a tale that should culminate in a joyous wedding but doesn't—in part to subvert the audience's expectations. No longer a tale of medieval romance, Rūmī's adaptation is about the relationship between master and disciple—between the Stranger and the Shah.[14] The stranger's role, like that of any good spiritual guide, is to estrange the Shah from his worldly attachments and to cultivate *adab,* loosely translated in its oldest sense as "custom" or "habit," which encompassed a form of ethics, urbanity, spiritual discipline, and even the literary knowledge of poetry and prose. Hence, to the extent that *adab* was a habitus of Islamization in Anatolia, as Sara Nur Yıldız has argued, it was partly rooted in the production of poetry.[15] This is especially true of the *Maṣnavī,* whose primary function is to instill spiritual discipline and knowledge in the listener. Hence, near the conclusion of this story, Rūmī directly beseeches God to help his audience cultivate such discipline, without which the world would burn.[16]

Still, this intervention might seem somewhat oblique. How exactly might one extract *adab* from a fanciful tale? Apparently, Rūmī's audience wondered the same thing. Halfway through the tale of the Stranger and the Shah, an unnamed disciple, widely regarded as Ḥusām al-Dīn, interrupts Rūmī's narration from within the text. Ḥusām al-Dīn (or his fictional counterpart) apparently wanted Rūmī to explain the master-student relationship more plainly, starting with Rūmī's own ecstatic encounter with Shams al-Dīn. Rūmī, however, retorts that answering such a request would be impossible—it would be like trying to offer proof of the sun (*shams*), which is its own proof. To foreground the dialogic character of these verses, I have labeled the speaking parts "Ḥusām al-Dīn" and "Rūmī" in my translation below; the original text, however, does not explicitly identify these figures. We might simply call these speakers "Master" and "Disciple" or perhaps, figuratively, even "Stranger" and "Shah," as the dialogue models a particular kind of relationship that the *Maṣnavī* seeks to reproduce. This act of reproduction—the creation of an interpretive community—is not immediately apparent in the following exchange, however. Instead, we most readily encounter an impatient Ḥusām al-Dīn, who simply wants Rūmī to explain spiritual ecstasy and the oblivion of selfhood (*fanā*) in God. But this task would not prove an easy one:

ḤUSĀM AL-DĪN:

"For the sake of years of conversation,
Speak again of spiritual ecstasy, from one of those enticing raptures [with Shams al-Dīn].

So that earth and heaven might laugh,
That mind and spirit and sight might swell a hundred times more."

RŪMĪ (*answering in Arabic*):

"*Do not burden me, for I am in a state of nonexistence* [al-fanā].
My comprehension is dazed, I can conceive of no praise.

Everything said by one without his faculties—
Whether he be reserved or vainglorious—isn't appropriate.

(*He switches to Persian:*)

There isn't a sober vein [in my body],
How should I explain that matchless Friend?

For now, leave the explanation of this separation,
and this broken heart, for a different time."[17]

Ḥusām al-Dīn, piping up for skeptical disciples the world over, didn't like how that sounded, apparently. He'd waited long enough for Rūmī to reveal the higher secrets of ʿAṭṭār and Sanāʾī—secrets that, frustratingly, the story of the Stranger and the Shah seemed only to conceal. A second time, he insists that there is nothing to be gained by making oblique references to Shams al-Dīn through the Shah's tale. Why not speak the truth outright? Rūmī replies that such an action would be impossible—even dangerous—for those who are not spiritually prepared. Ḥusām al-Dīn chafes at this, responding in Arabic, like his master, as if to perform his mastery of *adab*:

ḤUSĀM AL-DĪN (*answering his teacher, in kind, in Arabic*):

He said, "Give me sustenance, for I am ravenous,
And be quick: time is a slicing saber.

(*He switches back to Persian:*)

The Sufi should be a son of time, O friend.
There is no saying 'tomorrow' in one's duty on the Way.

Perhaps you are not a man of Sufism?
All comes to nothing if one tarries."

RŪMĪ:

I told him, "It's sweeter for the secret of the Friend to be cloaked.
Give ear to the details of this tale yourself.

It is sweeter that the secret of lovers
Be spoken in the stories of others [*dīgarān*]."

ḤUSĀM AL-DĪN:

He said, "Say it nakedly, made bare,
The recall of religion is better open than concealed.

Remove the veil and talk nakedly,
For I do not sleep with the beloved in a shirt."

RŪMĪ:

I said, "If you beheld him nakedly,
Nothing of you would remain. Not your bosom. Not your waist.

State your desire, but ask moderately.
A single strand of straw does not hold up a mountain.

If the sun, by which the world is illuminated,
Drew a little closer, all will be incinerated.

Seek not sedition, disturbance, and bloodshed.
Do not speak more of Shams al-Tabrīzī!"[18]

Obviously, in all likelihood Rūmī and Ḥusām al-Dīn did not converse in *mas̱navī* form. The exchange here is imaginative ("fictional," in today's parlance). But it is also more than that: it serves as a heuristic, a dialogic model, that allows one to interpret the story of the Stranger and the Shah in the proper light. One cannot directly speak of higher meanings, just as one cannot describe the "Sun" of religion, Shams al-Dīn. To understand the Sun (or Truth, or Love), one need but look at it. We therefore require the "stories of others"—in fact, the heuristic of others—to contemplate these meanings in an indirect manner, without forgetting that language itself is only another heuristic, circling around but never arriving at a true description of God.[19] Thus, the dialogue between "Rūmī" and "Ḥusām al-Dīn" is not an interruption of our previous tale but rather reveals that the Stranger and the Shah are analogues of "Rūmī" and "Ḥusām al-Dīn," who in turn serve as models for the audience's own disciple-master relationship with the *Mas̱navī*. The story of the Stranger and the Shah, therefore, is partly about Rūmī's audience—those who would speak with and from within the *Mas̱navī*, in its prescriptive voice, like our frustrated "Ḥusām al-Dīn."

Welcoming the Stranger

This is where a reading of the *Mas̱navī* as a miniature of Rūm begins to take shape. Here, in a versified exchange between "Rūmī" and "Ḥusām al-Dīn," we arrive at a guiding principle of the *Mas̱navī*: we need strangers to learn something important, something linguistically elusive, about ourselves in general and Islam in particular. Although Rūmī's concern is partly linguistic, he also took this lesson to heart in a more literal manner. As we have seen, he embraced not only stories about others but also the staggering variety of otherness that Konya had to offer. This meant he often treated simple craftsmen and illiterate people in the same manner as popular verses of poetry, commonplace narratives, and widespread musical forms: as though they concealed inner spiritual secrets. Despite confounding some of his more conservative followers, this attitude served both a pragmatic and an esoteric purpose, as it helped him to mix the diverse peoples of Konya into his project of charging everyday life with explicitly Islamic meaning.

It was his relationship with Ḥusām al-Dīn, the son of Akhī Turk, that truly exemplified this process. Despite their multifaceted differences, Rūmī often treated Ḥusām al-Dīn as the quintessential beloved. He publicly declared Ḥusām al-Dīn to be "my soul, my faith, my Junayd, my light, my master, the darling of God, the beloved of the prophets!" This extravagant praise must have brought disbelief to the faces of those present; Ḥusām al-Dīn apparently pulled aside the region's governor to explain, "Although it's not so, when Mawlānā [Rūmī] says it, it becomes so—a hundred times it becomes so!"[20] This unlikely relationship between master and student also produced a gradual transformation. For Rūmī, as we've seen, Ḥusām al-Dīn was the "grower" of the *Maṣnavī,* the one who drew out the tales of others in a manner his companions would find pleasing. Yet for Ḥusām al-Dīn, the change was even more radical. "I went to sleep as a Kurd and awoke as an Arab," he reportedly declared, in Arabic, of the relationship.[21] In other words, by following Rūmī and helping to produce the *Maṣnavī,* a native of Konya entered into the literary and theological spheres of the greater Islamicate world and, in turn, helped others in Rūm to do the same. Moreover, he also participated in shaping the increasingly prestigious literary culture of New Persian, entering into discursive and aesthetic spheres that were previously somewhat out of reach for a Kurd or a Turk born in Rūm. In short: he had cultivated *adab.*

What's most remarkable about the *Maṣnavī*'s first tale is that it represents and models this transformative relationship through subsequent performances of the *Maṣnavī.* That is, just as Ḥusām al-Dīn's relationship with Rūmī allowed him to participate in broadly circulating religious discourses and literary cultures, it also laid a foundation for the *Maṣnavī*'s audiences to do the same. Aflākī reports, for instance, that one way Ḥusām al-Dīn taught the *Maṣnavī* to others was by requiring them to recite it aloud with him, performing the roles of both "Rūmī" and "Ḥusām al-Dīn" at the same time.[22] In a literal sense, he guided others to engage with this literary and religious culture with his own voice, just as he preserved and transmitted it by writing in his own hand. The major implication is that the audience's reception of the *Maṣnavī,* which was chanted aloud, would be analogous to Ḥusām al-Dīn's reception of Rūmī, or the Shah's reception of the divine Stranger, or Rūmī's reception of Shams al-Dīn. It is primarily through this act of performance that the transformative encounter, wherein our spiritual states are revealed in the stories of others, even others who are different from "us," actually takes place.

It is therefore no coincidence that Rūmī presented himself in the same metaphoric terms he used to represent the Stranger in the *Maṣnavī.* He was, for his community, the quintessential stranger—not because he had come from Khorasan, but because, like the Stranger in the *Maṣnavī,* he viewed his authority as emanating from another realm. For instance, in one of his sermons Rūmī argues that because the entire world is but one house, traveling between rooms cannot make one a stranger. True strangers, he contends, are estranged from worldly attachments altogether—akin to the *gharīb* in the *Maṣnavī*'s first tale.[23] Tellingly, Rūmī's companions adopted this discourse as they reflected on his life. Thus, even after Rūmī's death, the poet ʿIrāqī proclaimed, "No one understood Mawlānā as he ought to be [understood]. He came into this world a *gharīb* and departed from it a *gharīb*."[24] Shams al-Dīn likewise thought of Rūmī as a stranger. "The secret of [Rūmī] is veiled as is the secret of Islam," he declared. "Like Islam, he has come as a *gharīb*. See how his secret shall be as [the hadith declares]: 'Islam began as a *gharīb* and will return as a *gharīb*. How blessed are the strangers!' "[25]

Just as important, Rūmī was also the "ingenious physician" (*ṭabīb-i ḥāẕiq*) who would mix his remedy—a particular discourse about Islam—into a more palatable form. In the *Maṣnavī*'s first story, that microcosmic form is a sweet sherbet (*sharbat*), the remedy a poison (but only to the uninitiated). However, in the macrocosm of Konya, Rūmī's palatable form was nothing other than the medicinal *Maṣnavī* itself, which aimed to reveal higher spiritual truths through its absorption of a variety of other poetic and theological works, including the popular sound of other didactic *maṣnavī*s. Put even more plainly, the first tale of the *Maṣnavī* thematizes not only its reception, as Ḥusām al-Dīn represents the *Maṣnavī*'s audience within the text, but also its own *composition*, depicted as the mixing of a sweet-tasting sherbet—the blended form of sundry literary adaptations and theological discourses—by an ingenious stranger-physician. In rewriting these works, in turning their narratives inside out, Rūmī aimed to reveal meanings that frequently worked against the expectations of his audience, who might be familiar with an "original" variant. The ultimate adaptation that Rūmī aimed to create, however, was a social one, as he sought to estrange his audience from preexisting worldly attachments and help them to cultivate *adab* by reflecting on the stories of others. The Shah, who receives the stranger with open arms, who kisses the stranger's face, who becomes the stranger's true beloved, is thus a figure of the audience. In this economy of metaphor, Rūmī is the stranger, the audience is the host, and performance is the praxis that knits the two together.[26]

J. L. Austin famously defined a performative utterance as one that "is, or is a part of, the doing of an action," whose paradigmatic example is saying "I do" during a marriage ceremony.[27] Hence, although the *Maṣnavī* is meant to be performed, either by chanting aloud or later by singing through the art of *āvāz*, it is also highly performative insofar as it describes a series of life-changing encounters with "others" and brings about what it describes through its own performance. For a Turk, Kurd, Armenian, or Greek in the time of Rūmī, listening to a performance of the *Maṣnavī* could literally mean welcoming the culture of strangers: both a discourse on Islam and a Persianate literary tradition steeped in the "strange meanings" of ʿAṭṭār and Sanāʾī. But it could also mean something far more straightforward: welcoming others into one's midst. As we've seen, when travelers like Ibn Baṭṭūṭa visited the Sufi hospice in Konya, they were sometimes treated to a performance of the *Maṣnavī*, chanted aloud by the official reciter, while they sat convivially in a spiritual repast. To perform the *Maṣnavī*, to recite it aloud, is potentially to perform, right from its first tale, an act of hospitality.

Rūmī alludes to such hospitality in a sermon from the *Fīhi mā fīh*. This sermon opens with the shocking claim that nonbelievers, including Greeks, can understand the essence of Rūmī's teachings even if they do not understand his exact words. Strikingly, as Rūmī declares, all people long for God, who is the true source from which we have been separated. In silence, before our longings come to language, there is no difference between Muslim and infidel. Because human speech cannot contain the divine, God himself must provide the path that leads to union with Him. And what is that path? "It is the story of a stranger [*gharīb*]," Rūmī explains. "It requires a stranger [*gharībī*] to hear, and be able to hear, the story of a stranger [*ḥikāyat-i gharīb*]."[28] We have heard part of this strange tale, from the mouth of a self-described stranger. It is Rūmī's *Maṣnavī*.

At the same time, in thirteenth- and fourteenth-century Konya, performances of music and poetry were opportunities for strangers and hosts, musicians and poets, indigenous and exogenous members of society to mix with one another. Performances were sites where Rūmī's audiences or companions could shape the *Maṣnavī*'s public reception in different ways—even by responding to it in a dialogic manner, much as Ḥusām al-Dīn does within the text. For instance, the official *Maṣnavī* reciter (*Maṣnavī-khwān*), even while chanting in a fixed poetic meter, could emphasize certain words or passages with minute inflections of his voice. This might seem like a small thing, but as Paul Zumthor reminds us, the human voice is not merely a conduit through which information passes but actually a medium of transmission in its own right.[29] Most medieval audiences experienced literary texts by listening to a voice, which could color a performance, through subtle emphases and other artistic choices, with a range of emotive states that were not textually inherent in any way. In this loose sense, to read the *Mas̱navī* aloud, in one's own voice, is to "adapt" it. The same can certainly be said of any musical accompaniment during or after such readings. When the Mawlaviyya practice of *samāʿ* was standardized in the manner that is still familiar today—sometime during the early modern period—participants began their remembrance of God by listening to an improvisation (*taqsīm*) on the *nay*.[30] Music allowed, and still allows, practitioners of *samāʿ* to reflect on Rūmī's poetry and on their own separation from God, but to do so in a locally contingent and aural mode, shaped by an individual musician on a given day.

Vocalists, sometimes with musical accompaniment, have even more freedom than reciters to mix the *Mas̱navī* into locally appealing musical forms and modes. In New Persian, the word for both "voice" and "song," *āvāz,* has a special relationship to the recitation of metrical poetry. It is through *āvāz* that singers have long performed the *Mas̱navī,* setting its words within a sophisticated modal system.[31] In many ways, the art of *āvāz* has informed the sound of the *Mas̱navī,* serving as another mode of address to audiences. In this sense, the *Mas̱navī*'s voice is still, to this very day, collaborative and communally contingent.[32] It is a voice that both belongs and does not belong to Rūmī and to his readers at the same time, shaped by the agencies of author, performers, and audiences alike.[33] Finally, it is also analogous to Ḥusām al-Dīn's voice in the performative dialogue of the *Mas̱navī*'s introductory tale, in that it allows its performers to participate in the adaptive process—the "mixing" of Islamic meanings into a locally palatable, communally contingent form. This kind of performative adaptation of an otherwise unchanging text is thus a mechanism of interpretation, but it is also one of *ownership,* of making the culture of "others" one's own. Performance enabled a reader, a singer, or a musician to take part in the hermeneutic endeavor of the *Mas̱navī* in ways that Rūmī himself could not anticipate or control.

Franklin D. Lewis has noted that scholars often complain that the *Masnavī*'s teachings are unorganized and unsystematic, that it's difficult to sift through and easily extract information from it.[34] Indeed, as Ḥusām al-Dīn's dialogue with Rūmī shows, impatient readers made the same complaint some eight centuries prior. What the *Masnavī* ultimately teaches is this ability, and this drive, to perform its hermeneutic maneuver for oneself: to mix the mundane, to mix the worldly, into an Islamic matrix of meaning. In this, the *Masnavī* seems to have been almost immediately successful, at least among a small coterie. Years later, Rūmī's son Sulṭān Valad (d. 1312) observed Ḥusām al-Dīn conversing with a group of people in his garden, telling simple stories about orchards and, presumably, horticulture. This is not, however, what reached Sulṭān Valad's ears. "All I heard from his blessed mouth [were] spiritual meanings and secrets," he reported of the miraculous, ecstatic state he had entered. Coming to his senses, he recalled a passage from his father's *Masnavī*, whose inner meaning was suddenly illuminated:

> Whatever the man in love speaks, the aroma of love
> Issues from his mouth into the realm of love.
>
> If he utters law, it all comes out as [spiritual] poverty,
> The fragrance of poverty comes from his sweet, enchanting speech.
>
> And should he recite blasphemy, it has the aroma of religion.
> And should he speak of doubt, his doubt is reborn as certainty.[35]

Sulṭān Valad had internalized the *Masnavī*'s "enchanting speech," a discursive mode that encouraged him, and others like him, to view his world through its hermeneutic frame—to look for, and thereby to create, meaning Islamically, even in everyday places such as Ḥusām al-Dīn's garden. The *Masnavī* teaches this interpretive mode, mixing the genre of exegesis (*tafsīr*) into something much more like a performative epistemology—one in which differences are made meaningful in Islamic terms, illuminating texts and lived experiences in equal measure. This is what it means to read the *Book of Ḥusām*: not necessarily to mine it for its historical content, but rather to view the matrix of its composition and hermeneutics as extending far beyond the static text that Ḥusām al-Dīn so lovingly recorded, folio by folio, in black ink.[36] To paraphrase Rūmī, the *Book of Ḥusām* may have entered the world, but was always a part and product of it.

A Miniature of Rūm

Just as the *Mas̱navī* presents a series of mirrored analogies, a fractal field of figures that shaped and were shaped by historical experience, this book treats the production of premodern literature and the cultivation of premodern interpretive communities as reflections of each other. It does so in part because this is how our premodern subjects theorized their own literary production. Thus, years after Rūmī's death, Aflākī was able to write both that Ḥusām al-Dīn "became cognizant of the mysteries and treasures of the [*Mas̱navī*'s] secrets" and that the six books of the *Mas̱navī* "were an explanation of [Ḥusām al-Dīn's] secret." The books, Aflākī asserted, "were revealed as a depiction of him."[37] In this view, the *Mas̱navī* and Ḥusām al-Dīn were commentaries on each other. The *Book of Ḥusām* offers us a case study in Anatolian literary history, one in which the voices of authors and audiences were important in asymmetrical ways, as they both shaped a dialogism that gave rise to a growing literary field. This is, of course, not the only way to read the *Mas̱navī*—far from it. However, I contend that it is the way we ought to read the *Book of Ḥusām*: that is, as both a product and a producer, signifier and signified, of the literary and musical cultures that circulated in Rūm.

This manner of thinking about literary production in premodern Anatolia—as dialogic and multimedial, a mode of composition that was shaped by multiple agencies and multiple voices—helps to break the mold cast by Ibn Baṭṭūṭa, in which the *Mas̱navī* appeared in Konya on account of Shams al-Dīn's holiness or Rūmī's singular literary genius. Instead, it spurs us to examine how cultures of poetry were produced in a more communal manner, shedding light on the historical ties that bound seemingly disparate literatures and audiences together. The dialogism that produced the *Mas̱navī*—part of an ongoing relationship between Ḥusām al-Dīn and Rūmī—is preserved not only by medieval hagiographies like that of Aflākī but also by the *Mas̱navī* itself, which models an analogous dialogue between "master" and "disciple" for its many audiences.

At the same time, the *Mas̱navī* theorizes its own performance across different media, as its organizing symbol, the dislocated *nay,* is not only textual but also sonic in character. Those who would make the *nay* "lament," who would chant the *Mas̱navī* aloud or even play musical instruments following its reading, therefore take part in this dialogue with the text. Like Ḥusām al-Dīn, they would also embody the *Book of Ḥusām*, albeit differently. However, the *Mas̱navī*'s "voice" could only be communal, as it was produced not only through the pen but also through a performance or an audible recitation and discussion between a teacher and their audience (see figure 1).

To some extent, as I have argued, the same dialogism that produced the *Mas̱navī* also produced the historical figure of Rūmī, whose agency was shaped by preexisting poetic and hospitable cultures in Rūm, by other literary works in Persian (such as the poetry of ʿAṭṭār and Sanāʾī), and by religious figures (like Shams al-Dīn) from elsewhere. As the following chapters will demonstrate, although the content of the *Mas̱navī* is not always locally oriented, its omnivorous adaptation of other sources, its transmutation of those sources into poetry and enticing sounds, and its ability to engage with heterogeneous audiences all reflect broad trends that spanned premodern Anatolia. In this light, Rūmī's manner of composing the *Mas̱navī* is particularly representative of a widespread pattern, the warp and woof of cultural production in Rūm, that would come to define the development of Anatolian Turkish and Middle Armenian literature in the next century. Significantly, many of the pioneering authors of Turkish literature were familiar with the *Mas̱navī* and in fact pursued a similar hermeneutic endeavor—via a strange mixing of sources—in part to demonstrate that Anatolian Turkish was fit to serve as a literary language within the Islamicate world.

Our literary history of Anatolia in the thirteenth century therefore begins with a practice of mixing and recombining the literary and musical cultures of "others." As we shall see, this practice generally aimed to produce a pleasing and recognizable sound and style, one that would be familiar to the ear and palatable to the audience. It often drew from a shared lexicon and shaped shared concepts across the New Persian, Anatolian Turkish, and Middle Armenian languages. It even helped to establish new standards for what poetry is and what it could mean for emerging literatures like Anatolian Turkish and Middle Armenian. Most important, this practice of adaptive composition infused these sonic and literary cultures with new meanings, thereby bringing diverse audiences into specific communal and confessional orientations. Adaptive composition, seen in this

FIGURE 1. A miniature from the *Ṣavāqib-i manāqib* (c. 1590–99), an abridged Turkish translation of Aflākī's *Manāqib al-ʿārifīn*, depicting a panorama in which different media act upon Rūmī's followers: the study and recitation of texts fill the top half of the frame, while musical performance facilitates the practice of *samāʿ* in the bottom half, alive with dizzying motion. Courtesy of The Morgan Library & Museum, New York. MS M.466, fol. 159r. Purchased by J. Pierpont Morgan (1837–1913) in 1911.

light, was not merely an activity constricted to the aesthetic realm: it was a communal and social mode of meaning making, with stakes for the production of religious knowledge in a heterogeneous urban environment.

Broadly conceived, to adapt, to mix, was to perform a kind of hospitality—but not one without self-interest. It was to welcome, with one's ear, the inviting call of another's voice. And as Ḥusām al-Dīn well understood, while he recited the *Book of Ḥusām* back to his master at the close of each day, it was also to make that voice, and its tradition, one's own.

CHAPTER THREE

LANGUAGES OF AFFINITY

The King's Speech

When Rūmī died in 1273, Persians, Greeks, Turks, Jews, and others flooded the streets of Konya to mourn the charismatic preacher and poet. Qur'an reciters read the holy verses; singers chanted funeral poetry composed by their deceased master; musicians accompanied the din on kettledrum (*naqqāra*), shrill woodwind pipe (*surnā*), and horn (*nafīr*).[1] It must have been an overwhelming experience for all involved, perhaps especially for Rūmī's son Sulṭān Valad. Sipahsālār's hagiographical account expresses the enormity of the event in miraculous terms, claiming that Rūmī's death was preceded by forty days of thunderous earthquakes.[2] Such reports have something of an apocalyptic flair, much like eschatological literature in the Jewish and Christian traditions, which presage epochal shifts by unsettling the very ground beneath our feet. Perhaps for some in the crowd it really did feel like the ending of an age.

One by one, as they joined the funeral procession, Jews recited the Torah and Christians read aloud from the Gospels. When questioned on their relationship with Rūmī, they reportedly answered: "We grasped the truth of Moses and the truth of Jesus and of all the prophets through his clear explanations. We witnessed in him the manner of the perfect prophets whom we had read about in our scriptures. If you, Muslims, say that the honorable Mawlānā is the Muḥammad of your time, we know him as the Moses of the age and the Jesus of the epoch."[3] The scene recalls, perhaps not coincidentally, a story from the *Maṣnavī* about the diverse birds in Solomon's retinue, who each marveled that the king could understand their speech. Gradually, as they conversed with Solomon, a strange transformation took hold. The birds, presumably once divided in speech, began to imitate their silver-tongued lord:

> All the birds, having quit their chirping,
> Spoke more eloquently with Solomon than [you with] your brother.
>
> To share the same language is [to share] kinship and connection;
> A man, with those who aren't intimates [*nāmaḥramān*], is like a captive.
>
> Oh, many Indians and Turks share the same tongue,
> Oh, many pairs of Turks are [still] like strangers.
>
> Thus the language of intimacy [*zabān-i maḥramī*] is itself different:
> It's better to be same in heart than same in tongue.[4]

The point of the tale, for Rūmī, was uncharacteristically simple. Speaking the same language (*ham zabānī*) pales in comparison to being one in heart (*ham dilī*), or possessing a shared framework for interpreting and making meaning out of the world. What Rūmī's hagiographers also stressed, it appears, is that their master ultimately succeeded in performing a Solomonesque function in Konya. Like that eloquent king, Rūmī had learned to communicate with different peoples on their own terms, joining the patchwork social fabrics of Rūm into something more cohesive. Seemingly, even those who did not convert to Islam—such as certain Armenians, Greeks, and Jews—had striven to emulate the strange preacher from Khorasan, who spoke, if not in their actual tongues, then at least something like a language of affinity, a tongue of kinship, in a resonant manner.

Sulṭān Valad, who initially ceded leadership of his father's followers to Ḥusām al-Dīn, would attempt to emulate his father as well, to varying degrees of success. On the occasion of Ḥusām al-Dīn's death in 1284, he appeared at a total loss on being left on his own. "After your passing, what will my state be like? And who will be the companion of my soul?" he pleaded with his father's dearest disciple, weeping bitterly. A litany of worry poured from his lips: "Whom will I sit with? From whom shall I seek true sustenance? Whom shall I tell the secret of the heart? With whom shall I find my company? And who will share my pain in this heart-rending, world-ending separation?"[5] His troubles ran deeper, perhaps, than he let on. How would he lay claim to his inheritance—the colossal literary, social, and theological achievements of his father? How do you succeed your father, especially when he is Our Master, Mawlānā, the incomparable Jalāl al-Dīn Rūmī?

From a modern perspective, one might assume that Sulṭān Valad was seized by an unyielding anxiety, an absolute need to grapple with the triumphs of his forefathers and overthrow them. After all, as the literary scholar Harold Bloom has argued, the history of Western literature is best understood as an unceasing rivalry between literary "fathers" and their successors—a basically Oedipal relationship, though Bloom has resisted this term.[6] "The greatest truth of literary influence is that it is an irresistible anxiety," Bloom writes, adding by way of example, "Shakespeare will not allow you to bury him, or escape him, or replace him."[7] For Bloom, influence (which shares the same root as *influenza*) is something that Western authors after Shakespeare cannot escape; hence, it becomes a site where authorial originality is both fetishized and called into question. By Bloom's logic, Sulṭān Valad would be a literary disappointment of sorts.

"Is there an original thought in Sulṭān Valad?" asks Abdülbâki Gölpınarlı, one of the foremost scholars of the Mawlaviyya. Sulṭān Valad, he rightly notes, walked closely in the footsteps of his father, repackaging many of Rūmī's ideas in the same style. "Of course," Gölpınarlı adds, "these are presented to us in a more sallow and lifeless state."[8] We find an echo of this refrain in the mouths of many others—seemingly even Sulṭān Valad himself, who denigrates courtly poets for treating composition as an aesthetic endeavor. "The poetry of the lover is all exegesis [*tafsīr*]," he stresses in a well-known poem, whereas "the poetry of poets is surely the stench of garlic [*taf-i sīr*]."[9] It seems that Sulṭān Valad thought of his craft in rather lukewarm and utilitarian terms. Modern appraisers have concurred, taking such statements at face value, as though a practice of *tafsīr,* a performative hermeneutics that encompassed audience and author alike, were not a major function of the *Maṣnavī.* Thus, although clearly admiring Sulṭān Valad as one of the earliest poets to compose in Anatolian Turkish, Gibb concluded that he "is one of those men whom I have described as being less a poet than a mystic teacher who taught through verse."[10] In this light, Sulṭān Valad's poetry is interesting and notable from a linguistic and theological standpoint but hardly a literary one. As Gibb explained in his first monumental volume on the history of Ottoman poetry, which appeared in London over a century ago, Sulṭān Valad's verses—including his work in Turkish—make "no attempt at literary grace of any kind."[11]

This view has only recently begun to change.[12] Lars Johanson was the first to trouble it, noting in a groundbreaking article in 1993 that we should not conflate Sulṭān Valad's dexterity as a poet with his "remarkable *linguistic creativity*" in fashioning some of the earliest verses of Anatolian Turkish in his *Dīvān* and in two of his three *maṣnavī*s, the *Ibtidā-nāma* and the *Rabāb-nāma.*[13] Still, even for Johanson, the basic assumption is the same. "Rūmī's activity was *poetically productive,* whereas that of some of his Turkish successors was largely *reproductive,* however creative they may have been in a strictly *linguistic* sense," he argues.[14] In poetic terms, for Johanson, Sulṭān Valad "necessarily remained in the shade of the great genius."[15] Likewise, Franklin D. Lewis, the preeminent Rūmī scholar in North America, initially reiterated Gibb's assertion, noting that "we sense that [Sulṭān Valad] is indeed more committed to the ideas than to the art of poesy." In Lewis's phrasing, he was "a generally competent Persian poet."[16] Generally, scholars have tended to view Sulṭān Valad's poetry as a kind of crude yet functional information-delivery system.[17]

Recently, however, in a paradigm-shifting essay, Lewis has offered a more dynamic look at Sulṭān Valad's literary production, taking him seriously as a poet. Explicitly arguing against a universal "assumption that Sulṭān Valad was a versifier, rather than a poet," Lewis sketches a picture of Sulṭān Valad as someone "born to poetry" and attuned to the musical cultures of Rūm, much like his father.[18] It is a perspective that has been sorely lacking over the past century. At the same time, this appreciation of Sulṭān Valad–as–poet has intensified the reading of the anxious son struggling to define himself against his literary and literal forefathers. For instance, Lewis observes that Sulṭān Valad chose to compose his first *maṣnavī,* the *Ibtidā-nāma,* not in the *ramal* meter of his father's masterwork but rather in the *khafīf* meter of Sanā'ī's *Ilāhī-nāma*—a gesture he calls "aggressively Oedipal," suggesting a hidden displeasure on Sulṭān Valad's part in his audience's request that he "imitate" the *Maṣnavī.*[19] It would seem that to rehabilitate the reputation of Sulṭān Valad's poetry, one must distance him from the imitation of his father, prizing originality above all.

Certainly, if one were to call Sulṭān Valad's poetry a product of *taqlīd,* blind imitation, he would have bristled. In different ways, even the earliest Ottoman poets would write disparagingly about this form of literary mimicry. Laṭīfī, who in 1546 completed an early Ottoman *teẕkire* (biography of poets), distinguished between poets who are people of God, and thus possess innate literary ability, and those who compose poetry through mere imitation.[20] In his view, even poets of natural ability end up reproducing, with subtle variations, the works of previous poets—the challenge resides in how one deviates from what has already been said. In fact, this is one way that Laṭīfī defines a true poet: "Through a pure disposition and the benefit of understanding, he imagines another poetic meaning from that [original] meaning and transports it from that art to another art," thereby dressing old metaphors and motifs in new garb.[21] As Walter G. Andrews has observed, for Laṭīfī, "this type of poet, the poet with the creative 'gift,' whether he writes original works or reveals an original dimension in the work of another, is always characterized by uniqueness of imagination."[22] From this perspective, the simple act of imitation does not itself make one a reductive poet; rather, early Ottoman poets could distinguish themselves even through a praxis of emulation (distinct from the pejorative sense of *taqlīd*), so long as they revealed hidden depths in or created new meanings from the works of other poets.[23]

Tellingly, pre-Ottoman sources on the Valad family—including Sulṭān Valad's own writings—exhibit no anxiety about any likeness between father and son. "Of all people," Rūmī reportedly told Sulṭān Valad in Arabic, "you resemble me most in constitution and nature."[24] This resemblance had a more generative meaning for our premodern subjects than terms like *taqlīd* or modern conceptions of "imitation" might suggest.[25] Whereas today's expectation is that Sulṭān Valad would have felt pressure to overcome, or at least try to match, his father's literary prowess, many premodern sources see no major conflict in his co-opting, or even merely reusing, Rūmī's poetic style(s) and content to serve the needs of his audience and followers. Hagiographic sources seek to valorize Sulṭān Valad not because he was different from Rūmī but rather because, in their view, he was essentially the same, capable of engaging deeply with the same source material and revealing the inner secrets of the Qur'an, the hadith, diverse works of Persian poetry, and the *Maṣnavī.* Thus, Aflākī rests Sulṭān Valad's spiritual authority largely upon his ability to interpret and engage artfully with the works of his father—in other words, to disseminate Rūmī's teachings throughout Anatolia. For "seventy complete years, without cessation or pause, he conveyed the discourse of his father through eloquence of speech and comeliness of expression," Aflākī reports. "He showed a miraculous hand in the explanation of secrets and interpretation [*tafsīr*] of the traditions," even through the selection of his representatives, whom he dispatched to other cities.[26]

In some ways, Rūmī provided the precedent for this activity, unsettling the notion of contrasting paternal production and filial reproduction (read: aesthetic *reduction*). After all, he likewise reproduced the style and meter of other poets, including ʿAṭṭār and Sanāʾī, to illuminate their "strange" meanings. But his adaptations also served another purpose. "Whoever busies themselves with the speech of ʿAṭṭār shall profit from the speech of Ḥakīm [Sanāʾī] and will reach an understanding of the secrets of those words," Rūmī declared, binding the two poets within the same hermeneutic circle. At the center of this circle was, of course, nothing other than the *Maṣnavī* itself. Therefore, as Rūmī continued, "whoever studies the words of Sanāʾī in complete seriousness will be well versed in the secret of the splendor of our words."[27] Hence, by adapting the styles and discourses of other poets, Rūmī placed himself within a particular literary genealogy, akin to the spiritual genealogies (*silsila*) that tied the founders of Sufi communities to the Prophet, retroactively constructing an unimpeachable authority. Rūmī's *Maṣnavī* opens another way of thinking about these chains of spiritual authority, as it fashions a poetic *silsila* that binds its interpretation to the interpretation of preexisting works of didactic poetry. That is, through a practice of literary imitation, adaptation, and emulation, Rūmī attempted to shape how his interpretive community in Konya received these other works.

Sulṭān Valad seems to have understood the function of emulation in similar terms. His companions had long observed that Rūmī had "composed *dīvān*s in many meters and quatrains" and that Sulṭān Valad had therefore done likewise, composing a *dīvān* of his own "by way of following [*mutāba ʿat*]," or emulating, his father.[28] For Sulṭān Valad, being a good disciple and being a good poet were not contradictory but rather two sides of the same coin: one could shape one's spiritual genealogy and literary authority by adapting, with subtle variation, the poetry of other poets. Therefore, regardless of the (unknown) psychological hang-ups that may (or may not) have informed a literary relationship between father and son, it is clear that poetic emulation served an important function for this interpretive community.

In fact, we know that Sulṭān Valad also wrote hundreds of poems in dialogue with and in response to individual poems by his father, honing his poetic voice in the process.[29] Sulṭān Valad might have continued to compose *ghazal*s, it seems, save for the fact that his followers desired an imitation of a different sort. "Eventually, the companions made an entreaty," he states. "Since, in following [*mutāba ʿat*] your father, you have [already] fashioned a *dīvān*," they pleaded, "it is necessary also to follow [*mutāba ʿat*] [him] in a *maṣnavī*."[30] Sulṭān Valad granted this request and composed a new *maṣnavī* around the year 1291. He signaled his soaring ambitions with its title, *Ibtidā-nāma,* or *The Book of Beginning.* As he makes clear from the outset, this adaptation's purpose would be exegesis, cloaked in the form of stories, much in the style of his father. Its subject matter would be somewhat different, however:

> My esteemed father and teacher and shaykh, the sultan of the scholars and the gnostics, Mawlānā Jalāl al-Ḥaqq wa'l-Dīn . . . commemorated the stories of past saints and described their miraculous deeds and stations [on the Way] in his *Maṣnavī.* His aim in [telling] their stories was to describe the miraculous deeds and stations of theirs and of those saintly comrades who were his intimate companions [*hamdam*], cordial friends [*hamnishīn*], and the same in heart [*hamdil*] as he.[31]

These companions were, he notes, none other than Shams al-Dīn Tabrīzī, Ḥusām al-Dīn Chalabī, Ṣalāḥ al-Dīn Zarkūb, and Burhān al-Dīn Muḥaqqiq. In other words, Sulṭān Valad interpreted the *Maṣnavī* not as part of an ahistorical, atemporal Sufi realm but rather as something more like the *Book of Ḥusām*: higher truths cloaked in historically rooted, locally contingent garb.[32] The *Ibtidā-nāma* doubles down on this principle, explicitly depicting the lives of Rūmī and his companions as a means of illuminating the audience's spiritual conditions. In other words, the *Ibtidā-nāma* is both a product of emulation and a *producer* of emulation, as it provides a model for others to "follow." As if to emphasize this point, Sulṭān Valad adapts a line from the opening tale of the *Maṣnavī*, now put in service as his very raison d'être for composing poetry:

> It is sweeter that the secrets of lovers
> be spoken in the stories of others.[33]

Therefore, since Rūmī had narrated stories about his predecessors from a bygone age, Sulṭān Valad would tell a complementary kind of tale: his *maṣnavī* would concern affairs that had occurred in his own time.[34]

These opening lines exhibit a different attitude toward imitation and originality, author and audience, than we find in most critical assessments of Sulṭān Valad's poetry. As the *Ibtidā-nāma*'s introduction suggests, Sulṭān Valad viewed "imitation" as a way of fashioning a new spiritual genealogy, of simultaneously constructing his own authority and reframing the authority of his predecessors in a particular light. To imitate, in this sense, was not to perform a reductive activity: it was to choose one's predecessors for oneself, to make their literary production part of one's own, and ultimately to shape the reception of each poet or religious figure within this genealogical chain.

Of course, it is possible that the audience's request for a new *maṣnavī* is a literary trope—a commonplace way of gesturing humility—rather than a historical reality.[35] Even so, the effect is the same: Sulṭān Valad inaugurated his career as a *maṣnavī* writer by reproducing the very origin story of the *Maṣnavī*, right down to his analogous choice of poetic meter, although he borrows this from Sanā'ī and not ʿAṭṭār. Had he composed in ʿAṭṭār's meter (as his father did), his *Ibtidā-nāma* would have sounded identical to the *Maṣnavī*, perhaps obscuring the effect of this imitative gesture. The point, I suggest, is that Sulṭān Valad demonstrated that his poetic authority issued from the same *sources* as did the authority of his father—that is, from his engagement with the higher secrets of ʿAṭṭār and Sanā'ī—and not only from the *Maṣnavī* alone. Thus, even his manner of claiming this authority, a claim advanced through the emulation of other poets, can be read as a subtle imitation of his father's own literary beginnings.

In the parlance of Sulṭān Valad, "to imitate" and "to follow" were the same, expressed by the same word—*mutāba'at*—which conjoined poets as intimately as rose and nightingale, moth and flame.[36] It is because and not in spite of emulation that he took up the pen to compose the *Ibtidā-nāma*.[37] "Another reason [for composing this *masnavī*] is that a disciple must adopt the character of his shaykh and follow [*mutāba'at*] the shaykh," he explains, "just as the faithful with the imam and the follower with the guide." Imitation takes many forms, such as "dressing in a robe, shaving one's head, performing *samā'*," or, as the existence of the *Ibtidā-nāma* suggests, even composing poetry.[38] There is little here to suggest that Sulṭān Valad felt locked in an Oedipal competition, or experienced an overwhelming anxiety, in following his father in this way. Nor is this act of *mutāba'at* merely "reductive" or "reproductive." Rūmī may have practiced *samā'*, but it was his son Sulṭān Valad who began to formalize and institutionalize it. Put simply, it was through the emulation of his father—a process that encompassed more than literary production alone—that Sulṭān Valad codified a particular manner of engaging with the teachings of Rūmī. As he seems to have understood, in emulation there is power.

Here, in this genealogical practice of adaptation, in which a poet shaped their legitimacy as a poet in part by co-opting the authority of previous poets, we find the contours of a larger story taking shape. For it was during this period that poets in Anatolia first admitted Turkish poetry to writing—and did so, moreover, by adapting Persianate literary forms and styles. In this labor, they constructed affiliations both for themselves in relation to their predecessors and for the Turkish language in relation to Persian and Arabic literatures. If we want to understand how and why Turkish deftly absorbed, and subtly reimagined, the literary codes of other languages in cities like Konya, we need to understand this denigrated mode of emulation better. Sulṭān Valad, the supposedly drier, less vital analogue of Rūmī, stands at the threshold of this story: how Anatolian Turkish, a stranger on the scene, made an early bid to become a literary language within the Persianate cultural sphere, long before the rise of the Ottomans.[39]

A Covenant of Voices

Sulṭān Valad came of age in a period of transition. He was only fourteen years old when Bābā Isḥāq, a charismatic Sufi leader, helped to foment a

Türkmen revolt against the Seljuks in 1240. The Seljuks failed to quash the rebellion themselves, instead relying on Frankish mercenaries to help them end it.[40] But the real victors of this conflict were the Mongols, who defeated the weakened Seljuk Sultanate of Rūm at the battle of Köse Dağ in 1243.[41] Their invasion triggered another wave of migrations to Anatolia, as nomads and urbanized Turks fled the Mongol incursions into Transoxania and Arran.[42] This upheaval marked Sulṭān Valad's youth, as a new influx of outsiders moved through the cities and country of Rūm. Cumulatively, these and earlier migrations presaged a cultural sea change too frequently assumed to be a teleological certainty: the ascendancy of Anatolian Turkish as one of the major literary languages of the Islamicate world.

Still, at the time of Rūmī's death the development of literary Turkish was far from certain. In fact, we can observe a fundamental ambivalence, if not outright hostility, toward the Turkish language at the end of the thirteenth century. Only three years after Rūmī's death, Meḥmed Bey, the son of a woodcutter named Ḳarāmān, fomented another rebellion against the Seljuks, which culminated in his taking the city of Konya by force.[43] Reportedly, one of his first acts was to issue a radical *farmān*, or decree. "After today," it declared, "no one shall speak in a language other than Turkish in the imperial council, the royal court and tribunal, the assembly and public square."[44] Had the rebellion lasted—it was put down the following year—his *farmān* might have represented a drastic shift in regional cultural production, with Persian and Arabic usurped by Turkish as an administrative and literary language. In the nationalist interpretation of this event, this was a moment of cultural awakening, a time when the Turkish people first shrugged off the heavy yoke of Persianate cultural hegemony.[45]

Yet the *farmān* is more nuanced than it first appears—if it existed at all. Ibn Bībī, the thirteenth-century historian of the Seljuks, quotes it not in Turkish but rather in *Persian.* Sara Nur Yıldız has suggested that Ibn Bībī may have been attempting to delegitimize the rebellion's authority by depicting Meḥmed Bey "as an illiterate Turk," incapable of running the affairs of the Seljuk court in Persian and therefore unfit to rule.[46] In this context, Turkish literature began to develop in Rūm only a few decades after Ibn Bībī depicted "courtly" or "literary" Turkish as a contradiction in terms. Why, then, did a new generation of poets, including prominent religious figures such as Sulṭān Valad and ʿĀşıḳ Paşa, compose Turkish poetry in Anatolia at that point?

Sulṭān Valad's practice of literary "following" provides us with a vital clue. In his works, a path forward lies not in usurping but rather in imitating—or more accurately, emulating—Persianate culture in other tongues, in other voices. An opportunity offered itself in 1301, when one of his companions asked him to compose yet another poetic adaptation. As this companion reasoned, Sulṭān Valad had already written the *Ibtidā-nāma* in the meter of Sanā'ī's *Ilāhī-nāma*. This time, he desired an adaptation of the *Maṣnavī* itself, since audiences had "grown accustomed to [its] meter from many recitations." By way of example, he cited the famous opening of Rūmī's masterpiece:

> Listen to this reed, how it laments,
> It tells a story of separations—[47]

The sound of the *Maṣnavī* must have resonated deeply with Sulṭān Valad as well, for he swiftly assented to the request. He titled this work the *Rabāb-nāma*, or *Book of the Rebec*, in a clear allusion to the musical opening of the *Maṣnavī*. However, although the *Rabāb-nāma* emulates certain aspects of the *Maṣnavī*, its organizing metaphor, the *rabāb*, hints at a more complex manner of engaging with, and ultimately rewriting and reinscribing, Rūmī's literary legacy to serve the needs of a new generation. At the same time, Sulṭān Valad's mode of "following" or "imitating" helps to shed light on a growing affinity between Turkic and Persianate cultural systems in Rūm. This linguistic and literary kinship—the result of a mixture of languages, aesthetic systems, and audiences—was not merely peripheral to a more authentically Turkish literary culture. On the contrary, it played a role in producing this culture *as* literary, at least according to a widespread and broadly recognizable set of poetic standards.

As we have seen, composing in the meter and style of a preexisting work was more than an exercise in aesthetic mimicry: it also performed a dual hermeneutic and genealogical function, binding together disparate texts within the same interpretive frame. It would be a mistake, however, to assume that Sulṭān Valad's ambition was simply to illuminate the multivalent *Maṣnavī*'s teachings in a self-effacing manner. Although he followed in his father's stylistic footsteps, he would compose the *Book of the Rebec* in more languages than New Persian alone. Instead, he crafted approximately 7,745 lines in New Persian, 35 in Arabic, 22 in medieval Greek, and 162 in Turkish, encoding these languages in variations of the lilting meter of his father's crowning literary achievement.[48] The *Maṣnavī* spoke in many voices, but the *Rabāb-nāma* would go further. It would speak in many tongues.

One should both gaze upon the *Rabāb-nāma*, whose unifying script graphically draws these disparate languages together, and hear it read aloud, to grasp the significance of its transformative adaptation.[49] When audiences listened to its recitation, they heard the stirring stresses of the catalectic *ramal* meter (– ᵕ – – / – ᵕ – – / – ᵕ –), the very sound of the Persian *Maṣnavī*, imprinted upon Turkish words. The Greek section follows the *Maṣnavī*'s form in a freer way: each line contains twenty-two syllables, with a caesura in the center after the first rhyme word, as we find in the rest of the *Rabāb-nāma*. Yet the medieval Greek portion does not try to (and in truth, cannot) match each foot of the *ramal* meter; it also breaks from the versification of Byzantine poetry, creating a pleasing aural space of its own. In a sense, Sulṭān Valad's employment of meter helps to fashion an aural genealogy, a sonic *silsila* (chain), that potentially links the *Rabāb-nāma* to the *Maṣnavī* in the ears of an audience, just as it creates underlying associations between the rhythms of Turkish, Arabic, and Persian poetry, matched by a complementary poetic sound and style in Greek. Although this might not strike a modern audience as especially meaningful, it perhaps bore an implicit argument for medieval ears: chiefly, that Turkish and Greek could imitate the *sound* of literature in different ways, at least from the perspective of a certain listening public in Konya, and thus perform and showcase their status as "literary" within a Persianate sphere. At the same time, this mode of adaptation suggested that Turkish and Greek were now fit to reveal higher spiritual meanings alongside literary Arabic and New Persian.

In some ways, this graphic and aural adaptation reflects a hallmark of Sulṭān Valad's general religious outreach. For instance, although he emulated his father, he rarely copied Rūmī exactly—even in his everyday economic transactions with others in Konya. Once, for example, Sulṭān Valad hired a group of "Anatolian" laborers to repair the roof of his madrasa. Aflākī describes these men as *rūmī*, a somewhat elastic term that often means "Greek" in Rūmī's writing but could also broadly describe other peoples of Rūm. In any case, while these *rūmī*s were working, Sulṭān

Valad slipped outside to discreetly monitor them. Eventually, one of the laborers became aware that someone was watching, and so he urged his companions to "do good work, for Mawlānā [Sulṭān Valad] is observing us." When Sulṭān Valad heard this, he was so pleased that he began to utter divine secrets in a rapturous state. Up to this point, the narrative resembles Rūmī's meditation on the meaning of "Dilku!," the cry of a Turkish merchant. Clearly, both father and son were partial to gleaning higher spiritual truths from unlikely sources, including the general population of Konya. However, Sulṭān Valad went a step further. Not content to uncover higher meanings for himself alone, he used this opportunity to teach those present a hadith in return, telling them that perfection is "to worship God as though you see Him, for although you don't see Him, He [still] sees you."[50] As he explained, the righteous shall be rewarded, even when the Master is not visible.

In other words, Sulṭān Valad taught the meaning of a hadith by using the very behavior of these workers as a way of illuminating its message. He not only used a linguistic, ethnic, or religious "other" to reach a higher spiritual state, as did his father, but also communicated his insights back to his audiences, potentially including the laborers themselves, using language and analogies they could understand. Though this is only one anecdote, it touches upon a broader pattern in Konya. Sulṭān Valad desired not to use "others" as a kind of literary heuristic but rather to teach new audiences about higher truths directly, either by sending followers to nearby cities to spread his father's message or by adapting the very utterances of those others to produce an explicitly Islamic meaning. In this sense he parallels, and in some ways escalates, his father's proclivity to mix with different peoples.

This escalation unfolds upon the expansive linguistic stage of the *Rabāb-nāma*, which draws both Greek and Turkish speakers into a similar hermeneutic fold. Far from distancing himself from his father, Sulṭān Valad welcomes Rūmī's "voice" into the Greek verses of the *Rabāb-nāma*, which mirror the *Maṣnavī*'s inaugural dialogue between master and disciple. In these verses, composed long after his death, Rūmī has ascended to paradise, and the role of the "disciple" is now ascribed to Sulṭān Valad, who, like Ḥusām al-Dīn, wishes to understand Rūmī's ecstatic spiritual state. "Tell us how you're managing yourself among the saints," Sulṭān Valad begs his father in Greek, since "your eyes behold God clearly, / you're so happy you're bursting from your clothes." So unshakable is his father's authority, Sulṭān Valad assures his audience, that whoever has business with Rūmī—whoever "buys and sells" their goods with him—will also live forever.[51]

But Rūmī does not grant his son's request. As with Ḥusām al-Dīn, the character of "Rūmī" instead offers a circuitous explanation of something else: in this case, how the celestial soul has no business with its corporeal counterpart, the body. Although Rūmī's poetry is replete with meditations on the duality between spirit and flesh, here the body assumes a different form. The Greek verses of the *Rabāb-nāma* call it a "tabernacle" (σκήνωμα), which must perish in order for the soul to return to its source. In this way, Rūmī rebukes his son for attempting to commune with those who have put off their earthly tents:

Sulṭān Valad's Perso-Greek verses:

ایپس ایپا ایذو بوسا لالس   تی یرفیس آپماس پو مس کالس
است یی تو سکینما کاتو بتی   اپشتی آبانو مریا پرپتی
است یی تسکینما مس ناخثی   که پشیشماش میتس آیس نفرثی
اپشیشی اختن خرا فتروثکن   آفن ارتن آبکی پکروثکن
پالی توپیای اپشیشی ستون دوبندو   نا خری پندا ایکی ستون بوثندو

A modern transliteration into the Greek script:

Εἶπες, ᾽Επά ἐδῶ πόσα λαλεῖς,
τί γυρεύεις ἀπ᾽ ἐμᾶς πού μᾶς καλεῖς;

Εἰς τή γῆ τό σκήνωμα κάτω πατεῖ,
ἡ ψυχή ἀπάνω μεριά πορπατεῖ·

εἰς τή γῆ τό σκήνωμά μας νά χαθῇ
καί ἡ ψυχή μας μέ τούς ἅγιους νά ᾽φραθῇ.

῾Η ψυχή ἀχ τήν χαρά φυτρώθηκεν
ἀφῶν ἦρτεν ἀπ᾽ ἐκεῖ πικρώθηκεν.

Πάλι τοῦ ὑπάει ἡ ψυχή στόν τόπον Του
νά χαρῇ πάντα ἐκεῖ στόν πόθον Του.

Translation from Perso-Greek to English:

You said, "How you talk and talk down here!
What do you want by calling us like this?

The tabernacle's rooted to the earth below,
The soul walks up above;

On earth our tabernacle will be lost,
And our soul will exult with the saints.

The soul springs from the seed of joy;
Since it's come from up there, it's bitter here.

Again the soul returns to His place,
To take joy forever there in His desire."[52]

There is more at work here than a simple lesson on the transience of the body or the duality of the body and the soul. As Dimitris Dedes has observed, Sulṭān Valad's word for our corporeal "tabernacle"—*skēnōma*—is used in a similar fashion in the New Testament.[53] For example, the author of 2 Peter 1:13–14 employs σκήνωμα as a metaphor for the temporary dwelling of the soul in the body, noting that he must soon put off his tabernacle and depart this vale of tears. Strikingly, Sulṭān Valad not only composed poetry in the Greek language but also remained cognizant of terms and imagery that would be familiar to—even resonate with—a Christian audience. Perhaps even more important, his multilingualism demonstrated to an initiated coterie of Muslim listeners that, much like Solomon with his birds, he was capable of teaching Greeks to be "same in heart," even if they necessarily differed in tongue.

This communicative strategy, a resonant mode of addressing potentially different audiences through poetry, is underscored at the conclusion of the Greek dialogue. Although Sulṭān Valad marvels at his father's heavenly discourse ("His soul speaks there like me"), Rūmī reminds him that language is a limited tool. Better to experience for oneself nonexistence, where language cannot go, than to confuse mere signifiers for the ineffable Signified:

ذن خوری ستغلوسا تا کالا توثیو　　　ایلا کاغو لییری ستون بوثندو
تس اذوکن تن پشیشندو ایزسن　　　تیس ایذو چاکوثن اولس نیکسن

Δέν χωρεῖ στήν γλῶσσα τά κάλλη τοῦ θεοῦ·
ἔλα κάγου, λυγερέ, στόν πόθον Του.

Τίς ἔδωκεν τήν ψυχήν του, ἔζησεν·
τίς ἐδῶ τσακώθην, ὅλους νίκησεν.

No tongue can describe God's graces.
Come on, graceful one, burn in His desire.

Whoever gave his soul lives on.
Whoever's been crushed in defeat down here has defeated everyone.[54]

While coded in the sound of the *Maṣnavī*, these verses are also evocative of a Christian voice, speaking from the New Testament. "When this perishable body puts on imperishability," Saint Paul writes in 1 Corinthians 15:54, "and this mortal body puts on immortality, then the saying that is written will be fulfilled: 'Death has been swallowed up in victory [νῖκος].' " In a similar vein, "Rūmī" speaks of the soul as having defeated (νίκησεν) all in the destruction of the body. Likewise, in 2 Corinthians 5:1–3, Paul writes, "For we know that if the earthly tent [σκῆνος] we live in is destroyed, we have a building from God, a house not made with hands, eternal in the heavens. For in this tent we groan, longing [ἐπιποθοῦντες] to be clothed with our heavenly dwelling—if indeed, when we have taken it off we will not be found naked." But in Sulṭān Valad's hands we find a nimble reversal: it is in God's longing (πόθος) that our earthly tent (σκήνωμα) is destroyed, although none of our corporeal trappings—clothing included—will be necessary in heaven.

In Sulṭān Valad's poetic voice one can hear the voices of others, his literary inscription evocative not only of the Koine Greek of the New Testament but also of the vernacular Greek spoken by potential audiences in Konya. Though he does not fundamentally alter the Christian idea of *skēnōma*, he does swing it into a new orbit of meaning making. In this light, the Christian *skēnōma* is not only compatible with Islam but also forms part of an Islamicate vocabulary, here potentially mobilized to communicate Rūmī's teachings to Greek Christians. The astonishing implication is that much like the *rūmī* laborers on the roof of the madrasa, the Greek *language* was capable of unveiling higher meaning in an Islamic discursive field. Significantly, it could do so in a manner that already resonated with Greek speakers even as it mimicked the style of a Persian *maṣnavī*.

A kindred vernacular speaks from the Turkish verses of the *Rabāb-nāma.* Like the Greek section, these verses open with an encomium to Rūmī, the Pole of the Saints, whose precious words are of great value. Just as wise Greeks who "buy and sell" with Rūmī will inherit eternal life, judicious Turks should surrender all their possessions to acquire Mawlānā's teachings:

اسلو کیشینك مالی سوزلر الر　　مالنی ویرر بو سزلاری الر
مال طپرق در بو سزلر جان درر　　اسلولر اندن قچر بندا درر

> The wealth of the prudent is words.
> [Such a person] gives up his wealth. He buys these words.
>
> A fortune is but dirt; these words are life.
> Prudent ones escape the former and dwell herein.[55]

These verses use economic metaphors evocative of the transactions between Rūmī and "others" in the bazaar and at the *khānaqāh.* Yet Sulṭān Valad invokes a more permanent kind of relationship—one in which Turkish speakers might "dwell" within Islamicate discourse—produced through his versifying efforts.

He continues to draw on this metaphoric language in the most cited passage from the *Rabāb-nāma,* in which he seemingly takes a step back from this endeavor. "Had I known Turkish," he says, "I would have given to you / the secrets that God entrusted to us." Therefore, he proclaims, his aim is that "through me, the impoverished may grow wealthy."[56] This supposed declaration of linguistic ignorance—ironically composed in the Turkish language—offers a master class in understatement. Although generally read as an admission that Sulṭān Valad felt uncomfortable outside his native tongue, the passage foregrounds his doubled awareness of the need to proselytize in an accessible manner and to reveal Islamic meanings where others might not. This meant, in part, that Sulṭān Valad remained cognizant of the languages and conceptual vocabulary of "others" even while drawing them into the sound and poetic style of the *Masnavī.* In fact, this supposed declaration of ignorance follows a poetic treatise, in Turkish, on the body-soul distinction, akin to that in his Greek verses. Just as he instructs his Greek audience, Sulṭān Valad urges Turks not to cherish their lives in this world, for the one who gives up their soul obtains a hundred more on the Way. So too does he envision the soul in familiar terms:

سن یتیجق کوده دن جانك اوچر　　قش کبی قندا دلرسا بیر ایچر
کندوزندن یوز صورت بر جان الر　　شهر الر بازار الر دکان الر
کندودن هم بیر الر هم کوك الر　　جان ایانقدر اکر کوده یتر

> While you sleep, your soul soars from your body,
> Like a bird, wherever it may wish, it eats and drinks.
>
> One soul, [drawing] from itself, takes on a hundred faces:
> It becomes a city, a bazaar, a shop,
>
> Out of itself, it turns into both sky and ground—
> The soul is wide awake, though the body drowses.[57]

Persian poetry features many analogies of the soul to a bird; Rūmī, for instance, likened the spirit (*rūḥ*) to a bird imprisoned in the cage of the body.[58] So too did pre-Islamicate and Islamicate Turkic cultures long associate birds with the soul. The mythological two-headed eagle, along with other birds of prey, held a variety of meanings for the Seljuk dynasty, in part because the eagle had been a totem of the Oghuz. At the height of Seljuk rule, the association between birds and the soul acquired a widespread visual imprint across Anatolia, with birds appearing on carved reliefs on several tombs, beginning with the mausoleum (*türbe*) of Emir Ṣalṭuḳ in Erzurum at the end of the twelfth century and continuing with the tomb of the Seljuk princess Khudāvand in Niğde around 1312. Miniatures of burial ceremonies from this period likewise depict the motif of the two-headed eagle.[59] As Katharina Otto-Dorn has suggested, these artifacts seem to reflect the shamanic beliefs that birds guide the soul to paradise and that the soul is transformed into a bird after death.[60]

It is possible to find echoes of these converging traditions in Konya, on glazed tiles depicting a two-headed eagle from the Seljuk palace and even among Sulṭān Valad's followers. Notably, a painting on the Qur'an stand used by the Mawlavī community depicts a double-headed eagle much like the one at the tomb of Princess Khudāvand. This stand dates to 1279/80—some two decades before Sulṭān Valad composed the *Rabāb-nāma*.[61] The soul-bird would therefore have been familiar to a Turkic audience, bearing various and complementary valences of meaning, in the same way as the "tabernacle" of the soul would be to a Greek one.

The *Rabāb-nāma* is therefore remarkable not only because of its dazzling linguistic dexterity but also because it accommodates the symbolic and semiotic languages of "others" within an Islamic hermeneutic framework. Rather than attempting merely to supplant other religious traditions and forms of devotion, it transforms the meanings of cultural differences without homogenizing the seemingly incongruous cultures of its audiences and languages. In the same vein as the *Maṡnavī*, it thus trains these audiences—speakers of Turkish, Persian, Arabic, or Greek—to look for higher meanings in unlikely places. After all, as Sulṭān Valad concludes in his Turkish section, it is possible for seekers of God to discern true religion and faith even in unbelief (*küfr*).[62] Meaning can be sussed out, it seems, even in the profane tongues of non-Muslims.

The most resonant metaphor for this activity—which bore currency from the cultural apex of the Seljuk court to the lowliest Armenian tavern—was the *rabāb*, the central image of Sulṭān Valad's poetry. We should recall that the *Maṡnavī* is the reed's lament. In this alchemy of metaphor—sound made text—Rūmī transmutes a musical culture into a verbal one, the song of the reed into New Persian words and sentences. This metaphor clearly spoke to Sulṭān Valad. "His excellency Mawlānā [Rūmī] said the reed laments, for it has become parted and fallen far from its reed bed and companions," Sulṭān Valad observes in the *Rabāb-nāma*'s Persian opening. "It laments its separation in exile [*ghurbat*]." Yet Sulṭān Valad does not recycle the figurative language of his father. In place of the reed flute, he offers his audiences a new instrument. The *rabāb*, he explains, is certainly more complex than the *nay*, but it is not only that. It is the very product of heterogeneity and hence can do something that the *nay* cannot: "Within the *nay* there is no more than one lament, but within the *rabāb* there are [many] laments and separations, because [the *rabāb*] is an assembly of *gharīb*s, each of which has been parted from its native country [*vaṭan*] and kind, such as skin and hair and iron and wood; all of these wail over and lament the separation from their kind. Therefore, the plaint and cry are greater in the *rabāb* than in the *nay*."[63]

If the *nay*, a single unbroken stalk, represents the discourse of the *Maṡnavī*, then its discourse is also of a single kind. As far as the *Rabāb-nāma* is concerned, the *nay* gives voice to homogeneous speech. That is not to label the *Maṣnavī*—or Rūmī himself—as monolingual. After all, independent of the Arabic and Persian verses of the *Maṣnavī*, Rūmī composed a number of macaronic poems (*mulamma'*)—which, as Johanson notes, "mix" together Persian and Turkish verses—and a handful of short *ghazal*s in Greek.[64] Unlike Rūmī, however, Sulṭān Valad had heard Greek and Anatolian Turkish since the days of his childhood. These languages, to different degrees, were *his* languages, allowing him to engage with the peoples of Konya in direct and intimate terms, even reaching potentially illiterate audiences. To draw these people into the spiritual mission of his father, Sulṭān Valad thus learned to speak not merely in the same language but also in a recognizable "voice," an intimate tongue, that would resound broadly across his diverse city.

This affinitive language is underscored by Sulṭān Valad's treatment of the *gharīb*, or stranger. In the opening of the *Maṣnavī*, the *gharīb* is a singular physician, a sun among shadows, who knows how to estrange the Shah from worldly attachment. As we've seen, Rūmī identified as a *gharīb* because he too severed his worldly attachments, he too sought to estrange his community from their previous affiliations. Sulṭān Valad, writing after Rūmī's death, subtly expanded upon this idea: in the *Rabāb-nāma*, estrangement is democratized, as the entire community now follows Rūmī's example, collectively singing many songs of separation. However, these "strangers" do not sing in the same manner. Nor do they form a single group. Instead, the *Rabāb-nāma* performatively foregrounds certain linguistic and semiotic differences, which Sulṭān Valad's teachings make discursively meaningful in Islamic terms even as they remain distinct from one another in a fundamental sense.

As one of the earliest works to encode Anatolian Turkish and medieval Greek as literary languages according to Persianate standards, the *Rabāb-nāma* offers a model for conceptualizing the complex relationships between diverse audiences and linguistic systems. Clearly, for Sulṭān Valad the *rabāb* is more than the sum of its parts, a random assemblage of *gharīb*s from elsewhere. Indeed, it is the very mechanism that draws these strangers together, even if they speak in many tongues: skin, iron, wood, and hair, Persian, Arabic, Greek, and Turkish. In fact, the secondary meaning of *rabāb* is *'ahd*, "covenant" or "oath," literally that which binds a people together.[65]

It is only through this covenant that *noise*—the discordant wailing of dissimilar voices—becomes recognizable as *sound*, harmonized through the lament of the *rabāb* and the pattern of metered poetry. Of course, this process works both ways. For Sulṭān Valad, poetry and music can likewise transform dissimilar individuals into a multiethnic and multilingual community, a society in which their polyvocal sounds bear meaning. Thus, in the heterogeneous *rabāb* we find a performative symbol for the creation of a literary culture and the formation of a religious community in tandem.

It is hardly coincidental that Meḥmed Bey's *farmān* captures far more scholarly and popular attention today than Sulṭān Valad's *Rabāb-nāma*. We have already seen the reason for this: Meḥmed Bey offers us an Oedipal reading of the past, in which the protonation must throw off the oppressive yoke of its forefathers so that its people might rediscover their "authentic" and "native" selves. This interpretation strongly resonates with a contemporary anxiety, found in nationalisms the world over, of falling under the influence of foreigners and thereby allowing the authenticity of an indigenous national spirit to be diluted. Of course, like nationalist understandings of Meḥmed Bey's *farmān*, this binary mode of viewing the world (native/foreign, authentic/influenced, us/them) is largely based on a fiction. Sulṭān Valad and his immediate audience did not think in such binary terms; they preferred more complex heuristics, capable of theorizing multilingualism through a praxis of speaking to many audiences in different poetic languages within a single literary work. It is through this compact of tongues, speaking differently but in concert, that an interconnected literary history of Anatolia takes shape.

A Language of Affinity

As we have seen, the *Rabāb-nāma* showcases a premodern manner not only of living with difference but of transmuting difference into something else entirely: a language of intimacy and affinity, or what Rūmī termed *zabān-i maḥramī*, which he distinguished absolutely from a mere monolingualism or even a "colingualism." Similarly, for Sulṭān Valad, it seems that to speak this language of affinity is not just to speak a language of similitude, although variations of the *ramal* meter, the enticing sound of the *Maṡnavī*, course through the heteroglossic verses of the *Rabāb-nāma*. Rather, it is to speak a poetic language in which a single hermeneutic frame can accommodate and incorporate heterogeneity. At its core, being *zabān-i maḥramī* allows one to navigate multiple linguistic and cultural systems by speaking in a poetic voice kindred to them all.

This notion of crosslinguistic kinship is reflected in the history of the term *maḥram*, which means a close relative: one who has permission to enter within the walls of a harem. A *maḥram* can be an ancestor, descendant, sibling, in-law, or stepparent, or simply someone who has shared one's wet nurse. Slightly differently, in the thirteenth-century Latinate world, the word *affinitas* signified a kinship, a relationship by marriage, or even a relationship by proximity—to someone who lived in or adjacent to one's neighborhood. Etymologically, *affinity* stems from the root *ad*, "to," and *finis*, "border" or "boundary." Thus, to speak a language of affinity is not just to acknowledge boundaries and borders within a relationship but to engage with such borders and sometimes to cross them. It is to shape a kinship of difference, to create a space for the linguistic, cultural, and religious diversity of one's community to produce (Islamic) meaning in a harmonious literary mode.

What Sulṭān Valad ultimately attempted to accomplish, even to a greater degree than his father, was to speak this intimate language across the walled neighborhoods (*maḥalla*) that segregated the peoples of Konya from one another. The genealogy he fashioned—the kinship he nurtured—was not one that extended merely chronologically back up the traditional Sufi chains (*silsila*) of authority, by which one established legitimacy via spiritual forerunners. Rather, Sulṭān Valad's radical *silsila* radiated outward, linguistically and ethnically, spatially and aurally. He sought to redefine both who might be included within local spheres of epistemic production and what languages could express the "literary" in a Persianate sphere. Moreover, he encoded this genealogy within the textual matrix of the *Rabāb-nāma*, in both its embodiment of multiple tongues and its very sound, allowing Turkish and Greek to "imitate"—or more accurately, "follow"—Arabic and Persian, much as a disciple (*murīd*) follows their guide (*pīr*).

Of course, this does not mean that the cross-cultural kinship thematized within and by the *Rabāb-nāma* is devoid of conflict or tension or, worse, is a forerunner of "tolerance" or "coexistence," those most lukewarm of modern values. Kinships do not distribute power equally—they are very often sites of complex and codependent forms of inequality. In much the same vein, those who were *maḥram*, and thus allowed within the harem, never enjoyed a universally equal autonomy, free of hierarchical relations. The very existence of the harem, and the kinship relations organized around it, is a potent reminder that power differentials do not vanish easily, if ever. In the case of poetry in medieval Rūm, although it was one thing to welcome the words and concepts of others into one's literary production, it was quite another to allow "others" to speak for themselves.

In Sulṭān Valad's voice, therefore, we can hear only distant echoes of these adjacent tongues. To grasp this speech more clearly, we must leave the city of Konya behind and travel to neighboring regions. Out in the countryside, as we venture through the rolling hills of Rūm, these voices begin to blend together, speaking in a poetics, a style, a sound uncoupled from any one language. If we listen closely, we can discern the stirrings of different kinships and kindred modes of literary production that would sound and resound throughout premodern Rūm.

CHAPTER FOUR

A BRIEF STROLL THROUGH RŪM

Sulṭān Valad sent his representatives to cities throughout Anatolia, spreading word of Rūmī's teachings and poetry. One such follower, Süleymān Türkmānī, is leaving Konya now.[1] He will travel about 125 miles northeast, perhaps crossing the recently constructed Kesik Köprü, a bridge built by the Seljuks over the river Kızılırmak, until he reaches Kırşehir, the city of prairies. There we will find poets such as Gülşehrī and 'Āşıḳ Paşa fashioning a new genealogy for literary Turkish and crafting a new language of affinity to be voiced through Turkish poetry. But before we arrive in Kırşehir, it is worth pausing to examine, however briefly, the adjacent poetic landscapes of Rūm.

This chapter serves as an intermezzo to our story, painting a broad picture of literary production through a series of vignettes at this moment in time. These vignettes are meant to be suggestive, teasing the panoply of ways in which literary cultures mixed and mingled together—even without the intervention of discrete figures one might recognize as "authors" today. In fact, with the exception of Yūnus Emre, who will appear near the end of this chapter's journey, the figure of the author recedes into the hazy distance as we venture forth. In its place, other kinds of storytellers, performers, and literary archetypes join us along the road. These guides present occasions to theorize the intersections between literary systems in different ways, even when authorial acts of adaptation remain unknown. Let us therefore tread briefly upon this terra incognita of performance and orality, though it is a world known primarily from later sources. What might a traveler have heard, moving through Rūm's cities and countryside around this time? And what was happening beyond the urban confines of literary production in Persian and Sufi circles?

The Minstrel and the Storyteller

Although the questions above are highly speculative, they have shaped the historiography of Turkish literature in important ways.[2] Mehmet Fuat Köprülü, a modern founding father of Turkish literary studies, differentiated rigidly between urbane poetry, produced within a Persianate cultural sphere, and the authentic Turkish culture of the country, expressed by wandering minstrels (*ozan*) who composed in syllabic meter (*hece vezni*).[3] To his credit, Köprülü maintained that a bridge existed between "high" and "low" Turkish cultures even while articulating his clear preference for those unlettered traditions which he viewed as more vital. "In this period," he asserted, "Anatolia was so permeated with an atmosphere of heroism that even the Seljuk rulers who were under the demoralizing influence of Persian culture could not give up their attachment to Oghuz customary law, and the old warlike traditions in their own palaces."[4] In Köprülü's eyes, any affinity between Persian and Turkish literatures was a symptom of encroachment, of the unfortunate shadow of Persian influence, on a "completely national, genuine, and widespread" Turkish spirit.[5] It is therefore not surprising that he used the term *taqlīd* (Turkish: *taḳlīd*), the simplistic imitation of one author by another, to characterize the Turkish adoption of conventions that were common in Arabic and Persian poetry.[6] As Paul E. Losensky notes, the most negative metaphor lurking behind *taqlīd* is the act of placing "a rope around an animal's neck."[7] The animal, pulled along by a stronger hand, simply has no choice in the matter.

For our purposes, the pressing issue is not that Köprülü's thesis relies on an overtly nationalist paradigm but rather that it assumes that "Turkish" and "Persian" cultural systems—at least, as we know them through their literary footprints—are irreducibly complex and ontologically distinct.

This assumption has proved markedly resilient. Thus, although scholars such as Ahmet T. Karamustafa and Ethel Sara Wolper have rightly deconstructed the supposed divide between "folk" and "elite" Turkic religious cultures, a broader critical assessment of the ways in which scholars conceptualize the indigenous and exogenous elements of early Turkic literature, and how this in turn colors what categories like "Turkic," "authenticity," and "artistry" mean, is still forthcoming.[8] In other words, there is no immediately apparent counterweight to the paradigm articulated by Köprülü, insofar as this dynamic is still framed in terms of a Turkish/Persian cultural binary, as though the origins of a particular set of literary conventions explain what is inherently "Turkish" or "Persian" about them.

However, when we move between the city and the country, the dividing lines between these cultural systems are not always so clear. Even Rūmī, a major representative of high Persian literary culture in Anatolia, mentions the *ḳopuz* (also spelled *ḳobuz*), a Turkic analogue to the *ʿūd*, or lute, in one of his macaronic poems. "One day I desire to sit alone at your side," he declares in a mixture of Persian and Turkish. "I'll play the *ḳobuz*, you'll drink the wine."[9] Rūmī would have learned some Anatolian Turkish as an adult, but he also may have brought knowledge of Turkish with him from Khorasan to Rūm.[10] Perhaps he was familiar, to whatever extent, with the "indigenous" Turkic cultures that supposedly did not flourish in urban centers of literary production. The *ḳopuz*, after all, was the very instrument of premodern performers of "authentic" Turkish poetry: the *ozan*. As we travel beyond Konya, we might find similar figures playing the *ḳopuz* and reciting poetry along the way.

If we were to encounter an *ozan* on our journey, it's hard to say what we'd hear, since our knowledge of these minstrels comes largely from later centuries. The same is true for the public storytellers known in Anatolia as *meddāḥ*s (Arabic: *maddāḥ*, meaning "panegyrist"), who would later recite prose narratives, sometimes on a raised platform, before a crowd.[11] Still, there are important clues, even at this early moment, that hint at a shifting poetic soundscape in Rūm. Most likely, a tradition of oral storytelling concerned with the period after the Turkic victory at Manzikert in 1071 began to coalesce in the thirteenth century. These stories—which we know today only through writing—depict the *ghāzī* (Arabic for "raider") ethos, which induced heroic fighters to wage battle on behalf of Islam in Rūm and the

Balkans, converting (or killing) swaths of the population in the process.[12] Such legendary stories would be fleshed out in works like the *Dānişmend-nāme,* reportedly recited to the Seljuk sultan ʿIzz al-Dīn Kaykāʾūs (d. 1279) in the mid-thirteenth century, and the *Baṭṭāl-nāme* and the *Ṣalṭuḳ-nāme,* which developed in some form over the following century (although the oldest manuscripts of these works date to later periods).[13] These (mostly) prose works harken back to their performative roots: various sections of the *Baṭṭāl-nāme* begin by invoking the *rāvī* (storyteller) who originally transmitted its tales orally, and the *Dānişmend-nāme* likewise depicts a past when storytellers (*rāvīler*) recited its narrative aloud.[14]

In some ways, the recitation and performance of Turkish literature may not have been so dissimilar to the performance of Persian literature. In 1360, for instance, a poet by the name of Yūsuf-i Meddāḥ composed a Turkish *Varḳa and Gülşāh,* adapting a popular *maṡnavī* that was written in Persian by ʿAyyūqī (c. eleventh century).[15] Yūsuf's Turkish tale, like its Persian counterpart, depicts two lovers—the manly Varḳa and the lovely Gülşāh—who must endure a painful separation. However, while *Varḳa and Gülşāh* is to some extent a Turkish translation of a Persian narrative, it is not a translation only of text. It is also a translation of *sound.* Yūsuf, as one of the earliest known figures to claim the title *meddāḥ* in Rūm, employed the metrical rules of *ʿarūż* in his Turkish (re)composition.[16] In his voice, his audience would have heard the same stirring *ramal* meter that patterns Rūmī's *Maṡnavī,* despite the fact that these works concern entirely different stories of separation. In a literal way—a legible and audible way—the soundscapes of Rūm converge in Yūsuf's performing voice.

The Hero and the Monster

Across Anatolia we hear echoes of analogous processes of mixing of disparate cultural systems. Our ears catch snatches of these kindred soundscapes even among the Türkmen and the descendants of the Oghuz tribes of Central Asia. If we were to find an untouched, "purely" Turkic culture, it would be among these Turkish speakers who occasionally caused the Seljuks (also of Oghuz descent) much trouble. Their masterwork, considered something of a protonational epic, is known today as *The Book of Dede Ḳorḳut,* brought to Rūm from Central Asia. This collection of tales, though recorded by Muslim hands, preserves many pre-Islamic Oghuz shamanic traditions. Generally, it depicts the heroic feats of the ruling class of the Oghuz long before they migrated to Rūm.[17] Dede Ḳorḳut looms, somewhere offstage, in these tales. He is the legendary leader of the Oghuz, and more: a shaman, a warrior-*khān*, even an *ozan*. He is said to have invented the *ḳopuz* and, indeed, is presented as the compiler of the book that bears his name.[18] Thus, in the figures of Dede Ḳorḳut and his companions, we encounter ideal blends of the Turkic music, poetry, and heroism that Köprülü so prized.

However, in some of these tales we also find unlikely kinships with other oral traditions in Rūm. It is therefore worth slowing our pace to examine such affinities more closely. Although the earliest copies of *Dede Ḳorḳut* date to the sixteenth century, Ibn al-Dawādārī, a Mamluk historian writing in the early fourteenth century, reported that Turks recited tales from a certain *Book of the Oghuz* to the accompaniment of music.[19] These stories, Ibn al-Dawādārī says, circulated "from hand to hand" among the Turks.[20] One in particular seems to have caught his ear:

> In this book occurs the story of a person named Dabakuz [Tepegöz] who ravaged the lands of the early Turks and killed their great men. They say he was an ugly and loathsome man with a single eye on the top of his head. No sword or spear had any effect on him. His mother was a demon of the ocean and his father's bonnet was of the skins of ten rams so as to cover his head. They have many well-known tales and stories about him, which circulate among them to this day and are learned by heart by their sagacious men who are skilled in the playing of their lute [*ḳopuz*].[21]

When the first manuscript of *The Book of Dede Ḳorḳut* came to light in the nineteenth century, readers quickly alighted on the parallels between Tepegöz and Polyphemus, the Cyclops of Homer's *Odyssey*.[22] The structural and narrative similarities are indeed striking.[23] In *Dede Ḳorḳut*, a young warrior named Basaṭ defeats Tepegöz by heating a spit in a fire, invoking the name of Muḥammad, and blinding the giant. He then attempts to sneak past the enraged giant at the entrance of the cave by cloaking himself in the skin of a ram, just as Odysseus clings to the wool on a sheep's belly to escape from Polyphemus's cave. Finally, much like Odysseus and Polyphemus, who are related to Zeus in different ways, Basaṭ and Tepegöz share a strange kinship: both were born of the same mother. Despite this, Basaṭ still strikes down his half brother in the end.[24]

What do we make of this cross-cultural correspondence? It is certainly possible that the Cyclops's eye is something of a Chekhov's gun: it exists in such tales to be blinded, and nothing more. Even so, some scholars have attempted to locate a singular, monocultural origin of the story, either Turkish or Greek.[25] Others have adopted a more nuanced approach, noting that these stories diverge in many instances and ultimately make different points.[26] Still other critics have pointed to linguistic clues that suggest a hazy relationship between these works—although it is unclear what, exactly, that relationship might be. For instance, C. S. Mundy has posited that the name Tepegöz, long thought to be a compound of the Turkish words *tepe* (top) and *göz* (eye), might instead derive from a truncated form of the Greek *sarantapēchos*, a word for "giant" that literally means "forty cubits." Whether or not this hypothesis is true, what's most remarkable is that subsequent Greek tales seem to have borrowed the Cyclops's name back from the Turkish language. Hence, we find at least two folktales in Greek about clans of giants known as the Τεπεκόζης (Tepekozēs) or Τεπεκόης (Tepekoēs).[27] In other words, regardless of the origins of our one-eyed monsters, it is clear that there existed some later interface—a chimeric mixing of oral traditions—between the Greeks and the Turks who recited these stories in Rūm. In certain cases, such as the appearance of Tepekozēs in later Greek (and even Armenian!) tales, interaction across this interface must have flowed in multiple directions.[28]

Hence, as we continue our stroll through the literary landscapes of Rūm, what seems to move across languages is not necessarily texts per se but rather what Franco Moretti calls "units that are much smaller or much larger than the text: devices, themes, tropes—or genres and systems."[29] Sometimes, this phenomenon might manifest as a proclivity to tell stories with a similar narrative structure, regardless of the language in question. At other times, such units are primarily aural, as in the adoption of another language's metrical system or mode of performance. Elsewhere, the affinity might stem from a shared lexicon or an overlapping understanding of what heroes should be like or how monsters should behave. In each of these cases, what should concern us are not static cultural origins but rather the strange affinities that *Dede Ḳorḳut* thematizes: those unlikely kinships not only between Basaṭ and Odysseus, Polyphemus and Tepegöz, but also between the intersecting oral traditions that circulated beyond the Persianate spheres of literary production. What we find is that Sufis were not the only poets who spoke a language of affinity that bridged, in different ways, multiple linguistic and cultural contexts. To some extent, a language of affinity had already begun to form among the peoples of Rūm. Moreover, this language transcended the Islamicate world, spreading among Christian peoples, including Armenians and Greeks.

The Warrior-Musician

We can hear this concordance of kindred voices speaking in different tongues as we continue on our way. Take, for instance, the romance of Digenēs Akritēs, born of a Syrian Muslim who converts to Christianity to marry a Byzantine princess.[30] The tale likely circulated orally for some time, in vernacular Greek, before it was written down as early as the twelfth century.[31] Digenēs, whose name is often translated as "two-blooded" or "twice-born," lives in the Byzantine borderlands as a fearsome warrior, undefeated in battle. Much like Dede Ḳorḳut, he is a virtuosic musician, adept at playing the lute (*labouto*), which at that time was perhaps not so different from the Turkish *ḳopuz*.[32] "He touched the strings with his bare hands," the narrator reports, for "he was well taught on instruments of music."[33] Frequently, Digenēs the Border Lord sings about the same subjects as his Persian and Turkish counterparts, and in a highly similar manner. He even complains, not unlike Rūmī, of the pains of separation. "Such is parting to all those who love," the story tells us. "It burns the soul and it subdues the heart, and separation wholly shatters reason."[34]

This declaration would be entirely at home in Turkish or Armenian poetry. For instance, Yūsuf-i Meddāḥ's Turkish adaptation *Varḳa and Gülşāh* is likewise concerned with the theme of separation. "I have lost my mind [and] senses," Gülşāh declares. "Alas, [my] state has become very difficult, your separation has burned me, [made me] helpless."[35] In both cases, separation "burns," destroying one's very capacity for thought. Similarly, both heroes sing and play the lute at highly affective beats in the story—moments of amorous initiation, union, separation, and sorrow.[36] Of course, despite sharing a common manner of representing separation, these romances still treat "infidels" as absolute enemies, to be crushed, if not slaughtered wholesale, without mercy.[37] Yet inscribed within the very bloodline of Digenēs is a literal kinship with Arabic and Islamicate culture, one that echoed across the soundscape of his home.[38] Scholars have posited a literary basis for this kinship as well, suggesting that another romance of borderland warfare, the Arabic *Dhāt al-Himma*, may have served as a possible source for the composition of *Digenēs Akritēs*.[39] In other words, these works also do more than showcase the "plasticity of identities in frontier environments," or inadvertently demonstrate the multicultural fluency of their creators, as Cemal Kafadar has posited.[40] I contend that such works exhibit a plasticity of their own—certainly one reflected in the social and religious fluencies of their protagonists, but also one encoded on a stylistic, structural, performative, and formal level. To put it simply, these literary and cultural systems "mixed" with one another no less than did the peoples who produced them. We can read the result of their mixing. In some cases, we can hear it.

These languages of affinity emerged from a landscape in which many communities tried, sometimes unsuccessfully, to navigate a diverse and politically volatile terrain. When Turkic groups began migrating westward in the eleventh century, culminating in the Seljuk conquest of Ani in 1064 and the defeat of the Byzantines in 1071, they provoked a wide array of complicated responses from local populaces.[41] Sometimes those responses may be expected: for instance, Matt'eos Uṙhayets'i, the twelfth-century Armenian chronicler, laments the terrible reign of Alp Arslān (d. 1072) and the destruction of settlements and lives by his military campaigns. Yet in the same chronicle, Matt'eos praises the Seljuk sultan Malik-Shāh (d. 1092), Alp Arslān's son, as a "kind and merciful" man, favored by God, who brought peace to Armenia after his father's reign.[42] Other relationships, no less complex, took root in more mundane ways. When Marco Polo traveled through Anatolia near the end of the thirteenth century, he simply noted that he found Armenians, Greeks, and Türkmens living together in villages and towns.[43]

Intermarriage in this period seems to have been, if not common, then at least common enough to provoke anxiety. We find such unions polemically thematized in stories such as *Digenēs Akritēs* and in the Armenian poem *Hovhannēs and Asha*, which depicts the love between a Christian man and a Muslim woman. Although this poem, which we encountered in the introduction, presents their love as illicit in the eyes of God and men, both Christian and Muslim are fluent in the speech of the other—a simple fact that escapes the otherwise moralizing or cautionary aspects of the poem. Arguably, what such examples reflect is a kind of plurality—albeit an often contentious and sometimes violent one—among the peoples who lived on different sides of these cultural "borderlands," which shaped the literary field in Anatolian Turkish, medieval Greek, and Middle Armenian. These kinships cannot be so easily expunged from the tales that developed and circulated in these lands, even when their narratives stress the absolute primacy of a Christian or Muslim hero above all others, as Kafadar has noted.[44]

The Middle Armenian romance *Patmut'iwn Farman Mankann* (*History of the Youth Farman*) showcases these entangled kinships even more clearly. Its protagonist, Farman Asman, whose name means "Edict of Heaven" (*Farmān-i Āsmān*) in Persian, is a warrior-musician much like Dede Ḳorḳut or Digenēs Akritēs. Farman "loved the sound [*dzayn*] of songs and melodies," the poem declares. "He kept many ensembles of minstrels [*gusanats'*] by him, / he played and rejoiced with his comrades."[45] Minstrels specifically and oral "secular" music generally were perhaps fairly commonplace in Cilician Armenia around this time, as Mkhit'ar Gosh condemned the performance of both in monasteries in his early thirteenth-century law code. For Mkhit'ar, minstrels and singing girls were "horrible for Christians to hear, let alone see."[46] On this evidence, he probably would not have liked the *Patmut'iwn Farman Mankann.* Its heroes not only sing extra- or non-Christian songs but also recite poetry in languages other than Armenian.[47] One character—another warrior-minstrel—even infiltrates the camp of his enemies in this manner. "He recites a Persian *qaṣīda* in a sweet voice," we learn of this sonic seduction:

> Many draw near him and gather there,
> They listen to the sound [*dzayn*] of the song and melody,
> They say, "Let's take and deliver him to the chief,
> So that he might rejoice in this sweet voice [*dzayn*]."
>
> He goes cheerfully and willing in heart,
> For the chief was a companion of the Great P'ōlat.

He goes and gladdens all who are there,
Until they give him a robe [*khalat'*] and treasured things.[48]

If the characters of this Armenian romance are heavily steeped in Persianate literary worlds, so too was their anonymous author. In fact, whoever composed the *Patmut'iwn Farman Mankann* seems to have loosely adapted the metrical system of *'arūż*—specifically, the *hazaj* meter—to imitate the sound of Persian poetry. As James R. Russell has posited, this adaptation of sound and meter also fulfilled an associative purpose, since the *hazaj* meter was used especially in stories featuring chivalric or manly deeds, primarily those associated with eros and battle.[49] One could, theoretically, hear the rapid pace of this meter and intuit what kind of story was about to unfold. In the case of *Patmut'iwn Farman Mankann*, this is exactly what happens: the sound of its performance announces its thematics, which are woven into scenes of wrestling, wooing, and warfare.

It is worth lingering on this observation. As we make our way through Rūm, we do not necessarily encounter poets translating *texts* from one language to another—although, as Yūsuf-i Meddāḥ's work shows, a loose form of translation certainly did facilitate cross-cultural exchange. Rather, we often encounter a kind of translingual migration of units both smaller and larger than texts: poetics, themes, meters, genres, narratives, words, and even sounds or modes of performance. Like the inhabitants of Anatolia, these units mixed together in observable ways. Even more, although many of these tales stress an absolute distinction between "us" and "them," "our people" and "their people," they mobilize similar styles, narratives, and characters to articulate this divide.

The Lone Stranger

The ubiquitous mixing of compositional units in Rūm allows us to view Köprülü's thesis in a different light. Travelers like Süleymān Türkmānī, whom we are still following, might have encountered oral poetry on their journey that did not strive for a Persianate sound but instead employed Turkish syllabic meter (*hece vezni*). Its foremost representative in Rūm, whom Kafadar calls "*the* classical poet" of Anatolian Turkish, was an enigmatic Sufi named Yūnus Emre.[50] He reportedly lived at the end of the thirteenth and the beginning of the fourteenth century, although imitators composed poetry in his name in subsequent periods. What little we know of Yūnus Emre comes largely from the poetry he composed in Turkish and from later sources.[51] Whereas scholars have criticized Sulṭān Valad for reductively "imitating" his father in clumsier verse, many have celebrated Yūnus Emre for his seeming disconnect, his apparent detachment, from an urban Persianate literary sphere. For instance, Köprülü declared that Yūnus Emre possessed a genius that was "completely Turkish" and "completely national," the result of a synthesis of Islamic Neoplatonism, which "gave Yūnus Emre his mystical and ethical principles," and the "Turkish popular element," which "provided his language, style, meter, and verse-form."[52]

In recent decades, some scholars have pushed back against Köprülü's "national" characterization, in part by drawing comparisons between the works of Yūnus Emre and of Rūmī.[53] However, this stroll through the literary landscape of Anatolia allows us to consider the poet's relationship to shared units of composition in a different way. Of course, Yūnus Emre certainly seems to represent himself as a lone figure, a destitute stranger (*gharīb*, or *garib* in an Ottoman Turkish transliteration), cast out of the urban centers of Islamic learning and Persian culture:

> I wonder, in this place, could there be a *gharīb* such as I?
> A broken-hearted, weepy-eyed one, a *gharīb* such as I?
>
> I passed through Rūm and Syria, all the lands on high,
> I searched greatly but found no *gharīb* such as I.
>
> May no one be a *gharīb*, may no one burn in longing's fire.
> My teacher, may no one be a *gharīb* such as I.
>
> My tongue speaks, my eyes weep, I myself burn for *gharībs*.
> Only my star in heaven is a *gharīb* such as I.
>
> How long shall I burn with this pain—till death come one day and I die?
> Only in my grave will I find a *gharīb* such as I.
>
> They'll say a *gharīb* died, they'll learn of it three days later.
> They'll wash, with frigid water, a *gharīb* such as I.

> O my Emre, cureless Yūnus. A cure can't be found for his agony.
> Come now, go from city to city, a *gharīb* such as I.[54]

Few poems go further in suggesting Yūnus Emre's reputation as a lone dervish than this one, as it paints the bleak life of a wanderer on a slow circuit from town to town, country to country. It is an image of the poet that seems to bolster his apparent detachment from the societies and peoples around him. But how closely should we read this representation into reality?

First, although our *gharīb* wanders far and wide, he is not in search of a home. More than anything else, the speaker seeks a counterpart—a kindred stranger "such as I." Given the widespread scope of social dispersion during this period in Rūm, one might think that finding such a figure would not be so difficult, were the poem truly about the phenomenon of exile or displacement. Mustafa Tatçı, the editor of the critical edition of Yūnus Emre's *Dīvān*, shares this view in his interpretation of the term *gharīb*. Noting that "the world is exile [*gurbet*]," he argues that *gharīb*s are those beings severed from the realm of the spirits, far from their source.[55] Hence, Yūnus Emre's identification as a *gharīb* probably has less to do with geographic displacement than with his separation from God on earth or his seeming inability to find kinship with others like himself.

In fact, a similar conception of *gharīb*s has long played an important role in Sufi thought. For example, one of the oldest manuals of Sufism in Persian, the late eleventh-century *Kashf al-maḥjūb* (*Unveiling the Hidden*), cites estrangement as a quality that every Sufi should cultivate. It presents John the Baptist, who is a prophet in the Qur'an, as the paradigm, since his "exile" (*ghurbat*) made him "a *gharīb* in his native country [*vaṭan*] and a stranger [*bīgāna*] to his own relations."[56] The *Kashf al-maḥjūb* elsewhere observes that the *gharīb* has no abode in this world or the next.[57] In the case of both Yūnus Emre and the wild prophet John, the *gharīb* serves as a model for others to emulate: one must become "estranged" from the world to practice true Islam, renounce one's ties to this material plane to find union with God. This is the great irony of Yūnus Emre's poem: to present himself as a *gharīb*, a stranger in total isolation, was to locate himself within a broad discourse on estrangement in the Islamicate world. In this context, it was to make a connective gesture by identifying as a wayfarer, or a Sufi. Most simply: it was to stake a claim about *belonging*.

Other poets articulated this claim in even more explicit ways. As we have seen, Sulṭān Valad conceptualized his followers as a community of strangers united in their mutual longing for God, even if they expressed this longing differently. It is therefore revealing that Christians also performed music and recited verse about strangers at this time—in particular, strangers one would do well to emulate. For instance, a thirteenth-century Greek hymn ascribed to the Byzantine historian Geōrgios Akropolitēs (d. 1282) depicts a lonely stranger wandering destitute, without hearth or home.[58] The processional hymn, which takes the perspective of Joseph of Arimathea and is sung during Holy Week, urgently repeats its refrain, "Give me this Stranger [ξένος]." A familiar narrative forms around this refrain:

> Give me this Stranger,
> Who from His youth has been received like a stranger.
>
> Give me this Stranger,
> Whom His kinsmen killed in hatred like a stranger.
>
> Give me this Stranger,
> Concerning Whom I am in perplexity, seeing the strangeness of His death.
>
> Give me this Stranger,
> Who knew how to take in the poor and strangers.
>
> Give me this Stranger,
> Whom the Jews, in their malice, estranged from the world.
>
> Give me this Stranger,
> That I may conceal Him in a tomb,
>
> Who being a Stranger
> Hath no place whereon to lay His head.[59]

Of course, this Stranger is not a wandering Sufi but rather the recently crucified Jesus Christ. Much like Yūnus Emre in his poem, Jesus wanders the country but finds no rest; his own kin do not recognize him; finally, he dies and is buried as a stranger. There are more direct associations that one can make between these works beyond the basic narrative structure, however. When later translators rendered the Greek hymn into Arabic, they used *gharīb* for *xenos*. Arab and Arabic-speaking Christians thus participated in shaping an affinitive discourse on estrangement, employing precisely the same vocabulary as their Muslim counterparts.

This shared lexicon of estrangement migrated into Middle Armenian. For instance, in the romance *Patmutʿiwn Farman Mankann*, our protagonist draws on this same Arabic term, now a loanword, to articulate his separation from kin. Surrounded by friends, Farman begins to weep bitterly when he remembers his distant father and mother. He thus laments his sad plight as a *gharīb*:

> Should the *gharīb* be lord over many cities
> And near him greatness never is lacking,
> His heart is always in dread, saying: "I am forlorn,
> I have no friend here, no complete love."
>
> [His] spirit severely yearns and [his] heart is willing,
> The poor one roams the land, consenting to his heart,
> Instead of sugar, he swallows bile and poison,
> He considers this sugar; it seems sweet to him.
>
> The *gharīb*, who has come to a foreign land,
> Is not even accepted by the earth; it does not agree [with him].
> Though he's been [like] Solomon in wit and wisdom,
> He appears to men as a fool, half-drunk and dumb.[60]

The Armenian *gharīb*, like Yūnus Emre and Jesus Christ, possesses an inner wisdom, a hidden authority, that goes unrecognized by others. Of course, in the case of Farman, who is a prince of Assyria, this authority is worldly and not spiritual. Still, in each of these examples the *gharīb* is defined neither by his separation from a geographic realm nor by a lack of mobility or isolation within his new environment. Rather, the *gharīb* is marked by separation, including an affective displacement from loved ones. This is, as Thomas Bauer has argued, a highly mutable state—one based on a conception of foreignness and otherness not in absolute, ontological terms but rather in terms of contingent relationships, feelings, and interactions.[61]

Although Farman's lament lacks the overt religious valences in the works of Yūnus Emre and Geōrgios Akropolitēs, its narrative structure follows a well-worn path. As the song progresses, the Armenian *gharīb* wanders the land without companion, only to die alone and be interred in the earth. Most important, the romance's author represents strangers in Farman's song by using a vocabulary specific to this genre in multiple cultures. He might have chosen an "indigenous" word in Middle Armenian, such as *ōtar* (stranger), *nzhdeh* (sojourner), or *pandukht* (pilgrim, migrant), but instead employs a term shared throughout Rūm to articulate separateness. We can say the same of Yūnus Emre. Instead of favoring a "purely" Turkish word for "stranger," he chose a term that already circulated across an array of languages—one that, much like the figure of the peripatetic poet, was most at home in motion.

Beyond Native and Foreign

Here our meanderings through Rūm arrive at a crucial point: although Köprülü drew a genealogy for Yūnus Emre, whom he connected linearly to a pre-Islamic Turkish culture, we find a more rhizomatic kinship in the poet's work. This kinship extends not only backward, to the syllabic meter of Turkish poets in Central Asia, but also laterally, connecting to the structures, vocabularies, themes, and concepts of adjacent languages in Rūm. In this light, figures such as the *gharīb* suggest a broad language of affinity, reflected here in a common understanding of what separation is, what it means, and how one should speak of it in verse. One therefore need not theorize the development of this affinitive language in terms of a onetime act of cross-cultural exchange—or worse, of the influence of a "dominant," active literary culture upon a "weaker," passive one. Rather, we ought to envision the literary field in more dialogic, interconnected terms: something like a kinship network distinguished not by pedigree—the supposedly absolute origins of each given literary culture—but rather by affinity, by a porousness to other languages and literary cultures within shared or adjacent geographic spaces.

Such affinities can help to reposition not only a major poet like Yūnus Emre in Anatolian literary history but also the Turkish literary tradition in relation to the integrative literary landscape of Rūm, examined here through the eyes of our strange guides. As we have seen, Köprülü—and many scholars after him—conceptualized Turkish literary history as a linear family tree, beginning with a singular, monolingual progenitor. In this framework, what is "foreign" to a literary system is that which intrudes from the outside—the foreign is "not us." However, what a modern perspective considers "foreign"—rigidly Turkic or non-Turkic—did not much interest our premodern subjects in Anatolia (at least, not in the same way that it interests modern readers). Yūnus Emre exemplifies this perspective: he identified as a *gharīb* because the term already had currency in other Sufi circles, particularly Persianate ones. So too did Armenians and Greeks adopt a similar discourse on estrangement in their literary production, in part because it had a widely resonant valence that transcended any single religious or linguistic context. In short, many literary cultures of Anatolia took shape through protracted exposure to and engagement with what is often (anachronistically) coded as nonnative. One cannot parse these cultures exclusively according to their real or perceived points of origin without losing something essential about their historical development, their gradual metamorphoses, within this multilingual space.

The literary codes of medieval Anatolia might therefore be best likened to the miscellany (from the Latin *miscere*, "to mix"), an assembly of disparate texts contained within the same manuscript, insofar as these codes collected an array of linguistic and cultural markers within themselves. By this analogy, both poems and poets are miscellanists—actors in the compilation of the literary code, selectively sampling from the other literary languages in their environment and from the experiments of previous poets to create new affiliations and associations. Thus, although Yūnus Emre composed verse in Turkish syllabic meter, he also wrote poetry using the metrical system of *ʿarūż*, such as the didactic *maṣnavī* ascribed to his name, and even evokes Rūmī in his *Dīvān*, placing himself within a poetic tradition whose boundaries were not marked by language alone. Simply put, even the most "Turkish" of the classical Turkish poets also drew from widely circulating units of composition, such as the trope of the *gharīb* and the genre of the *maṣnavī*, helping to shuffle them into new cultural and communal contexts.

Of course, poets did not need to claim direct kinships with other poets to form genealogical relationships across literary works or literary cultures. After all, as these peregrinations suggest, the mixing of diverse styles, narratives, and forms was a hallmark of composition in Anatolia in this period. Sometimes the simple adaptation of a poetics from another language—such as the Armenian or Turkish absorption of a meter from Arabic or Persian—was all that was needed to form an associative connection in the ears of an audience. It is therefore significant that poets often sought to make their entangled cultural and linguistic affiliations explicit in many of the earliest works of Anatolian Turkish poetry. As we shall see in the city of Kırşehir, which is just now visible on the road ahead, Turkish poets recombined various literary narratives, styles, and forms in the pursuit of such highly particular ends. They selectively drew upon the dazzling heterogeneity of Rūm—literary, linguistic, cultural, epistemic—and learned the alchemy of transforming difference into a Turkish language of affinity.

CHAPTER FIVE

KIRŞEHİR KINSHIPS

When Sulṭān Valad's representative Süleymān Türkmānī arrived in Kırşehir, he would have found a religiously and culturally thriving city, the streets thronging with Armenians, Persians, Turks, and Jews. On a warm day, the fragrant wind may have recalled through his nose the other name by which this place was known: Gülşehir, "City of roses."[1] Kırşehir boasted an endowed mosque, a *khānaqāh* (hospice), a *zāviya* (lodge), a *maktab* (school), and an imposing madrasa, atop which students traced the slow migration of stars. The city may have been rich in learning, but like many other regions of Rūm it was also flush with silver. After the Mongols defeated the Seljuks, Ghāzān Khān (d. 1304) established a mint in this region that produced small silver coins, stamped with the names of the Ilkhanid sovereigns.[2] These coins—known as *aḳçe*, "little white thing"—passed from hand to hand, city to city.[3]

Of course, coins were not the only currency that circulated here. Süleymān Türkmānī and his companions also labored to transmit the teachings and poetry of Rūmī throughout the area.[4] Thus, they established, in accordance with Sulṭān Valad's directive, a Sufi hospice in Kırşehir. It is possible that they felt somewhat crowded there. Ḥācī Bektāş (d. c. 1271), a Sufi from Nishapur, had migrated to Anatolia around the time of the Mongol conquests and settled near the city. He quickly became associated with a popular preacher named Bābā Ilyās, whose grandson

ʿĀşıḳ Paşa we shall soon meet. Rūmī's followers clearly felt some rivalry with Ḥācī Bektāş.[5] Aflākī, for instance, calls him a gnostic, a learned man, but one who "did not follow [*mutābaʿat*]" the religious law.[6] Still, despite the potential for friction, the followers of Rūmī and of Ḥācī Bektāş had something in common: both groups sought to spread knowledge of Islam among ethnically and religiously diverse audiences. Moreover, both did so by recontextualizing the symbolic vocabularies and devotional practices of those audiences, including Christians and Turks, within an Islamic interpretive framework.[7]

This chapter examines an analogous cross-cultural convergence and a complementary manner of transmitting knowledge in the literary production of Kırşehir. The rivalry it sheds light on, however, was not between the followers of different Sufi communities but rather between linguistic and literary systems. Gülşehrī (d. after 1318) and ʿĀşıḳ Paşa (d. 1333), two of the earliest poets of Anatolian Turkish literature, shall serve as our guides here, since both emerged as important authors after Süleymān Türkmānī's death around the turn of the century. A closer look at their poetry allows us to bring together the threads of our story so far: Rūmī's ubiquitous mixing of sources and audiences, Sulṭān Valad's manner of composing through emulation, and the widespread translation in Rūm of units both smaller and larger than texts. Most important, both ʿĀşıḳ Paşa and Gülşehrī fashioned poetic genealogies that help us to envision the origins of Turkish literature in Anatolia from a more emic perspective. As this chapter shall demonstrate, these poets were hardly anxious about using works of Persian poetry as their literary models. Nor did they attempt to differentiate Turkish literature from Persian literary production on ontological grounds. Instead, they desired to construct and emphasize affinities between Arabic, Persian, and Turkish literary cultures, which they accomplished in part by composing performative stories about genealogy, succession, and kinship. It was through and not in spite of kindred ties that these poets crafted a new authority, working with and for the Turkish language, to reveal Islamic meaning.

Persianate Genealogies for Turkish-Speaking Poets

What did it mean to be a poet in Kırşehir at this time? At least in some circles, it likely meant that one was skilled in the arts of Persian poetics.

Gülşehrī is exemplary in this regard. Although he is celebrated as one of the earliest poets to compose in Anatolian Turkish, he began his career by writing a *mas̱navī* in Persian, the *Falak-nāma* (*Book of the Celestial Sphere*).[8] Nor did he merely dabble in Persian poetry, as though he secretly longed to compose verse only in his mother tongue. Rather, Gülşehrī occupied himself with the most minutely technical aspects of poetic composition in Arabic and Persian, even going so far as to compose a treatise on *ʿarūż*, the metrical system that had come to define poetic production across much of the Islamicate world.[9] Simply put, he does not seem to have considered Persianate poetics to be "foreign" or "exogenous" to his "native" Turkic culture. Instead, he embodied multiple linguistic and literary worlds simultaneously.[10]

We know little else about Gülşehrī's identity—including, for instance, the precise location where he wrote his most famous works, though his pen name obviously suggests an association with Kırşehir. His given name is believed to have been Süleymān (Solomon), though even this is unsure. Today, Gülşehrī is best known for his Turkish adaptation of ʿAṭṭār's *Manṭiq al-ṭayr* (*Speech of the Birds*).[11] Although scholars often refer to this landmark as a translation or partial translation of ʿAṭṭār, we would likely not recognize it as a translation in any strict sense of the word.[12] Gülşehrī, for his part, at one point simply refers to his poem as a *teʾlīf*, meaning "composition," "compilation," or "book."[13] Moreover, rather than seeking to faithfully reproduce the narratives from ʿAṭṭār's frame tale, he changed the meanings of these stories in many ways—even, on occasion, criticizing deficiencies in the original work, as Vanessa Shepherd has shown.[14] Sometimes Gülşehrī departs from ʿAṭṭār's version altogether, choosing instead to elaborate on how members of urban confraternities in Anatolia ought to behave.[15] At other times, he infuses narratives from ʿAṭṭār's masterpiece with historical details more particular to Kırşehir at this time.

Take, for instance, ʿAṭṭār's famous story of a pious Muslim named Shaykh Ṣanʿān. In the Persian tale, Shaykh Ṣanʿān falls madly in love with a Christian woman in Rūm. She wants nothing to do with him, however, and declares that she could never love a Muslim. The shaykh is desperate. To placate the Christian, he casts off the precepts of his religion, choosing to wallow in the mud with pigs. Yet reduced to this pitiful state, the shaykh learns a strange lesson through the intercession of the Prophet. His path back to true religion emerges only after he severs all worldly attachments—including his attachment to the outward forms of religion.[16] Paradoxically, through his love of the heretical Christian he eventually realizes what it means to be a true Muslim, and he is ultimately freed from his crazed infatuation with her. In the end, his display of faith stuns his would-be Christian beloved. She converts to Islam on the spot and then promptly drops dead, no longer relevant to the narrative at hand.

Gülşehrī's adaptation of this story ends somewhat differently, however.[17] In his retelling, we find a curious change of scale: the pious shaykh inspires not one person but *seventy households* of Christians to become Muslims, perhaps reflecting a broad program of Islamization pursued by the Mawlavīs or Bektāşīs in the region.[18] What seems clear is that Gülşehrī's adaptation is as much about the people who are converted as about the restoration of the shaykh's faith. Consequently, the topicality of the Turkish *Manṭiq al-ṭayr* goes beyond its use of a locally comprehensible language.[19]

What Gülşehrī translated across languages was not necessarily ʿAṭṭār's words, then, but rather the *Manṭiq al-ṭayr*'s themes, characters, general structure, and poetics—units of composition that moved, much like the poets of Rūm, across multiple cultural and linguistic systems. He also recast these units, subtly altering their meanings, to speak to the needs of a local audience. This likely included members of Islamic confraternities; an elite readership versed in the Qur'an and Islamicate literature; and perhaps the Mongol soldiers in Kırşehir who used Turkish as a lingua franca, as A. C. S. Peacock has proposed.[20] At the same time, Gülşehrī's practice of unfaithful translation suggests more than a need to engage with local audiences as the sole reason behind this creative retelling. It seems that he desired most of all to be associated with the figure of ʿAṭṭār in overtly genealogical terms. As we shall see, Gülşehrī's practice of adaptive translation was an attempt not only to endow Turkish poetry with an aesthetic culled from Persianate literary production but also to fashion a particular kind of literary and spiritual authority for its author and other Turkish-speaking poets.

Gülşehrī manifests this genealogical desire in the story of six world-conquering men found in his Turkish *Manṭiq al-ṭayr*.[21] In this tale, he claims to be a great shaykh—presumably of Kırşehir—whose followers practice *samāʿ* at his house every evening. One day while out for a stroll, he reports, he was suddenly transported "to the mountain of the world."[22] There, in a dazzling garden, he encountered six world-conquering poets, who greeted him in turn. He names these men as Sanāʾī, Mawlānā (Rūmī), Niẓāmī, ʿAṭṭār, Saʿdī, and Sulṭān Valad, who had each composed a famous book. Gülşehrī, sadly, could not say the same for himself. Unworthy to join the ranks of these illustrious poets, he returned to the mortal realm. Only then did a stranger—in fact, a saint (*velī*)—approach and instruct him to compose a new *mas̱navī*, the *Falak-nāma*. At the saint's suggestion, he also selected the pen name of Gülşehrī. Thus named and with his *Falak-nāma* in hand, he went back to the mountain of the world:

> When, through this book, my renown was complete,
> I went and those six men I did greet.
>
> I inquired, "At last, what people are you?
> In this place, what do you desire?"
>
> One of them says: "I am Sanāʾī,
> Who is quite luminous in the *Ilāhī-nāma*."
>
> Another says: "O dear one, I am Mawlānā;
> My desirable book is the *Mas̱navī*."
>
> One of them says: "My taste has entered [the world]
> Through the *Makhzan al-asrār*. My name is Niẓāmī."
>
> Another says: "Here I am: ʿAṭṭār.
> Sweet in my hand, my fair *Manṭiq al-ṭayr*."
>
> One of them says: "I am Saʿdī, my fellow [poet].
> It is I who made the *Gulistān-nāma* elegant."
>
> One says: "[Sulṭān] Valad I am named,
> In the end, my *mas̱navī* you will have obtained."
>
> When they explicated their famous names,
> Each the flavor of his book did praise.
>
> The grace of the rose did I put on.
> Like the dove, like the nightingale, I broke into song:

"The name of your servant is Gülşehrī:
It is not a tax on sugar but rather its share.

And the *Falak-nāma* is the name of my book—
[Even] the taste of its salt is quite sweet."[23]

Scholars have interpreted this claim to literary affiliation in different ways. Shepherd, for instance, simply finds the story "interesting inasmuch as it mentions particular authors and works that influenced [Gülşehrī's] literary career."[24] Selim S. Kuru has advanced a more nuanced reading, noting that Gülşehrī makes no mention of this tale in the *Falak-nāma*, which he dedicated to the Ilkhanid ruler Ghāzān Khān.[25] Why, then, offer a fantastic account of the *Falak-nāma*'s origin in a different book? For Kuru, the answer lies in Gülşehrī's wish to be a poet-seer who illuminates hidden secrets. "Gülşehrī defies being considered a mere compiler or, to use a well-established term in Medieval European literary studies, a 'scriptor,' " he rightly posits. "Rather he aspired to be an author: [not] an author who writes a book . . . about the facts of this world (a historical narrative, for example) but a visionary one who can report about conditions in another world, following a specific Persian tradition of didactic verse-narratives as represented by the six authors discussed above."[26]

From the *Manṭiq al-ṭayr*'s account, there can be no doubt that Gülşehrī desired to be taken seriously as the seventh "world-conquering" poet. At the same time, he had already placed himself within a "Persian tradition" of writing didactic *maṣnavīs*, in the style of the other six poets, simply by composing the *Falak-nāma* years prior. What, then, is significant about a genealogy that links together these seven authors, and their respective *maṣnavīs*, in particular? Here we ought to recall other genealogical relationships among poets, and the works they produced, elsewhere in Anatolia. As we have seen, Rūmī positioned the *Maṣnavī* as the fulfillment of the *Ilāhī-nāma* and the *Manṭiq al-ṭayr* by imitating their style and adapting their content. Moreover, he instructed his followers to read the poetry of Sanā'ī and 'Aṭṭār to fully grasp the *Maṣnavī*'s secrets. In other words, Rūmī's poetic genealogy was not merely fictive: these works have direct hermeneutic and formal connections to one another. Nor was Rūmī the only figure to shape this genealogy. Sulṭān Valad, whose *maṣnavī* reached Gülşehrī last, placed himself at the culmination of this chain. Like Rūmī, he did so by expounding upon the secrets of the *Maṣnavī* and by imitating his father's works—a point he makes explicit in the introductions to the *Ibtidā-nāma* and the *Rabāb-nāma*.

Gülşehrī, by fashioning a genealogy within a work that is unquestionably an adaptation of ʿAṭṭār, laid claim to a similar poetic kinship. Although he desired to be a "visionary" author, as Kuru posits, he staked his authority upon this practice of emulation, in which literary works and their diverse authors are bound together according to a particular logic encoded within the very poetics of a text. Unlike Rūmī or Sulṭān Valad, however, Gülşehrī left his genealogy somewhat open ended. As he explains, he was the seventh poet in this chain but not necessarily the last. Others might therefore share in this literary kinship:

> Let he who desires to become eighth
> Come into [our] midst when he is able.[27]

"I would even be eighth," Gülşehrī concludes. "I would find my sustenance, myself content, in the world."[28] To join these elevated ranks, one needed to earn the name of a poet. An ordinary pen name, such as Zeyd or ʿAmr or Bekr, culled from life's quotidian spheres, would not do.[29] The name had to be unique. "Should he want a distinguished name, [there] is the name of Gülşehrī," he offers his audience, extending his own authority as a poet to those who might follow him.[30] Simply put, his poetic *silsila* (genealogy) serves as an invitation to other Turkish speakers: it calls on the audience to choose a new pen name, to inscribe that name at the end of this *silsila* of poets, and to compose verse in a similar didactic and literary mode, which in this case is the *maṣnavī* form. In other words, the Turkish *Manṭiq al-ṭayr* showcases a literary model, built on an open-ended genealogy of true poets, for emulation by other Turkish speakers. At the same time, it provides a foundation for poets of Anatolian Turkish to choose Persian poets, and not exclusively Turkic models of literary production, as their predecessors. Gülşehrī may have cultivated a kinship with the works of previous poets, but he ultimately extended it to all those who might later emulate his verses in the Turkish tongue.

Gülşehrī's praxis of "translation"—which in no small part concerned the transmission of authority from one language and poet to the next—also dovetails with the central theme of his work. The phrase *manṭiq al-ṭayr* did not originate with ʿAṭṭār, of course, but comes from the Qur'an, in the famous scene where Solomon succeeds David as king. Most significantly, this succession is observed not with great fanfare or a demonstration of military might but rather through the transmission of *knowledge*. Hence, when Solomon "inherited" David, he declared to his subjects: "Men, we have been taught the speech of the birds [*manṭiq al-ṭayr*], and we have been given of everything; surely this is indeed the manifest bounty" (27:16).[31] In other words, the speech of the birds is not literally a language. Instead, it is a symbol of the deep, divine wisdom of Solomon and thus a framework for viewing one's world, including the people who populate it, in a certain way. In the *Maṣnavī*, for instance, the heterogeneous birds of the sky grow unified in eloquence when Solomon teaches them his language—which, of course, is not a language at all but rather a way of being the same in heart (*ham dilī*), or sharing a way of seeing, thinking, and living with others. Thus, even an Indian and a Turk might understand each other if they learned to be one in heart from the right spiritual guide. The speech of the birds, Solomon's language of intimacy, creates kinship out of difference.

To the extent that this is subtext in the *Maṣnavī*, it becomes text in the Turkish *Manṭiq al-ṭayr*, particularly near the conclusion, in a highly performative manner. It is here that Gülşehrī, like many poets from this period, offers an explanation of why he composed the poem, and in his case thereby subtly extends his genealogy once more. His conclusion depicts a lush and fragrant garden—not so different from the garden of the six world-conquering poets—that enthralls his senses. Here he began to exercise his authority and to try his hand at composition. "I conversed deeply with the nightingale," he says. "Since it considered me a teacher / it learned the language of the birds from me."[32] The nightingale, of course, already spoke a language before Gülşehrī arrived on the scene. But, as Gülşehrī makes clear, the "language of the birds" (*ḳuş dili*) does not inhere in a single tongue:

> [As for] the *Manṭiq al-ṭayr* that ʿAṭṭār composed,
> He spoke the language of the birds in Persian.
>
> We, too, sang it for the sake of God,
> In a Turkish form, like the nightingale.

Since we made the *Falak-nāma* fit for a king,
A gilded throne and crown in Persian,

[And since] the language of Turks is finer than Arabic,
We made the *Manṭiq al-ṭayr* its fellow.

Because I shall not cease [in] this Turkish work,
I would not exchange it for Persian.

No one spoke such sweet words like this;
No one made a book grander than this.[33]

Therefore, much as "Solomon reproached the hoopoe" in the Qur'an, Gülşehrī challenges his audience: "Who could compose a book superior to this?"[34] Simply put, in Gülşehrī's eyes the Turkish *Manṭiq al-ṭayr* is no work of mimicry: it surpasses the Persian original, just as its language surpasses Arabic, which had long served as the prestige literary language of the Islamicate world. Crucially, what he "translates" into Turkish is not just the "allegory of the birds" that ʿAṭṭār created but also "the speech of the birds," which is the knowledge of Islam. This is a story about *succession*, in other words, as much as it is an allegory culled from Persian literature and rewritten for Turkish speakers in Rūm. Of course, all genealogies are ultimately stories of succession and inheritance. Thus, just as Gülşehrī inherits the mantle of Persian poets, so does the Turkish language inherit from Arabic and Persian the capability to reveal Islamic meaning. Turkish poetry could now articulate "the language of the birds," the knowledge of Islam that transforms its audience into kin.

As Barbara Flemming has observed, it is an undeniable fact that Turkish-speaking poets drew many (though not all) of their literary models from Persian poetry. The burning questions, she insists, are how and why.[35] In the case of the *Manṭiq al-ṭayr*, Gülşehrī couches his literary production in terms of succession, inheritance, and the transmission of Islamic knowledge from one language to another. Appropriately, then, King Solomon becomes something of an *ozan* in its final verses, holding the famed instrument of Dede Ḳorḳut in his hands. "O Solomon, tune the strings of that *ḳopuz*, / that we may learn this language of the birds," the verses implore, as though requesting a performance from a Turkish minstrel.[36] Perhaps there is also slippage here between King Solomon and the figure of the poet, who chose the distinguished name of Gülşehrī, as both were positioned to unlock hidden secrets through speech.[37] This request therefore speaks to the thrust of the entire work: the language of the birds, the language of poetry, also belongs to Turkish, by divine decree. And one who plays the *ḳopuz*, one who speaks Turkish to instruct an audience in Islam, inherits the mantle not only of Rūmī and ʿAṭṭār but also of Gülşehrī and Solomon.

Turkish Succession

Gülşehrī's genealogical engagement with Persian literature was not anomalous in Kırşehir. His contemporary ʿĀşıḳ Paşa fashioned a similar genealogy—although one that was less concerned with the pedigree of any single poet. Perhaps this was because ʿĀşıḳ Paşa came from a prominent family that was already infamous in the region. His grandfather was Bābā Ilyās, an itinerant preacher from Khorasan who played a major role in the 1240 revolt against the Seljuk regime. Whereas Bābā Ilyās incited social upheaval, his grandson would take another path, putting down roots in the multiethnic and multireligious city of Kırşehir.

In the past century, ʿĀşıḳ Paşa fell under the long shadow of Yūnus Emre, who is synonymous in the literary canon with an authentic Turkish poetic culture, seemingly distant from the creeping influence of the Persianate world. Conversely, ʿĀşıḳ Paşa is best known for his *Garīb-nāme* (*Book of the Stranger*), a monumental—but little read—Turkish *maṣnavī* of nearly 10,600 lines, composed in *ramal* meter.[38] Much like Sulṭān Valad's poetry, the *Garīb-nāme* has been dismissed as a reductive copy of the *Maṣnavī*, although it is structurally quite different. Even Mecdut Mansuroğlu, who was among the first scholars to understand the importance of Rūmī's and Sulṭān Valad's Turkish poetry, dismissed ʿĀşıḳ Paşa as "a mere imitator of Jalâladdîn Rûmî and Sulṭân Valad."[39] This mirrors the attitude of E. J. W. Gibb, who admired the scope and structure of the *Garīb-nāme* but was even more critical of its poetics. For him, its verses "read smoothly, and in matters of technique are on the whole tolerably correct; but poetry they are not." In Gibb's estimation, this was hardly surprising, as ʿĀşıḳ Paşa "naturally took Sultán Veled and Mevláná Jelál-ud-Dín as his models; they wrote in verse, so he did the same; they used a particular metre, so he used it also; they, engrossed in the didactic side of their work, wholly overlooked the artistic, so he did likewise." Thus, he concluded, the *Garīb-nāme* is a poem in "form alone."[40]

Of course, from a medieval point of view, there is little sense of poetics without form. Indeed, as we have seen, the adaptation of form served a vital role for poets, who were far from anxious about any resemblance between their work and that of others, in Turkish or in Persian. On the contrary, poets like Sulṭān Valad and Gülşehrī cultivated this resemblance, through a practice of literary emulation, an intentional "following" of other poets in Rūm, sometimes despite the language they used. Literary emulation was therefore generative: it helped to produce new works of Islamicate poetry in the Turkish language and, over time, to fashion Turkish as a literary language according to prevailing standards common to Arabic and Persian literatures.

Beyond Konya and Kırşehir, the labor of cultivating literary Turkish also unfolded at various courts both east and south of Anatolia. Yūsuf Khāṣṣ Ḥājib, whom we encountered in the introduction, produced one of the earliest works of Turkish literature by adopting the metrical system of *'arūż* in the eleventh century. So too did Maḥmūd al-Kāshgharī (fl. eleventh century) compile a monumental Turkish lexicon, based on the model of Arabic lexicons, which he dedicated to the 'Abbasid caliph al-Muqtadī.[41] Elsewhere, in late fourteenth-century Egypt, authors began to compose translations in Kipchak Turkish, again for a courtly audience, of Firdawsī's *Shāh-nāma* and the *Gulistān* by Sa'dī (d. 1291/2).[42]

Similarly, the Aydınid beylik (1308–1426), on the eastern shores of the Aegean Sea, patronized the composition of literary works in Persian, Arabic, and Anatolian Turkish alike. Moreover, the most notable Turkish poetry produced here—including a version of the *Kalīla and Dimna* in the 1330s and a translation of Niẓāmī Ganjavī's classic *Khusraw and Shīrīn*, completed in 1367 by the poet Fahrī—were clearly products of a court that emulated Persianate literary culture, seeking to re-create it in different ways.[43] As Sara Nur Yıldız has argued, these poets generally aimed to inculcate "aesthetic, ethical, and religious values," such as the knowledge of *adab*, in communities that were affiliated, to whatever degree, with the ruling elite.[44] The same is generally true of poets from the mid-fourteenth through the mid-fifteenth century at the Germiyanid court, which ruled another beylik in western Anatolia.[45]

Beyond the courts in Rūm, a refracted image emerges. Much like the translators at the Mamluk and Aydınid courts, Gülşehrī and 'Āşıḳ Paşa were versatile in many tongues. Their aim, however, was not to bolster Turkic claims to sovereignty, unlike Yūsuf or al-Kāshgharī, but rather to spread a message about Islam to their diverse, local audiences.[46] In other words, they endeavored to translate *adab* into a Turkish linguistic sphere in the heartland of Anatolia while navigating the same literary and aesthetic realms as their Arabic- and Persian-speaking counterparts. This kind of literary emulation thus served a pragmatic purpose, as it encoded their works in the styles and even the sounds of Islamicate poetry, creating a fuzzy set of aesthetic and aural affinities that performatively realized their genealogical claims. Implicitly or explicitly, the message of these early Turkish poets in Rūm was remarkably consistent: an Islamic episteme could now be revealed to Turkish ears, by Turkish tongues.

ʿĀşıḳ Paşa frames the *Garīb-nāme*, which he composed in 1330, in these very terms. Whereas Gülşehrī was primarily concerned with cultivating a hermeneutic relationship between himself and other poets, ʿĀşıḳ Paşa aimed to fashion connections between Arabic, Persian, and Turkish cultures of literary production. We find this new kinship form—an Islamic genealogy of language—taking root in the *Garīb-nāme*'s introduction. After invoking God, ʿĀşıḳ Paşa begins his genealogy, like the *silsila*s of almost all Sufi orders, with the Prophet Muḥammad, whom he praises as "the most eloquent speaker" among both Arabs and non-Arabs. Next, he briefly describes the scholars of religious law, the founders of Sufi orders, and all the shaykhs and saints, who each brought forth their secrets to compose works in Arabic and the languages of the *ʿacem*, which refers to all non-Arabs generally and Persians particularly.[47] It was through literary production, he claims, that Muslims in centuries past had escaped the snares of evil. ʿĀşıḳ Paşa then places himself, rather subtly, within this *silsila* of luminaries.

He does this by contrasting the past against the present—a time, he tells us, when a great many people are unable to comprehend higher, spiritual meanings. Therefore, he decided to compose a book in the Turkish language, for the benefit of all, with a few necessary caveats:

> Though spoken herein is the Turkish tongue,
> The stages of higher meaning [*maʿnī*] are indeed revealed.
>
> For you to know all stages of the Way,
> Do not revile the Turk and Tajik tongues![48]

This is where ʿĀşıḳ Paşa offers an entirely different perspective on literary Turkish than many of his predecessors to the east or south of Rūm. Notably, he does not attempt to marry the Turkish language to political power or territorial sovereignty. Instead, ʿĀşıḳ Paşa does something more radical: although he draws a genealogy between the Prophet and the production of Turkish literature, he does so in part to *decenter* the cultural and religious primacy of any single language. He proposes, in other words, a more lateral set of relationships, based upon mutual affinities between languages in their expressions of "truth" or "meaning." Or as he puts it in the *Garīb-nāme*'s conclusion:

> In every tongue there were regulation and rules:[49]
> All minds and intellects did fall for these!
>
> [Yet] no one has cared for the Turkish language,
> No one has ever been enraptured with Turks.
>
> Turks too did not know those languages,
> The narrow Way [and] those tremendous stages.
>
> So this *Garīb-nāme* began to speak
> That people of this tongue may know higher meanings too.[50]

Consequently, he warns, "do not assume that higher meaning is only in one tongue," and repeats that, for the adept, "there is higher meaning in every tongue," just as God can be found on every path.[51] Similarly, because no language has an absolute monopoly on the revelation of higher secrets, or "meaning" (*maʿnī*), he posits that "in every language" these secrets abide; the face of meaning shall not be concealed from those who seek.[52] This is why he names his *mas̱navī* the *Garīb-nāme*: not only on account of its marvelous and strange (*garīb*) stories but also because its higher meanings (*maʿānī*) were "*garīb* in the Turkish language."[53] These "strange" meanings, or at least ʿĀşıḳ Paşa's labor to unveil them in verse, are nothing less than Islam entering into a Turkish-speaking milieu.[54]

What is "foreign" for ʿĀşıḳ Paşa is not necessarily the *mas̱navī* form, Persianate poetics, or even the production of Turkish literature in Anatolia. In his verse we find no cultural parsing of shared compositional units, those building blocks of what Sheldon Pollock calls a "cosmopolitan" literary code, along an anachronistically rigid Turkish-Persian binary.[55] For ʿĀşıḳ Paşa, true alterity is not linguistic or literary at all but rather epistemic: it is the foreignness of Islam, presented as strange or a stranger, to a Turkish-speaking population. Like the *gharīb* in Rūmī's *Maṡnavī*, the epistemic figure of Islam enters the Turkish language to guide its own audience. In this sense, ʿĀşıḳ Paşa's work finds affinity with Sulṭān Valad's *Rabāb-nāma*, as the figure of the *gharīb* and the multilingual *rabāb* each simultaneously create a discourse about Islam and shape the community in which that discourse has meaning. In producing an Islamicate Turkish literature and a Muslim Turkish-speaking audience at the same time, it is the stranger, the outsider, that paradoxically forms the basis for a new kind of affiliation.

Kinship and Difference

Although scholars generally plumb the *Garīb-nāme* for its orderly cosmology or discussion of the Turkish language, there is a different thread that I wish to tease out here. One of ʿĀşıḳ Paşa's aims, as we have seen, was to decenter the primacy of any and every language in the capacity to unveil higher secrets. In fact, much as Gülşehrī constructed his own poetic genealogy through different stories about succession, ʿĀşıḳ Paşa thematized his proposed lateral relationship among the languages of Rūm in a tale from the *Garīb-nāme*, allowing us to conceive of their kindred ties in slightly different terms.

As this book has shown, the relationships between the peoples and literatures of Rūm often reflected an ethos of measured hospitality. Consequently, ʿĀşıḳ Paşa's language of affinity did not negate or whitewash the differences between people—linguistic, cultural, ethnic—but rather sought to preserve and accommodate difference within an Islamic hermeneutic frame. "Listen, O [you who] desires meaning," his story begins, commanding the audience to lend their ears.[56]

> Once upon a time, four people became travel companions,
> Setting out upon one road together.
>
> One of them was Arab, one Persian, one a Turkish man,
> And the other of these travelers was Armenian.

They didn't know one another's languages,
Nor did each understand what the other said.

Suddenly, as they were traveling together,
The four discovered an *akçe* on the ground.

They picked up the coin and kept going;
Listen to what they did when they arrived there.[57]

In a city brimming with abundant blessings, these companions unburdened themselves. Soon, at the rumbling of their stomachs, each recalled that silvery coin from the road. But when they brought forth the coin and placed it in their midst, ʿĀşıḳ Paşa tells us, their real trouble begins:

Their tongues were different, but what they desired was
  the same:
Listen to what each one said.

At first, the Arab spoke in his tongue:
[*in Arabic*] *O companions, give me grapes!*

The Persian said: [*in Persian*] *Let's buy grapes with this;*
It is well to sit and feast upon them together!

The Armenian said: [*in Armenian*] *I want [to eat] grapes;*
If you get grapes, let us buy . . . red ones.

The Türkmen said: [*in Turkish*] *Fetch grapes and let us feast;*
Let us set aside this small talk.

They didn't know what each other said;
One, hearing another's speech, didn't understand.[58]

This passage is dense with the same heteroglossia that the story thematizes. The Arab speaks, in verse, the Arabic language; the Persian, New Persian; the Armenian, Middle Armenian; and the Türkmen, Turkish. Of course, for all this speech to be possible, ʿĀşıḳ Paşa had to be familiar with these languages himself. But whereas he apparently embodied these multiple linguistic worlds, our travelers were not so fortunate. Soon they rose to their feet and began to beat one another with heavy blows. People from the street, hearing the noise, came running to observe this strange melee.

Although the travelers called out to the crowd, only one person could perceive their inner states:

> Someone was present in the midst who found
> The way to the heart of all people.
>
> God bestowed diverse tongues upon him;
> All affairs were absolutely revealed to him.
>
> He knew the languages of these [travelers] clearly,
> What each one desired was entirely evident.
>
> He came forward and said: "Hey, don't fight!
> Have patience; fall not at each other's throats.
>
> Give me the coin, that I may satisfy you
> And fetch what you desire."
>
> He took the coin and went to the garden,
> [Where] he sold that one *aḳçe*, purchasing grapes.
>
> When he brought the grapes, he placed them before [all],
> They became a remedy for the affliction of all.[59]

Thus the Arab, Persian, Armenian, and Türkmen were able to resume their companionable relationship, sitting and speaking and feasting with one another in harmony, thanks only to the intervention of a wise guide—a knower not merely of tongues but of hearts.

At the core of this vision of Islam we find a performative message. The linguistic origin of this story, appropriately enough, was not Turkish. In fact, ʿĀşıḳ Paşa's entire tale is an adaptation, a translingual migration, of a story from Rūmī's *Maṣnavī*. By transferring the story across languages, ʿĀşıḳ Paşa enacts its argument: other languages besides Persian, including Turkish, are just as capable of revealing Islamic meaning, even if they do so in a different manner. One might therefore read the entire story as a parable about Turkish literary culture in Anatolia in the early fourteenth century. Although Mansuroğlu criticized ʿĀşıḳ Paşa as a "mere imitator" of Rūmī, it was largely *through* such imitation that early Anatolian Turkish literary culture took shape—both in its absorption of various themes, styles, and literary forms and in the very justification of its existence. This does not mean that the *Garīb-nāme* was the product of *taqlīd*, or blind copying. Like any dexterous adaptor of poetic narratives and literary styles, ʿĀşıḳ Paşa rewrote this story in the service of a different purpose and for different audiences. In short, he mobilized the *Maṣnavī* to do something new.

This becomes clear when we examine Rūmī's original tale in the *Maṣnavī*, which differs from ʿĀşıḳ Paşa's version in several key ways. Rūmī depicts a Persian, a Turk, a Greek, and an Arab who come across a single dirham. In his telling, each traveler calls for grapes in his own tongue:

> A man gave one dirham to four people.
> One of them said, "I'll exchange this for a grape [*angūrī*]."
>
> Another one of them was an Arab;
> He said, "*La!* I want an *ʿinab*, not an *angūr*, O swindler!"
>
> That [other] one was a Turk, and he said:
> "Hey, [*in Turkish*] *that's mine*, I don't want *ʿinab*, I desire *üzüm*."
>
> That [last] one, a Greek [*rūmī*], said,
> "Set aside this fuss; we want *staphulē*."
>
> In dispute, those people started to brawl;
> They were heedless of the secret of names.[60]

The multilingualism in Rūmī's tale is largely confined to a single word: *grape*. Thus, in a literal manner, ʿĀşıḳ Paşa's story is more welcoming to the languages it describes. More strikingly, although Rūmī's companions, having barely declared their preference for grapes, are already at each other's throats, the behavior of the travelers in ʿĀşıḳ Paşa's version is entirely different: they share an assumption, entirely lacking in the *Maṣnavī*, that they will feast together, as they had already cultivated a familiar and hospitable relationship on the road. They are *yoldaş*, fellow travelers, even though they speak different languages.

The differences from the *Maṣnavī* multiply as ʿĀşıḳ Paşa's story progresses. Whereas in the *Garīb-nāme* a shaykh comes forward to purchase the grapes himself, no shaykh appears in Rūmī's telling. "If a lord of secrets had been there," Rūmī posits, "a venerable man of a hundred tongues, / he would have reconciled them," in part by commanding the absolute obedience of his audience:

Then he would have said, With this single dirham
I will purchase what all of you desire.

When you entrust your heart [to me] without deceit,
This, your dirham, will do much work.

Your one dirham shall [satisfy] four desires,
Four enemies shall become one through concord.

The things each of you speak create conflict and separation,
The things I speak bring you harmony.

So be silent, all of you! [*in Arabic*] *Be silent!*
Until I become your tongue in conversation.[61]

Arguably, in Rūmī's hands the Arab, Persian, Greek, and Turk represent all those who cannot understand the spiritual "meaning" hidden in words—the travelers are therefore "corporealists" or "people of the body" (*ahl-i jasad*), as Rūmī names them at his tale's end.[62] Although certainly evocative of Konya's diverse inhabitants, Rūmī's characters are somewhat fungible and figurative. They utter the different words for "grape" not necessarily for the benefit of Turkish, Greek, or Arabic speakers but rather to index the speech of others in general—that is, the speech of all those without a shaykh. *Had* a shaykh been present, he *would* have emerged as the sole authoritative voice and stopped the conflict. This, in fact, is the message of Rūmī's tale: the shaykh's authority is from heaven and is absolute; his unifying speech, which produces souls of the same heart, cleanses people of their material, worldly ways.[63]

ʿĀşıḳ Paşa, of course, does not contradict this message. But he does amend it somewhat, emphasizing not the shaykh's authority but rather the importance of accommodating difference in Islam and through Islam. Whereas Rūmī's shaykh would simply silence his audience, declaring that only his own speech brings unity, ʿĀşıḳ Paşa's shaykh explains what such unity means at length. It is not, in fact, the erasure of difference. Rather, for ʿĀşıḳ Paşa, communal or confessional unity is predicated upon the ability to welcome heterogeneity. As he explains, the cause of the strife was not linguistic diversity but rather the inability to understand such diversity in the proper way. Thus, he says, this story "is a parable for the state of people in the world," as all people desire the same thing.[64] "The light of all these eyes is from one Sun," he explains, "the vitality of all these peoples is from one Emir."[65] This is just as there may be a thousand candles but light is the same, or how the same water can sustain myriad plants, or how "by the wind of one sea there are a thousand waves; / when the wind ceases the sea still remains."[66] His final point is therefore quite simple:

> Then all creation is from one household,
> But creatures appeared in different guises.
>
> The knowledge of each one is variegated;
> From the knowledge of each comes desire for the Most Holy.
>
> He is the craving of the seventy-two sects,
> He is [who they] desire, love, and worship.[67]

Traditionally, the seventy-two sects are those religious communities that divide Islam. It is therefore up to the right guide to show both non-Muslims and Muslims that their yearnings are the same, just as their diverse languages contain the same potential to reveal Islamic meaning. In fact, we find this notion repeated throughout the *Garīb-nāme*, as ʿĀşıḳ Paşa reiterates that spiritual meaning (*maʿnī*) is not limited to a single people or language. Although many kinds of humans have been created, such as Turk and Tajik, Armenian and Circassian, Kurd and Mongol, these outer forms are deceiving.[68]

Consequently, he reports, although people seem different in kind, "the seeker of jewels does not pay attention to this."[69] The challenge, then, was not to speak in a manner that negated the linguistic density or ethnic differences of Kırşehir—it was to speak in a manner that acknowledged the diversity of the community and employed a language of affinity, capable of organizing those peoples around a particular interpretive framework. In other words, ʿĀşıḳ Paşa's lesson is not only for the audience—the traveling companions of Kırşehir—but also, just as notably, for the shaykh. At the same time, his language of affinity would have been recognizable, on the page and in the ear, to those familiar with the literary cultures of Arabic and Persian, as he composed in the *maṣnavī* form and used the *ramal* meter. Moreover, he opened a new pathway for others—Turkish speakers in particular—to voice this language for themselves, even in different ways than their Arab or Persian counterparts.

From a premodern perspective, it is therefore impossible to conceive of early Anatolian Turkish literary culture without taking into account its complex relationships with other languages in Rūm or with the Islamicate world at large. For Gülşehrī, these relationships were genealogical, since he viewed literary production in Turkish as the natural extension, and even succession, of poetic composition in Persian. The borrowing of Persianate literary conventions and the imitation of Persian poets were hardly reductive in Gülşehrī's eyes—these practices were generative and genetic, situated within a form of poetic kinship that extended across the languages employed by different poets. On the other end of the spectrum, ʿĀşıḳ Paşa likewise drew on Persianate literary models to compose his masterwork, in part by welcoming stories and styles favored by Rūmī into a sphere of Turkish literary production. However, he seems to have been concerned less with linear questions of succession than with crafting a more egalitarian basis for his authority. His genealogy grants all languages access to an extralinguistic, higher realm of Islamic meaning. ʿĀşıḳ Paşa's fictive kinships between literary languages are therefore based on adjacency and proximity, as all languages are displaced from God. Thus, anyone—be they Turk, Armenian, Persian, or Arab—could take part in the production of a multilingual Islamicate literary culture, in a myriad of tongues.

What unites these two poets, at least in terms of compositional praxis, is that they performatively envisioned these kindred relationships by selectively welcoming the aesthetics of other literary languages and the narratives of other poetic texts into their works. It is therefore worth recalling that a propensity to reenvision the literary cultures of others, in part to produce new meanings for local audiences, was already well established in Anatolia by this time. After all, Rūmī similarly forged a poetic genealogy for himself and for his *Maṡnavī* by following the meter of the *Manṭiq al-ṭayr*. We would do well not to think of Rūmī (or, by extension, Persian poetry) as "productive" while casting Sulṭān Valad, Gülşehrī, and ʿĀşıḳ Paşa (or, by extension, Anatolian Turkish poetry) as necessarily "reproductive" or "influenced." On the contrary, these praxes of literary emulation and adaptation were the coin of the realm. Like the silvery *akçe* that passed hands from Arab to Persian, Armenian to Turk, these practices were a kind of cultural currency, a fluency in multiple languages and literary cultures, that was commonplace among poets in Rūm.

The ability to perform this fluency to audiences, through the selective adaptation of other poetic cultures and versified sampling of other languages, thus served as an important ground on which poets constructed their spiritual authority both in Konya and in Kırşehir. It seems that this performative capability was often as significant as, and sometimes more important than, the language of composition.[70] Simply put, poets like Gülşehrī and ʿĀşıḳ Paşa found little conflict in their discerning emulation of Persian poets, since emulation served as the mechanism by which literary prestige and authority were translated to a new generation of authors, whether intra- or cross-culturally. So pervasive was the allure of emulation, it informed the authority of poets even in death. Reportedly, when ʿĀşıḳ Paşa died, Turks, Jews, Armenians, and other Christians joined his funeral procession (much as had happened at Rūmī's in Konya).[71] At least according to the narrative logic of this report, the mournful voices of these peoples mingled on the streets of Kırşehir in a cacophony of tongues, each presumably longing for the same thing: the guidance of their multilingual shaykh.

Of course, just because ʿĀşıḳ Paşa knew many languages does not mean that the Christians in his poetry had a true "voice" or a chance to speak on behalf of their real counterparts' variegated interests. For a more oppositional conception of literary production in Anatolia to emerge, we will have to travel again—this time, some 280 miles southeast, to one of the last strongholds of Armenian power in the region. Here, in medieval Cilicia, poetic representations of the relationship between Christians and Muslims do not paint so convivial a picture. Still, we shall see that Armenian poets reenvisioned and recontextualized multiple adjacent literary codes, much like Persian and Turkish poets, even while navigating the heteroglossic literary landscape in markedly different manners. Let us therefore be on our way, leaving the fragrant streets of Kırşehir behind, lest these other voices remain silent.

CHAPTER SIX

CILICIAN RIDDLES

> She is articulate, not animate.
> She travels widely, yet has no feet.
> Wherever the rich and royal be,
> She goes boldly forth. She speaks.[1]

We find ourselves on the northeastern shores of the Mediterranean Sea in Cilicia, a principality ruled by the Armenian Ṛubēnid dynasty, less than fifty years before Rūmī and his family entered Anatolia. Catholicos Nersēs Shnorhali (d. 1173), the head of the Armenian Church, has just composed a riddle—not in Classical Armenian but in a freer language, one whose spongelike form absorbed loanwords from Arabic, Persian, and Turkish in a way the literary language did not. Perhaps he looks down to watch his neatly inscribed letters drying, like the footprints of a small bird in wet sand. As he sits there, the answer must seem obvious. What speaks where men fear to tread? *T'ught'*. An epistle. A piece of paper.[2]

Shortly after becoming catholicos in 1166, Nersēs addressed his scattered flock in a *t'ught'* of his own. In some ways, his *General Epistle* (*T'ught' ĕndhanrakan*) would sow the seeds of a new narrative about the Armenian people. It addressed not only "all believers of the Armenian people who are in the east, dwelling in their own country of Armenia, and those wandering abroad in the western regions, and those in the midlands, circulating among speakers of other tongues," but even those scattered at the ends of the earth.[3] This gesture was not merely rhetorical. Since the collapse of the Armenian kingdoms around the mid-eleventh century, waves of his people had moved westward, resettling in Cilicia and in Rūm, where Armenian communities had long existed. Even the see of the Armenian Church and the institution of the catholicate had migrated to the fortress of Hṛomklay (Rumkale), overlooking the vividly green Euphrates River, on the eastern fringe of Cilicia.

These waves of dispersion presented a unique problem for the church. "In this time of evil and of diverse kingdoms," Nersēs laments in his epistle, "it is not possible to go around to all the parts of the world and preach the word of God as the holy apostles did":

> Our nation does not presently have a royal capital or assembly, which formerly allowed us to sit on the patriarchal and magisterial throne, and teach our people God's law as the first patriarchs and doctors did. But we are like the wild goat that has escaped from dogs and hunters to live in caves, lacking even villages and farms to supply our bare physical necessities. . . . We must therefore take care to advise and teach according to our rank and through our words to pour the milk of God into the mouths of the souls of our children in Christ. As already noted, it is impossible to do this in person.[4]

Nersēs sent his epistle to the prominent churches and cities of his day. Most likely, priests would have read aloud—and generally interpreted—his words to the faithful: to farmers and field hands, foot soldiers and governors, landowners and merchants. As our riddle suggests, the *General Epistle* would circulate where the catholicos could not. It would boldly call out transgression, avarice, and inequity. It would fear no governor, no king. However, by the twelfth century, the language of the epistle—a pristine Classical Armenian (*grabar*, the written language)—was generally a language of the elite. It was the holy tongue of the church, the lifeblood of the liturgy and the Armenian translation of the Bible. Yet as we shall see, Classical Armenian seems to have become opaque to general audiences by this time.

It is not coincidental, then, that Nersēs sought other ways of communicating with his scattered flock. Take, for instance, the riddle that we have just encountered. Its language, though not different from Classical Armenian by an order of magnitude, zips along at an easy gait, eschewing virtuosic command of the declensions and conjugations, the paradigms and vocabulary, of a higher literary register. The riddle's style, in a word, is simple. But its language also sings. In fact, this is one of the earliest known poems to be written in the Middle, or "vernacular," Armenian poetic register, a little over a century before Anatolian Turkish would show promise as a literary language in its own right. Nersēs's riddle, which thematically foreshadows its own broad circulation, anticipates a poetics that would travel across (and even beyond) Rūm, reaching audiences in ways that perhaps eluded the *General Epistle*, and all without feet.

This chapter sheds a selective light on this ascendant vernacular Armenian poetics: how it engaged in a project of meaning making, similar to the ones that we have observed in New Persian and Anatolian Turkish, and how it interfaced with its neighboring literary cultures in multiple ways. Just as Persian and Turkish poetry often taught its audiences to read—not only texts but also the world in which those texts moved—so did Armenian Christian poetry instruct its audiences in the fine art of interpretation, offering a lived-in hermeneutics of its own, and not so far from Konya. Moreover, Armenian poets used many of the same adaptive techniques as their Muslim counterparts, such as rewriting scripture as poetry and citing other poets (even Muslims) in their verses, in part to construct new interpretations of preexisting literary works and discourses. As we shall see, the earliest poets of vernacular Armenian likewise sought to forge a language of affinity—that is, to shape a poetics that could absorb cultural and linguistic differences—while welcoming heterogeneity into a coherent Christian worldview.

Armenian poets had good reason to engage with their audiences in new ways during this period. Although the Armenian Church had reestablished itself in Cilicia and was presiding over a remarkable flourishing of Armenian cultural production, its position was somewhat tenuous. Cilicia became an Armenian kingdom when Lewon II received one crown from the Byzantine emperor Alexius III Angelus and another from the Holy Roman emperor Henry VI at the end of the twelfth century. In the decades that followed, there would even be hope for a lasting alliance with the Mongols: King Het'um would travel to the court of the Great Khan

Möngke in Karakorum in 1253, seeking to establish a lasting alliance.[5] But these dreams, and Cilician fortunes, would be dashed after the Ilkhanid conversion to Islam. It would not be long until powerful opposition hemmed in the last Armenian kingdom on all sides. Cilicia would fall to the Mamluks of Egypt in 1375, and Armenians would not recover a form of statehood until the twentieth century.

Even in Nersēs's day, the future of Christianity in Anatolia seemed imperiled. Only in 1144, just east of Cilicia, the Syrian army of ʿImād al-Dīn Zangī had vanquished the Crusader state of Edessa. This conquest was a devastating blow to Christianity in the entire region and keenly felt in neighboring Cilicia. It was clear to Nersēs that he had to resist the encroachment of the Islamicate world—a world in which Armenians were being gradually outflanked and outnumbered. It also seemed obvious that he needed other ways of engaging with his audience—means that no single sermon, epistle, or even literary genre could ever offer. But how could he reinforce—or build anew—confessional boundaries to encircle his far-flung flock?

One solution was simply to reject, outright, everything that seemed antithetical to Christianity. This attitude is on display in one of Nersēs's most famous poems, the *Lament over Edessa*. Narrated largely from the perspective of Edessa itself, it minces no words in condemning Muslims as bloodthirsty and barbaric, a ferocious pack of "wolves in a flock of lambs."[6] Hence, when Zangī's army breached the city walls, they reportedly "slaughtered the youth and the little ones pitilessly; / they did not respect the gray hairs of the elderly / or the height of boys."[7] Yet Nersēs saves his harshest condemnation for the desecration of Christian churches. He laments that the invading armies polluted Edessa's holy temples, destroyed its altars, and trampled its crosses, all in the name of the Prophet:

> With a great voice they called out,
> With a shout, this they declared:
> "Good News to you today,
> Muḥammad, you oracle of the Divine.
> Again we reap that which we lost,
> Your own home and realm,
> From these errant peoples,

The worshipers of lifeless stone
With whose blood we filled the land,
According to the command of your Qur'an."[8]

In Nersēs's envisioning, Zangī's forces are outright demonic, literally dancing upon the blood-soaked ground while *ghāzīs* (Armenian: *ghazikk'*), religious warriors, tore the bodies of their victims to pieces.[9] The poem thus depicts Christians and non-Christians as opposed in breathtakingly violent terms, never to be reconciled in this life or the next. This is entirely the point, of course: the poem excoriates its enemies while commanding its audience to mourn the loss of Christian life. As in many works tinged with a shade of apocalyptic zeal, the message here is direct: keep the faith.

Still, Nersēs also had less polemical ways of responding to his changing world. Some of these, including a subtle practice of musical adaptation, should strike us as familiar. One night, before the sun rose opposite the fortress of Hṛomklay, he went out for an early-morning promenade. As he walked along the corridors of the fortress, a strange melody caught his ear. Nersēs had discovered the fortress's guards, standing together, singing a song—perhaps one that evoked light or even the sun itself. The song certainly was not Christian, but we know little about its subject matter. The medieval historian Kirakos Gandzakets'i (d. 1271), who recorded this story, simply calls this singing "useless."[10] Whatever the content of the song, it seemed to have unsettled Nersēs. If non- or extra-Christian songs were sung at Hṛomklay, one of the major strongholds of Cilicia and the seat of the Armenian Church, what corrupted form did the Armenian cultural landscape assume beyond its sturdy walls?

Nersēs may have had some idea; he was, after all, a musician himself.[11] "Since he was a wise man," Kirakos says, "he established in churches many [works] in a sweet air, hymns in a regal style [*khosrovayin ochov*], melodies, canticles, and verses."[12] In other words, Nersēs would not resort "to a bully pulpit" in addressing his fellow Armenians, as James R. Russell has shown.[13] Rather, he would adopt a more subtle approach. As Kirakos reports, Nersēs rebuked his guards by composing a new song—and by rewriting the Psalms—to serve a new function: "For this was the will of the saint [Nersēs], that so far as it is possible, no one should converse in worldly discourse, but rather [should be moved by] the scriptures, and not in drunkenness or other kinds of merrymaking. On account of this, [Nersēs] fashioned songs and taught these to those who were guarding the fortress, so that instead of useless tunes they might recite this, whose beginning is the Psalm of David, 'I remembered your name in the night, O Lord,' and thus [continues] sacramentally in succession, 'Awaken, my glory,' which now is recited in the hour of the Night Office in church."[14]

The section of the Night Office that Kirakos describes here, "Hishests'uk' i gisheri" (Let us remember in the night) and "Zart'ik', p'aṛk' im" (Awaken, my glory), is well known and still sung in the Armenian Church today. It reflects a common practice of composing hymns by quoting the Psalms, elaborating upon them, and setting them to music. In their earliest historical context, however, Nersēs's words also had a performative dimension. As the guards sang newly fashioned verses for their catholicos, they would have enacted exactly what Nersēs had commanded: remembering God and putting aside worldly pastimes in the middle of the night. "Awaken, children of light, in praise of the Father of light," the guards sang:

> Awaken, all you redeemed by blood, and glorify the Redeemer.
> Alleluia!
> Awaken, new people, singing new songs to the Renewer. Alleluia![15]

This is a hymn, in other words, that brings about the transformation it describes. Put simply, through biblical citation, the hymn evokes the formation of "new people" who find their voice *through* song, singing one of these very same "new songs." In the case of the guards, who were apparently compelled to put aside their "useless" music in favor of a Christian hymn, this particular "new song" would supersede whatever non- or extra-Christian music had occupied them in the weary hours before daybreak. The hymn therefore reflects a conversion—or at least a confessional consolidation—not just of people but also of certain poetic and musical cultures in Cilicia. It is an adaptation that both reframes how its audiences might engage with other musical cultures and provokes a different kind of relationship with scripture, removed from its biblical locus through various modes of rereading, recontextualizing, reinterpreting, and rewriting. Nersēs used culture to negotiate culture, to paraphrase Karla Mallette.[16]

In less obvious ways, Nersēs's *Lament over Edessa* does the same thing. Beneath its horrific narrative there lingers another story, evocative of a more dialogic, but no less contentious, relationship between Muslims and Christians. Nersēs was the great-grandson of Grigor Magistros, the Armenian adaptor of Arabic monorhyme, whom we encountered in the introduction. Exactly one century after the encounter between Grigor and "Manazi" in Constantinople, Nersēs composed his lament in alternating blocks of the same end rhyme, injecting some variation into his great-grandfather's innovation.[17] In the passage quoted above describing the destruction of Edessa's churches at the hands of Muslim conquerors, the rhymes largely end with *-in*, the bewitching sound of the letter *nūn* that had so captivated Grigor. Thus, although Nersēs's literary depiction of Muslims is certainly "militant," as Russell puts it, within the very matrix of his oppositional poetry lies another model for considering the relationship between the literary production of Armenians and those of "others."[18]

What's in a rhyme? Or more generally, what's in a sound? Sometimes, for complex reasons, the "new song" sounds much like the old one. Nersēs's literary production helps us to address these questions, in part because he lived during a cultural and linguistic sea change, which is the focus of this chapter. This transformation informed the early development of Middle Armenian literary culture as writers sought fresh ways of engaging with, and ultimately instructing, their audiences. But as with Hovhannēs's reply to Asha—"What does your apple have to do with me?"—there is a paradox at the heart of this story. To keep the Islamicate world at bay, poets after Nersēs began to adapt Islamicate works, styles, forms, themes, and discourses in their Middle Armenian compositions. The attempt to differentiate, in other words, was brought on by an intimate convergence between seemingly incongruous poetic cultures. And with this convergence came a clear and present need to accommodate difference within a coherent Christianizing hermeneutics.

Nersēs will serve as our first guide to Middle Armenian literary culture. He will be joined by an unusual second guide: Frik, an enigmatic and apparently lay poet thought to have lived in the latter half of the thirteenth century. These celebrated authors are among the earliest known to have composed "vernacular" Armenian poetry. At first blush, however, they have little in common. Nersēs, as the powerful head of the Armenian Church, rewrote the Bible as a collection of vernacular riddles. On the other end of the spectrum, Frik seems to brazenly rebuke God in his most famous poem, which borrows heavily from the tropes, themes, and vocabulary of Islamicate literature. Yet as we shall see, similar adaptive and interpretive practices undergird the works of these poets, allowing us to trace the decentralized development of these praxes across a broad literary ambit, spanning many genres and linguistic registers.

In fact, it is necessary to read these poets together for a more holistic conception of literary production in Anatolia to emerge: medieval Armenian poets, akin to their Muslim counterparts, composed in part to (re)interpret the complexity of their social and cultural worlds, as well as to offer pointed meditations on scripture for the instruction of their diverse audiences. Armenian poets show that just as this project of meaning making did not inhere in any single language or religious culture in medieval Anatolia, it was also not limited to any one literary genre or form. Equally as important, Nersēs and Frik demonstrate that various practices of literary adaptation in this region did not necessarily originate in the Persianate world, only later to trickle down to Christians. Instead, poetic gloss, citation, and adaptation provided indispensable tools for Armenian poets who desired to absorb, rewrite, or deflect Islamicate literary culture.

Poetic Gloss in Medieval Cilicia

Before the twelfth century, we know of only a few works written in the register of Middle Armenian.[19] However, the picture begins to look different by Nersēs's day. The erudite twelfth-century physician Mkhitʿar Heratsʿi, who studied under Nersēs and resided in Cilicia's capital, wrote his famous medical treatise, *Jermantsʿ mkhitʿarutʿiwn* (*The Consolation of Fevers*), not in Classical Armenian but in a vulgar or "rustic [*geghjuk*]" tongue so that it might be easily understood by all readers, as he explained.[20] It seems that authors in this period who composed in this "rustic" language, as opposed to *grabar*, the literary language, did so partly out of consideration for the potentially new audiences they wished to engage.[21]

The same may be true of Nersēs, whose writings are prodigious: he composed a long-form poem known as *Jesus, the Son*; a monorhymed epic poem about his family line; the *General Epistle*; sundry hymns and prayers; and a formal exegesis of the Gospel of Matthew—all in Classical Armenian. However, he wrote his effervescent and infinitely curious collection of riddles in the "rustic" language of Middle Armenian, which has a lexicon and some grammatical forms that differ at times from Classical. Nersēs not only versified his riddles as quatrains but also largely composed them in monorhyme, reproducing the rhyme scheme that his great-grandfather had adapted one century earlier. Moreover, he seems to have had a rather specific audience in mind. The medieval historian Kirakos Gandzakets'i claims that Nersēs "fashioned allegorical proverbs [*aṛak*] and riddles [*haneluk*] out of the scriptures, so that instead of telling fables or legends, people might recite [them] during wine bibbing and weddings."[22]

We have seen that Rūmī and Sulṭān Valad sought to train their audiences in a performative hermeneutics—one that, as Shahab Ahmed has observed, extended far beyond the traditional genre of exegesis (*tafsīr*).[23] This hermeneutics instead encompassed a manner of thinking, living, and being in thirteenth-century Konya. Above all, it aimed not only to accommodate difference (linguistic, cultural, conceptual) but also to transmute that difference into a language of affinity, in which heterogeneity would be brought within the apparatus of a particular interpretive framework. These poets may have composed a literary exegesis of scripture, but so too did they write a scriptural eisegesis of the world. However, half a century before Rūmī began this undertaking in Konya, an analogous project was already underway in Nersēs's literary production. His riddles reportedly circulated not only in manuscript form but also from mouth to mouth, wedding to wedding, in the public recitation of enigmas needful of interpretation. Whereas Nersēs's *General Epistle* relied upon the mediating presence of priests and bishops, his riddles could speak directly and "boldly" to a variety of peoples, perhaps without need of an interpreter.[24]

Both before and after the twelfth century, riddles enjoyed popularity in many literary cultures adjacent to Cilicia, not all of them Christian. Numerous Persian poets composed riddles in this period, including Sanāʾī (d. 1131), whose works circulated in Anatolia.[25] Sometimes these microhermeneutic exercises even infiltrated seemingly unrelated genres. For instance, the New Persian masterwork of the late tenth-century poet Firdawsī, the *Shāh-nāma*, contains scenes in which competitors challenge each other in riddling contests.[26] Important Byzantine authors also tried their hand at composing riddles in the twelfth and thirteenth centuries, including Theodōros Prodromos and Manouēl Holobolos.[27] And farther abroad, the *Codex Cumanicus*, initially compiled as a dictionary in the early fourteenth century by Franciscan monks or Italian merchants, preserves several riddles in the Cuman Turkish language, along with a Cuman translation of the Lord's Prayer.[28]

It seems that Middle Armenian was not the only nascent literary culture to have a predilection for enigmas. Nor was it the only one drawn to a genre that implicitly trains its audience in the art of interpretation. Perhaps the sheer abundance of riddling cultures prevalent throughout the premodern Mediterranean world suggested to Nersēs his unique intervention in Armenian letters. Certainly, folded into his riddles are a number of subjects—candles, eggs, books, writing, the sky, bread—that are common staples of the genre in many languages. However, Nersēs's riddles are set apart from those of many cultures in a significant way, as his collection is more than a random assemblage of metaphorically veiled objects. In fact, it represents nothing less than a poetic reimagining of the Bible, rendered in an accessible Middle Armenian form.

The collection thus opens with a riddle about God, who ransoms a thief with his own life. It is followed by poems on Satan, Paradise, Adam and Eve, the Tree of Life, the Sun, the Moon, Clouds, the World, Time, Man, Woman, Thought, Spring, Summer, Fall, and Winter. These initial riddles, as Russell has observed, loosely rehearse the order of the Creation.[29] Nersēs even lavishes incredible attention on the Bible as a whole. Riddle after riddle, the collection guides us through the Book of Genesis in operatic detail (with individual riddles on Cain and Abel, Enoch, Noah, Noah's ark, the Tower of Babel, Melchizedek, Lot, Abraham, Isaac, Jacob, and Joseph). Subsequent word puzzles chronologically restage scenes from Job, Exodus, Numbers, Psalms, Joshua, 1 Samuel, 2 Samuel, Chronicles, 1 Kings, Jonah, Daniel, Jeremiah, Matthew, Mark, Luke, John, Acts, 1 Corinthians, and even Revelation. The hagiographic *Lives of the Prophets*, a collection of legends about figures from the Old Testament, makes a suggestive appearance, as do major texts in the Armenian tradition, such as Movsēs Khorenatsʿi's *Patmutʿiwn hayotsʿ* (*History of the Armenians*).[30] In this microcosmic collection of riddles, we are treated to a sampling of the books in Nersēs's library, their stories retold as vernacular poetry.[31]

The Soviet scholar Asatur Mnatsʿakanyan has observed that the modern Armenian word for "riddle," *haneluk*, is related to the verb *hanel*, meaning "to draw or pull out," "to remove," or "to divulge."[32] In this, it has an etymological correspondence with *exegesis*, which means "to take out" (from *ex-*, "out," and *hēgeisthai*, "to lead"). Certainly, Armenian readers plumbed the invisible depths of such puzzles, looking to extract hidden meanings from them, even through extended periods of silent vexation.[33] As Mnatsʻakanyan notes, in the margin of Matenadaran MS 8652, folio 58v, one reader boasts, "O brother, for half an hour I racked my brain, and by [the grace] of God I discovered the [solution] to [these] riddles. Trust in God, that you may find them too." Below that, a different hand has written: "If you had really discovered the solutions, you would have actually written them. If you haven't figured it out, don't brag."[34]

Would the secluded torture of a monk be reborn as a boisterous public affair? One cannot say for sure, although Kirakos's thirteenth-century *History* at least suggests that this was the case. It is not difficult to imagine a jostling crowd shouting out answers while the riddle reciter playfully teased, corrected, and offered hints, guiding the public to seize upon the correct reading. Still, whether done in public or in private, grappling with riddles would have borne an undeniably interpretive, and even epistemic, dimension. As Winfried Rudolf has noted, riddles "impart encyclopaedic knowledge concerning the properties and the classification of things" even as they rely on "semantic ambiguity" that keeps the audience guessing, which teaches readers to seek deeper correspondences between signs inscribed in the Book of the World.[35] In this sense, the literary genre of riddles had a clear exegetical value in the medieval period, as it heuristically guided readers to "reveal the hidden mysteries of things," in the words of Aldhelm (d. 709/10), the bishop of Sherborne.[36]

In medieval Armenian, riddles were known under a broad umbrella of names, such as *haneluk* (riddle), *aṛeghtsuats* (enigma), *ban tsatsuk* (hidden discourse), *aṛaspel* (myth or fable), and *aṛak* (proverb or enigma), the term favored by Nersēs.[37] One idea is obviously common to all: the subject must be treated as an analogue for, a heuristic for thinking about, something else. Here is one example of how this worked:

> I pass away, I die,
> Again I rise, revitalized.
> Toward heaven I raise my eyes,
> In many offshoots I do shine.[38]

With this riddle's overt evocation of resurrection, we might initially assume that Christ is the solution. But the poem describes the life cycle of *wheat*, whose grain falls to the ground only to rise again, pushing up to the sky in copiously branching stalks and shoots. Even in its simplicity, however, a dense cluster of associations lies at the heart of the wheat-Christ-resurrection correspondence. Most immediately, Nersēs's mysterious "proverb" evokes another mystery, spoken by Christ in John 12:24: "Very truly, I tell you, unless a grain of wheat falls into the earth and dies, it remains just a single grain; but if it dies, it bears much fruit." In the Armenian Church, priests chant these words during the requiem service, a liturgy in remembrance of the deceased; they would have been familiar and emotionally resonant to Cilician Armenians. Moreover, farmers brought grain offerings, the fruits of their lives, to the church, which would then be transformed as Communion, the bread of life, for the faithful. The riddle's veiled correlations are multifold, as they simultaneously evoke the labor of field hands, the burial of loved ones, the growth of wheat, the resurrection of Christ, and the eternal life to come. In effect, the riddle offers an audience the chance to reflect on the true nature of the Sacrament, but not by way of sermonizing or through a formal exegesis of John 12:24.

Unlike Nersēs's long-form poetry, with its biting condemnation of non-Armenians, his riddles exhibit a more polemically playful approach. Who calls aloud like a Syriac priest? A crow.[39] What lives in a mosque and a house of bone? A turtle.[40] Who speaks Arabic and sings songs? The swallow.[41] In this vein, Nersēs lifts up, brings down, or slyly mocks a wide array of peoples: Franks ("Like a wolf who devours porkers / and desires garlic with every morsel"), Greeks ("Every one of their titles is 'Lord' [Greek: *kyr*], / but they wouldn't dare to rise and piss at night"), Syrians ("They're vainglorious and accomplish nothing / but are quite clever in [their] shops"), and even Armenians (a "daring" people, yet one indifferent to Syrians).[42] From the perspective of Christian didacticism, these correspondences help to illuminate the hidden natures of people and things, but they do much more: they train their audiences to understand the world's ambiguity as another code, the veiled language of creation, which reveals the true natures of things through their likenesses and dissimilarities to other things.[43] Like any written language, this one can be read and taught to others. The difference is that these riddles impart this instruction not overtly but covertly, through a coiled economy of metaphor. Moreover, they do so in a poetic idiom that people might readily understand.

Of course, we do not know how most individual readers or listeners engaged with these riddles on a granular level. Still, Nersēs's collection offers a few valuable clues. Many of its riddles guide their audience to undertake a particular kind of interpretive labor—one that glosses scripture and the milieu of medieval Cilicia at the same time. Take, for instance, the following riddle, on the beheading of John the Baptist:

> There was a whore, sure in eloquence,
> And she was a hideous ornament of ruin.
> Binding a kettledrum [*guz*] like a troubadour [*gusan*],
> She severed a head like a murderer.[44]

On the simplest level, the answer is Salome. When she danced alluringly on the occasion of King Herod's birthday, he was so pleased by the display that he offered to grant anything her heart desired. After consulting with her mother, Salome named her request: the head of John the Baptist, served on a gleaming platter (Matthew 14:6–8; Mark 6:22–25).

Salome is a relatively minor figure; her name is not even given in the Bible. Still, for medieval audiences familiar with scripture, the riddle's solution was probably obvious. That does not mean, however, that this riddle contained no surprises. In fact, it implicitly poses a number of subtle enigmas that require different kinds of knowledge to solve. Why, for instance, is Salome depicted as a prostitute? Astute readers—or at least anyone with a Bible handy—might realize that this particular defamation is extrabiblical. Many Christians associated Salome with the Old Testament figure of Jezebel, a vain and villainous queen who persuaded her husband, King Ahab, to abandon God. Things did not end well for her: one day, after adorning makeup, she was thrown from her window and trampled to death by horses (2 Kings 9:33). Because Jezebel painted her face, some Christians would later slander her as a prostitute. The correlation was reinforced by the author of Revelation, who condemns a certain "Jezebel" for misleading people into sexual immorality (Revelation 2:20). Thus, in the first two lines of this riddle, Nersēs plays on this typology, linking Salome to Jezebel through prostitution. Her beauty and her dancing bring about cataclysmic ruin.

In other words, the riddle not only demands—or seeks to encourage—knowledge of scripture but also demands—or seeks to produce—a nuanced typological *reading* of scripture, in which different books of the Bible (2 Kings, Matthew, Mark, Revelation) converge to inform a particular interpretation. Moreover, this interpretation extends beyond a static binary of getting the riddle "right" or "wrong." Indeed, it unlocks a moralizing lesson on sexuality and seduction, serving up a heavy-handed commentary on the adornment of women's bodies in particular, as well as the dangers of certain forms of entertainment.

Other mysteries, and hidden caverns of meaning, now expand into view. Why, for instance, does Salome play the kettledrum? And for that matter, why is she likened to a troubadour? Salome does not play any instrument in the Bible. Moreover, at least from a linguistic perspective, the kettledrum and the troubadour are not only extrabiblical but also extra-Armenian. *Guz*, the loanword that Nersēs uses for "kettledrum," is a Persian term (*kūs*). This hefty instrument was used during military campaigns and at times of royal feasting. During warfare, it was generally tied to elephants or camels (hence the expression "to bind the *kūs* on the elephant," *kūs bar pīl bastan* in Persian, meaning "to prepare or set out for battle").[45] For Nersēs, the *kūs* also had a particularly anti-Christian resonance: in his poem *Lament over Edessa*, the Muslim forces who conquer Christian Edessa make their kettledrums (*gos*) thunder with great relish.[46] Similarly, the word for "troubadour" that Nersēs uses is of Parthian pedigree (*gōsān*), referring to one of a class of musicians who, at one time, circulated throughout the Caucasus and the Persianate world.[47] The *gusan* and the kettledrum, whatever their historical presence in medieval Cilicia, suggestively represent a musical culture that was antithetical to Nersēs's project of musical and literary production. Here Nersēs not only indexes this culture through his riddles but furthermore ties it to a world of vice. The message is clear: we ought to busy ourselves with riddles that subtly rewrite and reread scripture and not with the seductive sounds, the sensual dancing and singing of a Salome.

In this manner, Nersēs adapts, cites, and paraphrases the Bible to promote a particular manner of viewing the world and the people who populate it, including both Christians and Muslims. For example, early in his collection he recasts a story from Genesis to conform to a more immediate milieu:

It was equally pure as the clouds,
Straight, it was, as a minaret [*mnaray*].
There it brought winds, sweetly savored,
Seventy and two rivulets.[48]

Though the answer is "a tower," it is clear from the riddle's placement in the collection that it serves as an extended riff specifically on the Tower of Babel, opening multiple layers of meaning for different audiences. The first line evokes Genesis 11:4, in which the Tower of Babel reaches to the clouds and beyond: "Then they said, 'Come, let us build ourselves a city, and a tower with its top in the heavens.' " It is not necessary to know the line to solve the riddle, of course, so long as one is at least cursorily familiar with the account. Still, access to Classical Armenian would allow a more learned reader to appreciate the highly coordinated relationship between the riddle and scripture. Yet the next line leads us into a territory removed from the Biblical locus. For the Israelites, the salient God-affronting religious towers were ziggurats, pyramidal stepped temples built by their enemies, such as the Babylonians. In Nersēs's polemical rendering, the riddle opens to admit the Islamicate world by likening the Tower of Babel to a minaret. Perhaps this minaret-Babel correlation also teased a different kind of anticipation, no less polemical: if the Babylonians (or, more simply, the proud and haughty) fell by divine decree, so might the adversaries of Cilicia. Nonetheless, the riddle does not envision a return to the idyllic days before the multiplication of minarets across Rūm. Instead, it ends with seventy-two "rivulets," representing the tradition that seventy-two languages resulted from Babel's fall, in a cacophonic mingling of tongues that almost seems fortuitous. After all, the riddle implies, the languages of the world are "sweetly savored."

Herein lies a riddle of another sort, equally worthy of our mental labors. In the microcosmic world of vernacular riddles, we glimpse the sparks of a new literary tradition that would emerge in Cilicia and spread throughout Rūm—and all without "feet." This tradition, of course, would become the corpus of Middle Armenian poetry, which is riddled with styles, sounds, loanwords, concepts, themes, and forms absorbed from adjacent literary cultures. However, Middle Armenian literature would not merely admit the poetics of others into an Armenian milieu but also sift and separate this poetics, much like a medieval English *hriddel*, or "sieve," and recombine its units within a Christian interpretive framework. As we shall see here and in the final chapter, the early body of Middle Armenian poetry offers its own exegesis "by other means"—one that might be learned in a tavern or at a wedding feast, and one whose form wriggled its way into the lives of Cilician Armenians, reaching even those on the fringes of the last Armenian kingdom. This was the dawning of a covert hermeneutics, a new language of affinity, voiced by Armenian tongues.

Quoting the Poetry of Others

Nersēs helps to inaugurate the story of the emergence of a Middle Armenian poetic culture, and its subsequent transformations in the late thirteenth and early fourteenth centuries, by giving it some necessary historical grounding in medieval Cilicia. But whereas we know a great deal about him, the same cannot be said of many other early adopters of Middle Armenian as both a written and a poetic language. In fact, we know so little about some of these figures that it is difficult to tell their tales without looking at, first and foremost, what has attracted the attention of modern readers to their works, which have often served as inkblot tests for the present historical moment.

One such test has acquired a visual imprint outside the Mesrop Mashtots' Institute of Ancient Manuscripts in modern-day Yerevan. Here, statues of the premodern Armenian intellectual forefathers stand tall, the gatekeepers of the manuscript library and the canon of texts it houses. Largest and in the foreground is Mashtots', the early fifth-century inventor of the Armenian alphabet and the institute's namesake, alongside his disciple Koriwn.[49] Farther up the hill, flanking the library's entrance, gather an imposing cast of figures: T'oros Ṛoslin the miniaturist (fl. thirteenth century), Grigor Tat'ewats'i the theologian (fl. fourteenth century), Anania Shirakats'i the mathematician (fl. seventh century), Movsēs Khorenats'i the historian (fl. fifth century or later), Mkhit'ar Gosh the lawgiver (fl. twelfth and early thirteenth centuries), and, most enigmatically, Frik the poet (see figure 2).[50]

The subjects of the other statues are busy with various objects (a manuscript, a codex, an astrolabe), but Frik simply stares ahead with

FIGURE 2. Six statues, literal and figurative giants of an Armenian intellectual tradition, watch over the entrance of the Mesrop Mashtotsʻ Institute of Ancient Manuscripts.

dark-rimmed, haunted eyes (see figure 3). His left hand is half extended outward, incompletely mimicking the gesture one adopts in the Armenian Church while praying, as though something were holding him back. As depicted here, Frik evokes, more than any other figure in our historical diorama, the tortured witness of medieval Armenians, who were subjected to waves of invading forces—Franks, Turks, Mongols, and others—on their ancestral lands and in their dispersion. The statue thus adopts a silent and brave stance against the vicissitudes of fate—and for many readers, God—which is the subject of Frik's perhaps most famous poem.

Of course, this statue of Frik is an idealization, representing an icon of Armenian bravery in the face of an indifferent, even malevolent universe. In actuality, we know little about this poet, save what might be gleaned from his poetry.[51] Scholars have therefore struggled to place him geographically. Archbishop Tirayr, the compiler of the critical edition of his poetry, suggested in 1952 that Frik had migrated from the Caucasus to

FIGURE 3. The statue of Frik at the Mesrop Mashtotsʻ Institute of Ancient Manuscripts.

Hachn (Turkish: Haçin), north of Adana in Cilicia.[52] Other scholars, such as Ashot Hovhannisyan and Hakob Zhamkoch'yan, have not embraced this hypothesis, although they agree that Frik's lexicon, idiomatic phrases, and use of grammar largely conform to the Middle Armenian used in Cilicia. Zhamkoch'yan, for one, posits that Frik was born and lived a good deal of his early life somewhere in the vicinity of Cilicia, perhaps in a region under Mongol control.[53] However, it appears that Frik did not stay in place: he praises the virtues of being a "voluntary mendicant" in his verses and seems to allude to sojourning widely near the frontier of Rūm, the Caucasus, Iran, and Syria.[54] So too did his poetry travel: the first printed book of Armenian poetry, published in 1513 in Venice, is largely a collection of Middle Armenian poems that includes verses by Frik and a large number of riddles by Nersēs Shnorhali.

Arguably, Frik offers an Armenian analogue to Yūnus Emre, and not only because the passage of time has obscured the biographical details of both figures. For one, Frik is widely thought to stand at the beginning of a new literary tradition: the development of Middle Armenian, a "vernacular" language whose literary use, like that of Anatolian Turkish, was frequently modeled upon preexisting literary conventions (a process that Sheldon Pollock has termed literarization).[55] Moreover, like the poetry of Anatolian Turkish, which seems to have emerged as a written language at the same time that it was fashioned into a literary language, Middle Armenian poetry burst upon the scene replete with words, themes, tropes, and styles culled from Arabic and Persian literature. Perhaps the most notable affinity between these poets, however, is their retrospective status as national figures. But whereas Yūnus Emre has come to embody the moment when the pre-Islamic *ozan* gave way to the popular poet of Turkish Islam, Frik stands at the cusp of a transition initially marked by the decline of Armenian sovereignty, during which the first glimmers of secular Armenian literature are thought to have appeared. In fact—regardless of how one precisely dates these figures, whose works come to us in manuscripts from later periods—the historical moment that they represent is the same: the end of the thirteenth century, when new vernacular poetic cultures dawned in Rūm.[56]

Despite their respective nationally central positions in Turkish and Armenian literary history today, both poets also engaged, in formative ways, with Persian literary cultures. Whereas Yūnus Emre drew upon preexisting literary tropes, themes, and styles to insert himself, as a Turkish speaker, into the heteroglossic realm of Sufi poetic production, Frik pulled Persianate and Islamicate discourses into a Christianizing realm. As we have seen, Nersēs undertook a similar labor when he adapted extra-Christian songs and melodies to strengthen his flock's confessional boundaries. Frik, however, was cut from a different cloth. According to the claims of his poetry, he never studied under any priest.[57] His poetry, though of a didactic and devotional nature, also dares to engage with other literary worlds in more direct ways. Consequently, I shall read Frik's poems not as autobiographical documents, as much of Armenian literary criticism has done over the past century, but rather as I have read the riddles of Nersēs: that is, as hermeneutic exercises that work upon their audiences in a certain manner. In this respect, Frik's precise locations (inside or outside Cilicia) matter less to this story than the ways that his poetry potentially engaged with speakers of Middle Armenian across a broad zone, starting from Cilicia and extending eastward, toward the Caucasus, Syria, and Iran, where Armenians came into contact with the Persianate world.

One poem by Frik, a much-discussed work in the genre of wisdom, or "instruction" (*khrat*), affords a unique glimpse at how Armenians read, translated, and adapted works of Persian poetry in particular. Like much of his work, this poem begins with a condemnation of the world, whose false pleasures heap hot coals upon our heads in the life to come:

> Come, let us cast off this deceitful life, that we not be deceived.
> Let us go to that place we desire, where we have hope that we may live.
> This life has fooled many—never does it say "enough."
> Seek to find a means in this life that you not be despised in the next.
> As long as you remain happy in this world, you'll be bitter and weeping in the next;
> As long as you indulge yourself here, great torment is stored up for you there.
> Many were hoaxed by this world; they became fodder for the fire in the next.[58]

The poem continues in this vein, intensifying the dichotomy between "this world" and "the next" for several more lines. The litany is interrupted only by God, who speaks directly, and terrifyingly, to the audience of the poem: "You take My holy and formidable name in your corrupted mouth," He rebukes the audience, promising to scatter their ashes to the wind. "How could I be like you, you drunkard, dog, and whore?"[59] It is an understatement to say that one is meant to feel increasingly unsettled as the poem winds toward its conclusion.

However, like any repentance poem worth its salt, this one offers the promise of respite near the end. Frik counsels himself to spill the wine from his head and not to consider "luck" (*baghd*) or "fate" (*talef*) his friends. Now sober, he instructs his audience to do the same: "When you possess ears of the heart that surpass the ears of the head, / you must listen, brothers: do not be fooled in the world here."[60] Only "instruction," or wisdom, can guide the soul to reach salvation:

> [For] that person who is wise, all of this counsel [*khrat*] is enough,
> He gives ear to the heart and keeps it many years.
> But if you do not make use of this [counsel], count it as the wind;
> Near the senseless and ignorant, it is not even worth a palmful of feces.[61]

One might then suppose that the poem would conclude in a predictable fashion. Instead, in the next four lines we find one of the greatest enigmas in all of medieval Armenian literature. Perhaps even Armenian scribes were startled when they reached the conclusion of the poem: one reader simply wrote "It is Persian" in the margins of the early seventeenth-century manuscript that records the following lines. This is what Frik's audience found:

> Յարմուտ պախի էշխի ջուզնէ քուրա՛ նա՛ քուշանդ,
> Լաղար սիֆաթան ու ժիշտ խուրա՛, նա՛ քուշանդ,
> Գարաշիղ իսադիղի զի քուշտան, մագրէզ,
> Մուրդ, արպուաթ հարանչի վաիրա՛ նա՛ քուշանդ։[62]

> *Transliteration into the Roman script:*
>
> *Harmut pakhi ēshkhi juznē k'ura nak'ushand,*
> *Laghar sifat'an u zhisht khura, nak'ushand,*
> *Garashigh isadighi zi k'ushtan, magrēz,*
> *Murd, arpuat' haranch'i vaira nak'ushand.*

Of course, these lines are not Armenian at all but rather Armeno-Persian: Persian written in the Armenian script (see figures 4 and 5). The mystery

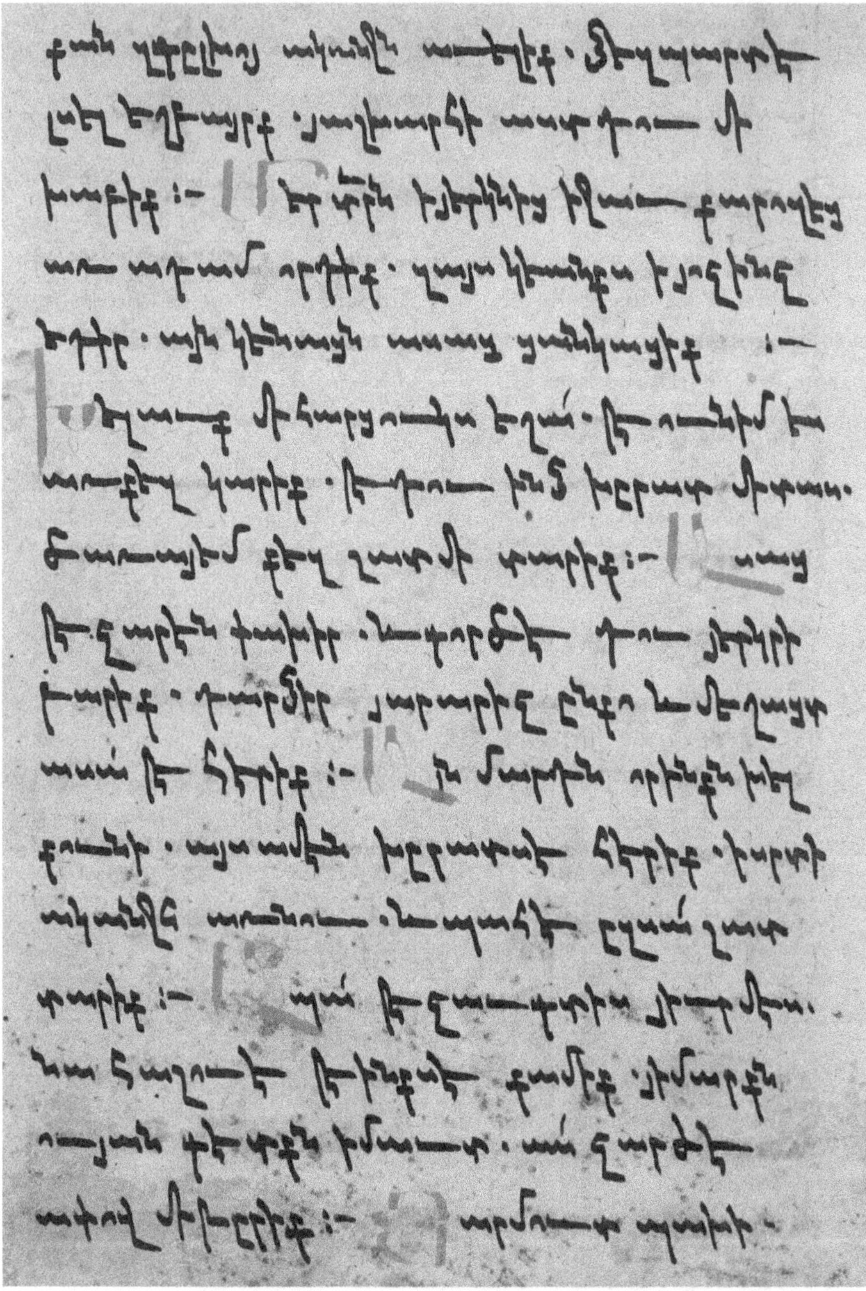

FIGURE 4. A poem by Frik, including the first two words of an Armeno-Persian quatrain in the lower right-hand corner. MS Armenian F. 16, fol. 121v. Courtesy of The Bodleian Libraries, The University of Oxford.

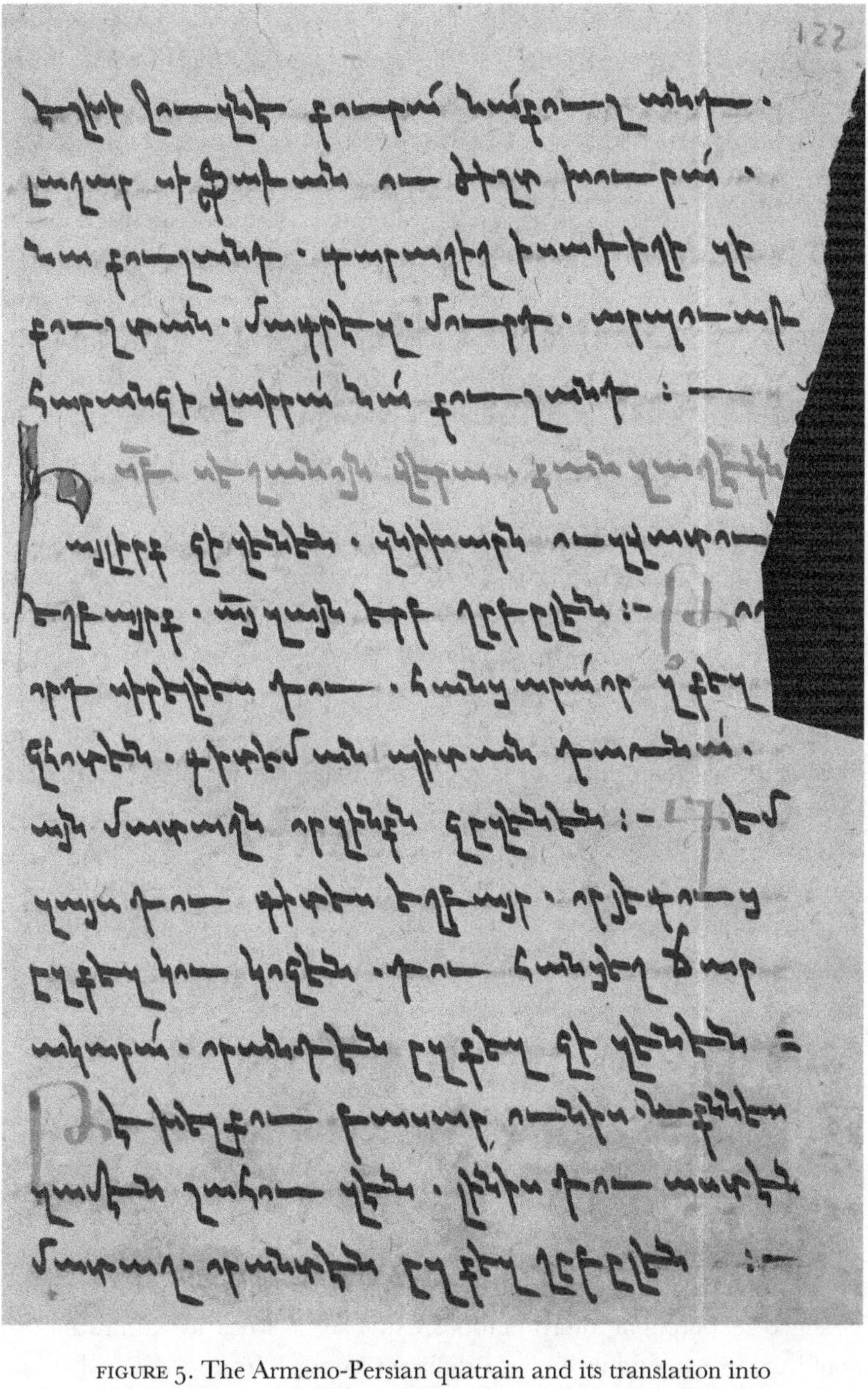

FIGURE 5. The Armeno-Persian quatrain and its translation into Middle Armenian. MS Armenian F. 16, fol. 122r. Courtesy of The Bodleian Libraries, The University of Oxford.

behind this quatrain has vexed scholars for many years. What were Persian verses doing in an apparently late thirteenth- or early fourteenth-century Armenian poem? Could Frik, whose poetry is highly saturated with Persian loanwords, be its author? Or was the Persian quatrain an addition by a later scribe?[63]

The answers are not entirely clear even today. Still, soon after the publication of the critical edition of Frik's *Diwan* in 1952, scholars realized that the following poem, which is preserved in a seventeenth-century manuscript at the Bodleian Library, is an Armenian translation and gloss of this Armeno-Persian quatrain.[64] Moreover, it is accompanied by a truncated version of the didactic Armenian poem that *precedes* the quatrain, in the same meter and style, using vocabulary and grammar characteristic of early Middle Armenian poetry. What these scholars realized, in other words, is that Frik's poem comprises four distinct sections: first, a Christian meditation on the transience of the world; second, a Persian quatrain written in the Armenian script; third, a translation of the quatrain into Middle Armenian; and fourth, a brief poem in Middle Armenian that reiterates the major themes of the first section.[65]

Several breakthroughs soon followed. In 1963, Babgen Chʻugaszyan attributed the quatrain to an unnamed daughter of Fażlallāh Astarābādī (d. 1394), a Persian mystic who founded the Ḥurūfī movement, which was popular especially among Bektāşīs in Anatolia.[66] One scholar found another variant, in a copy of the *Dīvān* of Khāqānī (d. 1190), a Persian poet attached to the court of the Shirvānshāh in the Caucasus.[67] Suddenly, after years of mystery, the enigmatic quatrain seemed to appear everywhere. It turned up in the Persian *Dīvān* of the poet Nesīmī (d. 1417), who was likely of Türkmen descent, and again in the *Dīvān* of Sarmad Kāshānī (fl. seventeenth century), who migrated from the Caucasus to India.[68] The quatrain has even been ascribed, on rare occasion, to Rūmī.[69] It is probably best, then, to describe it as one of the so-called wandering quatrains: popular poems that circulated broadly, making their homes as stowaways in the works of others.[70]

The migration of a quatrain from *dīvān* to *dīvān*, poet to poet, subtly changed its potential interpretations. After all, a word in Rūmī's mouth could mean something entirely different coming from, say, ʿĀşıḳ Paşa. Context is everything. This is especially true in the case of *this* wandering quatrain, which moved not only from one collection of poetry to another but also from one linguistic and religious milieu to another. To see how its ascription to Frik changes its meaning, one must first carefully attend to one of its common variants in the original Persian:

در مسلخ عشق جز نکو را نکشند　　لاغر صفتان زشت خو را نکشند
گر عاشق صادق ز کشتن مگریز　　مردار بود هر آنکه او را نکشند

In the slaughterhouse of love, they sacrifice none save the good,
The scrawny, ill-tempered ones they do not kill.

If you're a sincere lover, don't flee the killing.
Anyone they do not sacrifice is carrion.[71]

In the most general terms, the primary conceit is that the obliteration of the self is something that "sincere lovers" should seek out. The unworthy, those with meager bodies and wicked characters, are not able to die in the slaughterhouse of love (or in love's "kitchen," *maṭbakh*, in the Armeno-Persian text). Those who flee become "carrion," rotting away, their lives a waste. Hence, one commenter has observed, the quatrain plays on a basic tenet of mystical Islam: those who love God must seek self-obliteration (*fanā*) in the radical presence of the divine.[72]

Stunningly, in his quotation of the quatrain in Persian, Frik initially seems to accept this conceit wholesale. But as we move from his quotation to his translation, which immediately follows the Armeno-Persian text, a different story emerges. Here Frik takes the opportunity not only to render the Persian poem in a Middle Armenian idiom but also to recast its imagery for a Christian milieu. This becomes clear in his subtle emphasis on a "holy altar," which replaces the "kitchen" or "slaughterhouse" of the Persian quatrain, as well as in his rendering of "sacrifice," which bears a different connotation here:

Ի սուրբ սեղանոյն վերայ քան զաղէկն այլ իրք չի զենեն,
Զ՟նիհարն ու զվատուժն, եղբարք, Աստուծոյ զայն ե՞րբ ղըբըլեն։
Թ՟ ողորդ սիրելի ես դու, հանց արա, որ զ՟քեզ չի խոտեն,
Գիտեմ՞ անպիտան դառնայ այն մատաղն, որ զինքն չի զենեն։

Upon the holy altar, they sacrifice none save the good,
Since when do they make the gaunt and scrawny acceptable to God,
brothers?

If you're a sincere lover, act so they don't scorn you,
I know the sacrificial offering [*matagh*] they don't sacrifice is worthless.[73]

In the Armenian Church, the *matagh* is a young animal—often a lamb—that clergymen flay, cook, and distribute to the poor for sustenance. It therefore symbolizes Christ, the sacrificial lamb of God, who died to redeem the world. In Frik's remarkable translation, the "sincere lover" is not obliterated in *fanā* but rather becomes a participant in this redemptive work. Some commenters have observed that the lover hence becomes a martyr, giving their life to uplift the faithful. As Chʿugaszyan writes, Frik has "very subtly and masterfully replaced the Muslim character of the final line, 'anyone they do not sacrifice is carrion,' with a Christian one: 'I know the sacrificial offering [*matagh*] they don't sacrifice is worthless.'"[74] Or in Russell's later phrasing, "The message has crossed the bridge of the translator from Muslim to Christian territory, as it were."[75]

Clearly, translation plays a vital role in "translating" this message from an Islamicate to a Christian domain. It does not diminish the body of secondary literature on Frik, however, to observe that translation does not play the only role. As Chʿugaszyan's analysis suggests, it is precisely where Frik does *not* translate—where he deviates from a practice of faithfully reproductive translation—that the transplantation of the quatrain onto Christian terrain occurs. One might wonder, given the apparent need for such deviation, why Frik decided to cite, translate, and gloss this quatrain in the first place. Why not simply rewrite the poem, in Armenian, to match the Christian sensibility of his audience and leave it at that? Why bother to welcome a Muslim voice into his poetry at all? There is so much that we do not know—about Frik, his audience, and his poetic milieu—that we cannot answer these questions fully. However, a closer examination of his praxis of quotation and translation suggests a few possibilities.

As we have seen, discrete practices of literary adaptation were commonplace in Anatolia, including the incorporation (*tażmīn*) of lines from preexisting poems into new compositions. Similar practices that emerged later, under the rubrics of *istiqbāl* (welcoming), *javāb-gūʾī* (speaking in reply), and *naẓīra-gūʾī* (speaking in parallel), likewise allowed poets to "willingly and publicly acknowledge the voice of the other," in Losensky's phrasing, while advancing a divergent point of view.[76] Moreover, we have seen that poets did not repurpose the verses of others merely for aesthetic reasons. Rūmī, for instance, defended *tażmīn* as an essentially Islamic activity.[77] Similarly, the earliest Turkish poets in Rūm adapted Persianate poetic styles to place themselves within a particular literary genealogy and to spread knowledge of Islam among their diverse audiences. In Frik, we find an inversion of these practices: literary adaptation served to counter Islamization by providing room within Christianity for the recitation and audition of Islamicate poetry.

This picture becomes clear only in the final section of Frik's poem, which serves as a gloss that weaves the primary themes and even the vocabulary of the first three sections into a cohesive whole. It thus reiterates Frik's insistence on renouncing "this world," thereby transforming the Persian quatrain into a Christian *vanitas* poem:

> You certainly know this, brother, that tomorrow they will summon you.
> Find such means for yourself, lest they sacrifice you in the next world.
> If you have sense and are clear sighted [*basar*; Persian: *baṣar*], and you examine every gain and loss [*zēn*; Persian: *ziyān*],
> You will become a sacrificial offering [*matagh*] in this world, so that they accept you in the next.[78]

The poem continues in this vein for another eight lines, warning the audience that all their deeds are recorded in a ledger to be reviewed and judged by the divine council (Persian: *dīvān*) of the heavenly host.[79] In other words, Frik's reading of the Persian quatrain, like its accompanying (un)faithful translation, shores up the dichotomy between this world and the next, where one will be accepted or flayed. His gloss seals the Persian poem into a Christian hermeneutic matrix.

The three linguistically Armenian sections of this work therefore each take up a different hermeneutic labor. First, the opening section introduces the framework in which the wandering quatrain should be understood. Second, the Armenian translation showcases the kind of interpretive transformation of the Persian verses that must take place in the audience's minds. Finally, the last section provides a coda to the entire interpretive exercise. In other words, Frik's poems do not simply Christianize the Persian quatrain by placing it within a Christian context. Nor do they inscribe a

Christian reading upon the quatrain by rewriting the original. Rather, in a systematic fashion, they guide the audience to read the wandering quatrain—in the original Persian!—through Christian eyes. Hence, Frik's poetry bears an affinity to the earliest Armenian vernacular poems from Cilicia—the riddles of Nersēs—in that it subtly offers a kind of "instruction" in the fine art of interpretation. In this case, however, the poet provides a model for interpreting—or reading in a Christian light—even extra- or non-Christian literature.

This helps to explain why Frik includes a transliteration of the original quatrain alongside its Armenian translation, with both contextualized by a poetic introduction and conclusion. It also sheds light on why he might bother to incorporate an Islamicate poem, composed in another language, within his literary production at all. Perhaps Frik simply wished to show, à la Grigor Magistros's adaptation of the Bible in monorhyme, that he could produce literary works that would be poetically competitive within a Persianate literary sphere. After all, his adaptation of the Persian quatrain would not have occurred in a vacuum: if he was familiar with this poetry, it is likely that other Armenians, perhaps even his "brothers," enjoyed the recitation and contemplation of Persian verses as well. In this light, Frik's poetry sublimates, in fact transforms, such enjoyment within the proper hermeneutic context. One might conceivably now be ready to discern the veiled message within Khāqānī, Nesīmī, or Rūmī: repent, flee life in this world, and be grounded more firmly in the Christian faith. Put differently, Frik's poem provides an interpretive framework that extends far beyond a single Persian quatrain. Like Nersēs, he teaches his audience something more complex: the ability to marshal religious and linguistic heterogeneity into a decidedly Christian worldview.

Reading a Crooked World

Frik was not alone in "translating" the translations of literature from other languages into a Christian hermeneutic frame. Khachʿatur Kechʿaṛetsʿi, a late thirteenth- and early fourteenth-century clergyman who resided in the Caucasus, composed poetry in a similar manner. Khachʿatur considered the Classical Armenian translation of the Greek *Alexander Romance* to be an unbecoming work of "pagan" literature, though he encouraged audiences to view Alexander as a precursor to Jesus Christ. For this reason, somewhat akin to Frik, he composed a series of vernacular quatrains to gloss the text.[80] These monorhymed quatrains, known in Armenian as *kafa*s, are woven throughout the Armenian translation of the romance in one early fourteenth-century manuscript, expanding upon the narrative without altering it directly. Other *kafa*s attributed to Khachʿatur, though perhaps the work of later poets, draw on figures and scenes from the Bible to reframe the romance in a Christian light. In other words, these *kafa*s do more than comment on the Classical Armenian translation. Arguably, they translate it.[81]

Khachʿatur shares another similarity with Frik: both poets advanced a Christian worldview by drawing, not coincidentally, from an Arabic and Persian lexicon. For instance, Khachʿatur warns his audience to be wary of two Arabo-Persian concepts: *charkh* (Armenian: *chʿarkh*), the wheel of fortune, and *falak* (Armenian: *falakʿ*), the celestial sphere, whose movements shape human lives.[82] At least in Khachʿatur's hands, these loanwords bear an unabashedly didactic message: although life might bring joy today, eventually the wheel of fortune will move again, and all happiness will turn to sorrow. In the face of an indifferent universe, the only thing to do is to repent and turn to God for mercy. Both words thus evoke the ancient notion of the Wheel of Fortune (Latin: *Rota Fortunae*) yet here are mediated through languages—and as we shall see, poetic sensibilities—that were geographically and temporally immediate to the Caucasus and Anatolia at this time.

Frik draws from this same vocabulary in one of his most iconic poems, "Ĕnddēm Falakʿin" ("Against Fate"). He too offers a searing look at the hardships of life in a wicked age, condemning the celestial sphere—or Fate (*Falakʿ*)—as a "crooked judge."[83] Modern readers have generally seized upon "Ĕnddēm Falakʿin" as representative of a gradual inclination in Armenian poetry to address social concerns, a form of soft secularization, in which the unjust universe, *Falakʿ*, serves as a coded substitution for God.[84] For better or worse, this poem has become synonymous with Frik. However, like Khachʿatur, he did not employ this term neutrally.[85] Instead, as we shall see, he guides his audience to reflect on Arabo-Persian terms for the universe in a pointed manner—a manner that both provokes a reevaluation of modern assumptions about this poem and helps to bring into legible relief a broader pattern of literary adaptation in Middle Armenian.

"O *Ch'arkh,*" his poem begins, "when you turn against man, you dig a pit for him the entire day."[86] The verb that Frik uses for "to turn" or "to incline" (*tsṛil*), which in Middle Armenian can also mean "to go mad," evokes the fatalistic revolutions of fortune's wheel. It also has a revealing root: *tsuṛ*, "crooked." Indeed, in the first half of Frik's poem, Fate's crookedness is its defining quality, as the poem's primary conceit is reversal. In righteous fury, the poet thus unleashes a powerful complaint against *Ch'arkh/Falak'*, personified as an evil agent who props up despots to torment the realm:

> O *Ch'arkh,* you gild the house of the evil entirely with gold,
> You cast the righteous in the land down, where they collect scraps.
> He who is not suited to be a swineherd you make a fearsome horseman,
> And without laborers [to assist], you dismantle the home of just men.
> *Falak'*, if I curse you, "He," they say, "is a man gone astray."
> Otherwise why do you always gaze angrily at the wise man?
> The ignorant and ignoble [*nak'as*] man you make lord in this world,
> You scatter the bread of wise men on peak or in valley.
> Now my affairs have grown difficult, for the Tatar has become king;
> He plundered all the realm and made crooks grow mighty.
> Yet even he does not remain; *Falak'* is devoted to no one.
> It strikes, and hurls [rulers] down, and considers no one king.
> O *Ch'arkh,* how can I trust you now, when you keep no intimates?
> You take no vow [*ghawl*]; you have neither oath nor creed, O you deceiver.
> You place him whom you love today upon a golden throne.
> Tomorrow, when you cast him from your sight, you level him with the ashen earth.[87]

Frik employs Persian vocabulary throughout the poem in specific ways. This is especially true in his description of foreign rule over the land. Even the powerful *sahip diwan* (transliterated from Persian as *ṣāḥib dīwān*), who held the highest administrative position in the Ilkhanate, is not spared by the revolution of the Heavenly Wheel, no matter how great his *siasat'* (Persian: *siyāsat*), or administration.[88] No epistle and no pen (Persian: *qalam*), the accoutrements of the court, can save one from Fate.[89] In this selective use of Persian loanwords, Frik advances a particular message. Yes, the world is unjust. Yes, the righteous are scattered, exiled from their homes, in search of a new and uncertain future. But just as important, the enemies of the righteous—the Tatar, the ignoble (Persian: *nākas*), the *ṣāḥib dīvān*—will not remain in power forever. They too must fall. In other words, Frik's poem reflects the most common motif of Christian *vanitas* literature: all life is transient. At least in this capacity, the poem is therefore didactic, advancing an oblique form of Christian instruction.

Of course, in the first half of this poem, Frik condemns *Falakʿ* as a "crooked [*tsuṛ*] judge" whose wicked rulings corrupt the world.[90] When his litany of Fate's wrongdoing reaches its climax, however, we find a strange reversal: Fate offers its own complaint against Frik. This ending, which is vital to understanding the poem as a whole, does not square well with the common interpretation that Frik wanted merely to criticize his creator. In fact, the most significant anthology of medieval Armenian literature in English does not even include this portion of the poem.[91] Yet Fate's complaint against Frik is essential, as it simultaneously informs a particular reading of *Falakʿ* and differentiates the poem from a Persian and Turkish literary milieu in which fate's crookedness is a common motif.

"Whatever you do is crooked [*tsuṛ*]," Frik complains of Fate, but then is cut short.[92] In some manuscripts the poem splits at this point, creating two distinct halves. One manuscript even gives the second half a title, "[THE] REPLY," in red letters, signaling the reader to attend carefully to what follows.[93] Another manuscript heralds the beginning of this section, and its divergence from Frik's initial complaint, with a red symbol.[94] *Falakʿ*, apparently fed up with Frik's slander, now begins a robust defense of its authority:

> *Falakʿ* gives a reply: "Cease your howling, ignorant old man.
> In all my days as *Falakʿ*, I haven't seen one more errant than you.
> There was another before me, that formidable Father, who wrote [what he had ordained] for you.
> You hold me accountable for your crimes, [saying] that *Falakʿ* is a crooked [*tsuṛ*] judge.
> Do you not know that [*Falakʿ*] is from the Creator? He makes mighty whomever he desires."

Again *Falak*ʿ declared to paupers and kings:
"God is the giver of good, who establishes all who are mighty.
Although I am *Falak*ʿ, I cannot even toss you table scraps.
The command is from God that I prepare a king for you,
And when God does not command it, who can offer you a scrap [of bread]?"[95]

Frik is forced to concede this logic. He then redirects the thrust of the complaint, acknowledging both the justness of God and the inequity of humankind:

*Falak*ʿ, who can blame you? All is well that you do,
But it is on account of our sins that God looks at us with anger.
You discern the occasion for giving, you know what is proper and who is worthy.
It only seems this way to us, that you are not a righteous judge.[96]

"The blameless King God, by his reckoning, establishes all," Frik counsels his audience.[97] Rather than condemn *Ch*ʿ*arkh,* therefore, he begs for its mercy and its intercession. In essence, Frik asks *Ch*ʿ*arkh* and *Falak*ʿ to help him become a better Christian, even if that means living in hardship:

Turn wickedness from me, and change the old to new,
Whether it be evil or good, easy or hard, in this life.
All comes from you. You are the cause, God the judge.
One wise pauper is better than a thousand wealthy fools.[98]

Ultimately, what we witness in these final lines is a reversal of the position on *Falak*ʿ's agency in the world. We are warned to not even describe fate as "crooked," at the risk of going astray ourselves. It is only God who can intervene in our lives; the very concept of *Falak*ʿ or *Ch*ʿ*arkh* has no power. In this sense, the turning of the celestial sphere, which both erects crooked kings and topples good men, is merely an effect of the sins of humankind. Or, to put it simply, the idea of *Falak*ʿ has been absorbed into a Christian worldview.

Typically, because *Falak*ʿ is an extension of God's will, this poem has been interpreted as an indirect rebuke of the Creator, carefully walked back in the final lines.[99] There are at least two fundamental problems with this interpretation. The first is the presumption that Frik's intention was indeed to get away with criticizing his God, although the majority of his poetic corpus—a sizable body of poetry that is rarely read today—is essentially didactic (*khratakan*) and devotional.[100] Its thrust is largely to impart lessons about Christianity or articulate different expressions of Christian devotion in a vernacular idiom for the benefit of its audience. We would therefore need to assume a kind of insincerity on Frik's part, and a half-hearted gesture to conceal the true nature of his theodical conclusion: creation is wholly crooked and was never just to begin with. Simply put, this interpretation is not consistent with a complete reading of the poem. Second, and more important, this interpretation ignores a large body of Persian and Turkish poetry that likewise concerns the "crookedness" of *Falak*ʿ, a charge interrogated and ultimately rejected as untenable by Frik.[101]

Take, for instance, a famous poem by Khāqānī, composed while he was in prison, that uses the trappings of Christianity to appeal to an unnamed Christian ruler. "*Falak* is more crooked than the writing of Christians," it begins, evoking the Greek, Armenian, and Georgian scripts, which are read left to right, unlike Arabic and Persian.[102] Although quite different from Frik's poem in tone and theme, Khāqānī's poem also features a prominent reversal. First he flirts with the idea of devoting himself to Christianity, a religion he knows quite intimately, as his mother was a Nestorian Christian who converted to Islam. Then, to secure the intercession of a powerful Christian patron to allow him to visit Jerusalem, presumably after freeing him from his "imprisonment" in the Caucasus, he proceeds to make a dazzling show of his erudition: he offers to compose a commentary on the Gospels in Syriac, he proposes to send an epistle on the Trinity to be read aloud in Baghdad, and he even performs a typological reading of the Old and New Testaments. Of course, though he likens his trials in prison to the suffering of Christ, Khāqānī has no real intention of becoming Christian. All of this serves as a prologue to a dramatic climax, the moment of repentance when this dizzying erudition is flipped on its head:

> Enough, O Khāqānī, of corrupting madness,
> For Satan indoctrinates with madness.
>
> How can a vile companion care for Jesus?
> How can an evil vizier instruct Dārā?

Do not speak this blasphemy. Renew the faith.
Utter: I beg God's forgiveness for this request![103]

Quite obviously, the opening line—"*Falak* is more crooked than the writing of Christians"—is tongue in cheek. It is, after all, the heretical writing of Christians that is the truly crooked element of Khāqānī's poem. Khāqānī falsely positions himself—with a knowing wink—as a devotee of this crooked writing, adopting the perspective of a Christian to examine his unjust incarceration. Yet by opening a space to investigate transgressive Christian teachings, he also positions himself to call for the renewal of his faith. He has been tested, much like Shaykh Ṣanʿān in the famous tale by ʿAṭṭār, only to emerge triumphantly as a true Muslim—even as he continues to beseech his patron by invoking the latter's Christian beliefs.

Frik does something analogous, for an entirely different purpose, in his poem against fate. Although he presents it as a complaint against *chʿarkh* or *falakʿ*, he ultimately instructs his audience not to think of Fate as crooked. In fact, he strongly implies that those who do are "crooked" themselves. Who, we might ask, perennially described *falakʿ* as "crooked" in this period? The most immediate answer, at least in the literary realm, is the authors of a substantial body of Islamicate poetry. Khāqānī's verses are replete with the motifs of *chʿarkh* and *falakʿ*, as are many of significant works of Persian literature. In Firdawsī's *Shāh-nāma*, which was known to Armenians in Erznka, fate (*bakht*) is deeply malevolent (*badkhwāh bakht, bakht-i shūm*) and fortune is hunchbacked (*kūzhpusht*), grotesquely deformed in its indifference to human suffering.[104] The theme is common in Persian poetry. Thus a quatrain attributed to ʿUmar Khayyām (d. 1131) similarly laments:

No one has ever prevailed upon the Wheel of Heaven [*charkh-i falak*],
And the earth has never become satiated from swallowing men.[105]

So too did Turkish poets compose poetry on fate's fickleness. Most notable is the *Çarh-nāme* (*Book of the Wheel*) attributed to Aḥmed Faḳīh, who perhaps lived in the late fourteenth century. Much like Frik, Aḥmed Faḳīh repeatedly reminds his audience that all who come into the world must leave it. Many labor in vain because of *Çarh* (the Wheel): even great kings like Solomon cannot flee the fate of all flesh.[106]

Simply put, this fateful lexicon was common in poetry throughout the Persianate world at this time. Like Khāqānī, who flirts in his poetry with Christian ideas without becoming Christian, Frik adapts a Persianate and Islamicate lexicon without abandoning his religion either.[107] At the same time, by glossing this vocabulary in his poetry, Frik subtly glosses poetic discourses that condemn fate as "crooked." Thus, his poems offer an interpretive stance, as they instruct audiences to listen with the "ears of the heart" and not the ears of the head, to read according to the spiritual senses, now trained to seek the hidden Christian meanings in Islamicate or Persianate source material. Frik therefore offers a glimpse of an emerging Armenian language of affinity—one that accommodated linguistic, cultural, and religious differences within a particular hermeneutic frame.

In this, Frik's poetry shares an even more obvious affinity with Armenian riddles, which diverse authors began to produce, in versified Middle Armenian, after the twelfth century. After all, in English, the words *read* and *riddle* are doublets, as they both derive from a common root. Riddles, in a real way, teach you to read. Indeed, in a similar mode, this early corpus of Middle Armenian poetry does the same. But whereas the encyclopedic scope of Nersēs's riddles subtly instructs its audience to read scripture in a particular way, Frik's verses guide the reader to understand another kind of instruction, adapted from a Persianate literary sphere, in explicitly Christian terms. His is therefore a meaning-making endeavor akin to that of Rūmī, Sulṭān Valad, ʿĀşıḳ Paşa, and Gülşehrī, who fashioned languages of affinity that accommodated cultural difference in terms of Islam. Yet as the poetry of Nersēs and of Frik suggests, the stakes of this hermeneutic exercise encompass more than the reading of words. Their poems offer manners of theorizing the world beyond texts: destiny, fate, luck, the universal flow of time, the unceasing rotation of the celestial sphere, that will bear us all away. Theirs is a poetics that opens a space, within the Islamicate world, to be a Christian.

CHAPTER SEVEN

AN EDUCATION IN ERZNKA

It is time to tread where Bahā᾽ al-Dīn, Rūmī's father, would not: the multilingual and multireligious city of Erznka (contemporary Erzincan), home of many "bad people."[1] While still a significant cultural and mercantile center (Marco Polo was particularly impressed by its baths and buckram), it was no longer exactly an Armenian metropolis by the thirteenth century.[2] Situated northeast of the Cilician frontier, beyond the rule of an Armenian kingdom, Erznka was a mother city without children—a place that, for the moment, was fundamentally in between. It had fallen into the hands of the Mongols, who allowed the populace to maintain some autonomy under Ilkhanid control. Eventually, however, it will be swept up in the wake of Ottoman expansion, which has already begun to unfold, just offstage.

What would Bahā᾽ al-Dīn have found had he been cajoled into exploring its winding streets, its urban confraternities, its bazaar and public square? In some ways, had he been more adventurous, certain aspects of the city might have struck him as familiar. However, since Bahā᾽ al-Dīn is not here, we shall walk the streets of fourteenth-century Erznka in his stead. As we tread its circuitous passageways, roads, and routes, we encounter a small crowd ahead. Out of the din, a beckoning voice reaches our ears, chanting a passage from the *Shāh-nāma* (*Book of Kings*) of Firdawsī (d. 1020), which is largely considered *the* Persian epic today. We find ourselves enchanted by the lilt, the rise and fall of the *mutaqārib* meter, patterning the epic's sound. When the performance ends, a group of Armenian speakers break off from the crowd. They seek out another poet, an Armenian by the name of Kostandin Erznkatsʿi, and confront him with a familiar request.

As Kostandin explains, after these "brothers" had listened to the performer chanting the *Shāh-nāma* "aloud," or "with a voice," they were left wanting more, and so they asked him to compose a new poem using the same style and sound. "The brothers asked [me], 'Recite a poem to us in the voice [*dzayn*] of the *Shāh-nāma*,' " Kostandin reports. He then offers a pithy instruction: "I wrote these words. Read them in the voice of the *Shāh-nāma*."[3]

Later, Kostandin appears before this audience again, his composition complete. Let us suppose for a moment that we are among Kostandin's brothers, seated in a semicircle before him. What might cross our minds as his performance begins? Most likely, we would be keenly attentive to two elements of this adaptation. First, and more technically, is its sound (or "voice"), the musical and rhythmic chant that a performer employs. In this case, the performance's "voice" should produce an uncanny aural convergence, creating a sonic kinship between Middle Armenian and New Persian poetry.[4] Second, we would probably listen, rather intently, for how this new poem might diverge from its source material. Of course, all literary adaptations must do this somehow. The pleasure of a skillful adaptation, however, lies in the ways that the poet opens a suggestive space, one of dialogue and difference, between the new poem and the old.

To our delight, as Kostandin begins to speak, his adaptation does not disappoint on either front. His words resound with the *Shāh-nāma* but also gracefully weave a different worldview with its seductive style and sound. This is apparent from the moment that Kostandin's stentorian voice fills the room:

> In the name of the uncreated and mighty God,
> In the name of the Father and the Son, who is the only begotten,
>
> In the name of the eternal, true Holy Spirit,
> Who are a single dominion, powerful in tribunal.

I began to recite a poem to my beloved ones alike,
To open doors to you through marvelous counsel,

To string together pearls and luminous gems,
To show you the beautiful discourse of instruction [*khrat*].

We must heed the words of the sages,
We must willingly distance ourselves from the ignorant.[5]

Kostandin's talent is on full display here as he makes overt gestures to his source material while completely changing its meaning. As James R. Russell has observed, his invocation of "the uncreated and mighty God" is a subtle revision of the *bismillāh* (in the name of God), recited before all but the ninth sura of the Qur'an, and of its Persian variant in the *Shāh-nāma*'s first lines.[6] "In the name of the Lord of life and wisdom [*khirad*]," Firdawsī writes at the start of his epic masterpiece. "Thought cannot soar higher than He."[7] Kostandin's adaptation leaves no doubt of his work's Christian orientation. This is a poem, he signals to us, that will be grounded in the "only begotten" Son of God.

Just as Kostandin's words convey a semiotic playfulness, rich with carefully differentiated meaning, so too does the sound of his voice. In emulation of the *Shāh-nāma*, he adapted the catalectic *mutaqārib* meter (˘ – – / ˘ – – / ˘ – – / ˘ –) to compose this poem, throwing out some of the most basic principles of Armenian versification in the process. Unlike Persian, Armenian does not have long or short vowels. Theo M. van Lint has shown that for Kostandin to achieve an approximation of *ʿarūż*, he needed to place an unusual stress on the second and third syllable of each foot, corresponding to the long syllables of a truly quantitative meter.[8] The true coup of his composition, in other words, is one that cannot be written down. Rather, this adaptation needs a human voice to come alive, animated by a staccato cadence that navigates the space between dissimilar metrical systems.[9] Hence the immediacy of Kostandin's instruction: "Read [these words] in the voice of the *Shāh-nāma*." We the audience are invited to take part in this adaptive labor by reciting the Armenian *Shāh-nāma* in the same manner as the Persian original. Indeed, according to Kostandin's report, we are already part of this labor. After all, "we" asked for this poem: we presumably first glimpsed the possibility of its "voice" speaking in new ways.

This adaptive feat is one of the more notable in medieval Armenian literature. Kostandin not only rewrites Persian poetry for a new purpose and a new audience but, unlike Frik, even names his source of inspiration, creating a genealogy between the new work and the old. In the context of national literary history, everything that transpires here is absolutely extraordinary. Yet from the perspective of an integrative literary history of Anatolia, there is hardly anything unusual about what Kostandin describes. From this vantage point, one is struck by the familiarity of this dynamic between poet and audience, generative of poetry. After all, throughout this book we have observed similar praxes of literary composition, based on analogous relationships between poets and their publics, in other cities. Moreover, this dialogue between poet and audience was not simply an aesthetic endeavor but also an epistemic and social undertaking: a communal negotiation over what things are meaningful, how they are meaningful, and to whom they are meaningful. Kostandin's *Shāh-nāma* is no different.

Of course, by the time that Armenian audiences might have desired an Armenian *Shāh-nāma*, the literary scene in Rūm had changed in ways both sweeping and subtle. Sulṭān Valad was nearing the end of his life, having dispatched his followers to spread Rūmī's teachings throughout Anatolia—including to Erznka.[10] The *Maṣnavī*, with its proclivity to mix new meanings into old stories, was gradually securing its reputation among even Turkish audiences, who had begun to compose poetry in the *maṣnavī* form. Nascent literary cultures, such as those of Anatolian Turkish and Middle Armenian, were making their impressions upon the palimpsestic literary landscape. And with the admission of these languages to writing, their respective literary cultures developed in rather decentralized fashion, even as they so often took their cues about what was "literary" from other poetic cultures. A new era of literary production in Anatolia was dawning, and its outcome was hardly inevitable or certain.

When Kostandin rewrote the *Shāh-nāma* in Middle Armenian, in the early fourteenth century, he too had been shaped by this transformed environment.[11] Probably around fifty or sixty years old, he had a lifetime of learning behind him—and not all from a particularly "Armenian" milieu—that informed his poetic praxis in many ways. What, then, might this praxis reveal about Kostandin and about the city in which he came of age? We have already seen how this region, in the previous century, had shaped the sensibilities of a Persian poet in Konya. But how did another, later Rūm produce an Armenian poet in Erznka by similar means?

By reconstructing the literary education of Kostandin Erznkatsʿi, this chapter offers a culmination of our journey. It shows that many processes that informed cultural production within the Arabic-Persian-Turkish literary sphere were never unique to that sphere. At its core is a summative argument: to understand Kostandin's development as a poet, we would do well to place him in dialogue with his contemporaries—and not only with Armenians. Many of the poets whom we have met along the road—especially Rūmī—therefore return in this chapter, to serve as counterpoints to Kostandin. Though they produced works that are formally dissimilar, shaped by different needs, theologies, and audiences, a similar conception of poetry's utility in society undergirds their compositions. Kostandin matters, in other words, not only because he sheds a different kind of light on Armenian literary history but also because he brings the multilingual, multireligious literary landscape of Anatolia into revealing relief. In Kostandin's voice we can discern nothing less than a robust premodern theory and praxis of poetry, by now widespread throughout Rūm.

A Theory of Poetry

To understand how Erznka shaped Kostandin as a poet, one must begin at the start of his life. Van Lint, the foremost expert on Kostandin, places his birth sometime between 1240 and 1250, around when the Mongols assumed control of the city.[12] This was, in more ways than one, a tumultuous time. A devastating earthquake thundered across the region in 1251, and then another in 1254, sending the residents of Erznka scrambling through the streets in panic.

At some point, Kostandin decided to leave his worldly life behind and become a monk. It is possible that he had already joined a monastery by the time the earthquake of 1254 struck. Although we cannot say for certain, perhaps it was the prominent monastery of Tirashēn, located near the Euphrates River just eight kilometers south of Erznka.[13] Had Kostandin rushed from his cell during the earthquake, pressed into a jostling crowd together with his spiritual brothers, a large monastic complex would have greeted him. Its sturdy church, with large and small vaulted domes, would have been a reassuring sight, as would the warren of monastic cells and guesthouse for pilgrims near the entrance, all of which were encircled by a formidable wall. In the fourteenth century, various scriptoria at monasteries like Tirashēn would place Erznka on the map as a center of cultural production for the Armenian Church. However, as we shall see, the manuscripts produced and preserved here did not represent the only literary culture that would shape Kostandin's life.

The few biographical details about him that have survived are shrouded in mystery. Here is what we know: When he was fifteen years old, still a "young lad" (*manuk tghay*) by his own report, an otherworldly encounter upended his life more than an earthquake ever could.[14] Kostandin was alone in his cell one evening, either on the cusp of sleep or preparing for bed. Suddenly, a radiant stranger appeared before him. This stranger, also a young man, shone beautifully, like the sun. As Kostandin's eyes adjusted to the light in his cell, he more clearly beheld this luminous youth (*manuk*), "seated upon a throne, like a king."[15] The visitor, Kostandin explains in a famous poem, was clearly from a higher realm. Astonished at the youth's glory and radiance, Kostandin immediately prostrated himself, making three requests of this divine stranger:

> I said: I am a sinner [Persian: *gunāhkār*]; you are king. I have sinned against you.
> I said: I am sick in spirit and have found you, my physician.
> I said: I am poor, and have always needed [your] word.
> Grace me, this slave, with a share, a portion, and a robe.[16]

The physician, dressed in "clothes of the sun" (*aregaknazgest*), gave no verbal reply.[17] Instead, the radiant being rose silently from his throne to tread upon Kostandin's recumbent body.[18] Though Kostandin labored to draw the visitor into dialogue, his efforts were fruitless. The youth only answered him "in a sweet voice" (*k'aghts'r dzaynov*) with a single command—"Go!"—thus waking Kostandin from his reverie.[19]

This experience seems to have shaken Kostandin to his core, leaving him senseless, devoid of reason, and full of longing for days on end. When would the divine youth return? And why had he cast Kostandin into the painful abyss of separation? Many sleepless nights and tearful hours followed. Kostandin found that he could not confess his vision even to his monastic brothers. Instead, he girded his belt and applied himself to study, poring over the books at his disposal for an explanation. At the end of this soul-searching he reached a conclusion that, by modern standards, might seem rather bizarre. Kostandin realized, quite unexpectedly, that he had become a poet:

> Suddenly, for whoever wanted it, I could recite poetry
> Such that I was astonished by my own arrangement of words;
> With love and great hope I tried my hand at this poetry,
> I gave up my spirit in exchange, and attained that Spirit at last.[20]

"My speech [*ban*] came to me, as manna for me, from that light," he writes, drawing us into the scriptural heart of his newfound talent.[21] *Ban*, the term he uses synecdochically for his poetry, also denotes "reason," "oration," "discourse," and "word." In fact, it can mean *the* Word: *ban* is the Armenian equivalent of Logos, the divine Word, whose order undergirds the Christian universe. After all, it is the bread of life, as Christ names himself in John 6:48–51, which sustains the soul for eternity, unlike the manna that the Hebrews ate in the desert. "One does not live by bread alone," Christ admonishes in the Armenian translation of Matthew 4:4, "but by every word [*ban*] that comes from the mouth of God." Kostandin reaches a similar conclusion: his poetry is a divine gift, the word of God and a reflection of Christ—whom some commenters have identified as the luminous boy in the vision.[22]

Not everyone appreciated Kostandin's higher calling, however. "Some slander me out of jealousy," he tells us in the heading of his vision-poem. "They say, 'How does he recite such poetry, since he has not studied with a teacher [*vardapet*]?' "[23] This complaint presumably strikes at the question of who, in the eyes of the church, was allowed to be a poet. Many of Kostandin's poems are explicitly concerned with the instruction (*khrat*) of their audience(s). But as Van Lint has observed, teachers of church doctrine were expected to have undergone rigorous training, which likely included the memorization of many foundational texts, before attempting to instruct others.[24] It was therefore perhaps on shaky ethical grounds that Kostandin claimed divine sanction of his literary endeavors. Not surprisingly, his vision also seems to have elicited a fervent response. "Some are wicked toward me; they gnash their teeth over me," Kostandin claims near the end of his poem. "And to some it seems right to spill my blood," he chillingly adds, "[so] their desire may come to pass . . ."[25]

Yet Kostandin makes no attempt to defend his education. Nor does he appeal to his monastic credentials, however slight. Instead, he flips this complaint on its head by reminding his audience that it is one thing to labor but it is entirely different to receive "grace from the Spirit."[26] The implication is striking: Kostandin claims greater authority to compose poetry than a monastic scholar has, as he drinks "without lips" from a bottle of wine and is "intoxicated [*sarkhōsh*] in that love" offered to him by the divine physician.[27] In Kostandin's eyes, "whoever is a thief of this treasure [*gandz*] or is treacherous toward me / is against God."[28] It is his enemies, then, who are found wanting:

> They are blind in the eyes of the soul, in mind foolish and ignorant,
> For who has the sense or this grace that is with me?
> I am an earthen vessel; there is treasure [*khazinay*] filled in me,
> That which I recite, through the spirit, is the manna of the awesome Lord.[29]

This is the story as Kostandin tells it. It is not, however, the only story worth telling. Recent scholarship on Kostandin has been occupied with one question in particular: where did this vision come from? Scholars have cast a wide net when reading his poem, searching for its sources and analogues in both Armenian history and neighboring religious traditions.[30] Yet Kostandin's vision-poem is significant for reasons that have received less attention. Chiefly, it sheds light on how a coterie of Armenians in medieval Erznka conceptualized their literary production—how they theorized the meaning, value, and function of poetry—in a manner entirely consistent with their immediate Persian and Turkish contemporaries in the late thirteenth and early fourteenth centuries.[31] In other words, regardless of its cultural or religious origins, the poem reflects a widespread theory of literary production, which Armenians had come to shape locally in medieval Erznka.

Throughout this book, I have examined a particular kind of poet: charismatic figures who were not attached to courts and did not receive patronage to write in rhyme. They obviously did not compose poetry because they had no choice, as though swept up in a lyric frenzy, nor write to support themselves financially, nor take up the pen merely because poetry was in vogue (although it clearly was). Rather, their composition of poetry was often tied to the production of knowledge, as it advanced a way of thinking and being in the world, including engaging with "others" both within and outside one's own community. Poetry, this book has argued, therefore often guided its audience in how to read both texts and the social contexts in which they were embedded.

The choice to compose poetry that aspired to such lofty epistemic heights was not without controversy—which poets sometimes courted. Rūmī, for one, reportedly challenged the supremacy of the Qur'an over his poetry in strategic ways. He offered a fiery rebuke to a follower who remarked that the *Maṣnavī* was only a commentary (*tafsīr*) on the Qur'an: "O dog! Why is [the *Maṣnavī*] not [the Qur'an]! O jackass! Why is it not [the Qur'an]? O [brother of a] harlot! Why is it not [the Qur'an]!"[32] In Rūmī's eyes, the *Maṣnavī* does something equivalent and analogous to scripture, insofar as it draws from the same divine wellspring of meaning. Of course, not all poets were so bold. Others, such as Sulṭān Valad, merely claimed special status for Sufi poetry: because it comes from the love of God (and not from the love of the self), it has the power to unveil hidden spiritual meanings. Recall Sulṭān Valad's maxim: "The poetry of the lover is all exegesis [*tafsīr*]," whereas "the poetry of poets is surely the stench of garlic [*taf-i sīr*]."[33] This is what the production of "real" poetry meant, at least among a small but influential coterie in Konya: real poetry is handed down from a higher realm and refracts a glimpse of the divine secrets beyond language.

A similar idea animates Kostandin's verses. Take, for instance, his self-portrait as "an earthen vessel" in whom "treasure" is filled. As some commenters have observed, this declaration evokes 2 Corinthians 4:7, in which the apostle Paul rests his authority on divine grace.[34] "But we have this treasure in earthen vessels," Paul writes, "so that it may be made clear that this extraordinary power belongs to God and does not come from us."[35] Kostandin's assertion of poetic authority relies on the same claim: he sees with the "eyes of the soul" precisely because he is filled with the treasure that comes directly from God, which no amount of bookish learning can surpass. One must instead drink "wine without lips" and encounter the ineffable for oneself, much as Yūnus Emre desired to swim "in the sea of Truth" and not follow the legalistic study of religious scholars.[36] Kostandin thus advances and in fact reshapes a theory of literature that was common among premodern poets in Rūm: poetry, in its revelatory and epistemic dimension, supplements and even supersedes other forms of knowledge production.

Kostandin weaves this outlook into the language he employs, including his claim that his words are a treasure from on high. Strikingly, he does not use the Classical Armenian word for "treasure" (*gandz*), as he would in the following stanza; nor does he use the Greek word from 2 Corinthians (*thēsauros*). Rather, he chooses a term of Arabic origin: *khazīna*, meaning both wealth that is "stored" or "laid up" (that is, treasure) and "treasury."[37] This choice is illuminating. Though the line clearly paraphrases Saint Paul, it also refracts an Islamicate milieu. In fact, the Qur'an (15:21) speaks of divine treasures and treasuries (*khazāʾin*) in a complementary manner. "Naught is there, but its treasuries are with Us," God proclaims, "and We send it not down but in a known measure."[38] Whether we know it or not, the verse implies, all of creation is doled out from God's divine treasuries. This verse impressed itself deeply upon poets in Anatolia. Rūmī, in his exegesis of it, even preaches that humans possess "handfuls and scraps from the treasuries [*khazāʾin*] of the attributes of God," including wisdom and speech, which are slowly depleted in the course of everyday life. At night, while we rest, beings must come from the celestial sphere to replenish our provisions.[39] In this light, all things—even artistic capacities—come from the treasuries of God.[40] What makes intellectual labor possible, then, is the continuing interface between the celestial treasuries and human society, which is mediated by angelic intercessors, or "peddlers of God," as Rūmī calls them.[41]

Of course, not all treasures are equal. Nor do all people enjoy the same access to these heavenly storehouses. "Intelligence [*ʿaql*] comes in two intelligences," Rūmī explains in the *Maṣnavī*. "The first is acquired [*maksabī*], / that you learn like a youth in school."[42] Through books and teachers, through the sweat of one's brow, one accumulates this learning gradually. Yet as he continues, "The other intelligence is the blessing of God; / its fountain is within the soul."[43] This wisdom is the treasure of God and comes effortlessly and unmediated.[44] Quite obviously, the knowledge that Kostandin lays claim to—the ability to reveal meaning through poetry—is of the latter variety.[45] His idea of poetic composition is marked by a conceptual and lexical convergence—a space that opens in both Islam and Christianity, though one that is not unique to either historically. It is in this space that Kostandin, a Christian in the Armenian monastic tradition, displaces bookish study with a claim to possess divine treasure, a treasure that *generates* poetry and cannot be earned by any amount of work. His is a poetics of experience. Hence Kostandin claims that he can reveal something which his monastic brothers, busy at the scriptoria in medieval Erznka, could not. And that his poetry, which comes from the divine treasuries of God, does something that other forms of knowledge production do not.

In the Garden of Minstrel-Nightingales

Did Kostandin ever leave the monastery? Or did he attempt to compose his divine words within its sturdy walls? Although the details of his life are unclear, we have at least some idea of whom he might have met and spent time with in his late adolescence and early adulthood. It would hardly have escaped Kostandin that one of the most luminary Armenian poets of the age, the erudite Hovhannēs Erznkats'i Pluz, came from his city and had certain designs for it.

Hovhannēs was born around 1230, which made him at least a decade Kostandin's senior. Unlike Kostandin, the monastically trained Hovhannēs had attained the rank of *vardapet* (doctor or teacher of the church). He traveled extensively between Erznka, Jerusalem, and Georgia and was renowned by both king and catholicos in Cilicia. There was good reason for this: Hovhannēs was an intellectual giant, keenly attuned to cultures of literary production both east and west of Erznka. His writings thus cover a dazzling breadth of subjects, ranging from an Armenian summary of the *Rasāʾil ikhwān al-ṣafāʾ* (*Epistles of the Brethren of Purity*), a tenth-century compendium of philosophical and scientific treatises in Arabic, to his learned *Hawakʿumn meknutʿean kʿerakani* (*Compilation of Commentary on Grammar*), which includes a section on poetics and music based partly on various interpretations of the Greek *Art of Grammar* by Dionysius Thrax.[46] Like Kostandin, Hovhannēs was clearly the product of multiple worlds—although this does not mean that those worlds were the same.

We first encountered Hovhannēs during our initial sojourn through Rūm. As we recall, he composed a poem in Middle Armenian on the importance of being hospitable toward the *gharīb*, or stranger, in one's midst. It is therefore revealing that he helped to organize an Armenian confraternity in Erznka—an organization that transformed potentially dissimilar men into "brothers," forging kinship bonds rooted in community and religious covenant rather than blood.[47] Moreover, Hovhannēs seems to have modeled this brotherhood explicitly on the Islamicate *akhī* or *futuwwa* movement, as Seta B. Dadoyan and others have demonstrated.[48] These were the same institutions that offered hospitality to travelers like Ibn Baṭṭūṭa as they journeyed through Rūm. Hovhannēs even wrote a series of rules to govern this brotherhood—in part because Muslim fraternal groups penned such treatises of their own—which bears a lofty heading: "The Statute and Regulations of the Concord of the Brothers, Who through Divine Love Were United in Brotherhood with One Another in This Metropolis, Which Is Called Eznkay [Erznka], in the Year 729 [1280]."[49] This constitution, including its supplemental "canons and instructions" (*kanonkʿ ew khratkʿ*) that he composed for "mature, worldly youths," commands adherents to observe the same principles that guided Islamicate brotherhoods: they were to love God and care for one another, attend church and obey its commandments, honor their parents, care for the sick, orphans, and the poor, offer hospitality to outsiders, and learn from visitors, both Christian and non-Christian alike.[50] It therefore seems, in the words of Rachel Goshgarian, that the Erznka fraternity reflected "the Armenian Church's attempt to restructure its own institutions" in light of the popularity, if not ubiquity, of Islamicate urban brotherhoods in Anatolia.[51] This brotherhood developed, at least in part, to accommodate differences of many kinds.

One can observe a complementary—though not symmetrical—form of hospitality that informed literary production. Like many other poets of his time, Hovhannēs composed poetry to interact with and instruct his audience in accessible ways. In fact, he tells us so much himself: "Come, that I may give you instruction [*khrat*] from the word [*ban*] of God," he declares at the start of one oft-cited poem:

> I know that every man cannot learn from scripture [*i grēn*].
> That is why I wrote this, so you may hear it from me.[52]

The poem goes on to narrate, at a lively clip, a story about the expulsion of Adam and Eve from paradise. As it unfolds, we learn that the Fall of Man was redeemed by the sacrifice of Christ, essentially making the narrative one of salvation history. This straightforward retelling of the Bible ends with a familiar claim. Hovhannēs wrote this poem, he asserts, at the request of one of his brothers, who "was upon the way" and needed guidance.[53]

It is not difficult to imagine a figure like Kostandin in this very position: a young poet fresh from the monastery, hungry for a different manner of producing knowledge and a different manner of transmitting it. Seated in a spacious room with other young men, hospitable trays of grapes and sweetmeats arrayed before them, he may well have listened to his elder Hovhannēs reciting stories from the Bible, retold in a poetic idiom so that they "may hear it" in a different way.[54] At least on a generational level, then, this is a story of succession. On one side is the generation of poets such as Hovhannēs and Sulṭān Valad, who were born and began to compose literature at about the same time. On the other are figures like Kostandin and Gülşehrī, the generation that came immediately after, who grew up in a different Rūm than the one of their literary and literal forefathers. In the particular case of Erznka, this is the story of an Armenian scholar, trained by the brightest minds in the church, who transmitted another kind of knowledge to a group of urban "youths" in an increasingly Islamicized and Persianized milieu.

Of course, we do not know what—if any—kind of relationship Hovhannēs and Kostandin actually had. Still, as Van Lint has shown, there is good reason to think that members of the Erznka brotherhood regarded the writings of Hovhannēs and Kostandin as related. The earliest known collection of Kostandin's poetry, copied in 1336 by a certain Baron Amir Pʻōlin in Tabriz, opens with a sermon by Hovhannēs, implicitly staging the entire compendium under a homiletic light.[55] It is immediately followed by one of Kostandin's didactic poems. Revealingly, just as Hovhannēs narrates the story of Adam and Eve in his poetry, so does Kostandin retell the Fall of Man in the first poem of this collection, expanding the scope of salvation history to include other significant events from the Bible. It seems reasonable, then, to depict Kostandin as a natural torchbearer of Hovhannēs's work, continuing the elder poet's project of adapting lessons from scripture in a poetic idiom.

But this, once more, is not the whole story. After all, Sulṭān Valad likewise continued in the literary footsteps of Rūmī, even as he attempted to draw Greeks and Turks into a more prolonged dialogue. Kostandin similarly engaged with his audience in fresh ways. Tellingly, what he most frequently adapts is not scriptural in origin but rather came from a shared culture of poetry and performance—one that had gradually coalesced over the previous century and now expressed itself ubiquitously in Rūm, even in Erznka. To the extent that Kostandin was a kind of poetic successor to Hovhannēs, he was equally the inheritor of a vast literary confluence: the mixture and merger of multiple literary cultures, poised to become something new.

Although I have been examining a particular kind of poetry so far—one that instructs its audience to discern "higher" meanings in unlikely places—it is not necessarily the kind that audiences always craved. Poetry, at its core, often held a social function: it brought people together to enjoy one another's company and to revel in song and dance, even during politically uncertain and unsettling times. Kostandin's audience repeatedly asked him to compose such poetry, hinting at an intersecting literary landscape that extended far beyond the boundaries of the "Christian" or the "Armenian." Though he somewhat begrudgingly granted these requests, it is illuminating that a body of convivial poetry widely attributed to Kostandin does not appear in the explicitly devotional manuscript copied in 1336.[56] Yet these poems are essential for understanding the milieu in which Kostandin's poetic sensibility emerged, endowing him with a perspective on verse that even his elders, such as Hovhannēs, do not seem to have shared.

Revealingly, Hovhannēs's overt didacticism is nowhere to be found in these convivial poems. Instead, Kostandin depicts himself and his companions gathered in a lush and vibrant garden, seduced by the graceful movements of a lovely dancer, with nary a monastery in sight. "Such a poised, pleasing sapling, / lovely in countenance, has come to me," he sings. "No other man alive has seen / that which my eyes beheld."[57] He offers a rapturous feast for the senses as the poem continues, focusing his attention on the movements of this supple dancer, drawing on loanwords from Arabic, Persian, and Turkish as he sings:

> When I see her, dancing with charm [*nāz*],
> A moonlike visage [*ṣūrat*], black [*siyāh*] in hair,

I rise, lute [*sāz*] in hand, to face her,
[Saying], "I shall willingly be [your] slave."[58]

At the poem's conclusion, Kostandin confesses that he has recited others of its kind at such gatherings (*zhoghov*).[59] As though to excuse this exercise, he blames his "transitory, errant poetry" on his audience. "There are brothers, affectionate to us, / who desire a worldly poem [*ashkharhi ban*] in writing," he explains in the poetic equivalent of a light shrug. "Because of this, I recited / many a poem of love in a well-known voice [*dzayn*]."[60]

Kostandin seems to have shared his audience's desire to hear the melodic "voices" of others in many ways. These voices speak to a mode of literary production and performance that had become commonplace in Rūm. It is not merely that Kostandin's poems are replete with words from other languages but rather that these loanwords double as key terms in an intersecting culture of poetic performance. For instance, in another poem Kostandin sits in a fragrant garden surrounded by intoxicated companions. "Cupbearer, fill and offer the cup," he supplicates while regaling his audience with "a thousand stories."[61] Kostandin's term for "cupbearer" (*sāqī*) comes to us either from Persian or through the intermediary of Turkish, his "garden" (*bāghcha*) and "myriad tales" (*hazār dāstān*) are of Persian origin, his "cup" (*qədḥā*) entered the Classical Armenian lexicon from Syriac, and the "wine" (*gini*) is Armenian—they all mix together here in an intoxicating brew. This poem even thematizes the commingling of its styles and sounds. "Minstrel!" Kostandin bellows in a later verse, employing the Arabic and Persian term *muṭrib*, which also means "musician" or "singer." He continues: "Tune the six-stringed guitar [Turkish: *çaşta*] / so the slender one may dance upon the square [Arabic: *maydān*]."[62] Nor does the slender dancer sing necessarily Armenian songs. "Her lips bear a *parda*," Kostandin declares, using a Persian term for "melody." "Dulcet and sweet [Persian: *shīrīn*] is her voice."[63] And then he gives perhaps the most tongue-in-cheek line in all of medieval Armenian literature. In this garden, he acknowledges, "there are many minstrel-nightingales [*muṭrib bulbul*]; they speak many poems of love."[64]

The nightingale, represented here by the Persian loanword *bulbul* and not the native Armenian *sokhak*, is an apt representative of this polyphonic garden of poetic performance. In Persian, Turkish, Greek, and Armenian verse from this period, the nightingale often represents the poet—an amorous harbinger of song. "In the garden of the beloved, I am a nightingale [*bülbül*]," Yūnus Emre pronounces. "I came to rejoice and sing in the beloved's garden."[65] We find similar expressions in the poetry of others: "Because he is my rose and rose garden," Rūmī sings, "I became a singing nightingale [*bulbul*]."[66] In an analogous fashion, Digenēs Akritēs built his home in a garden full of songbirds. The sweet voice of his wife, we are told, surpassed even the warbling of nightingales. Much like Kostandin in the scene he envisions with the lovely dancer, Digenēs joins his wife by playing the lute. "When the sound of the lute turned into dance tunes," we are told, "the lovely girl rose from her couch at once. . . . I'm quite unable to describe her movements, / the turning of her hands, her shifting feet; / these were done lightly, following the music, / while twists accompanied the striking lute."[67]

Arguably, in Kostandin's verse there emerges an intersecting milieu in which audiences gathered to hear—even to request!—an intermingling of poetic and musical traditions: something like a converging Arabo-Perso-Greco-Turko-Armenian poetics that formed and re-formed in manifold ways. Poetry therefore not only reflects but potentially enacts the "mixing" of cultures and languages. Hence Kostandin is a "minstrel-nightingale," but he is also accompanied by a slender dancer whose own "sweet voice" bursts with familiar melodies while he plucks the *sāz* and his companion plays the *çaşta*—the Turkish or Kurdish term for the Persianate *shashtār*. In these lyrics and sounds, the "Armenian" commingles with the "Persian," the "Turkic," the "Greek." Indeed, at least in these worldly poems, Kostandin and his audience do not seem to care about parsing their literary and musical cultures in rigidly ethnic, linguistic, or religious terms. They instead embody a multiplicity of poetics in their performing and performative voices.

But the garden of poetry was not a frictionless open market of exchange, fraternity, and conviviality. To the extent that Kostandin sings in a kindred voice, cognizant of other poetics and other peoples, at times he seems uneasy about these intersections. Hence his words are "transitory" and "errant." As we have seen, with convergence comes a palpable need to differentiate—to mark new limits for what is "Christian" and what is "Muslim," or between what is Persian, Turkish, Greek, or Armenian, at a time when such distinctions were not always apparent in music or poetry. Kostandin felt this imperative even as he articulated a shared poetic language for the enjoyment of his brothers. It was clear to him that he needed to instruct them to do certain kinds of interpretive work—even in ways and in places that Hovhannēs had not envisioned. And so a different praxis of adaptation and a different form of cross-cultural mixing began to take hold in his mind.

A Praxis of Poetry

Kostandin's new praxis, exhibited in the devotional manuscript copied in 1336, is showcased in one of his most famous poems. The work bears a simple heading: "This poem tells of Christ through the example of the rose."[68] Here too Kostandin depicts a fragrant garden on the verge of spring. And here too do the birds burst into song, intoxicated by the ravishing aroma of a blossoming world. Yet all is not peaceful in the garden.

One freshly budded flower, the jealous violet, hatches a plot to kill the rose before it can bloom. The mountain cowslip, the meadow saffron, the water lily, and the narcissus all conspire to assist in this evil deed. Fortunately, their plan never comes to fruition. At the last minute, a warbling nightingale (Persian: *bulbul*) bursts into the garden with good tidings. "The rose has awoken from sleep in his verdant tent!" it proclaims.[69] The wicked flowers disperse, put to shame. Meanwhile, the nightingale swoops to the side of the rose, singing in intoxicated revelry:

> Love is the tree and love the flower, and love the voice [*dzayn*] of birds in the tree,
> Love is the rose and love the *bulbul*, perched lovingly over the rose.[70]

The rose greets the nightingale in kind: "I too am lord of love, thus the center of my heart is yellow."[71] After all, love does not come without some degree of sorrow, just as there is no rose without thorns.

S. Peter Cowe, in an influential article, rightly observes that Kostandin is the first Armenian poet known to have adopted the rose and the nightingale in his verse, which he seems to have modeled explicitly on Islamicate poetry.[72] The sudden appearance of these well-worn figures in Armenian poetry at this time is not surprising. As we have seen, a culture of poetic adaptation had taken root in Anatolian soil over the previous century, facilitated by the interventions of particular poets, the intersections of different audiences, and the circulation of units larger and smaller than texts across literary systems. Thus, what is unusual—and highly revealing—is not necessarily the appearance of the rose and the nightingale in Kostandin's poetry but rather what he does with them. Gradually, as the poem continues, the nightingale fades from view. Then the bird disappears entirely. In its stead, the rose tells us, wise men enter the garden:

Those physicians [*hak'ĕmnin*] pick me, bear me off, mix me with sugar,
And fashion a rose conserve [*kulpashak'ar*], and keep [me] as a remedy for the heart's pain.[73]
Then they bake me in fire and make a sherbet for the market;
[Some] buy me and carry me off, [as] a remedy for every affliction of the infirm.

And they extract the water of my heart and pour me in glass bottles;
They sell me as rose water, [for] I have the fragrance of immortality.
For this reason I freely bare the center of my heart, which is yellow.
Whoever sees my heart exposed, let him come and hear my woes.[74]

In the place of the rose garden, we now encounter a world of shops and stalls, the jostling panoply of the marketplace. In the place of the poet-nightingale, we meet the *hak'ĕm* (Persian: *ḥakīm*), or physician, who knows how to mix an enticing remedy—a palatable medicine—for "the heart's pain." And in the place of the rose, flourishing in its native garden, we find rose conserve, the flowery paste of petals and sugar that is used as a cure "for every affliction of the infirm." Finally, the rose makes a striking command: anyone who glimpses its heart should listen to its tales of sorrow, the fundamental complaint (*gangat*) of love and of lovers.

What are we to make of these lines? Medieval audiences, it seems, had difficulty interpreting the rose's speech. This is not altogether startling—after all, Kostandin's "brothers" had probably listened to poems about nightingales before and may have had certain expectations for the theme. But Kostandin quite clearly did not wish to compose only "worldly" poetry, devoid of instruction (*khrat*), for his affectionate brothers. He therefore insists, in the heading of the next poem in his collection, that listeners attend to his words more carefully. "A concise exegesis on the rose," he writes, girding his belt to correct misunderstanding. "I fashioned this for the unlearned," he explains, "for they thought that the poem of this rose was of the world [*marmnaw(orats')*, more literally "of the body"]. So for that reason, I wrote this."[75] We are then treated to a remarkable metamorphosis as Kostandin leads us almost line by line through the original poem, carefully bringing its hidden meanings into the light of day:

> Brother, give ear and take heed, that I may recite an explanation [*meknut'iwn*]:
> Who is the crimson rose, or who are those flowers?
> Or who is the love of the rose, or who is the voice of the nightingale?
> Or who are those flowers that took flight from the rose?
>
> The flowers who gathered: those are the priests of the old law;
> And the inflamed crimson rose: this was Jesus, the only begotten of the Father.
> The violet who assembled all the flowers alike:
> That was the disciple Judas, who betrayed the celestial king unto death.
>
> And "*the nightingale suddenly arises and cries over the rose*":
> That was the trumpet of the resurrection, which resounded at dawn;
> The rose, who "*rent his green tunic [Persian / Turkish:* qabā*] and donned satin [Persian / Turkish:* aṭlas*] and scarlet [Persian / Turkish:* qirmizī*]*":
> That was Christ, who, by his blood, arose in heaven from the dead.[76]

As Kostandin's explanation continues, the familiar tale of the rose and the nightingale miraculously transmutes into the story of Christ's crucifixion, resurrection, and ascension. Thus, as Kostandin explains, the flowers who fled from the rose were "the soldiers, who became like the dead at [his] fearsome voice."[77] Other flowers were Jews who converted to Christianity or the demons who "trembled with terror" at Christ's resurrection.[78] Much like Hovhannēs, who realized that not everyone can learn from scripture, Kostandin uses a familiar poetic tableau to instruct his audience—in this case, by overlaying the panorama of Christ's final days on earth upon the rose-and-nightingale trope, which previously was not part of the symbolic vocabulary of Armenian Christianity in Rūm. It is clear that Kostandin, like Hovhannēs, wished to transmit knowledge of Christianity to his spiritual "brothers" through the medium of poetry.

Yet Kostandin departs from Hovhannēs's praxis in important ways. For instance, the poem that Hovhannēs composed on Adam and Eve follows a linear narrative path. Though couched in a poetic form and pleasing rhyme scheme, the poem does not attempt to transform a Persianate poetics into mystical Christian signifiers. And why should it? If the aim was truly to transmit knowledge of Christianity in a simple manner, to clarify scripture and church doctrine for the unlettered, why crowd the scene with a hodgepodge of distracting metaphors? After all, as Kostandin begrudgingly admits, the presence of his rose and nightingale seems to have thrown the audience for a loop, as they interpreted these figures in accordance with "the flesh" or "the world" and not through the "eyes of the soul."[79] So why write like this at all?[80]

To address these questions, one must look beyond the horizons of Armenian literary production once more. In essence, Kostandin's audience had difficulty seeing the rose and the nightingale in a Christian light: their expectations for the poem were too firmly established. Kostandin, however, was hardly the only poet to struggle with this problem. Rūmī also rewrote popular tropes and stories, particularly from the well-known *Kalīla and Dimna*, knowing full well that his adaptations would "oppose the received way in which the fables are read," as Christine van Ruymbeke has observed.[81] In the most blatant example, Rūmī acknowledges his audience's familiarity with one story from the *Kalīla and Dimna* while shattering any preexisting expectations about what it means. "You would have read [this story] in the *Kalīla*," he warns his listeners, "but that / is the tale's rind and this is the kernel of [its] spirit."[82] True to form, what follows is no longer a simple tale of three fishermen but rather a complex meditation on ritual ablution.

In essence, as Rūmī tells us elsewhere, he sought not merely to show audiences what popular stories "really" mean but rather to free them from overly relying on outward appearance. Those who cleave too tightly to external form, to the most literal meanings of words and stories, might as well complain that the characters of Kalīla and Dimna, who are both jackals, cannot actually speak.[83] To insist on a literal reading of their (frankly impossible) discourse would only double down on a paradox. It would be acting, Rūmī tells us, like a king who hears a fable about a miraculous tree and then wastes his resources to acquire its nonexistent fruit.[84] The tree—the outward form of our stories—is ultimately only a heuristic and hence should serve as a tool for accessing higher secrets beyond the field of language. Rūmī thus disavows a slavish dependence on literalism and literary form:

> O brother, a tale is like a cup for measuring goods,
> and within it spiritual meaning [*maʿnī*] is like grain.
>
> A wise person shall acquire the grain of meaning.
> He shall not notice the measure, though it may be taken away.
>
> Give ear to what transpires between the nightingale and the rose,
> Although no speech is evident in that place.[85]

Rūmī's point here is simple: roses and nightingales do not converse in New Persian sentences. Nor do they speak in Anatolian Turkish, nor in Middle Armenian, nor in any other language. Instead, the symbolic discourse of the rose and the nightingale provides a vital clue that a different game is afoot. The rose and the nightingale are, in no uncertain terms, also heuristics: they signal to an audience to look beyond narrative and uncover another pattern, another mode of meaning making, that is lurking somewhere past the words themselves.

As I have argued throughout this book, one purpose of adapting preexisting literary works was not merely to impart instruction in an entertaining manner but also to make audiences participants in extracting the "kernel" of a story's spirit. Put simply, poetic adaptation obviously aimed to teach audiences to understand preexisting units larger and smaller than texts in new ways. Moreover, such compositional practices trained readers and listeners to generate such meaning for themselves. Kostandin's poetry is therefore revealing for what it doesn't do. He might have simply written the original poem to make its Christian resonances plainer. But Kostandin eschewed this option. The deficiency was not in his poem but rather in how his audience fixated on its outward form: its "flesh" or "body." They weren't reading it right.

And so Kostandin led his public on a journey back through the principal lines of his poem, culminating in a return to its strange ending. In a similar vein as Rūmī's rewriting of a tale from *Kalīla and Dimna* to comment on ritual ablution, Kostandin reimagines the poetics of the rose and the nightingale as a complex rumination on the divine sacraments, the only remedy for the sorrows of heartache. "Whoever sees my heart exposed, let him come and hear my woes," the rose laments, much as the *nay* commands us to listen to its complaints in the *Masnavī*. Though formally different in nearly every important way, these works are similar insofar as they seek to reveal meaning in seemingly mundane places, extracting divine secrets from prosaic sources.[86] Kostandin and Rūmī both felt the drive to mix, to rewrite, and to recombine. More important, they both used their compositions to impart that drive to others.

The unusual ending of Kostandin's poem encapsulates this drive perfectly. In fact, the poem thematizes this transformation, a kind of alchemy that turns one thing (a poem on the rose and the nightingale) into another (a meditation on divine secrets). Though wise men may enter the garden and sell its roses as medicine in the market, their labor is anything but mundane. Kostandin thus invites his audience to reread his original verses with fresh eyes:

> *"Those physicians [*hakʿĕmnin*] pick me, bear me off, mix me with sugar,*
> *And fashion a rose conserve [*kulpashakʿar*], and keep [me] as a remedy for the heart's pain."*
> That was the body of Christ, the bread of life of Mass,
> And the physicians are the priests, the remedy and the doctor of the sinner.
>
> *"Then they bake me in fire and make a sherbet for the market;*
> *[Some] buy me and carry me off, [as] a remedy for every affliction of the infirm."*
> That was the blood of Jesus, the atoner of the transgressor's sins,
> Which all of those sick in sin shall take and be made well.
>
> *"And they extract the water of my heart and pour me in glass bottles;*
> *They sell me as rose water, [for] I have the fragrance of immortality."*
> Those are the soldiers, who pierced [me]; streams of water and blood burst forth;
> That water was the sign of the baptismal font, our eternal salvation.[87]

The simplicity of Kostandin's commentary belies the complexity of the instruction he seeks to bestow. The rose has long been a symbol of God in Persian poetry, playing on a visual pun between a word for "rose" (*gul*) and a word for the divine, or the "All" (*kull*).[88] Kostandin extends this metaphor to its most logical Christian conclusion: if Jesus is the rose, then the sundry products distilled from the rose—conserves, sherbets, and rose water—must therefore be analogues of communion and baptism, those remedies for sin.

The correspondence here is apt. Roses were one of the four Galenic cordial flowers, prized for their medicinal properties throughout the premodern Mediterranean world.[89] It is unlikely that Kostandin and his brothers did not use such aromatic products in Erznka. Muslims and Christians would have settled their stomachs with a little rose conserve after an unpleasant meal, just as they would have occasionally perfumed their homes with a sprinkling of rose water. On one level, then, Kostandin's exegesis is clearly a commentary on the sacraments of the Armenian Church. We are to reflect on the holy body and blood of Christ as medicines akin to floral remedies that were already consumed by Muslims, Christians, and Jews in medieval Rūm. Kostandin here translates the everyday wares of the bazaar, the economic heart of Erznka, into a Christological framework. However, on another level he guides his audience to reflect on rose products in terms of Christ's body and blood. His is a project of correspondence construction, akin to the poetry of Nersēs Shnorhali, and the correspondence cuts both ways.

What Kostandin's poem teaches, then, is how to get at "the kernel of [the] spirit" of things—including a shared poetic language in Anatolia, the rituals and sacraments of the Armenian Church, and even the everyday, aromatic wares of the bazaar. Its hermeneutic is expansive, overflowing from the hidden wellsprings of a text (or a voice) and moving outward into the social and spiritual world of medieval Erznka. Kostandin may have fretted that his "worldly" songs were devoid of "instruction" or that he was neglecting his divine calling by acting as merely another "minstrel-nightingale" in the garden of Rūm. But perhaps he also reassured himself with the knowledge that his audience was capable of discerning *khrat*, instruction, even in unlikely or unexpected places—including those convivial gatherings that mixed multiple poetic cultures together.[90] After all, in poetry, nightingales still sing of God.

The Wisdom of Poetry

Our story ends with one final adaptation, informed by a theory and praxis of poetic composition that could not be contained within any single linguistic or cultural context. Kostandin is poised to give a performance, and we, his audience, have gathered round. This time we have a good idea of what he will chant, since we asked for this composition ourselves. And when Kostandin opens his mouth and begins to recite—

> In the name of the uncreated and mighty God,
> In the name of the Father and the Son, who is the only begotten[91]

—we are delighted and astonished in equal measure. He has pulled it off. We hear many voices in his voice, including the alluring cadence of the *Shāh-nāma*, the sound of the Persian epic of epics, rendered in a Middle Armenian idiom. However, Kostandin's voice reveals more than his stunning poetic prowess. In his performance, if we listen carefully, we can discern a broad pattern that had shaped literary production in Rūm over the previous century and had now converged to reinvent itself again, this time through the Armenian voicing of a Persian epic.

As we have seen throughout our journey, poetry in Rūm often gestated particular forms of knowledge within audiences, such as *adab* (Arabic for "manner" or "way of conduct"), *khirad* (Persian for "wisdom"), and *khrat* (Armenian for "instruction"). Such "wisdom" crucially transformed the intersecting poetic languages of Anatolia—with their ubiquitous mixing of compositional units smaller and larger than individual texts—into a language of affinity, a framework that reified certain forms of religious difference even while dissolving boundaries in the linguistic, cultural, and aesthetic realms. Thus, in Kostandin's hands the rose and the nightingale are not mere allegories for biblical narratives. Rather, his adaptations serve as guides to interpreting the words, the aesthetics, the ideas, and the symbolic languages of many peoples living in a shared space. His poetry enables audiences to navigate not only cultural and religious difference but also cultural and religious convergence. Poetry makes convergence permissible, or meaningful in the right way.

This is essentially what Kostandin's *Shāh-nāma* does: it teaches its audience to reflect upon the original text and upon their lives simultaneously.

Kostandin does not forbid us to listen to Firdawsī's *Shāh-nāma*, though he does mediate and subtly change our experience of it. Hence, as Kostandin reports, he composed this poem only to offer "the beautiful discourse of instruction [*khrat*]."[92] But in this attempt to impart wisdom, something strange happens. Troublingly, as Kostandin continues to sing, he seems to condemn a world not so different from his own:

> This cupbearer [*saghi*] sits among the great assembly [*jamyiat'*];
> [His] words false, he brings nothing of value [*ghimat'*].
>
> A draft of death is in the wine he shares;
> In more ways than one, those who drink it grow tipsy.
>
> They are dead in soul but seem alive—
> Whoever imbibes from those bottles of wine.
>
> They have grown inebriated [*sarkhōsh*] by their heart's desire [*murat*];
> They have fallen, with a heavy charge, into a great, ill mire.
>
> They do not possess the eyes of the mind, they do not look here and there,
> They do not know—they are bound, in a dungeon, in iron![93]

Kostandin's intention is to counsel and to warn: we must not love this world, and we must not consort with those he calls "the ignorant," who have fallen under the spell of worldly pleasures.[94] As Van Lint has posited, it could hardly have escaped Kostandin's public, who once asked him to compose love songs "in a well-known voice," that these lines seem to present an inversion of their "ethical as well as aesthetic values."[95] Thus, whereas the *saghi* (Persian: *sāqī*) once brought the pleasure of companionship and wine, he now serves death and decay. Meanwhile, since fools "do not possess the eyes of the mind," they cannot even discern their spiritual state to realize what is happening.

Kostandin's adaptation, only eighty-eight lines in total, largely hammers home this single point: death awaits us all. Even a "mighty *pādishāh*" such as the Ilkhanid ruler Ghāzān, who is the only historical figure named in the poem, cannot escape its icy grip.[96] On first glance, especially in comparison with the rich narrative worlds of Firdawsī's *Shāh-nāma*, this might seem something of a letdown. However, there is reason to suppose that such didacticism was not so unexpected—or unwelcome—to Kostandin's audience. After all, he had been steadily training his brothers to extract hidden meaning—*khrat*, instruction—from poetry for some time. The brothers were hardly green in this mode of instruction or composition. Even more important, they had good cause to expect "instruction" from an Armenian *Shāh-nāma* in particular.

This is because Firdawsī also placed a high premium on the cultivation of wisdom, which he called *khirad*, a term derived from Middle Persian, like the Armenian *khrat*. As we have seen, Firdawsī opens his *Shāh-nāma* by invoking God as the "Lord of life and wisdom [*khirad*]." Immediately after, he praises wisdom in an encomium that casts the entire epic in a particular light:

> Now, O sage [*khiradmand*], the time is right
> For reciting the worth of wisdom [*khirad*].
>
> For as wisdom [*khirad*] is better than all else God gave you,
> It's best to render it praise, if you're on a just path.
>
> Wisdom finds the way; wisdom thrills the heart,
> And, in both worlds, wisdom guides your hand.[97]

Like Kostandin, Firdawsī commands his audience to distance themselves from the ignorant, as those who "possess no wisdom [*khirad*]" cause much harm.[98] "The sober label [the ignorant one] mad," Firdawsī councils, warning that fools are ostracized even by their kin.[99] In the works of both poets, instruction and wisdom (*khrat*/*khirad*) serve as the organizing principles of society, the forces that align the soul with the celestial order, and the lenses through which we must read poetry. "Wisdom is the eye of the soul," Firdawsī concludes. "When you look / without eyes, you will not sojourn through the world merrily."[100] Much later, in the city of Erznka, Kostandin would offer the same advice to his Armenian brotherhood. The ignorant, he declares, "do not possess the eyes of the mind" and therefore do not "look here or there," in this world or the next.[101] The aim of both *Shāh-nāma*s, then, is to restore the audience's sight.

In short, Kostandin's emphasis on instruction—the exact, didactic heart of his poem—is not an aberration but rather an adaptation of Firdawsī's epic. And in this labor he is anything but unique. As the literary historian

Nasrin Askari has observed, during this period "numerous works were composed on the model of the *Shāhnāma*, emulating its form, metre, language, and style, but focused on different mythical, historical, and religious figures."[102] Diverse poets mined the *Shāh-nāma* especially for its perceived didactic content, some in cities not so distant from Erznka. For instance, in 1335, Ḥamdallāh Mustawfī composed the *Ẓafar-nāma*, a versified history from the days of the Prophet to the time of Ilkhanid rule. He wrote it in Qazvin, just south of where Kostandin's early collection of poems would be copied in 1336. Mustawfī not only repeatedly cites Firdawsī and employs the *Shāh-nāma*'s meter but also imitates its invocation to God, following this with praise of wisdom (*khirad*), just as Kostandin does. Of course, Mustawfī presents his poetry as a mirror for princes not to an urban confraternity, as Kostandin does, but instead, as he claims, to the Ilkhanid court near Qazvin. It is clear that these poets created new *Shāh-nāma*s to instruct different audiences for different ends—and the wisdom they revealed likewise meant different things to their dissimilar publics.

It is hardly unusual that a multilingual Armenian poet in a region where Persian literature was popular—and where such adaptive techniques proliferated—would compose poetry in this manner. Nor is it unusual that such an Armenian poet would choose the *Shāh-nāma*, a touchstone of literary adaptation during this period, as the basis for composing a new poem on wisdom. After all, Kostandin's praxis of adaptation is essentially no different than that of his contemporaries: he borrowed liberally from literary works that circulated between Khorasan and Rūm, rewriting them for the instruction of his local audience but preserving a kindred relationship between the new poem and the old, encoded on formal, lexical, and thematic levels. This is the entire thrust behind his mode of composition: the new poem putatively carries the inner meanings of the old poem even while discarding parts of its "rind," or narrative particularity. And so the new composition advances an implicit claim: it succeeds, works alongside, and sometimes rivals the authority of the original text. Of course, when that original text was the Bible or the Qur'an, this was no small undertaking.

Given his peers to the west in Konya and to the east in Qazvin, Kostandin's praxis as a poet, not to mention his conception of poetry, achieves one last alchemical transformation: it begins to look ordinary. In fact, most everything that he did looks rather ordinary in a comparative light. And if he is ordinary—at least to the extent that he followed and reinforced a broad pattern—then so too are his contemporaries. Gülşehrī is ordinary. Yūnus Emre is ordinary. Sulṭān Valad is ordinary. Even Rūmī, in this sense, is ordinary. Though divided in different generations, all of these poets grappled with similar concerns about their communities, compositions, and calling as a poet. They lived only short distances from one another and often shared aesthetic, theological, and intellectual tool kits. Their development as poets consequently followed pathways that were common but not unique to medieval Rūm. After all, as the proliferation of *Shāh-nāma*s suggests, the more we trace currents of literary adaptation elsewhere, the more Anatolia begins to look ordinary too.

Kostandin's literary education, like that of his peers, helps to make this pattern of composition legible today. Like Hovhannēs, he realized that "every man cannot learn from scripture" and that the role of literature in a robust society was thus to instruct as well as to entertain.[103] Like Nersēs Shnorhali and Frik, he recognized the utility of composing poetry in locally accessible and resonant ways, of speaking both literally and figuratively in a language that people could comprehend. Like ʿĀşıḳ Paşa and Gülşehrī, he intuitively grasped that poetry is tied to the production of knowledge and can help to translate an episteme across languages. Like Sulṭān Valad, he believed that true poetry comes from on high and therefore serves a revelatory function in society. And like Rūmī, he recognized the need to train an audience to read texts for more than their outer form. Kostandin thus guided his brothers to suss out divine meanings in everyday places, both from preexisting literary tropes and from the sights, sounds, and stories of premodern Erznka.

The relationships between poets and their communities transfigured the literary landscape of Anatolia on a macro scale, just as they shaped the individual lives of poets and their audiences on a micro scale. For both Kostandin and Rūmī, it was not only a sunlike stranger from a distant realm who gifted them with a particular theory and praxis of poetry. Instead, something more like this land, the milieu that shaped their lives, bestowed upon them an ability and desire to compose verse. From the country he called home, Kostandin learned that composition is a meaning-making endeavor with high stakes: in his context, one that sought to sort and sift, to differentiate and divide urban life according to a shifting stance on what was acceptable for Christians (and Muslims) to hear, to see, and to reproduce. This was Kostandin's most keenly intuited lesson, the guiding force of his literary production, and the supple wisdom underlying his *Shāh-nāma*. Poetry does not serve a merely didactic or missionary function, although it was closely tied to trends of Islamization and counter-Islamization in medieval Anatolia. Rather, poems are the very matrices of meaning, the microcosmic windows through which one peers at the world. To adapt the poetry of others is, in no small way, to dare to change that world and its inhabitants. Including, of course, oneself.

EPILOGUE

Poetry from the Inside Out

Though it is wingless, featherless,
It goes faster than the swallow.
It roams aimlessly from country to country,
It returns, it comes, bringing many guests.
—*Nersēs Shnorhali*

O Solomon, tune the strings of that *ḳopuz*,
That we may learn this language of the birds.
—*Gülşehrī*

The answer to Nersēs's avian riddle found above and in this book's epigraph is *mitkʿ*—reason, advice, mind, counsel, idea. Or, if one prefers, meaning.[1] The riddle suggests a manner of thinking that cannot be confined but instead bursts forth to soar over diverse terrains below. This way of thinking is not predetermined—it does not seem to have a destination; it loops idly back and forth, moving in multiple directions, airy and light, tracing rhizomes in the sky. Meaning cannot be controlled—at least not permanently. It does, however, do something. Meaning, the poem suggests, organizes our thoughts—"guests" in Nersēs's parlance—just as it beckons others from distant realms. Meaning is a force; it works on the world. This force takes a literal turn in the poem's concluding lines: "It draws out the water of rivers from rivers, / it levels fortress, home, and hill." Meaning is transformative, terraforming, and mobile.

A complementary though somewhat different idea runs through the verses of Gülşehrī. For him, the language of birds is more than a mere assemblage of words. It is the language that lies beneath language, an organizational principle of creation, and the source of meaning. Moreover, this language has a genealogy: it is transmitted by special figures who receive it directly from the divine. In this book, those figures have been poets. Because we the audience do not enjoy such direct access, we must acquire meaning in a different way. And so we need poets, who so often happen to be charismatic leaders in their religious communities, to tighten the strings of their lutes and to sing a few carefully chosen words—to teach us to hear the song, to discern the pattern, behind the words.

This book has told a particular story about those poets who sought to make "meaning" out of difference at a pivotal moment in the literary history of medieval Anatolia. Many have been misunderstood as mere versifiers or misconstrued as figures who valued literature only for its so-called propagandistic dimension. Yet as I have shown, these poets and their coteries were adept at engaging one another, in rewriting canonical texts such as the Qur'an and the Bible, and in subtly responding to or co-opting the literary models of others. These poets matter, even if their aesthetics do not delight or inform audiences today in the same manner as they once did, in part because they demonstrate that a widespread process was at work: a mode of composing literature via the adaptation of preexisting literary works and codes, transforming difference into languages of affinity. Awash in a world of others, poets in Anatolia became dazzling readers of cultural, religious, and linguistic heterogeneity—and so did their communities.

In bringing to light this alternate account of composition, this book also brings to light a different Anatolia, one whose agency was subtly felt across the literary production of its heterogeneous peoples. Anatolia was the nexus of a convergence, a conflux of historical currents that gradually transformed the demographic, linguistic, political, and religious ecosystem. In this gestalt, these changes had a profound effect on literary production and consequently on knowledge production, spurring the lateral movement and reconfiguration of "wisdom" across many languages. Of course, the agency of a place—let alone a place as large and diverse as medieval Anatolia—is hardly the same as the agency of a poet or other author. Places do not write words, after all. People do. But as we have seen, places shape poets and their communities. Places inscribe their intangible scripts upon individuals: repeating sets of variables that persist longer than the span of a normal life. Call it a baseline, an iterative, a meter, or a mode. Call it a pattern: the framework that makes improvisation possible.

Let us return, one last time, to the story of Hovhannēs and Asha, which was likely composed around when or shortly after our story reached its conclusion. Asha asks Hovhannēs to love her. "It will be sweet," she promises in Armenian. And Hovhannēs is sorely tempted by this proposal. He feels an undeniable attraction to Asha's voice, which shares the same underlying meter as his own. Her voice, like his, is the product of many mixings, obliquely refracting the encounters between multiple peoples over the previous century.

Yet Hovhannēs and Asha cannot—and never really could—act freely on this attraction. The picture is always more complicated, and not just because one is an Armenian and the other a Turk. In a sense, the poem is less about two star-crossed lovers than about the societies in which they live. Gradually, figures from these seeming peripheries loom into view. The first is Hovhannēs's mother, who comes forth to admonish her son:

> [Here] is Hovhannēs's mother, boy.
> She wears a cloak over sackcloth,
> Wandering the monasteries above,
> Promising incense and candles.
>
> [*His mother speaks:*] "Monks, say: I have sinned.
> Deacons, say: Lord, have mercy.
> Perhaps he will gather his wits,
> And my Hovhannēs will return home."
>
> He uttered not one "Lord, I have sinned."
> Only: "Allah!" And "Shahidullah!"
> Then [all] spoke this reply:
> "Hovhannēs has no way out."

> [*His mother speaks:*] "Hey Hovhannēs, hey my son,
> Return home and say: 'I sinned!'
> Your priest bellows there:
> 'Asha has fallen after him.' "[2]

What becomes clear, in this communal back-and-forth, is that these peripheral figures are not actually peripheral. They are central to the escalation and resolution of this conflict. Love is not merely a family affair, after all, but one that involves the monks, the deacons, and even the priests of Erznka, who each have a share in Hovhannēs's precarious situation. His mother therefore commands these clergymen to reaffirm their creed. Her message is simple: when the boundaries of the community are at stake, everyone is accountable and all must speak words of repentance: "Lord, I have sinned."

Still, Hovhannēs does not acquiesce so easily. He knows he should not consort with Muslims. Yet—having met Asha—he feels that his situation has changed. Straightaway he pleads his case to his mother, appealing directly to their bond of kinship. He knows he has done wrong, and therefore asks her to pardon—to make *ḥalāl*, in his words—the milk he nursed from her body as a babe. He cannot repay this heavy debt:

> Ah, my mother, I'm your servant,
> Pardon me your milk, which I drank.
> My wits were seized and I went mad,
> There's nothing I can do for you.[3]

But his mother is not moved. The mere evocation of old kinship bonds and admission of fault are not enough for her. These bonds must be not dissolved but renewed. Moreover, and most important, their renewal should come through the formal intervention of the church. "I'll bring you an Armenian daughter," she promises him, if he will only renounce Asha. "I'll have you blessed a married priest."[4] Again Hovhannēs declines. There is none like Asha, who possesses "the tongue of the nightingale [Persian: *bulbul*]" and a waist "slender as a Frank's."[5]

Here is the crux of the problem: Hovhannēs has drunk his mother's milk, but he has also heard Asha's voice. He should not have done both. Now opposing claims compete for his affiliation, presenting divergent possibilities for living and belonging in medieval Rūm. Hovhannēs cannot simply return to the monastery, as though sealed away from the worlds beyond his own. Nor, at this point, can the nascent literary cultures of Anatolia be so easily disentangled from one another. In a relatively short time, swept up in waves of literary adaptation, what I have called a praxis of measured hospitality, these cultures have also changed in many ways.

Asha is suggestive of this shift. In the hands of another poet—ʿAṭṭār or Gülşehrī—she might serve as a simple heuristic, the empty vessel of Hovhannēs's desire who tests his faith, for but a moment, before his glorious restoration as a true Christian. However, at least in the context of this dialogic poem, the lover from another religion is no longer only a heuristic. Asha is not even other. She is known. She has a family and a community, and her kinship networks correspondingly assume a historical density in this poem. Asha even names her family members, one by one, as if to clarify herself to Hovhannēs. "They call my grandfather Mullā," she slyly tells him:

> My brother they call the city's viceroy [Persian: *shaḥna*],
> And they call me Asha,
> And my sister Zuluta,
> My mother Fatma,
> And my father they call Qāḍī Mullā.[6]

Her family members similarly exert their wills, even to the point of corporal punishment, upon Asha. She must heed reason, they tell her. The Armenian cannot defend her or offer her help, they tell her:

> Asha was sitting by the window,
> Face in palm, weeping deeply,
> "Today my father, the *qāḍī*, beat me, saying:
> 'Why do you love the son of an Armenian!'
> Look, for once, would Hovhannēs,
> deaf in ear, hurry in his coming?"[7]

Asha's voice might beckon to others, resound with others, sound like others. But the origin of her voice—the body—is not so free. The individual and social body can be disciplined, made to bend in ways that voices, airy and shapeless, often seem to resist. And so, in this poem that openly and performatively celebrates many voices, we find a concomitant struggle to reassert one set of affiliations over another. Of course, this has been our story all along.

To read the literatures of Anatolia—or the literature of any place—from the inside out is, quite obviously, to read them for more than the information they contain. It is to read poetry for what it does—for how it works on its audience in a particular place and time, and how its audience works on it. However, to the extent that poetry is something that shapes community, it is necessarily part of what Cemal Kafadar calls "a socially constructed dialectic of inclusions and exclusions."[8] As this book has shown, the poetry of Anatolia frequently enacted an exclusionary function even in its most inclusive gestures. Poetry often shaped interpretive frameworks that accommodated certain types of heterogeneity—linguistic, cultural, aesthetic—while reinforcing religious boundaries. In the end, not all differences were impassable. But not all differences were permeable either.

Hovhannēs and Asha anticipate a future in which those differences would continue to be negotiated in many ways. Still, in moving beyond the etic boundaries imposed by national literary history, one finds that "difference" does not vanish. Beneath the surface, other boundaries, genealogies, and hierarchies must inevitably remain. In other words, the premodern counterweight to the modern analytic categories of "the national" or "the monolingual" is not necessarily to be found in the equally modern values of cosmopolitanism, tolerance, or coexistence. The proposed ethical and humanist correctives to our present historical moment, in which populist nationalism is undergoing a global resurgence, are not the solutions that our premodern counterparts sought for themselves, in part because the challenges they faced were also different. A literary history of the premodern that merely supplemented the nation form with a toothless, multicultural conviviality would therefore still be etic. In the case of medieval Anatolia, it would also be fictional.

This book has sought, then, to model an emic alternative. It has argued that to understand what boundaries existed between figures like "Hovhannēs" and "Asha," it is necessary to examine the ways in which our premodern subjects drew and redrew boundaries for themselves—how these figures theorized what boundaries are, what boundaries do, and what boundaries demand of the voyagers at their thresholds. As we have seen, the primary mechanism for organizing literary history—the taxonomic family tree—was originally developed to graph formal differences in the natural world. However, literary "boundaries," mediated through the composition of poetry, are obviously not the same as other kinds of limits, such as the naturally occurring borders created by impassable geographic terrains. The boundary in literature is not always morphological or analogically grounded in principles that mirror nature. Instead, it is often a speech act. It is a mode of address, a way of fostering a dynamic and dialogic relationship between poet and audience, that incubates a particular interpretive stance.

Here is another way of putting it: the boundary in literature is not a line in the earth. It is a way of looking *at* the earth, of sorting and differentiating multiple literary fields. To adopt this "sight" was to read the world, through poetry, as a kind of tender palimpsest. After all, even the gentlest scraping of a blade across the world's surface could yield startling, transformative meanings, hidden just beneath the outer form of things. At the same time, the basic premise of this operation, which seeks equally to reveal the hidden spiritual meanings in both scripture and society, generally presupposes an engagement with one scriptural canon over another. Meaning still has a genealogy, even if its potential for signification may not always be possible to control. Hence, Yūnus Emre's nightingale may sing of the Friend, but Kostandin's nightingale sings of Christ.

As this book has argued, the negotiation of these boundaries therefore necessitated a corresponding engagement with multiple other interlocutors in the literary field, whether this dialogue unfolded implicitly or explicitly, consciously or unconsciously, and whether it involved agents that were authors, audiences, texts, or literary codes. Moreover, this engagement had a technical component, finding expression through multiple praxes of literary adaptation. Hence, a diverse portfolio of adaptive techniques often set the terms of how this polyvocal dialogue would unfold, at least insofar as it sought to make cross-cultural contact legible in a particular manner. Many of these practices—such as citation, paraphrase, translation, gloss, and quotation—are well known in scholarly discourse today. Others are less common in Western literary criticism, such as *tażmīn*, yet are represented by rich premodern terminology in Arabic, Persian, and

Turkish. Still other practices, such as the graphic and sonic translation of meter and rhyme across languages, have no precise critical terminology. However, as I contend, one ought to think of this portfolio as greater than the sum of its parts. Compounded over time, these practices helped to shape a widespread sense of what "the literary" is—what the literary looks like, what it speaks of, and what it sounds like—across multiple languages and religious communities. These innumerable and selective acts of "adaptation," so often read as individual and isolated incidents, therefore construct more than texts: they inform the development of literary "codes" themselves. Just as important, these adaptive acts have the potential to facilitate the migration and multiplication of literary codes across languages and cultural contexts.

To view the literary field in this manner—as a network of interlocutors (human and inhuman) rather than a canon of discrete texts—is thus to reenvision one final boundary: the boundary that we draw around the literary "tradition" itself. Whereas the way in which these poets negotiated difference might not have direct ethical or political application today, how they conceptualized what is "literary," in theory and praxis, has never been more relevant to literary studies in a globalized age. After all, to adapt the literatures of "others" is to understand the literary field, including the boundaries around any single literary tradition, as basically mutable. It is to see "tradition" as a kind of process. For much of the past century, at least as regards medieval Anatolia, scholars have often cast this process as the uninterrupted handing down of discrete texts along monolingual and monoethnic pathways of transmission. This conception reflects the etymology of *tradition*, which derives from the Latin *traditio*, meaning "a giving up, delivering up, surrender."[9] However, it is useful to recall that *tradition* and *treason* are doublets, sharing the same root. The "tradition" can transmit itself—can hand itself over—synchronically as well as diachronically, simultaneously betraying its own linguistic, cultural, and geographic boundedness and suggesting new possibilities, even new tellings, for its texts and poetics in other tongues.

This critical perspective—which our premodern subjects often implicitly shared—is fundamentally provisional. It reflects a recognition that no one can have the last word in composition, just as the dialogic literary field cannot be sealed off from new interlocutors. Meaning will eventually slip beyond the author's control, just as the literary code will not allow its potential significations to conform to the intentions and ideologies of only a single community. When we gaze at the literary field of Anatolia in this light, the boundaries of the tradition begin to blur, disaggregating into a fuzzy set of characteristics that mix with other fuzzy sets. From this vantage point, the literary landscape extends horizontally outward in multiple directions, teasing few predetermined trails beneath our feet. The terrain ahead is open and uncertain. Yet as the poets of Anatolia well understood, in uncertainty one can find possibility and freedom too.

Only one option is left to Hovhannēs. He mounts a final appeal, traveling to Erznka to address Asha's elders and plead the case for her hand. He does so, however, in an unusual and even comic manner:

> Mad Hovhannēs, when he heard this,
> Hit the road to Erznka;
> [His] head uncovered, [his] hat in hand,
> He went and stood before the Khan.
>
> He saluted the king;
> They swiftly received his salute.
> He seized the tail of the gray horse,
> He recited a poem [*kafa*] to every hair.[10]

Hovhannēs does not evoke the Qur'an or promise to become a Muslim. Rather, he recites poems—hundreds and hundreds of monorhymed quatrains—known as *kafa*s. We have no idea what they are about, but their content is not so important here. What matters instead is that this recitation allows him to perform a kind of poetic "madness" before a potentially hostile audience.

In other words, through the recitation of poetry, Hovhannēs establishes a positionality that will inform his relationship with the Khan. This positionality carries a distinct message: Hovhannēs is not a heretic with hidden ruses up his sleeve. He is instead a character in a story that would be familiar to this audience: the lovestruck madman, willing to transgress any boundary to reach the hem of his beloved's skirt. In this (strictly) literary realm, his transgressions are not only forgivable but necessary. After all, the protagonists of such stories must journey down the path of crookedness, where boundaries dissolve like midmorning dew, only to arrive safely back at the shores of orthodoxy. Hovhannēs is able to stake this position and lay claim to Asha's hand only by co-opting and speaking in this poetic language. Poetry provides him with both the medium for expressing this affective state and the leverage to insert himself into a new community. In speaking this way, he establishes a kind of poetic reciprocity between himself and the Khan even while coming from a place of difference. He now speaks in a kindred voice.

Soon after this performance, their story comes to an end. Asha commands Hovhannēs to enter the mosque and promenade with the *mullā*s; he counters by lamenting that he has forgotten the Psalms; she consoles him by promising, at last, to become a Christian. Order and orthodoxy are restored. Yet the simplicity of this ending belies a more complex reality. The poem, like much of Anatolia during this brief time, exists in an in-between state in which multiple and mutually exclusive outcomes seem equally possible. The narrative teeters in a superposition of Hovhannēs's potential conversion to Islam and Asha's potential conversion to Christianity. Eventually, however, the moment ends. The box opens and the wave function collapses. A choice must be made, and this choice, like all choices, bears consequences for individual and community alike.

Our characters would not seem to get a happy ending—at least not one that would ever be free of strife, conflict, or friction. But their marriage would, for a time, be generative. In the coming centuries, poetic registers of Middle Armenian, Anatolian Turkish, and medieval Greek would proliferate differently across the literary landscape, just as poets would continue to engage with Persianate aesthetics in many ways. Although the literary landscape would change, an underlying dialogism and praxis of adaptation, emulation, and counterpoint between languages would hardly recede from the scene. If anything, these practices would only flourish.[11] In other words, the true union, the lasting union, would not be the one between Hovhannēs and Asha's bodies following their promised marriage in a Christian church. The real union had already happened. It happened when Asha addressed Hovhannēs in Middle Armenian and he addressed her in Turkish. It happened when Hovhannēs stood before the Khan and decided that in order to negotiate a position in this community, the best course was to recite poetry. And it happened in the composition of this very poem, in which an Armenian voice and a Turkish voice converse, unsettling the boundaries of their world once more.

ACKNOWLEDGMENTS

One of my aims in writing this book, and perhaps my clearest idea in the beginning, was to show how much a community can shape the act of composition. And so I feel happy to pull back the curtain, at least a little, on the composition of this book and reveal the support, labor, encouragement, and advice that many interlocutors put into it. In particular, I am grateful to my mentors, who, having performed the herculean task of shepherding my ideas into a dissertation, continued to push and inspire me as I embarked on this new project. I am especially grateful to Kathryn Babayan, who planted several seeds that grew, eventually, into a different story than the one I expected to write. Without her support and critical eye, this project would likely be very different and perhaps would not exist. My heartfelt thanks to Kevork B. Bardakjian—with whom reading and discussing Armenian poetry has been one of the joys of my education—for always being willing to think through any problem with me. I express my gratitude to Catherine Brown, Kader Konuk, and Karla Mallette, who each read from this project in its various stages, challenged me to think about my material in fresh ways, and inspired me to take this story in new directions. This book would not exist without the National Endowment for the Humanities, to which I will always be thankful for awarding me a fellowship during the 2016–17 academic year. Of course, the views expressed in this publication do not necessarily reflect those of the NEH.

Cameron Cross gamely read the earliest drafts of my earliest chapters, offering much helpful advice, suggestions on poetic translation, and energizing conversation before anyone else had laid eyes on these pages. Austin O'Malley and Matthew Thomas Miller also read this book from front to back, and then a little more on a second round, each time helping me to fine-tune the narrative and case studies throughout. Sergio La Porta, Alison Vacca, and N. İpek Hüner Cora carefully read this book as well; I am grateful for their discerning feedback and for allowing me to read my text through their eyes, both of which improved this story immensely. İpek also kindly allowed me to revisit some of my Turkish translations with her, as did Zeynep Oktay Uslu with a few verses near the end of this project; I am thankful for their suggestions in my search to find a fitting poetic register in translation.

Much later in the process, Peggy McCracken generously played the role of respondent at my book workshop, teaching me much about my own writing and helping me to realign some of the book's larger claims.

Gottfried Hagen has offered much helpful commentary over the long haul of this project, as have Armen Abkarian, Samet Budak, Murat Cankara, Jay Crisostomo, Dzovinar Derderian, Ahmet Barış Ekiz, Shahla Farghadani, and Christopher Sheklian. William Stroebel kindly provided Greek translations for my chapter on Sulṭān Valad, as well as spirited conversation on literary imitation and adaptation. Thanks also to Panagiotis Agapitos, who helped me to think through the aural adaptation of Sulṭān Valad's Greek, and to Fr. Seraphim Dedes, who answered many questions about Byzantine hymns and hymn writing. I've been enriched by talking shop, whether about Anatolia or Ann Arbor, with Jonathan Brack over the years. And I'd be remiss not to thank Leslie Stainton, who initiated me into the art of writing nonfiction, through her own example, not so many years ago.

I was additionally helped, in significant ways, by several institutions I acknowledge here. The Center for Armenian Studies (CAS) at the University of Michigan awarded me a Simone Manoogian Foundation postdoctoral fellowship in the earliest stages of this project, which allowed me precious time to read, to translate, and to reconsider what I thought I knew about medieval Anatolia. My present and past colleagues from CAS—Armen Abkarian, Maral Aktokmakyan, Richard Antaramian, Sebouh David Aslanian, Kathryn Babayan, Kevork Bardakjian, Marie-Aude Baronian, Ali Bolcakan, Tamar M. Boyadjian, Murat Cankara, Etienne Charrière, Yaşar Tolga Cora, Dzovinar Derderian, Karen Jallatyan, Jeremy Johnson, Tuğçe Kayaal, David Leupold, Gerard Libaridian, David Low, Arakel Minassian, Mehmet Polatel, Hakem Al-Rustom, Vahe Sahakyan, Arsène Saparov, S. Ruken Sengul, Anoush Suni, Ronald G. Suny, Melanie S. Tanielian, Alison Vacca, Murat C. Yildiz, and several other graduate students and fellows—were vibrant interlocutors throughout this project, and many of our conversations have found their way into these pages. I have additionally taken inspiration from conversations with Salam Rassi and Alberto Rigolio during our stay at the Hill Museum and Manuscript Library in 2017. The Bodleian Library, the Hill Museum and Manuscript Library, and the Mesrop Mashtots' Institute of Ancient Manuscripts each hospitably facilitated my research in different ways. The National Association for Armenian Studies and Research (NAASR) and the Knights of Vartan Fund for Armenian Studies (FAS) generously supported the indexing and proofreading of this book.

I had the pleasure of working with two wonderful editors at Yale, Sarah Miller and Jaya Aninda Chatterjee, whom I thank for believing in this book and supporting it throughout its production. I'm also grateful to Ash Lago and Eva Skewes, who did much meticulous work to bring it to press; to Juliana Froggatt, for her sagacious copy editing; to Ann-Marie Imbornoni for her guidance during the production of the book; and to Nicole Scholtz, for teaching me to make maps. In truth, there are so many individuals who provided assistance, in ways both large and small, that it is impossible to name them all without, perhaps, wearing out my welcome. Nevertheless, I hope it suffices to say that I have benefited from many other colleagues and friends, near and far, who have helped me to think and write better than I ever could have alone.

This project has also been made possible in less tangible ways. I wrote a great deal of this book in the normal places—research institutions, cramped offices, and so on—but the lion's share of it was completed at the Ann Arbor Public Library, with a hot coffee from Sweetwaters, by the window. My thanks to William Runyan, busy with his own project on global Yiddish literature, who kept me company for much of the process. I especially thank my parents, Jan Bedrosian and Steve Pifer, my sister, Kate, and my departed grandmother Margaret Pifer, for their love and support throughout this project.

Last, I dedicate this book to Knar, dearest friend: I find that it is hard to recall, exactly, all of the time I spent physically writing this story or what those long hours felt like. But it is easy to remember the moments that bookended each of those days, at home together with Dzovig and with you. And to me, that has always been the real adventure.

NOTES

Introduction

1. All translations are my own unless otherwise stated. It is worth noting that the Library of Congress's transliteration system treats the Armenian letter յ as an *h* in the initial position but as a *y* in subsequent positions within a word: thus Hovhannēs, not Yovhannēs, although both reflect the Classical and Western Armenian spelling of the name. Hovhannes is the transliteration of the Eastern Armenian orthography.

For the portion of the poem translated here, see Hovhannēs Erznkats'i, *Hovhannes Erznkats'i,* 163–64, lines 9–25. This work is usually ascribed to the thirteenth-century poet and theologian Hovhannēs Erznkats'i, though the attribution is contested. James R. Russell, for instance, instead credits the fourteenth-century poet Hovhannēs T'lkurants'i. See Russell's discussion and translation of the poem in *Yovhannēs T'lkuranc'i and the Mediaeval Armenian Lyric Tradition,* 105–6. See also S. Peter Cowe's translation and discussion on attribution ("The Politics of Poetics," 389, 400–403, 401n101, 403n106).

2. Hovhannēs Erznkats'i, *Hovhannes Erznkats'i,* 164–65, lines 26–30. In an exact transliteration (with Western Armenian pronunciation), the Turkish reads: "Eōru, eōru, geawur oghli, Geōt'ur bizdēn muhal sozi, Sēn Hovhannēs, k'ēshish oghli, Bēn miwsiwrman[,] mōlla ghĕzi."

3. We might hear the distant voice of a third interlocutor in this speech: *khōsh* is, of course, of Persian origin. Though such vocabulary was not "indigenous" to the Armenian language, it was widely used in Middle Armenian.

4. See also Sergio La Porta's brief discussion of this poem and its rhyme scheme, "Conflicted Coexistence: Christian-Muslim Interaction and Its Representation in Medieval Armenia," 114.

5. Similarly, other stanzas adopt rhyme schemes common in Persian and Turkish poetry (*aaba, aaca*), teasing the audience with a culturally liminal poetics. Cowe first observed that the poem "manifests a stanzaic rhyme pattern characteristic of Turkish folk poetry" ("Politics of Poetics," 389). See also his illuminating study on the complex relationships between Armenians and Muslims in medieval Anatolia, "Patterns of Armeno-Muslim Interchange on the Armenian Plateau in the Interstice between Byzantine and Ottoman Hegemony." On the interstitial quality of poetic discourses in medieval Anatolia, see also Michael Pifer, "The Rose of Muḥammad, the Fragrance of Christ."

6. On the westward migration and settlement of Armenians in the eleventh century, see Thomson, "The Influence of Their Environment on the Armenians in Exile in the Eleventh Century."

7. Vardan Arewelts'i, *Ashkharhats'oyts' Vardanay Vardapeti*, 9–50. "Armenia" had long served as an ancient and early medieval toponym, defined in different ways over the centuries in Greek, Armenian, and Arabic sources.

8. My use of geographic terms such as "Anatolia" and "Rūm" follows Cemal Kafadar, "A Rome of One's Own." Kafadar notes, "The word 'Rum' or *diyār-ı Rūm* for defining a cultural as well as a physical space (the lands of Rome, limited over time to the eastern Roman lands, i.e., Byzantium) was adopted from earlier Arabo-Persian usage but now stretched by Turkish speakers to refer to the zone that they inhabited and in large part also governed. . . . In that sense, the usage of 'Rum' in our late medieval and early modern sources can indeed be identified most of the time with the current delineation of Anatolia, with the same attendant vagueness about its boundaries, but only those to the east or the south" (9, 18). Hence, my use of "Anatolia" is not meant to obscure other territories or toponyms that overlapped historically with this geography. See also Sergio La Porta's discussion of the difficulty of deploying certain broad geographic terms, such as "the Mediterranean" or "Armenia" ("A Fish out of Water? Armenia(ns) and the Mediterranean," 70–71).

9. On the circulation of scholars and texts among Anatolia, Central Asia, and the Middle East, see also A. C. S. Peacock, "Islamisation in the Golden Horde and Anatolia."

10. On the role that Mongol rule played in shifting medieval Anatolia's cultural and literary landscape eastward, see the recent study by A. C. S. Peacock, *Islam, Literature and Society in Mongol Anatolia*. For a detailed and interdisciplinary study on the interaction of Turks with Byzantine society, see Rustam Shukurov, *The Byzantine Turks, 1204–1461*.

11. The seminal work on the diminution of Byzantine power in Anatolia is by Speros Vryonis, *The Decline of Medieval Hellenism in Asia Minor and the Process of Islamization from the Eleventh through the Fifteenth Century*. For broad introductions to this period, see also Claude Cahen, *Pre-Ottoman Turkey*; Cahen, *The Formation of Turkey*.

12. On the beylik period, see İsmail Hakkı Uzunçarşılı, *Anadolu Beylikleri ve Akkoyunlu, Karakoyunlu Devletleri*.

13. E. J. W. Gibb, *A History of Ottoman Poetry,* v.

14. Joseph von Hammer-Purgstall, *Geschichte der osmanischen Dichtkunst bis auf unsere Zeit.*

15. Gibb, *History of Ottoman Poetry,* vii.

16. Gibb, *History of Ottoman Poetry,* vii–viii.

17. The seed of Browne's study germinated after he read John Richard Green's *A Short History of the English People,* which in his words was a work that "any writer may be proud to adopt as a model." Green's *History* chiefly aimed to replace some well-worn figures and events from premodern historiography—kings, queens, and wars—with an emphasis on its titular namesake, the "people." See Edward G. Browne, *A Literary History of Persia,* vii–viii.

18. Browne, *Literary History of Persia,* viii.

19. The previous edition of Pʻapʻazean's *History,* published in 1907, did not include the modern period. The 1910 edition is especially notable because it also expands upon the late medieval period, largely ignored by the *Hayotsʻ patmutʻiwn* (History of Armenia) of Lēo (Aṛakʻel Babakhanean), the first comprehensive national history of Armenia to be composed in the twentieth century. The late medieval period held Pʻapʻazean's interest in part because he believed it was the dawn of secular Armenian literature. Subsequent scholarship has not supported this reading, however.

20. There is a long-standing precedent for this kind of narration in Armenian historiography, both in the premodern period and now. For a critique of modern Armenian histories based on the nation form, see Sebouh David Aslanian, "From 'Autonomous' to 'Interactive' Histories."

21. Thomas Sergeant Perry, *A History of Greek Literature,* 1. One year later, Karl Krumbacher published a far more monumental work, *Geschichte der byzantinischen Litteratur von Justinian bis zum Ende des Oströmischen Reiches,* which has remained the most comprehensive history of Byzantine literature until today. For a thoughtful overview and critique of the "Krumbacher paradigm," see Panagiotis A. Agapitos's "Contesting Conceptual Boundaries," which argues in part for the inclusion of Byzantine Greek literature within European literary history.

22. William Wright, *A Short History of Syriac Literature,* 2.

23. The intention of this series was to position literary history as the logical counterpart to national history, erected upon the same cornerstone—the people. As the editors explain: "There is for every nation a history which does not respond to the trumpet-call of battle, which does not limit its interests to the conflict of dynasties. This—the history of intellectual growth and artistic achievement—is less romantic than the popular panorama of kings and queens, finds its material in imperishable masterpieces, and reveals to the student something at once more vital and more picturesque than the quarrels of rival parliaments. . . . If all record of a nation's progress were blotted out, and its literature were yet left us, might we not recover the outlines of its lost history?" (Browne, *Literary History of Persia,* series title page). While national history chronicles the feats of a people or the major events that punctuate a nation's life, literary histories of this period generally strive to represent its introspective heart and brain.

24. One might therefore assume, because of this insular focus on the (proto-) nation, that such histories are generally uninterested in other literary traditions. However, this is not the case. Gibb, for instance, starts his literary history not with Turkish poets but rather with Jalāl al-Dīn Rūmī and his son Sulṭān Valad, who were both Persian. In some ways, this unlikely beginning for a literary history of the Turkish people was unavoidable, as both Rūmī and Sulṭān Valad were early adopters of Turkish as a literary language in Anatolia. Consequently, while asserting that the "true genius" of the Turkish race "lies in action, not in speculation," Gibb explains the curious convergence of Turkic and Persian literary cultures by doubling down on an ontological distinction between the two. "The Turks forthwith appropriated the entire Persian literary system down to its minutest detail," he therefore observes; though they "did not pause to consider whether this Persian culture was really in harmony with their own genius, they did not even attempt to modify it to suit that genius; on the contrary, they sought to adapt the latter to it, and to force themselves to think upon Persian lines and to look upon things through Persian eyes." Still, in Gibb's estimation, the tradition that emerged from this Persian-Turkic convergence was at its core quintessentially Turkic. In fact, as he ironically posited, the most Turkic thing about the Turkish literary tradition was its single-minded "fidelity" over five centuries to the Persianate aesthetics it adopted. See Gibb, *History of Ottoman Poetry,* 6–8.

25. The parallels between this model and national history are quite clear. As Cemal Kafadar has observed in the case of Anatolia, the basis of ethnic or national identities is often conceived of "as an original stock and descendants going through a linear series of adventures in time and, along the way, clashing with other original stocks and descendants going through similarly linear series of adventures" (*Between Two Worlds,* 27).

26. See also Kafadar's discussion of the problem of influence in the study of Anatolian history, in *Between Two Worlds,* 19–28.

27. René Wellek and Austin Warren, *Theory of Literature,* 51.

28. Mehmet Fuat Köprülü, "Method in Turkish Literary History," 65. See also Köprülü, *Early Mystics in Turkish Literature.* For an extensive critical review of the Köprülü model, see especially Devin DeWeese's foreword to *Early Mystics in Turkish Literature.* For a detailed examination of Köprülü's approach to literary history, see also Selim S. Kuru, "Fuat Köprülü ve Eski Edebiyat I."

29. This body of literature is too expansive to survey comprehensively here. For some starting points, see, in the field of social history, Nicolas Trépanier, *Foodways and Daily Life in Medieval Anatolia;* in art and architectural history, Patricia Blessing and Rachel Goshgarian, *Architecture and Landscape in Medieval Anatolia, 1100–1500;* Antony Eastmond, *Tamta's World;* Ethel Sara Wolper, *Cities and Saints;* in intellectual history, Seta B. Dadoyan, *The Armenians in the Medieval Islamic World*; in religious studies and history, Alexander Daniel Beihammer, *Byzantium and the Emergence of Muslim-Turkish Anatolia, ca. 1040–1130;* Goshgarian, "Beyond the Social and the Spiritual"; Kafadar, *Between Two Worlds;* Ahmet T. Karamustafa, *God's Unruly Friends;* Dimitri Korobeinikov, *Byzantium and the Turks in the Thirteenth Century;* Tijana

Krstić, *Contested Conversions to Islam;* La Porta, "Conflicted Coexistence." My use of *Islamicate* follows Marshall G. S. Hodgson, *The Venture of Islam*, 59.

30. Although this body of scholarship has enriched how we understand Muslim-Christian interaction in the Ottoman period, there still exist relatively few investigations into the convergence of literary cultures in this region and even fewer that treat each "group" in any given comparative set with equal attention. This picture is gradually beginning to change, however, thanks in part to three important volumes that devote some space to the question of literary production in medieval Anatolia: A. C. S. Peacock, Bruno De Nicola, and Sara Nur Yıldız, *Islam and Christianity in Medieval Anatolia;* Peacock and Yıldız, *Islamic Literature and Intellectual Life in Fourteenth- and Fifteenth-Century Anatolia*; Peacock and Yıldız, *The Seljuks of Anatolia.*

31. Many critics have productively opened vistas in the study of Anatolian, Mediterranean, and world literary history by illuminating the migration of literary forms (such as the *ghazal* or the *maṣnavī*), styles (such as Arabo-Persian prosody), tropes (such as the rose and the nightingale), genres (such as frame tales or chivalric romance), and discourses across linguistic boundaries. Another increasingly prevalent trend is to read Turkish, Persian, and Arabic literatures together, against the grain of national history, as a comparative set, based on formal and intertextual grounds.

For instance, C. Ceyhun Arslan has recently drawn on intertextual theory to disrupt the paradigm of influence studies in Ottoman literature, which tends to privilege Arabic and Persian literature as authentic and original and Turkish literature as derivative and reductive ("Canons as Reservoirs"). Murat Umut Inan, in a complementary manner, has drawn on intertextuality to rethink a pervasive assumption that early Ottoman poets reductively imitated Persian literature and hence produced a derivative literary culture ("Rethinking the Ottoman Imitation of Persian Poetry").

Still other scholars have expanded the boundaries of the Arabic-Persian-Turkish comparative set, in part by considering how non-Muslims composed poetry by drawing from Islamicate literary styles and genres. Here too is the scholarship voluminous, but for an orientation to cross-cultural exchange and literary production in the field of Armenian studies, see B. L. Chʿugaszyan, *Hay-iranakan grakan aṙnchʿutʿyunner;* Cowe, "Patterns of Armeno-Muslim Interchange"; Cowe, "Politics of Poetics"; Dadoyan, *Armenians in the Medieval Islamic World*; Armanush Kozmoyan, *Hayotsʿ ev parsitsʿ mijnadaryan kʿnarergutʿyan hamematakan poetikan;* Michael Pifer, "The Age of the *Gharīb*"; Russell, "An Armeno-Persian Love Poem of Grigoris Aghtʿamartsʿi"; Russell, *Yovhannēs Tʿlkurancʿi;* Theo Maarten van Lint, "The Gift of Poetry." For a comparative look at Armenian and Arabic literary production elsewhere in the Mediterranean world, see Tamar M. Boyadjian's study *The City Lament.* On shared narratives in Armenian, Arabic, Greek, and Syriac historiography, see Alison Vacca, "The Fires of Naxčawan."

At present, even the geographic boundedness of "Anatolian" literature is under reassessment. This placement of Anatolia within a more global context of literary production can be seen in different ways in the work of Gottfried Hagen (as mirroring other vernacularization movements around the globe; see "Updated Prolegomena to a Social Prehistory of the Ottoman Language"), Mimi Hanaoka (as part of historiographic patterns throughout the Persianate world; see "The View from Anatolia"), and Muhsin J. al-Musawi (as part of literary production across the expanse of Islamicate civilizations; see *The Medieval Islamic Republic of Letters*).

32. Peacock, *Islam, Literature and Society in Mongol Anatolia.* Peacock's concern rests exclusively with Islamicate literature in Arabic, Persian, and Turkish and what literary production in these languages can tell us about the Islamization of Anatolia under Ilkhanid rule. In other words, his study is interested in literature as a particular kind of historical source: one which demonstrates that the Mongols played a crucial role in the Islamization of Anatolia, which Peacock understands as not only a process of conversion but also the entrance of Islam into the cultural sphere; one that allows us to connect intellectual history in Anatolia to the broader Islamicate world; and one that he argues can show "the initiation of a process described as 'Sunnitisation' whereby, backed by the might of the state, a distinctively Sunni religiosity was increasingly propagated" (10). Because Peacock's study was published after this book entered into the final stages of its production, I have had occasion to cite it only sparingly here; nevertheless, it remains an important work, especially as it brings to light unpublished case studies from Turkish literary production in the mid-to-late fourteenth century.

33. Until recently, two paradigms have largely dominated discourse on Muslim-Christian interaction in medieval Anatolia, though not equally. The most prominent rubric comes from Vryonis, who, in his oft-cited *Decline of Medieval Hellenism in Asia Minor,* generally examines Muslim-Christian interaction as a series of destructive encounters that eroded the Byzantine social fabric. On the other end of the spectrum, Frederick W. Hasluck, in his *Christianity and Islam under the Sultans,* emphasizes peaceful religious accommodation between Muslims and Christians, which he understands as shaping "heterodox" forms of Islam that bridged otherwise separate religious cultures. Hasluck's work has recently gained a newfound appreciation and assessment, as reflected in David Shankland's three-volume *Archaeology, Anthropology and Heritage in the Balkans and Anatolia.* At the same time, scholars such as Tijana Krstić have questioned some of the underlying assumptions in the Hasluck paradigm, including its reliance on notions of syncretism and heterodox devotional practices. Krstić thus proposes reconceptualizing "syncretism," post-Hasluck, "from its simplistic interpretation as an 'equipoise' that obliterates the tension in inter-faith relations (especially when it comes to the issue of conversion) to a term that takes into account and brings forth constant negotiation of differences that underlined everyday life in the Ottoman Empire" ("The Ambiguous Politics of 'Ambiguous Sanctuaries,' " 249).

34. Hovhannēs Erznkatsʿi, *Hovhannes Erznkatsʿi,* 208.

35. This claim is reported by Shams al-Dīn Aḥmad Aflākī, *Manāqib al-ʿārifīn,* vol. 1, 291.

36. See especially Bakhtin's "The Problem of Speech Genres."

37. My use of the term *integrative* draws inspiration from Joseph F. Fletcher's classic essay "Integrative History." I'm grateful to Sebouh D. Aslanian for bringing it to my attention.

38. For Pollock, vernacular languages become "literary" in part by engaging with a "superposed" cosmopolitan cultural formation ("India in the Vernacular Millennium," 46). Hence, as he describes in his seminal *Language of the Gods in the World of Men*, the "cosmopolitan vernacular" is "that register of the emergent vernacular that aims to localize the full spectrum of literary qualities of the superposed cosmopolitan code" (26).

39. For an overview of Grigor Magistros's life and education, see Avedis K. Sanjian, "Gregory Magistros."

40. See Abraham Terian's critical edition of Grigor's poem, Grigor Magistros, *Magnalia Dei*, 10–12. See also Cowe's discussion of Grigor's literary production in the broader context of Armeno-Muslim literary interchange ("Politics of Poetics," 384–85).

41. Grigor Magistros, *Magnalia Dei*, 34.

42. Grigor Magistros, *Magnalia Dei*, 35.

43. Grigor Magistros, *Magnalia Dei*, 35.

44. Michael Pifer, "Introduction: A Movable Armenia."

45. Cowe, "Politics of Poetics," 385–86.

46. "We [Turks] forgot our distinctive national character in the middle ages under Persian influence and, since the Tanzimat [the Ottoman reform movement between 1838 and 1878], under European influence, popular Ṣūfī literature, like everything related to, or derived from, the people, has been neglected, even regarded with contempt," Köprülü argues in *Early Mystics in Turkish Literature*, lii. For a rebuttal, see Inan's article "Rethinking the Ottoman Imitation of Persian Poetry," in which he critiques the modern understandings of literary imitation as reductive. Finally, for a searing analysis of the concept of "influence" in Ottoman historiography, see Kafadar, *Between Two Worlds*, 19–28.

47. Sheldon Pollock, "Sanskrit Literary Culture from the Inside Out."

48. For a critical overview of the concept of the Persianate sphere, as well as a historical tour of the spread of the Persian language, see Nile Green's "Introduction: The Frontiers of the Persianate World (ca. 800–1900)." He rightly notes that Armenian engagement with the Persian language was selective; he is, however, somewhat reticent about theorizing this relationship aside from mentioning a handful of well-known examples, stating that most of the Persian loanwords in the Middle Armenian lexicon were mediated through Turkish. In this assertion, Green mirrors an argument most notably advanced by Andrzej Pisowicz, who has suggested that several Arabic and Persian words may have entered the lexicon of Kostandin Erznkatsʿi, an Armenian poet who appears in chapter 7 of this book, through the intermediary of Turkish ("How Did New Persian and Arabic Words Penetrate the Middle Armenian Vocabulary?"). However, as Theo M. van Lint has noted, Kostandin's poetry has approximately 140 loanwords of Arabic and Persian origin but only one or two of Turkish origin ("Kostandin of Erznka," 68). It seems, then, that if some of Kostandin's

"Persian" vocabulary was indeed mediated through the Turkish language, as Pisowicz has posited, he was therefore somewhat discerning in how he used it, preferring as it were a Persianate vocabulary over an explicitly or coincidentally "Turkic" one. In the spirit of Green's intervention, there is ample room for a broader reconsideration of Middle Armenian's role in the Persianate literary world (even in cases where Turkish may have served as an intermediary between the two languages). On Persian loanwords in Armenian, see also Ṛ. A. Ghazaryan and H. M. Avetisyan's invaluable dictionary of Middle Armenian, *Mijin hayereni baṛaran.*

49. There is a growing body of scholarship on adaptation in premodern Persian and Ottoman Turkish literary production, most (but not all) of which focuses on the late medieval or early modern period. For the Persian case, see especially the seminal study by Paul E. Losensky, *Welcoming Fighānī;* see also Domenico Ingenito, " 'Tabrizis in Shiraz Are Worth Less than a Dog' "; Franklin Dean Lewis, "The Rise and Fall of a Persian Refrain"; Riccardo Zipoli, *The Technique of the Ǧawāb.* For the Ottoman Turkish case, see Edith Gülçin Ambros, "*Naẓīre*"; the essential essay by Walter G. Andrews, "Other Selves, Other Poets, and the Other Literary History"; Walter Feldman, "Imitatio in Ottoman Poetry"; M. Fatih Köksal, *Sana Benzer Güzel Olmaz.* On "imitation" as a mode of engagement between Turkish and Persian literary cultures, see Inan, "Rethinking the Ottoman Imitation of Persian Poetry"; Victoria Rowe Holbrook, "Originality and Ottoman Poetics." For a complementary reappraisal of poetic "imitation" in Ottoman poetry, see Saliha Paker, "On the Poetic Practices of 'A Singularly Uninventive People' and the Anxiety of Imitation," "Terceme, Te'lîf ve Özgünlük Meselesi," and "Translation as *Terceme* and *Nazire,*" an illuminating article on translation as adaptation. Finally, for the Byzantine conception of literary imitation, see Herbert Hunger, "On the Imitation (*Mimesis*) of Antiquity in Byzantine Literature"; Andreas Rhoby and Elisabeth Schiffer, *Imitatio—Aemulatio—Variatio.*

50. Salam Rassi, "Justifying Christianity in the Islamic Middle Ages," 75.

51. On the Syriac adoption of wine poetry, a common genre in both Arabic and Hebrew, see David G. K. Taylor, " 'Your Sweet Saliva Is the Living Wine.' " This period of "renaissance," though contested as part of a broader narrative of cultural decline, took place in the eleventh through thirteenth centuries. Anton Baumstark argues that a "renaissance" in Syriac literary culture occurred, to a large degree, as a result of engaging with parts of the Christian West, such as Byzantium and the Crusaders (see *Geschichte der syrischen Literatur, mit Ausschluss der christlich-palästinensischen Texte*). More recently, scholars such as Herman Teule ("The Interaction of Syriac Christianity and the Muslim World in the Period of the Syriac Renaissance"; "The Syriac Renaissance") and Hidemi Takahashi ("The Reception of Ibn Sīnā in Syriac") have nuanced this view by shedding light on the interface between Syriac and Islamicate literary cultures.

Of course, not all Christian poets desired to reproduce the aesthetic values of Arabic literature. For instance, Salam Rassi has shown that the Syriac poet ʿAbdīshōʿ bar Brīkhā (d. 1318) once responded to Islamicate literature by refusing to emulate it. In the preface to his *Paradise of Eden,* ʿAbdīshōʿ claims that Arab poets ridiculed the Syriac language and said it would never produce literature as great as the *Maqāmāt* of Muḥammad al-Qāsim ibn ʿAlī al-Ḥarīrī (d. 1122). In response, ʿAbdīshōʿ decided to compose a body of poetry in an entirely new style. Rassi argues that this refusal to imitate the *Maqāmāt* reflects "an attempt to affirm Syriac literature's cultural autonomy from Classical Arabic models, which ʿAbdīshōʿ viewed as culturally hegemonic." Still, as Rassi observes, ʿAbdīshōʿ also composed texts in Arabic and drew on literary conventions popular in Arabic in some of his other Syriac compositions ("Justifying Christianity in the Islamic Middle Ages," 37–40).

52. Shotʿa Rustʿaveli, *The Man in the Panther's Skin,* 3. I have modified this translation, based on Marjory Scott Wardrop's fn. 4, to prefer the more literal "orphan pearl" over her rendering of *margaliti oboli,* "pearl of great price."

53. Mary J. Carruthers, *The Book of Memory,* 1–17, 246.

54. Nor was this the only "Persian tale" to circulate in Georgian at the time. In the early twelfth century, the Persian romance *Vīs and Rāmīn* was loosely translated—that is, heavily adapted—into Georgian as *Visramiani.* This "translation" would prove highly popular in Georgian literary culture, inspiring subsequent adaptations of the same tale well into the early modern period. On the translation and reception of *Vīs and Rāmīn* in Georgian, see Inga Kaladze, "The Georgian Translation of *Vis and Rāmin.*" On the multivectored and fragmentary adaptation of this romance in subsequent works of Persian literature, see Cameron Cross, "The Lives and Afterlives of *Vis and Rāmin.*"

55. Raymond P. Scheindlin, *The Song of the Distant Dove,* 13.

56. Petrus Alfonsi, *The Disciplina Clericalis of Petrus Alfonsi,* 104.

57. On the potential Arabic sources used in Alfonsi's work, see John Tolan, *Petrus Alfonsi and His Medieval Readers,* 73–91.

58. The *Kalīla and Dimna* was widely popular in Anatolia and Europe at the time; its structure was adapted in the composition of other frame tales, such as the *Disciplina Clericalis,* and it was translated into Castilian as *Calila e Dimna* for Alfonso X in 1251. Jalāl al-Dīn Rūmī also adapted the *Kalīla and Dimna* in his *Maṣnavī,* partly in an effort to teach his audience to find spiritual meanings in popular and accessible source materials. See Christine van Ruymbeke, "The *Kalīla wa Dimna* and Rūmī."

59. On the linguistic and cultural complexity of frame-tale technology, see David A. Wacks, *Framing Iberia.*

60. Geoffrey Chaucer, *The Canterbury Tales,* 180.

61. For a detailed analysis of Griselda's "translation" from Italian to Latin to English, see Alison Cornish, *Vernacular Translation in Dante's Italy,* 159–64. As Cornish observes, the adaptation of this tale across languages is what Rita Copeland has termed "secondary translation." In her classic study, Copeland defines this process as an author's use of "techniques of exegetical translation to produce, not a supplement to the original, but a vernacular substitute for that original" (*Rhetoric, Hermeneutics, and Translation in the Middle Ages,* 179).

62. Chaucer, *Canterbury Tales,* 181.

63. Yūsuf Khāṣṣ Ḥājib, *Wisdom of Royal Glory,* 253.

64. On this achievement in Turkish letters, see Talat Tekin, "Determination of Middle-Turkic Long Vowels through *'Arūḍ*."

65. The *Dīwān lughat al-turk* by Maḥmūd al-Kāshgharī (fl. eleventh century), another monumental work of early Turkish literature, also draws parallels between the Arabic and Turkish languages. The introduction's metaphor for literary production in the Turkish language—a Turkish racehorse galloping neck and neck beside the stallion of Arabic letters—suggests an aspiration to compete in the same arena. Of course, such a race becomes possible only when the audience is able to recognize similar sets of rules in play for both competitors. See Maḥmūd al-Kāshgharī, *Compendium of the Turkic Dialects,* vol. 1, 71.

66. Similarly, within the Perso-Turkish comparative set, Inan has argued that "intertextual concepts like appropriation, imitation, or adaptation operated in the Ottoman world as mechanisms of literary productivity and creativity and significantly contributed to the flourishing of poetry" ("Rethinking the Ottoman Imitation of Persian Poetry," 685). As we shall see, these "mechanisms" also played a foundational role in literary production prior to the Ottoman Empire, and among authors of not only Turkish poetry but also Persian and Armenian.

67. Grigor Magistros, *Magnalia Dei,* 33.

68. Kafadar, *Between Two Worlds,* 5.

69. Aflākī, *Manāqib al-'ārifīn,* vol. 1, 24.

70. Many scholars have posited that this request is a technical instruction, since Kostandin composed his Armenian *Shāh-nāma* in part by loosely emulating the *mutaqārib* meter. See, e.g., Manuk Abeghyan, *Hayots' hin grakanut'yan patmut'yun,* 552–54; Russell, *Yovhannēs T'lkuranc'i,* 7; Van Lint, "Kostandin of Erznka," 260–62.

Chapter 1: Stranger Encounters

1. Ibn Baṭṭūṭa, *The Travels of Ibn Baṭṭūṭa, A.D. 1325–1354,* 430; for the original Arabic, see Ibn Baṭṭūṭa, *Riḥlat Ibn Baṭṭūṭa,* 294. Translations of Ibn Baṭṭūṭa here are by Gibb, with a few exceptions as noted.

2. Ibn Baṭṭūṭa, *Travels,* 431; Ibn Baṭṭūṭa, *Riḥlat Ibn Baṭṭūṭa,* 294.

3. Shams al-Dīn Aḥmad Aflākī, *Manāqib al-'ārifīn,* vol. 1, 87.

4. A. J. Arberry, *Discourses of Rūmī,* 6.

5. Afzal Iqbal, *The Life and Work of Jalal-ud-din Rumi,* 129.

6. As John Stuart Mill argued in 1833, "Eloquence supposes an audience; the peculiarity of poetry appears to us to lie in the poet's utter unconsciousness of a listener. Poetry is feeling, confessing itself to itself, in moments of solitude, and embodying itself in symbols, which are the nearest possible representations of the feeling in the exact shape in which it exists in the poet's mind" ("Thoughts on Poetry and Its Varieties," 348). See also the discussions on Mill and lyric poetry in Virginia Jackson, *Dickinson's Misery,* 9, 129–33; Anne Janowitz, *Lyric and Labour in the Romantic Tradition,* 33–61.

7. In a complementary manner, Franklin Dean Lewis has argued that Rūmī's poetry should not be read as "emerging orphically, outside of time" ("Towards a Chronology of the Poems in the *Dīvān-i Shams,*" 150).

8. Many sources tell us a great deal about the life of Rūmī, but three early hagiographies in particular stand out. The earliest hagiography, the *Ibtidā-nāma,* was written by Rūmī's son Sulṭān Valad, who eventually led Rūmī's followers after his father's death. The next is Farīdūn ibn Aḥmad Sipahsālār's *Risāla-yi Sipahsālār,* which was reportedly written by a little-known figure who knew Rūmī personally. Finally, the third is Aflākī's *Manāqib al-ʿārifīn,* which he began to compose around 1318. Aflākī, curiously, makes no mention of Sipahsālār, however, leading some to suppose that the latter's hagiography may be a later work. Despite this, Sipahsālār's account is often credited as being less miraculous than Aflākī's and therefore more "historical." Franklin Dean Lewis, who wrote the most detailed study of Rūmī in English, makes this argument in terms of historicity, noting: "Sepahsâlâr's life of Rumi presents us with a far more sober history than the contemporaneous account of Aflâki, who constantly lends his credence to incredible supernatural events associated with Rumi and Shams. As such, we may place a greater degree of faith in Sepahsâlâr, despite the uncertainty about the years of his companionship with Rumi and the date of composition of his 'Treatise,' and assume him, for the purpose of reconstructing the events of Rumi's life, to be generally more reliable than Aflâki" (*Rumi,* 249). My concern here is somewhat different, however, as I seek not to sift "history" from "hagiography" but rather to examine the attitudes that Rūmī's family and followers had toward their own literary production—how they conceptualized and theorized their literary activity, in other words, even though one cannot take the historicity of these accounts at face value. In this, my approach shares an affinity with that of Şevket Küçükhüseyin, who has stressed the importance of hagiography in illuminating the "mindset" of Sufis in Konya ("Some Reflections on Hagiography with Reference to the Early Mawlawī-Christian Relations in the Light of the *Manāqib al-ʿārifīn*").

9. Sanāʾī's *Ilāhī-nāma* is better known as the *Ḥadīqat al-ḥaqīqa.*

10. Aflākī, *Manāqib al-ʿārifīn,* vol. 2, 740.

11. Here Aflākī quotes the original opening of the *Maṣnavī,* which commands the audience to listen to "*this* reed" (*īn nay;* my emphasis) and not to "the reed" (*az nay*), which would become a common variant in later centuries. Reynold Alleyne Nicholson, for instance, initially used the latter variant before preferring the former. See his discussion in Rūmī, *Maṣnavī,* vol. 7, 8–9; see also Muhammad Esteʿlami, "Understanding Rumi's *Mathnawi,*" which provides a valuable overview of the difference in meaning between the original opening of the *Maṣnavī* and its later variants. For consistency, my subsequent translations of the *Maṣnavī* preserve the original line.

12. Aflākī, *Manāqib al-ʿārifīn,* vol. 2, 740.

13. Aflākī, *Manāqib al-ʿārifīn,* vol. 2, 742.

14. Before the twelfth century, the followers of a charismatic Sufi leader would often disband or regroup after his death. However, that century and the following one witnessed

a dramatic transformation, as the teachings of charismatic Sufis were gradually institutionalized, in a more enduring fashion. See especially Erik S. Ohlander, *Sufism in an Age of Transition.* For cogent studies of Sufism's beginnings and subsequent development, see also Ahmet T. Karamustafa, *Sufism;* Karamustafa, *God's Unruly Friends;* Nile Green, *Sufism.*

15. Rūmī, *Masnavī,* 2: 1. All citations of the *Masnavī* follow Nicholson's critical edition and adopt the same pattern: *Masnavī,* book number: line number(s). Translations, however, are my own.

16. Aflākī, *Manāqib al-ʿārifīn,* vol. 2, 742–44.

17. Rūmī, *Masnavī,* 5: 1.

18. Rūmī, *Masnavī,* 4: 1–6.

19. Rūmī, *Masnavī,* 6: 2.

20. Lewis, *Rumi,* 216.

21. Aflākī, *Manāqib al-ʿārifīn,* vol. 2, 738.

22. Rūmī, *Masnavī,* 1: 1–4. Here my choice to render *shikāyat,* "complaint," as "lament" is meant to foreground both the auditory and poetic dimensions of the *nay*'s song.

23. For an accessible overview of *samāʿ*, see Leonard Lewisohn, "The Sacred Music of Islam"; for an introduction to the debates in Islam on the lawfulness of music, see Amnon Shiloah, "Music and Religion in Islam"; for a general description of the Mawlavī practice of *samāʿ*, see Talât Sait Halman and Metin And, *Mevlana Celaleddin Rumi and the Whirling Dervishes.*

24. Numerous commenters have observed that the reed stands for the figure of the poet. In the words of Muhammad Esteʿlami, "The reed is the poet—Rūmī himself—and anyone who shares his same awareness of separation from God" ("Understanding Rumi's *Mathnawi,*" 10).

25. Aflākī, *Manāqib al-ʿārifīn,* vol. 1, 12. "Darkness, temptation, fantasy, depraved passions, and deviation appeared," Bahāʾ al-Dīn preached, "because reason is a stranger [*gharīb*] while the body is in its own country and that country is one of devils." It is clear from the sermon's context that Bahāʾ al-Dīn is speaking of himself. Thus, when he says that "reason is a stranger," he not too subtly implies that other Muslims unjustly marginalized his own practice of Islam. On the figure of the *gharīb*, see Franz Rosenthal, "The Stranger in Medieval Islam."

26. For a detailed chronological and critical overview of the Valad family's itinerary, see Lewis, *Rumi,* 55–74.

27. Aflākī, *Manāqib al-ʿārifīn,* vol. 1, 18.

28. As Friedrich Meier has argued, music occupied a somewhat ambivalent position in Bahāʾ al-Dīn's teachings: he seems to have accepted that music could guide one to achieve a particular spiritual state but still held that it should not be relied upon too heavily (*Bahāʾ-i Walad,* 45–46).

29. Certain instruments and forms of music were controversial since the earliest days of Islam, and the *mizmār* was no exception. See the brief discussion in Amnon Shiloah, *Music in the World of Islam,* 32–33.

30. Aflākī, *Manāqib al-ʿārifīn,* vol. 1, 29.

31. Ethel Sara Wolper rightly cautions that although Rūmī and his father tended to describe buildings in Anatolia in extremely "hierarchical and stratified terms," we should bear in mind that "in reality, there could have been no simple one-to-one relationship between buildings and their audiences" (*Cities and Saints,* 20).

32. Oya Pancaroğlu, "Devotion, Hospitality and Architecture in Medieval Anatolia."

33. Wolper, *Cities and Saints,* 1–2.

34. Wolper, *Cities and Saints,* 12. Along similar lines, Wolper posits that in many Anatolian cities, the "symbiotic relationship among dervishes, non-Muslims, and Türkmen groups gave the dervish lodge prominence within the city," serving as an institutional space that was capable of incorporating outsiders into the fabric of urban life.

35. Ibn Baṭṭūṭa, *Travels,* 416; Ibn Baṭṭūṭa, *Riḥlat Ibn Baṭṭūṭa,* 283.

36. Ibn Baṭṭūṭa, *Travels,* 426; Ibn Baṭṭūṭa, *Riḥlat Ibn Baṭṭūṭa,* 290–91.

37. Ibn Baṭṭūṭa, *Travels,* 418–21; Ibn Baṭṭūṭa, *Riḥlat Ibn Baṭṭūṭa,* 285–87. Urban confraternities were not alone in this practice. In the city of Yazmir, for instance, an amir bestowed a Greek slave and silken robes upon Ibn Baṭṭūṭa (*Travels,* 446).

38. Ibn Baṭṭūṭa, *Travels,* 430; Ibn Baṭṭūṭa, *Riḥlat Ibn Baṭṭūṭa,* 293–94.

39. Ibn Baṭṭūṭa, *Travels,* 450; Ibn Baṭṭūṭa, *Riḥlat Ibn Baṭṭūṭa,* 307. Gibb translates *samāʿ* as "song," but its explicitly spiritual connotation is important here.

40. Ibn Baṭṭūṭa, *Travels,* 427–28; Ibn Baṭṭūṭa, *Riḥlat Ibn Baṭṭūṭa,* 291–92.

41. Aflākī, *Manāqib al-ʿārifīn,* vol. 1, 24.

42. Seta B. Dadoyan has posited that Hovhannēs attempted to transform and co-opt the *futuwwa* reform project of the ʿAbbasid caliph al-Nāṣir (d. 1225), which had spread throughout Anatolia at the time, for Armenian Christians ("A Case Study for Redefining Armenian-Christian Cultural Identity in the Framework of Near Eastern Urbanism"; "The Constitution for the Brotherhood of Erznkay [1280] by Yovhannēs Erznkacʿi"). Rachel Goshgarian has also examined the brotherhood movements in Anatolia through a comparative lens and has convincingly shown that they should not be studied in isolation from one another ("Beyond the Social and the Spiritual"; "Futuwwa in Thirteenth-Century Rūm and Armenia").

43. This transliteration reflects the Arabic and Persian spelling of *gharīb.* From its Armenian spelling, the loanword would be transliterated as *gharip.*

44. Hovhannēs Erznkatsʿi, *Hovhannes Erznkatsʿi,* 154.

45. The Armenian word *kafa* reflects a corruption of the Arabic loanword *qāfiya,* an elastic term that refers to a poem's use of rhyme. Hence, this poem not only draws from a widespread lexicon of estrangement shared by speakers of Persian, Arabic, Turkish, and Armenian but also seems to have developed from a convergence of musical and literary cultures among these peoples. For a detailed study of *kafa*s in Armenian literature, see Hasmik A. Simonyan, *Hay mijnadaryan kafaner*; for a shorter overview, see S. Peter Cowe, "Politics of Poetics," 383.

46. Hovhannēs Erznkatsʿi, *Matenagrutʿiwn,* 404. See also Dadoyan's discussion of this passage in *The Armenians in the Medieval Islamic World,* vol. 3, 89.

47. Aflākī, *Manāqib al-ʿārifīn,* vol. 1, 25. Āqshahr, whose toponym no longer exists, is not to be confused with the city of Akşehir. See Lewis, *Rumi,* 69–71.

48. On the Valad family's arrival in Konya, see Lewis, *Rumi,* 71–74.

49. Aflākī, *Manāqib al-ʿārifīn,* vol. 1, 296.

50. Aflākī, *Manāqib al-ʿārifīn,* vol. 1, 395.

51. Aflākī, *Manāqib al-ʿārifīn,* vol. 1, 88.

52. Aflākī, *Manāqib al-ʿārifīn,* vol. 1, 167.

53. Aflākī, *Manāqib al-ʿārifīn,* vol. 1, 489.

54. Jalāl al-Dīn Rūmī, *Kitāb-i fīhi mā fīh,* 74.

55. Farīdūn ibn Aḥmad Sipahsālār, *Risāla-yi Farīdūn ibn Aḥmad Sipahsālār,* 68–69.

56. Arberry, *Discourses of Rūmī,* 5.

57. Lewis, "Towards a Chronology of the Poems," 161.

58. Annemarie Schimmel, *The Triumphal Sun,* 43. Similarly, Talât Sait Halman cautions against reading this passage as a nationalistic confirmation, which sometimes appears in Turkish scholarship, that Rūmī wrote verse simply because Turks appreciated poetry. As Halman observes, Rūmī composed poetry in Persian for a group of friends and disciples first and foremost, though he still desired to engage more broadly with the different peoples in Konya ("The Turk in Rumi / Rumi in Turkey," 274).

59. Aflākī, *Manāqib al-ʿārifīn,* vol. 1, 207. A slightly more prosaic translation of the verse would be "You brought me from Khorasan [to be] next to Greeks, / so that I mix with them, and offer a pleasing religion." Rūmī uses the word for Greeks (*yūnānī*) here and not the term for a person from Rūm (*rūmī*), but the passage's context at least implies the people of Rūm more generally.

60. Annemarie Schimmel, "Christianity VII." Schimmel has also posited that Rūmī's *Dīvān* contains an allusion to the Gospel of Matthew, as it urges the faithful to turn the other cheek when someone strikes their face. Numerous scholars have commented on Rūmī's knowledge of Christianity: see Leonard Lewisohn, "The Esoteric Christianity of Islam"; John Renard, *All the King's Falcons;* Schimmel, "Jesus and Mary as Poetical Images in Rumi's Verse." For an extensive bibliography on the relationship between Rūmī and Christianity, see Lewisohn, "Mawlānā Jalāl al-Dīn Rūmī."

61. On a possible literary antecedent for Rūmī's use of Turkish words in Persian verses, see István Vásáry, "The Beginnings of Western Turkic Literacy in Anatolia and Iran (13th–14th Centuries)," 250.

62. Rūmī, *Kitāb-i fīhi mā fīh,* 97.

63. Aflākī, *Manāqib al-ʿārifīn,* vol. 1, 476–77.

64. Aflākī, *Manāqib al-ʿārifīn,* vol. 1, 109.

65. In other words, Rūmī understood such bawdy verses as mystical signifiers in their own right—regardless of the original intent of their (unknown) authors. If this attitude perplexed his companions in the thirteenth century, it has also confounded contemporary scholars. In fact, Rūmī composed multiple erotic tales in the *Masnavī,* but few scholars have

attempted to analyze, or even acknowledged, these stories within the broader context of Rūmī's interpretive practices. The major exception is Mahdi Tourage, whose study *Rūmī and the Hermeneutics of Eroticism* is the defining work on the nexus between eroticism and mystical signification in Rūmī's poetry.

66. Aflākī, *Manāqib al-ʿārifīn,* vol. 1, 153, 484.

67. Aflākī, *Manāqib al-ʿārifīn,* vol. 1, 356.

68. Aflākī, *Manāqib al-ʿārifīn,* vol. 2, 709–11. That goldsmith, Ṣalāḥ al-Dīn Zarkūb, later became one of Rūmī's spiritual guides.

69. As Jawid Mojaddedi observes, "While ʿAṭṭār's *Asrārnāma* contains a citation from the Qurʾān approximately every 250 couplets and Sanāʾī's *Ḥadīqat al-ḥaqīqa* every 150 couplets, Rūmī's *Mathnawī* contains a Qurʾānic citation on average every 30 couplets" ("Rūmī," 367). On Rūmī's citation practices, see also Nargis Virani, " 'I Am the Nightingale of the Merciful,' "; on the *Maṣnavī*'s approximately seven hundred citations from the hadith, see Badīʿ al-Zamān Furūzānfar, *Aḥadīṣ-i Maṣnavī.* This practice of citation and quotation perhaps led to the mistaken impression among Rūmī's followers that the *Maṣnavī* is simply an exegesis of the Qur'an, which he vehemently denied (Aflākī, *Manāqib al-ʿārifīn,* vol. 1, 291).

70. See Lewis's brief discussion of this attribution in *Rumi,* 468–69.

71. Aflākī, *Manāqib al-ʿārifīn,* vol. 1, 221. Qāniʿī's surviving work is his versification of the *Kalīla and Dimna,* which he composed for the Seljuk court.

72. Of course, Qur'anic citation is common in the didactic-mystical *maṣnavī* genre. This report is therefore perhaps more reflective of a certain type of attitude that Rūmī and his followers wished to rebuke than indicative of an actual confrontation between Rūmī and Qāniʿī.

73. Shahab Ahmed, *What Is Islam?,* 445.

74. Ahmed, noting that the *Maṣnavī* is not a "formal *tafsīr,*" has argued that it is "*the* historical exemplar of creative and explorative engagement with the Qur'ān—that is, of exegesis by re-imagining, re-configuring, re-presenting, re-formulating, re-valorizing, and re-narrating." It is, in his view, "a Qur'ānic exegesis *by other means*" (*What Is Islam?,* 306, 307). Jamal J. Elias has also reevaluated *tafsīr* beyond any rigid definitions of genre ("Ṣūfī Tafsīr Reconsidered"). Finally, see Amidu Sanni's discussion of the different poetic and hermeneutic functions of *taḍmīn* (Persian: *tażmīn*) in Arabic poetry ("Again on *Taḍmīn* in Arabic Theoretical Discourse").

75. Aflākī, *Manāqib al-ʿārifīn,* vol. 1, 207–8.

76. Lewis, *Rumi,* 327.

77. Undeniably, the cultivation of poetry and music was important to the Seljuks of Rūm, whose appreciation of these things is reflected in not only their patronage of poets such as Qāniʿī but also various forms of art. For instance, in an article on Seljuk architecture, Scott Redford observes that "the tiles of the pavilion of Kılıç Arslan II featured representations of mythic beasts such as griffons and harpies, but also of the activities of court: music making, dancing, hunting on horseback and other court scenes" ("Anatolian

Seljuk Palaces and Gardens," 235). Other Seljuk tiles and candlesticks from the twelfth and thirteenth centuries depict similar tableaux (Sheila R. Canby et al., *Court and Cosmos: The Great Age of the Seljuqs*, 160–62).

78. Aflākī, *Manāqib al-ʿārifīn*, vol. 1, 208.

79. ʿAlī Akbar Dihkhudā offers *tarkīb*, "composition," and *taʾlīf*, "compilation," as definitions of *āmīkhtan* (*Lughat-nāma*, vol. 1, 162–63). See also his entry on *dar āmīkhtan* (vol. 10, pt. 1, 333).

80. On intertextuality in Persianate poetry, see Domenico Ingenito, " 'Tabrizis in Shiraz Are Worth Less than a Dog' "; Franklin Dean Lewis, "The Rise and Fall of a Persian Refrain"; Paul E. Losensky, *Welcoming Fighānī*; Riccardo Zipoli, *The Technique of the Ǧawāb*.

81. Losensky, *Welcoming Fighānī*, 106–7.

82. Losensky, *Welcoming Fighānī*, 107. Losensky partly bases his discussion of *sariqāt* on Zipoli's succinct study (*Technique of the Ǧawāb*, 9–12).

83. Losensky, *Welcoming Fighānī*, 108. As Losensky notes, the distinction between adaptation and plagiarism was sometimes hazy. The eleventh-century literary critic Ibn Rashīq, for instance, limited "the question of plagiarism to the theft (*sarq*) of what is original (*badīʿ*) or out of the ordinary," whereas "most themes, images, and metaphors (*al-maʿānī*, 'topoi and tropes') belong equally to all poets, and only a particular turn of phrase or conceit can be an object of intentional borrowing" (105). However, Losensky observes that even in cases of adaption, if the author not only improves upon the original but also hides all traces of "borrowing" or "theft" to begin with, the work in question can be considered original. For an overview of the terms *istiqbāl*, *naẓīra-gūʾī*, *javāb-gūʾī*, *tatabbuʿ*, and *sariqāt*, see *Welcoming Fighānī*, 105–14.

84. Losensky, *Welcoming Fighānī*, 108.

85. Bruno Latour, *Reassembling the Social*, 59–60.

86. Aflākī, *Manāqib al-ʿārifīn*, vol. 1, 208. A variant of the first couplet can be found in Rūmī, *Masnavī*, 3: 2709; the second couplet, which incorporates Arabic from the Qur'an (26:63), is in *Masnavī*, 3: 2700.

87. Aflākī, *Manāqib al-ʿārifīn*, vol. 1, 356.

88. This reveals an important way that the Mawlavī community conceptualized their master's literary production, regardless of the historical accuracy of Aflākī's report.

Chapter 2: The Macrocosmic *Masnavī*

1. Rūmī, *Masnavī*, 1: 35.

2. For an overview of the Arabic and Persian sources that Rūmī used in his composition of the *Masnavī*, see Badīʿ al-Zamān Furūzānfar, *Maʾākhiz-i qiṣaṣ va tamsīlāt-i Masnavī*. See also the discussion by Franklin Dean Lewis, *Rumi*, 287–91.

3. Although Ḥusām al-Dīn had presumably never heard the *Masnavī*'s first tale before, he almost certainly recognized its content and sound as familiar. Rūmī composed his rhymed couplets in the catalectic *ramal* meter (– ⏑ – – / – ⏑ – – / – ⏑ –), one of the customary meters

used for didactic narratives. As Bo Utas has noted, the choice of a poetic meter "seems to add a mode, a tone to the poem—a little like the choice of key for a piece of music" (" 'Genres' in Persian Literature, 900–1900," 223). In this case, the meter would likely have suggested a contemplative mood, suitable for a work of didactic poetry. At the same time, the *Maṣnavī* would have sounded, true to Rūmī's promise, exactly like the poetry of ʿAṭṭār. For an analysis of the poetry's musicality in Rūmī's *Dīvān,* see Fatemeh Keshavarz, *Reading Mystical Lyric,* 100–137.

4. See the short overview by Furūzānfar, *Maʾākhiz-i qiṣaṣ va tamṣīlāt-i Maṣnavī,* 3–6.

5. Niẓāmī ʿArūżī, *Chahār maqāla,* 118–23.

6. Amin Azad Sadr has advanced a similar argument in a different manner, demonstrating that the opening tale of the *Maṣnavī* provides a hermeneutic key that is essential to understanding the work as a whole. As Sadr argues, the first story of the *Maṣnavī* "follows a textual strategy designed to jam, frustrate, and confuse a reader-centered interpretation of the narrative. It accomplishes this through the establishment of an overt narrative topic to which the Model Reader's intertextual encyclopedia has conditioned him or her to be sensitive. The text then performs a series of discursive, narrative, and actantial techniques and maneuvers that the Model Reader's intertextual frames based on this topic are unable to process" ("Love, Death, and Submission," 46). Though I agree with Sadr's conclusion that the *Maṣnavī* frustrates the reader's—or listener's—attempt to interpret it using their personal "intertextual encyclopedia," my concern here is with contextualizing this hermeneutic maneuver within the social dynamics, and in some cases the actual performance, of the *Maṣnavī* in medieval Konya. In other words, I intend to suggest how the *Maṣnavī* promotes a hermeneutic method that extends beyond its own textual corpus.

7. Rūmī, *Maṣnavī,* 1: 63–65.

8. Rūmī, *Maṣnavī,* 1: 68.

9. Rūmī, *Maṣnavī,* 1: 73–74.

10. Rūmī, *Maṣnavī,* 1: 101.

11. Rūmī, *Maṣnavī,* 1: 99.

12. Rūmī, *Maṣnavī,* 1: 202.

13. Aflākī similarly depicts Khiḍr as a *gharīb* in one of his miraculous tales. In this account, a dervish by the name of Shams al-Dīn ʿAṭṭār is listening to Rūmī preach a sermon about Khiḍr when he notices a *gharīb* sitting in the corner. This strange person is conversing with himself, confirming audibly that everything Rūmī says is true. Suddenly, it dawns on Shams al-Dīn that the stranger is Khiḍr himself. When he approaches the saint to beg for his help, Khiḍr replies that Shams al-Dīn should instead seek the assistance of Rūmī, who is the source of Khiḍr's own instruction. With that, the strange saint suddenly vanishes (Aflākī, *Manāqib al-ʿārifīn,* vol. 1, 344). While Khiḍr's appearance as a *gharīb* in this report serves to bolster Rūmī's religious authority, it also reinforces the notion that important Islamic figures could seem strange even to other Muslims. Often, the *gharīb*s who appear in hagiographic accounts of Rūmī, as well as in his own literary production, are people with the true authority of Islam.

14. Rūmī thought of the relationship between the *Maṣnavī* and its audience in similar terms. He predicted that after his death, for instance, the *Maṣnavī* would become the shaykh of Konya. See Aflākī, *Manāqib al-ʿārifīn,* vol. 1, 409.

15. Sara Nur Yıldız, "Aydınid Court Literature in the Formation of an Islamic Identity in Fourteenth-Century Western Anatolia," 231–35.

16. Rūmī, *Maṣnavī,* 1: 78–79.

17. Rūmī, *Maṣnavī,* 1: 126–31.

18. Rūmī, *Maṣnavī,* 1: 132–42.

19. For Rūmī, it was impossible to put the mysteries of Love or Truth into direct speech. "Whatever I say to explain or describe love, / I am ashamed of when I encounter love," he noted in his conversation with Ḥusām al-Dīn, later continuing, "While the pen rushed in writing, / when it encountered love, it was cleft in two" (*Maṣnavī,* 1: 112, 114). If these verses seem circumlocutory, skirting around at a point, there is a reason. Rūmī, seven hundred years before Jacques Derrida, addressed the slippery nature of language in similarly recursive, performative terms—by describing, in an elusive manner, language's inability to provide direct access to an extralinguistic Truth, or Reality.

20. Aflākī, *Manāqib al-ʿārifīn,* vol. 2, 770.

21. Aflākī, *Manāqib al-ʿārifīn,* vol. 2, 737.

22. Aflākī, *Manāqib al-ʿārifīn,* vol. 2, 880.

23. Jalāl al-Dīn Rūmī, *Kitāb-i fīhi mā fīh,* 52.

24. Aflākī, *Manāqib al-ʿārifīn,* vol. 1, 400.

25. Aflākī, *Manāqib al-ʿārifīn,* vol. 1, 308–9. For a discussion of this hadith, see Franz Rosenthal, "The Stranger in Medieval Islam," 59–63.

26. Of course, this is not the only way to interpret the meaning of the Shah, the stranger-physician, the handmaiden, and the goldsmith. In a concise monograph dedicated entirely to the exegesis of this single tale, ʿAbbās Khayrābādī offers multiple overlapping interpretations of these figures. For instance, in one interpretation, the Shah is a Sufi wayfarer (*sālik*), the handmaiden the carnal self (*nafs*), the physician the spiritual guide (*pīr*), and the goldsmith worldly attachment: without the guidance of the *pīr,* it's impossible to sever one's material attachments, in other words. However, the Shah can also represent the soul (*rūḥ*), the handmaiden the carnal self (*nafs*), the physician love (*ʿishq*), and the goldsmith the body (*tan*)—that is, love leads the soul away from the body; in another interpretation, the Shah represents Muslims, the handmaiden Islam, the physician the Prophet, and the goldsmith corruption in religion. Finally, in a more historically contingent reading, Khayrābādī suggests that the Shah represents Love, the handmaiden Rūmī, the physician Shams al-Dīn, and the goldsmith the allure of study or worldly knowledge. Clearly, as Khayrābādī implies, the tale can mean different things in different contexts (*Sirr-i dilbarān,* 62–66). The Ottoman scholar Kenan Rifai likewise identifies the physician in part as Shams al-Dīn, and thus the encounter between the stranger and the Shah represents the encounter between Shams and Rūmī (*Listen,* 16–17). My argument here is that the story means something particular when we examine it not only as a text but also within the historically contingent

dynamic of performing the *Maṣnavī* in Konya. In public readings of the *Maṣnavī*, we find a historical parallel to the master-student dynamic that prevails in three of Khayrābādī's interpretations, even as that dynamic necessarily took on a different form. In this sense, the relationship between Shams and Rūmī anticipates the relationship between Rūmī and Ḥusām al-Dīn, the "author" and the "audience" of this tale.

27. Austin, *How to Do Things with Words*, 5.

28. Jalāl al-Dīn Rūmī, *Kitāb-i fīhi mā fīh*, 100.

29. Paul Zumthor, *Oral Poetry*, 5.

30. Although we know little about how the early Mawlavī community practiced *samāʿ*, it is clear that Rūmī's companions often recited his *ghazals* while dancing. It seems there was an early precedent for reciting the *Maṣnavī* in these contexts as well. Long after Rūmī's death, Aflākī describes falling ill (albeit in highly miraculous and metaphoric terms); he was on the brink of death until Rūmī's grandson ʿĀrif Chalabī visited his sickbed and commanded him to recite the *Maṣnavī* and perform *samāʿ*. Thus, after reciting the *Maṣnavī*, Aflākī found that the fires of separation were extinguished within him; he recovered shortly thereafter (*Manāqib al-ʿārifīn*, vol. 2, 953–54).

31. Gen'ichi Tsuge, "Āvāz." On the relationship between *āvāz* singing and *ʿarūż* versification, see Gen'ichi Tsuge, "Rhythmic Aspects of the *Âvâz* in Persian Music"; Ehsan Yar-Shater, "Affinities between Persian Poetry and Music."

32. Mohammad Reza Shajarian, widely regarded as one of the twentieth century's masters of *āvāz*, describes the relationship between vocalist and musician in precisely such dialogic and responsive terms, as though the two were in rapt conversation with each other. See Rob Simms and Amir Koushkani, *The Art of Avaz and Mohammad Reza Shajarian*, 214–15. For a technical overview of *āvāz*, see Lloyd Miller, *Music and Song in Persia*.

33. Even though Sufi texts were frequently products of broader Persianate or Islamicate cultures, as Michael Frishkopf has noted, "Ṣūfī music often draws upon local culture. Thus music of Sudanese Qādirīs sounds Sudanese; in East Africa, the same *ṭarīqa* spread among the non-literate population via colloquial devotional poetry. South Asian *ṭarīqas*, such as the Chishtiyya, draw upon Hindustani musical materials" ("Music," 520).

34. Lewis, *Rumi*, 394–95.

35. Aflākī, *Manāqib al-ʿārifīn*, vol. 2, 746, quoting *Maṣnavī*, 1: 2880–82.

36. Aflākī, *Manāqib al-ʿārifīn*, vol. 1, 496–97.

37. Aflākī, *Manāqib al-ʿārifīn*, vol. 1, 496; vol. 2, 628.

Chapter 3: Languages of Affinity

1. Shams al-Dīn Aḥmad Aflākī, *Manāqib al-ʿārifīn*, vol. 2, 593.

2. Farīdūn ibn Aḥmad Sipahsālār, *Risāla-yi Farīdūn ibn Aḥmad Sipahsālār*, 113.

3. Aflākī, *Manāqib al-ʿārifīn*, vol. 2, 592.

4. Rūmī, *Maṣnavī*, 1: 1204–7.

5. Aflākī, *Manāqib al-ʿārifīn*, vol. 2, 807.

6. On the literary "father" against whom the poet must struggle, see Harold Bloom, *A Map of Misreading,* 19. On his resistance to the term "Oedipal," see Bloom, *The Anxiety of Influence,* xxii.

7. Bloom, *Anxiety of Influence,* xviii.

8. Abdülbâki Gölpınarlı, *Mevlânâ'dan sonra Mevlevîlik,* 59.

9. Sulṭān Valad, *Ibtidā-nāma,* 65. Sipahsālār cites this passage in his hagiography of the Valad family (*Risāla-yi Farīdūn ibn Aḥmad Sipahsālār,* 71–72). On this seeming distaste for poetry, see also Sulṭān Valad, *Dīvān-i Sulṭān Valad,* 17–18.

10. E. J. W. Gibb, *A History of Ottoman Poetry,* 153.

11. Gibb, *History of Ottoman Poetry,* 147.

12. From an entirely different perspective than Gibb's, M. S. Fomkin has shed needed light on the reception of Sulṭān Valad's poetry in medieval Anatolia while productively abstaining from the question of his artistic merit. Citing some 105 copies of works by Sulṭān Valad, Fomkin posits that "written sources give us all the reason to believe that the Turkic poetry of Sultan Veled was well-known and fairly popular in a specific socio-cultural milieu in medieval Anatolia. The role of his Turkic verses in the further emergence and development of Turkish poetry cannot be denied" ("On the Literary Fate of Works by Sultan Veled," 30).

13. Lars Johanson, "Rūmī and the Birth of Turkish Poetry," 28.

14. Johanson, "Rūmī and the Birth of Turkish Poetry," 25.

15. Johanson, "Rūmī and the Birth of Turkish Poetry," 27.

16. Lewis, *Rumi,* 240.

17. For example, Hülya Küçük, in an article from 2012 in the *Mawlana Rumi Review,* cites Gibb and repeats his assessment of the quality of Sulṭān Valad's poetry. Küçük posits that "Sulṭān Walad did not want to write books at all, and did so only to follow the example of his father and on the insistence of his close friends"; his poems therefore "show a certain lack of exuberance, ecstasy, and a dearth of fascinating descriptions." Still, Küçük observes that Sulṭān Valad did not merely "repeat" Rūmī's teachings but rather "re-interpreted and rephrased them" ("Sulṭān Walad's Role in the Foundation of the Mevlevi Sufi Order," 25–26).

18. Franklin Dean Lewis, "Solṭân Valad and the Poetical Order," 27.

19. Lewis, "Solṭân Valad and the Poetical Order," 31. Lewis identifies three primary ways that Sulṭān Valad differentiates himself from Rūmī: "(1) the *Ebtedâ-nâme* is in the *xafif* meter, slightly different than the *ramal* of Rumi's *Maśnavi* (in the second foot); (2) the poem does not begin as his father's *Maśnavi* does, but rather reasserts the propriety of beginning with a traditional doxology; and (3) it points to a hybrid and quasi-secret spiritual lineage that had not been publicly divulged before the writing of this text" (33).

20. Laṭīfī, *Tezkiretü'ş-Şu'arâ ve Tabsıratü'n-Nuzamâ,* 485.

21. Laṭīfī, *Tezkiretü'ş-Şu'arâ ve Tabsıratü'n-Nuzamâ,* 103.

22. Walter G. Andrews, "The *Tezkere-i Şu'arā* of Latifi," 89.

23. For a discussion of Laṭīfī's views on artful poetry, see Andrews, "*Tezkere-i Şu'arā* of Latifi," 81–92.

24. Aflākī, *Manāqib al-ʿārifīn,* vol. 2, 785.

25. This fact is underscored by Johanson's reluctance to label Rūmī an "imitator," which has an undeniably negative connotation in the modern era. "Rūmī simply had, from the beginning, a highly developed, functioning literary instrument at his disposal, by which he could also exert direct influence in Qonya," Johanson notes. "This statement is, of course, not tantamount to saying that he was an imitator. As we know, Rūmī himself developed the available poetic vehicle to a high degree of perfection and created a masterly clear and simple style" ("Rūmī and the Birth of Turkish Poetry," 25). However, as Paul E. Losensky has shown, in the early modern Persianate world, practices of imitation extended far beyond a reductive notion of *taqlīd.* Corresponding to the European *imitatio,* a portfolio of imitative techniques emerged, all of which allowed poets to innovate their verses by replicating, with subtle deviations, what had been composed by other poets. See especially Losensky, *Welcoming Fighānī,* 100–133.

26. Aflākī, *Manāqib al-ʿārifīn,* vol. 2, 786.

27. Aflākī, *Manāqib al-ʿārifīn,* vol. 1, 220.

28. Sulṭān Valad, *Ibtidā-nāma,* 20.

29. Lewis, *Rumi,* 239. As Lewis notes, Istanbul University Library MS 1205 preserves at least 350 poems of this nature. It is worth observing that the title of this particular manuscript, "The Poetic Contest between Rūmī and Sulṭān Valad," supposes a competition, though hardly a zero-sum game, between father and son.

30. Sulṭān Valad, *Ibtidā-nāma,* 20.

31. Sulṭān Valad, *Ibtidā-nāma,* 19.

32. Sulṭān Valad has not been alone in reading the *Maṣnavī* this way. For example, Kenan Rifai also understands the meaning of its first story in terms of these personages: "The mysteries of Shams are in the meaning of this story," he writes. "For Shams of Tabriz is the divine physician of this tale, and the other arrogant, crude doctors are the luckless whose enlightenment is not yet possible, they are those whom the light of gnosis has not yet reached" (Rifai, *Listen,* 28).

33. Sulṭān Valad, *Ibtidā-nāma,* 19.

34. Sulṭān Valad, *Ibtidā-nāma,* 20.

35. Lewis, "Solṭân Valad and the Poetical Order," 30–31.

36. William C. Chittick has posited that even Shams al-Dīn treated following as "the key attribute" his audience should cultivate ("The Real Shams-i Tabrizi," 51–52).

37. On the emulation of Rūmī in the works of subsequent poets, see Losensky's article "To Revere, Revise and Renew," which sheds light on the adaptive practices of the seventeenth-century Ṣāʾib Tabrīzī. "In following the path of 'Mawlawī's way of writing', Ṣāʾib recognizes the past master's authority, and voluntarily undertakes a literary apprenticeship," Losensky argues (10). "To train himself in Rūmī's style, he composes a *jawāb* or response that utilizes the same meter and rhyme scheme as one of his mentor's *ghazals.* This discipline in the techniques of language and form (*ṭarz*) then results in a profound metamorphosis of thought and content (*fikr*)."

38. Sulṭān Valad, *Ibtidā-nāma,* 20.

39. Certainly, the Türkmen brought musical, poetic, and other storytelling cultures with them when they migrated to Rūm. Even so, the question of when and to what extent Turkish was first employed as a literary language in Anatolia remains contentious, to put it mildly. Mehmet Fuat Köprülü maintained, on highly speculative grounds, that a culture of Turkish literary production must have existed "since the earliest period of the Seljuks," although he acknowledged that "virtually nothing" of these hypothetical texts has survived today (*Early Mystics in Turkish Literature,* 207). Many scholars have followed suit, particularly Mecdut Mansuroğlu, who placed other early poets of Turkish literature, such as Şeyyād Ḥamza, Dehhānī, and Aḥmed Faḳīh, alongside Rūmī and Sulṭān Valad in the thirteenth century ("Anadolu'da Türk Dili ve Edebiyatının İlk Mahsulleri"; "Calāladdīn Rūmī's türkische Verse"; introduction to Aḥmed Faḳīh, *Çarhname*; "The Rise and Development of Written Turkish in Anatolia"; *Sultan Veled'in Türkçe Manzumeleri*). Others have emphasized that the Türkmen must have introduced their own literary cultures to Anatolia and, moreover, that the relationship between literary production in Anatolia and literary production in Central Asia was open and ongoing (see, e.g., Zeynep Korkmaz, "Selçuklular Çağı Türkçesinin Genel Yapısı"). This perspective has gradually complicated the equally simplistic counterassumption that Turkish literature in Anatolia began singularly with Rūmī and Sulṭān Valad.

More recently, methods of dating and attributing works to particular authors have been subject to much scrutiny. Semih Tezcan, for instance, has rejected Köprülü's thesis, arguing that with the exception of Sulṭān Valad and perhaps Yūnus Emre, we do not possess reliable information about poets who wrote in Anatolian Turkish in the thirteenth century ("Anadolu Türk Yazınının Başlangıç Döneminde bir Yazar ve *Çarḫ-nāme*'nin Tarihlendirilmesi Üzerine"). Scholars continue to nuance this view as well, especially in light of new manuscript evidence. Mustafa Koç has posited that *Behcetü'l-hadayık* was completed in 1286, slightly over a decade after Rūmī's death, making it, for now, among the earliest reliably dated literary works written in Turkish in Anatolia ("Anadolu'da İlk Türkçe Telif Eser"). Still, the fact remains that we possess relatively little information about the state of Turkish as a literary language in thirteenth-century Anatolia, especially in comparison to the fourteenth century, when, the manuscript record suggests, there was increasing literary production in Anatolian Turkish. See Sara Nur Yıldız's brief discussion of the need for more rigorous codicological methods and manuscript evidence in the study of this period ("Battling *Kufr* [Unbelief] in the Land of Infidels," 330–31 n9). Finally, see the critical discussion of the rise of early Turkish literature and the problem of dating in A. C. S. Peacock's *Islam, Literature and Society in Mongol Anatolia,* 147–87.

40. Ahmet Yaşar Ocak, "Social, Cultural and Intellectual Life, 1071–1453," 357. On the Bābāʾī revolt, see Ocak, *La révolte de Baba Resul, ou La formation de l'hétérodoxie musulmane en Anatolie au XIIIe siècle,* later revised and published in Turkish as *Babaîler İsyanı.*

41. For historical background to this period, see Claude Cahen, *Pre-Ottoman Turkey,* 269–79.

42. For a brief overview of these migrations, see Ocak, "Social, Cultural and Intellectual Life," 360–65.

43. Cahen, *Pre-Ottoman Turkey*, 280–92.

44. Ibn Bībī, *Al-Awāmir al-ʿalāʾiyya fīʾl-umūr al-ʿalāʾiyya*, 597.

45. For a critical overview of the nationalization of Meḥmed Bey's *farmān*, see Sara Nur Yıldız, "Mongol Rule in Thirteenth-Century Seljuk Anatolia," 45–51. On the *farmān*'s language politics, see Yıldız's "Karamanoğlu Mehmed Bey."

46. Yıldız, "Mongol Rule in Thirteenth-Century Seljuk Anatolia," 49.

47. Sulṭān Valad, *Rabāb-nāma*, 1.

48. There are many studies of the Turkish and Greek poetry of Sulṭān Valad; to begin, see M. S. Fomkin, "On the Literary Fate of Works by Sultan Veled"; Fomkin, *Sultan Veled ī ego tiurkskaia poeziia;* Gibb, *History of Ottoman Poetry*, 141–63; Mehmet Fuat Köprülü, *Türk Edebiyatı Tarihi*, 263–65; Mansuroğlu, *Sultan Veled'in Türkçe Manzumeleri*; Carl Germanovich Salemann, "Noch einmal die seldschukischen Verse"; Dimitri Theodoridis, "Versuch einer Neuausgabe von drei griechischen Doppelversen aus dem *Dīwān* von Sulṭān Walad." On the multilingualism of later Turkish poets, see Barbara Flemming, "Languages of Turkish Poets."

49. Scholarship has generally emphasized the graphic dimension of Sulṭān Valad's linguistic adaptation, though its auditory dimension was arguably no less important. On his composition of poetry in multiple languages in the same script, see Matthias Kappler, "Graphic Adaptation in Sultân Veled's Greek and Turkish Verses," 227.

50. Aflākī, *Manāqib al-ʿārifīn*, vol. 2, 801–2.

51. Sulṭān Valad, *Rabāb-nāma*, 438. I thank my colleague William Stroebel, who graciously provided all the translations here of Sulṭān Valad's Greek poetry.

52. Sulṭān Valad, *Rabāb-nāma*, 439; transliteration in the Greek script from Dimitris Dedes, "Τά ἑλληνικά ποιήματα τοῦ Μαυλανᾶ Ρουμῆ," 13. For legibility, I have slightly modified the spacing in ʿAlī Sulṭānī Gird-Farāmarzī's edition of the *Rabāb-nāma*, which divides Greek words in two in a few cases. I have also changed the spelling of some words in the Perso-Greek text (e.g., *īzū*, ἐδῶ or "here," instead of *āpzū*, which might be readable only as a truncated "from here"), in consultation with Dedes's transcription of the Perso-Greek verses and accompanying transliteration ("Τά ἑλληνικά ποιήματα τοῦ Μαυλανᾶ Ρουμῆ," 14).

53. Dedes has suggested that Sulṭān Valad's use of this term suggests contact between the Sufi lodge in Konya and the nearby Christian monastery of Saint Charitōn ("Τά ἑλληνικά ποιήματα τοῦ Μαυλανᾶ Ρουμῆ," 5–6).

54. Sulṭān Valad, *Rabāb-nāma*, 440; transliteration from Dedes, "Τά ἑλληνικά ποιήματα τοῦ Μαυλανᾶ Ρουμῆ," 15. Here too I have preferred a minor change in spelling, in consultation with Dedes's transcription of the Perso-Greek verses (14).

55. Sulṭān Valad, *Rabāb-nāma*, 446. See Mansuroğlu, *Sultan Veled'in Türkçe Manzumeleri*, 17, for a transliteration of these verses into the modern Turkish script; xxii-lxii, for facsimiles of the *Rabāb-nāma*'s Turkish verses, which include a handful of spellings that are different from those in Gird-Farāmarzī's edition of the *Rabāb-nāma* and which I have preferred in one case here (*kişinüñ*, which also appears with a final *nūn*).

56. Sulṭān Valad, *Rabāb-nāma*, 451.

57. Sulṭān Valad, *Rabāb-nāma,* 449. Here too I have made a few minor changes in spelling (e.g., *gibi* instead of *bigi*), following Mansuroğlu, *Sultan Veled'in Türkçe Manzumeleri,* 22, and the related facsimiles therein.

58. Rūmī, *Maṡnavī,* 5: 841-42.

59. Katharina Otto-Dorn, "Figural Stone Reliefs on Seljuk Sacred Architecture in Anatolia."

60. Otto-Dorn, "Figural Stone Reliefs," 115.

61. Otto-Dorn, "Figural Stone Reliefs," 120, 123.

62. Sulṭān Valad, *Rabāb-nāma,* 454.

63. Sulṭān Valad, *Rabāb-nāma,* 2.

64. Johanson, "Rūmī and the Birth of Turkish Poetry," 29–36.

65. Dihkhudā, *Lughat-nāma,* vol. 7, 10456.

Chapter 4: A Brief Stroll through Rūm

1. For a short discussion of Süleymān Türkmānī and Sulṭān Valad's other representatives, see Abdülbâki Gölpınarlı, *Mevlânâ'dan sonra Mevlevîlik,* 44; Hülya Küçük, "Sulṭān Walad's Role in the Foundation of the Mevlevi Sufi Order," 44–47. On the spread of the teachings of Rūmī and Sulṭān Valad, see also A. C. S. Peacock, *Islam, Literature and Society in Mongol Anatolia,* 103–7.

2. For instance, Karl Reichl, a pioneer of scholarship on medieval orality among Turkic peoples, has posited that while we can now access medieval oral culture only through texts, one difference between Turkic oral poetry and its European counterparts is that a culture reminiscent of "medieval orality is still alive in Turkey, both in song and in epic or romance" ("Medieval Turkish Epic and Popular Narrative," 682; see also Reichl's valuable studies on Turkic orality and poetic recitation *Singing the Past* and *Turkic Oral Epic Poetry*). For a study on the signs of orality and oral performance across different genres of writing, see Arzu Öztürkmen, "Orality and Performance in Late Medieval Turkish Texts." Finally, see also İlhan Başgöz's collection of essays *Turkish Folklore and Oral Literature.*

3. Köprülü made this position clear on numerous occasions. For instance, in his influential *Early Mystics of Turkish Literature,* he argues: "While the elite who received a *madrasa* education in the great civilized centers of Anatolia cultivated a taste for the refined products of Persian literature and tried to write works of the same kind, the great mass of the people remained almost total strangers to it. Not only the nomadic Turkmen tribes and the march tribes who guarded the frontiers with Byzantium, Armenia, and Georgia, but also a large part of the urban population could take no pleasure in the literature of a language that they did not understand. Consequently, a number of simple and rudimentary Turkish works of a religious or heroic nature, as well as heroic poems, were written for them. The wandering *ozans* [minstrels], who for centuries had, with *kopuz* in hand, satisfied the aesthetic needs of the people, kept the old Turkish traditions alive throughout Anatolia in a vigorous and devoted manner" (210). See also Köprülü, "Ozan."

4. Köprülü, *Early Mystics in Turkish Literature,* 211.

5. The full sentence reads: "Beneath a veneer apparently borrowed from Arabic and Persian culture, Turkish life in Anatolia in the Seljuk period was perhaps a bit primitive, but it was completely national, genuine, and widespread" (Köprülü, *Early Mystics in Turkish Literature,* 210).

6. See, for instance, Mehmet Fuat Köprülü, *Türk Edebiyatı'nda İlk Mutasavvıflar,* 1, 168–69. Köprülü briefly describes the New Persian absorption of Arabic poetic models in similar terms ("Arûz," 640).

7. Paul E. Losensky, *Welcoming Fighānī,* 108.

8. As Karamustafa has argued, "There are serious problems with this 'two-tiered' model of religion. The assumption of an unbridgeable separation between high, normative and low, antinomian religion serves to obscure rather than clarify the true nature of the deviant dervish groups and the process of their emergence in the aftermath of the Mongol invasions," as it tends to strip "this particular mode of dervish religiosity of its specific features and renders it immune to analysis by suggesting that it is essentially indistinct from the 'popular' versions of other religious trends such as millenarianism and messianism" (*God's Unruly Friends,* 9). See also Wolper's overview of Köprülü's thesis in *Cities and Saints,* 6–13.

9. For the original poem, see Mecdut Mansuroğlu, "Mevlâna Celâleddin Rumî'de Türkçe Beyit ve İbareler," 210–11, 215–16. See also the short discussion of this line in Lars Johanson, "Rūmī and the Birth of Turkish Poetry," 30. On Rūmī's composition of poetry in Turkish, see also Mansuroğlu, "Calāladdīn Rūmī's türkische Verse"; Mansuroğlu, "The Rise and Development of Written Turkish in Anatolia"; Mehmed Şerefeddin [Yaltkaya], "Mevlânâ'da Türkçe Kelimeler ve Türkçe Şiirler."

10. As Johanson speculates, "We may suppose that J̌elāleddīn Rūmī brought Persian *(P)* and East Oghuzic (Khorasan) Turkic *(TE)* with him, and that he acquired knowledge of West Oghuzic, Anatolian Turkish *(TW)* and even Greek *(G)* in Qonya. We know nothing about the relationship between his competence in *TW* and *TE*" ("Rūmī and the Birth of Turkish Poetry," 24).

11. On the figure of the *maddāḥ,* see P. N. Boratav, "Maddāḥ."

12. See Cemal Kafadar's comparative reading of frontier literature, including his discussion of the Greek romance *Digenēs Akritēs* in relation to Turkish *ghāzī* narratives, for a broader overview of this ethos (*Between Two Worlds,* 65–90). Köprülü also provides a succinct overview of the "historical" romance genre in *The Seljuks of Anatolia,* 40–52.

13. Irène Mélikoff-Sayar has posited that legends about the Dānişmendids were recorded in the thirteenth century and then compiled and revised in the fourteenth century, although the earliest known copy of the *Dānişmend-nāme* was not produced until the fifteenth century (*La geste de Melik Dānişmend,* vol. 1, 53–70).

14. See Yorgos Dedes's short discussion of these performers (*Battalname,* vol. 1, 52) and his extensive introduction to and translation of the *Baṭṭāl-nāme.* See also Mélikoff-Sayar, *La geste de Melik Dānişmend,* vol. 2, 8.

15. For an English introduction and translation (facing the original Turkish), see Yūsuf-i Meddāḥ, *Varqa ve Gülşāh.*

16. On Yūsuf-i Meddāḥ's adoption of *'arūż* and use of Persian vocabulary, see Grace Martin Smith's introduction to Yūsuf-i Meddāḥ, *Varqa ve Gülşāh*, 18–20.

17. On heroism and the rise of what might be termed heroic literature in medieval Anatolia, see Gottfried Hagen, "Heroes and Saints in Anatolian Turkish Literature."

18. Reichl, "Medieval Turkish Epic and Popular Narrative," 687–90.

19. The two sixteenth-century manuscripts are held in the Vatican Library (MS Turco 102) and in the Saxonian State and University Library Dresden (MS Ea.86). For transcriptions of both, see the edition by Semih Tezcan and Hendrik Boeschoten, *Dede Korkut Oğuznameleri.*

20. Translation by Geoffrey Lewis, in *The Book of Dede Korkut*, 21. For the original Arabic, see Ibn al-Dawādārī, *Durar al-tījān wa-ghurar tawārīkh al-azmān*, 55.

21. Translation by Lewis, in *Book of Dede Korkut*, 21; see also Ibn al-Dawādārī, *Durar al-tījān wa-ghurar tawārīkh al-azmān*, 55.

22. For comparative studies of the Tepegöz-Polyphemus relationship, see Jo Ann Conrad, "Polyphemus and Tepegöz Revisited"; Heinrich Friedrich von Diez, *Der neuentdeckte oghuzische Cyklop verglichen mit dem Homerischen*; Wilhelm Grimm, "Die Sage von Polyphem"; Michael E. Meeker, "The Dede Korkut Ethic"; C. S. Mundy, "Polyphemus and Tepegöz."

23. See Mundy, "Polyphemus and Tepegöz," 295–98, for a succinct overview of the narrative structure in these tales; Conrad offers an even more comprehensive comparison in "Polyphemus and Tepegöz Revisited," 289–92.

24. Odysseus is the great-grandson of Hermes, a son of Zeus; Polyphemus is Zeus's nephew.

25. For instance, Diez, in his 1815 comparative study of the Turkish and Greek tales, posits that the origin was indeed Turkish (*Der neuentdeckte oghuzische Cyklop*), though this theory was met by many dissenting voices. For a short overview of discussions on this subject, see Mundy, "Polyphemus and Tepegöz," 279–83.

26. Meeker, "Dede Korkut Ethic."

27. Mundy, "Polyphemus and Tepegöz," 288. On Greek folktales about the Tepekozēs, see R. M. Dawkins, *More Greek Folktales*, 12–24.

28. James R. Russell has observed that Armenian folktales feature a Cyclops named T'ap'agöz, possibly reflecting "the influences of the Turco-Moslem milieu in which the Armenians lived, as well as, perhaps, the infiltration of the Homeric story of the Cyclops itself through both literary sources and the oral folklore of the Greeks of Cappadocia and Pontus" ("Polyphemos Armenios," 36).

29. Franco Moretti, "Conjectures on World Literature," 57. Moretti's insight into the global diffusion of the novel's form—that is, as a literary *form* and not merely as a translated text—has perhaps been overshadowed by the more controversial aspects of his methodology of "distant reading," such as its Eurocentrism or his insistence that "if, between the very small and the very large, the text itself disappears, well, it is one of those cases when

one can justifiably say, Less is more. If we want to understand the system in its entirety, we must accept losing something." Although I do not share Moretti's drive to comprehend the world-literary system in its "entirety" and do not think literary studies will or should ever let the text "disappear," I do contend that to understand the integration of literary cultures in Rūm at this time, we ought to account for movable "units that are much smaller or much larger than" the texts themselves. These units are often marked by a certain cultural ambiguity and in some cases belong to a shared or overlapping lexicon that is the result of the mixing of peoples and languages in this region.

30. For an English translation and introduction to the Grottaferrata version of *Digenēs Akritēs*, see Denison B. Hull, *Digenis Akritas*. For a more recent translation, based on both the Grottaferrata and Escorial versions, see Elizabeth Jeffreys, *Digenis Akritis*.

31. On the romance's development, see Roderick Beaton, *The Medieval Greek Romance*, 30–51.

32. The ethnomusicologist Joachim Braun, noting the dearth of information about Byzantine musical instruments, has used miniatures to shed light on Byzantine organology. In particular, he has compared a lute in a miniature from an eleventh-century copy of *Barlaam and Josaphat* likely produced in Constantinople to four-string, pear-shaped lutes (*kobza*, known as *kobuz* to the Uzbeks and *kobiz* to the Kazakhs) in miniatures from seventeenth-century Ukraine ("Musical Instruments in Byzantine Illuminated Manuscripts," 321–22). For salient references to the lute in the Greek variants of *Digenēs Akritēs*, see Jeffreys, *Digenis Akritis*, 284, 302, 304, 324.

33. Hull, *Digenis Akritas*, 44.

34. Hull, *Digenis Akritas*, 24.

35. Yūsuf-i Meddāḥ, *Varqa ve Gülşāh*, 131, lines 912–13.

36. The correlation of musical performance with these particular affective states may help to explain why Rūmī famously begins the *Mas̱navī* with the *nay*'s complaint on separation and not with the customary praise of God. The pains of separation, in this formal and generic sense, must be expressed immediately through song—they simply cannot be suppressed. This pattern extends to various medieval Greek romances: Belthandros (romanized as Velthandros from modern Greek), the protagonist of *Belthandros and Chrysantza*, sings of his bitter separation from country and kin while playing an instrument similar to the lyre, just as the protagonist of the Greek romance *Libistros and Rodamni* sings at moments of parting. See Gavin Betts, *Three Medieval Greek Romances*, 7, 173.

37. The *Baṭṭāl-nāme* provides another example of this. Its hero, Jaʿfar, mounts a horse in the middle of the night; to the alarm of his mother, he heads for Rūm, a land of infidels. Eventually, he reaches a monastery, where he is greeted by a monk named Shammās (Deacon). To Jaʿfar's surprise, the monk is hospitable, offering bread, grapes, and other delights. After night falls, the monk leads Jaʿfar into a room where he finds "a *masjid* with a *mihrab* properly arranged" and a Qur'an on its stand. Shammās takes off his monastic garments and dons Sufi robes, leading the call to prayer and relating many tales about Rūm before dawn. From the perspective of the narrative, the episode prefigures Jaʿfar's violent

conquest of Rūm and proselytization of Islam. Thus, in the very next scene he begs God for the strength to seize Rūm and to "destroy its churches and build mosques and madrasas in their place." However, even this triumphalist and militant narrative cannot erase a plain ambiguity: Shammās, despite living in a monastery, is already fluent in the devotional practices of Islam. Furthermore, it is from Shammās, whose name preserves his Christian background and who stands at the threshold between Islam and Christianity, that Jaʿfar learns not only of the country he is to overthrow but also that outward appearances can be misleading. For an English translation, see Dedes, *Battalname*, vol. 1, 107. A similar account, featuring a dervish and a Christian monk, appears in the *Vilāyet-nāme* (see Abdülbâki Gölpınarlı, *Manakıb-ı Hacı Bektâş-ı Velî*, 55).

38. Kafadar, in reading *Digenēs Akritēs* alongside Turkish *ghāzī* narratives, first observed that the boundary running between these Christian and Muslim worlds "is more remarkable for the ease with which one can cross it than for its rigidity" (*Between Two Worlds*, 81–82).

39. Henri Grégoire and Roger Goossens, "Byzantinisches Epos und arabischer Ritterroman."

40. Kafadar, *Between Two Worlds*, 82.

41. On the interactions between the Türkmen and local non-Muslim populations, see Claude Cahen, *Pre-Ottoman Turkey*, 202–15.

42. Mattʿeos Uṙhayetsʿi [Matthew of Edessa], *Armenia and the Crusades*, 137.

43. Marco Polo, *The Travels*, 18.

44. Kafadar has productively argued that the purpose of such frontier literature "is, among other things, an attempt to gain hearts and minds; it is always possible that the pure-hearted infidel will join your fold. He or she is not necessarily an enemy to the bitter end" (*Between Two Worlds*, 82).

45. Shushanik Nazaryan, *Patmutʿiwn Farman Mankann*, 65, lines 141–43. We know very little about the origin of this romance, but it was composed in Middle Armenian and makes liberal use of Persian loanwords, including in some of its end rhymes. The earliest known copy is from the fifteenth century.

46. Mkhitʿar Gosh, *The Lawcode (Datastanagirkʿ) of Mxitʿar Gosh*, 254–55. On the figure of the minstrel in premodern Parthian and Armenian contexts, see Mary Boyce, "The Parthian Gōsān and Iranian Minstrel Tradition"; on Armenian minstrels in the late medieval and early modern period, see Theo Maarten van Lint, "The Gift of Poetry."

47. The romance makes no mention of Armenians; moreover, its characters have names similar to those found in Firdawsī's *Shāh-nāma*, as James R. Russell has discovered ("The Šāh-nāme in Armenian Oral Epic"). Conspicuously absent is any evocation of Christianity, save for a brief encomium at the end. See also Russell's translation of the *Patmutʿiwn Farman Mankann* and discussion of its meter ("The History of the Youth Farman").

48. Nazaryan, *Patmutʿiwn Farman Mankann*, 136, lines 772–80. Pʿōlati Hndi, who has died at this point in the narrative, is one of Farman's primary antagonists.

49. As Russell argues, "Armenian has no short and long vowels or syllables, so its basic poetic forms have been syllabic; but the regularity of stress can be manipulated to produce an imitation of quantitative meter. . . . This heroic effect, employed in PFM [*The History of the Youth Farman*], sets a suitable mood, since the action of the poem moves back and forth between action scenes—jousting and fighting, narrow escapes, clever tricks and fast moves—and more tranquil episodes: love letters and expressions of longing." ("History of the Youth Farman," 204).

50. Kafadar, *Between Two Worlds,* 5.

51. On attempts to reconstruct Yūnus Emre's life and his reception over time, see Zekeriya Başkal, "Claiming Yunus Emre"; *Yunus Emre,* 81–141.

52. Köprülü, *Early Mystics in Turkish Literature,* 322.

53. See, for instance, Başkal, *Yunus Emre,* 36–46. Other scholars have demonstrated Yūnus Emre's interface with the Islamicate and Persianate worlds in different ways. In his study on Yūnus Emre's lexicon, Sait Hurşid argues that of a base vocabulary of 2,500 words, only 1,119 are of Turkic origin—the others are from Arabic (967), Persian (381), Greek (10), Latin (3), Armenian (2), and German (1) (*La langue de Yunus Emre,* 61–64). For a nuanced critique of the Köprülü paradigm and an examination of how Yūnus Emre's poetry created boundaries and mediated knowledge between different reading and listening publics, see Zeynep Oktay Uslu, "The *Şaṭḥiyye* of Yūnus Emre."

54. Yūnus Emre, *Yûnus Emre Dîvânı,* vol. 2, 361.

55. Yūnus Emre, *Yûnus Emre Dîvânı,* vol. 1, 550.

56. ʿAlī ibn ʿUs̱mān Hujvīrī, *Kashf al-maḥjūb,* 45.

57. Hujvīrī, *Kashf al-maḥjūb,* 184–85.

58. This hymn is an adaptation of a homily by Epiphanios (see *The Lamentations of Matins of Holy and Great Saturday,* 33–51).

59. Epiphanios, *Lamentations of Matins of Holy and Great Saturday,* 53. The hymn's discomforting and disquieting blame of Jews for the treatment of Jesus finds its scriptural parallel in Matthew 27:24–25.

60. Nazaryan, *Patmutʿiwn Farman Mankann,* 167–68, lines 1045–56.

61. Thomas Bauer, *Die Kultur der Ambiguität,* 347.

Chapter 5: Kırşehir Kinships

1. Under the Seljuks, the village of Gülşehir was part of Kırşehir Province, and these toponyms seem to have been used "near-synonymously" in the medieval period (A. C. S. Peacock, *Islam, Literature and Society in Mongol Anatolia,* 159n53).

2. On the coinage minted under Ghāzān and his successors, see Sheila S. Blair, "The Coins of the Later Ilkhanids."

3. Rudi Paul Lindner calls the thirteenth century in Anatolia a "silver age," when as many as ten mines produced an abundance of coins. Their common name—which can

also be transliterated as *akça*—is a reference to the purity of Anatolia's silver (*Explorations in Ottoman Prehistory*, 88–89).

4. For a brief overview of Süleymān Türkmānī's life and activity in Kırşehir, see Ethem Erkoç, *Âşık Paşa ve Oğlu Elvan Çelebi*, 53–54.

5. On this intermittently fraught relationship, see the chapter by Judith Pfeiffer, "Mevlevi-Bektashi Rivalries and the Islamisation of the Public Space in Late Seljuq Anatolia."

6. Shams al-Dīn Aḥmad Aflākī, *Manāqib al-ʿārifīn*, vol. 1, 381.

7. For instance, the historian Speros Vryonis has observed that local Bektāşīs and Christians shared a number of practices, which lent these Muslims, in his words, a "good propaganda advantage" in the Islamization of Anatolia: "They equated the twelve imams with the twelve apostles; the virgin birth of Christ with that of Balīm Sultan, the second founder of the order. They considered Hadji Bektash a reincarnation of Saint Charalambus. As the Christians had a Trinity, so did the Bektashis, consisting of God, Muhammad, and Ali. And, of course, Bektashi mysticism, as was true of most Islamic mystical orders, ultimately derived much of its mystical doctrine from Neoplatonism, in which the Godhead created the world by emanating from itself: It is obvious how eclectic and syncretistic Bektashism was, and how accommodating and latitudinarian it was" (*The Decline of Medieval Hellenism in Asia Minor and the Process of Islamization from the Eleventh through the Fifteenth Century*, 372). Vryonis suggests that Bektāşīs were also able to preserve older Türkmen traditions—such as the ecstatic dancing of shamans through the performance of *samāʿ*. But whereas he characterizes many of these affinities as "obviously incidental or accidental parallels," we might adopt a different approach: namely, viewing such affinities as attempts to accommodate and eventually transform differences within the same hermeneutic frame.

8. Moreover, like other *maṡnavī* writers in Rūm, Gülşehrī composed this work in the *ramal* meter, using Sanāʾī as his model. See Gülşehrī, *Gülşehri ve Felek-nâme.*

9. The only known manuscript of this treatise is preserved in the İstanbul Millet Kütüphanesi, *Farsça yazmalar*, no. 517, fols. 46v–61v.

10. Other Turkish poems attributed to Gülşehrī, such as a work on the deeds of Akhī Evren, likewise employ the *maṡnavī* form (see Franz Taeschner, *Gülschehrîs Mesnevi auf Achi Evran*). It is worth noting that this attribution has been contested, however.

11. Rūmī was far from the only poet to emulate ʿAṭṭār's *Manṭiq al-ṭayr.* For a survey of those who drew inspiration from it in Turkish, including a short discussion of Gülşehrī, see Berrin Uyar Akalın, "The Poets Who Wrote and Translated Mantiku't Tayr in Turkish Literature."

12. Christopher Shackle, for instance, has called Gülşehrī's *Manṭiq al-ṭayr* a "translation" that is about "the same length as the original, which it follows in metre and to which it appears to be quite faithful in style, although in places divergent in content." At the same time, he rightly notes that "creative imitation" often played a more important role than translation in the interface between Persian poetry and other literatures in the premodern era ("Representations of ʿAṭṭār in the West and in the East," 176).

13. Gülşehrī, *Gülşehri'nin Mantıku't-Tayr'ı*, vol. 2, 654, line 4416. On the concept of *te'līf* in Ottoman literature, see Saliha Paker, "On the Poetic Practices of 'A Singularly Uninventive People' and the Anxiety of Imitation." See also Selim S. Kuru's short discussion of *te'līf* and translation in relation to Gülşehrī, "Destânı Mesnevîde Anlatmak," 203–4.

14. Vanessa Margaret Shepherd, "The Turkish Mystical Poet Gülşehrī with Particular Reference to His Manṭiq al-Ṭayr," 59–99. For more comparisons of the stories in the *Manṭiq al-ṭayr*s of ʿAṭṭār and Gülşehrī, see Akalın, "Poets Who Wrote and Translated Mantiku't Tayr," 171; Kemal Yavuz, "Çeşitli Yönleri ile Mantıku't-Tayr ve Garib-nâme Mesnevileri," 347–48.

15. Gülşehrī, *Gülşehri'nin Mantıku't-Tayr'ı*, vol. 2, 398–446.

16. On the transgressive lesson of Shaykh Ṣanʿān, see Claudia Yaghoobi, "Subjectivity in ʿAttār's Shaykh Sanʿān Story in *The Conference of the Birds*."

17. Gülşehrī, *Gülşehri'nin Mantıku't-Tayr'ı*, vol. 1, 48–112. See also Shepherd's discussion of this adaptation, "Turkish Mystical Poet Gülşehrī," 103–9. Sara Nur Yıldız suggests that the tale, with its emphasis on unbelief, may represent a subtle "underlying religious polemic against Christianity" ("Battling *Kufr* [Unbelief] in the Land of Infidels," 347).

18. Gülşehrī, *Gülşehri'nin Mantıku't-Tayr'ı*, vol. 1, 110. See also the short discussion of this scene in Peacock, *Islam, Literature and Society in Mongol Anatolia*, 206.

19. In fact, Gülşehrī adapted several tales from Rūmī's *Maṣnavī* and other works by ʿAṭṭār in a similar manner, bringing disparate narratives into a locally relevant interpretive frame (see Shepherd, "Turkish Mystical Poet Gülşehrī," 101).

20. Peacock, *Islam, Literature and Society in Mongol Anatolia*, 163.

21. Gülşehrī, *Gülşehri'nin Mantıku't-Tayr'ı*, vol. 2, 380–98.

22. Gülşehrī, *Gülşehri'nin Mantıku't-Tayr'ı*, vol. 2, 382, line 2562.

23. Gülşehrī, *Gülşehri'nin Mantıku't-Tayr'ı*, vol. 2, 392–94, lines 2630–41.

24. Shepherd, "Turkish Mystical Poet Gülşehrī," 164.

25. Selim S. Kuru, "Portrait of a Shaykh as Author in Fourteenth-Century Anatolia," 191. See also Kuru's earlier analysis of this story, "Gülşehrî the Seventh Sheikh of the Universe."

26. Kuru, "Portrait of a Shaykh as Author," 192.

27. Gülşehrī, *Gülşehri'nin Mantıku't-Tayr'ı*, vol. 2, 396, line 2660.

28. Gülşehrī, *Gülşehri'nin Mantıku't-Tayr'ı*, vol. 2, 396, line 2662.

29. Gülşehrī, *Gülşehri'nin Mantıku't-Tayr'ı*, vol. 2, 396, line 2664.

30. Gülşehrī, *Gülşehri'nin Mantıku't-Tayr'ı*, vol. 2, 396, line 2665.

31. A. J. Arberry, *The Koran Interpreted*, vol. 2, 77.

32. Gülşehrī, *Gülşehri'nin Mantıku't-Tayr'ı*, vol. 2, 652, lines 4401–2.

33. Gülşehrī, *Gülşehri'nin Mantıku't-Tayr'ı*, vol. 2, 654, lines 4408–13.

34. Gülşehrī, *Gülşehri'nin Mantıku't-Tayr'ı*, vol. 2, 656, line 4419.

35. Barbara Flemming, "Old Anatolian Turkish Poetry in Its Relationship to the Persian Tradition," 49.

36. Gülşehrī, *Gülşehri'nin Mantıku't-Tayr'ı*, vol. 2, 656, line 4428.

37. As noted, Gülşehrī occasionally seems to refer to himself by the name of Süleymān (Solomon), prompting speculation about his identity. However, Shepherd has posited that in cases where Gülşehrī explicitly refers to both Solomon and the language of the birds, he probably has the Qur'anic Solomon in mind. Still, there appears to be some overlap here, as Gülşehrī/Süleymān more or less assumes Solomon's ability to impart the language of the birds to others. See the discussion in Shepherd, "Turkish Mystical Poet Gülşehrī," 26–30.

38. The title could alternatively be translated as *Book of the Strange.*

39. Mecdut Mansuroğlu, "Turkish Literature through the Ages," 92. In contrast, Mansuroğlu more enthusiastically asserts: "Yûnus Amra was the greatest figure in [the thirteenth] century. He is regarded as the best Turkish popular mystic poet. His art is essentially one of the people, i.e. it is Turkish. It was through his mystical verses that there developed a tradition of writing poems in the language of the people and in the popular syllabic metre, which did not lose its power even in the period when Persian influence was at its height" (90).

40. Gibb, *A History of Ottoman Poetry,* 185.

41. Maḥmūd al-Kāshgharī, *Compendium of the Turkic Dialects.*

42. For overviews of Turkish literary production and the circulation of popular narratives in the historiography of medieval Egypt, see Ulrich Haarmann's brief "Turkish Legends in the Popular Historiography of Medieval Egypt" and more detailed version of the same study, "Alṭun Ḫān und Čingiz Ḫān bei den ägyptischen Mamluken."

43. On literary production at the Aydınid court, see Sara Nur Yıldız's groundbreaking "Aydınid Court Literature in the Formation of an Islamic Identity in Fourteenth-Century Western Anatolia." See also Barbara Flemming's classic study on Fahrī, "Faḫrī's *Ḫusrev u Šīrīn* vom Jahre 1367," translated into English by Vanessa Karam, with some revisions by Flemming, as "Old Anatolian Turkish Poetry in its Relationship to the Persian Tradition," and then by John O'Kane as "Faḫrī's *Ḫusrev u Şīrīn* from the Year 1367."

44. Yıldız has posited that the cultivation of literary *adab* at court could have reached a broader audience, though she acknowledges that "the small number of manuscript copies of some of these works indicates a rather limited circulation" ("Aydınid Court Literature," 199).

45. See, e.g., Halil İnalcık, "The Origins of Classical Ottoman Literature."

46. That al-Kāshgharī sought to shore up Turkic sovereignty might not be immediately apparent. Yet he famously cites an apocryphal hadith in which the Prophet Muḥammad commands all to "learn the tongue of the Turks, for their reign will be long" (*Compendium of the Turkic Dialects,* vol. 1, 70). For the 'Abbasid audience of his Turkic lexicon, which had recently witnessed the Seljuk conquest of Baghdad, this injunction could not have been more on the nose.

47. 'Āşıḳ Paşa, *Garib-nâme,* vol. 1, pt. 1, 4–5.

48. ʿĀşıḳ Paşa, *Garib-nâme*, vol. 1, pt. 1, 6–7. "Tajik" is often translated as "Persian," although its meaning in this period was certainly multifaceted (see John Perry, "Tajik I").

49. The polysemous terms that ʿĀşıḳ Paşa uses here, *żabṭ* (regulation) and *uṣūl* (rules), can also connote senses of, on the one hand, writing or spelling and, on the other, vocalizing the Arabic script, musical tone, or musical mode.

50. ʿĀşıḳ Paşa, *Garib-nâme*, vol. 2, pt. 2, 954–55, lines 10560–63. See also the discussion and translation of this passage in Peacock's *Islam, Literature and Society in Mongol Anatolia*, 161–63.

51. ʿĀşıḳ Paşa, *Garib-nâme*, vol. 2, pt. 2, 956–57, lines 10575, 10570.

52. ʿĀşıḳ Paşa, *Garib-nâme*, vol. 2, pt. 2, 956–57, line 10572.

53. ʿĀşıḳ Paşa, *Garib-nâme*, vol. 2, pt. 2, 924–25.

54. As Kemal Yavuz observes in the notes to his edition of the *Garīb-nāme*, its correlation of Islam with "strangeness" is reinforced by the famous hadith "Islam began as a stranger and it will return as a stranger as it began; therefore blessed are the strangers!" (ʿĀşıḳ Paşa, *Garib-nâme*, vol. 2, pt. 2, 925). For a discussion of this hadith, see Franz Rosenthal, "The Stranger in Medieval Islam," 59–63.

55. Sheldon Pollock, *The Language of the Gods in the World of Men*, 26. I am grateful to Gottfried Hagen for encouraging me to think about Pollock's argument in relation to medieval Anatolia. Hagen draws on Pollock's terms *literization* (the admission of a language to writing) and *literarization* (the development of a language as literary) to conceptualize the emergence of literary Turkish in Anatolia in his paper "Updated Prolegomena to a Social Prehistory of the Ottoman Language." See also Peacock's brief discussion of Pollock and the applicability of his model to early Anatolian Turkish in *Islam, Literature and Society in Mongol Anatolia*, 149–51.

56. ʿĀşıḳ Paşa, *Garib-nâme*, vol. 1, pt. 1, 138–39, line 601.

57. ʿĀşıḳ Paşa, *Garib-nâme*, vol. 1, pt. 1, 140–41, lines 610–14.

58. ʿĀşıḳ Paşa, *Garib-nâme*, vol. 1, pt. 1, 142–43, lines 621–26. The Armenian text is not entirely clear here, containing a mixture of easily recognizable words and others that are not well attested. I have read *elük* as the Middle Armenian *aluk*, generally meaning "bright red," and the Persian verb *kharīm*, "let us buy," as opposed to Yavuz's reading of *ḥazīm*. However, the only thing that is certain is that the Armenian is likewise speaking of his desire for grapes. This is obvious in the phrasing "hagūg küzim / tī hagūg carnūs." In Armenian, this would be transliterated as խաղող կ'ուզեմ, թէ խաղող կ'առնուս (I want grapes / if you get grapes).

59. ʿĀşıḳ Paşa, *Garib-nâme*, vol. 1, pt. 1, 144–45, lines 632–38.

60. Jalāl al-Dīn Rūmī, *Maṣnavī*, 2: 3681–85. *Angūr*, ʿ*inab*, *üzüm*, and *staphulē* are the words for "grape" in Persian, Arabic, Turkish, and Greek, respectively. I have transliterated the Greek term directly from Greek rather than preserving Rūmī's spelling in the Persian script (*istāfīl*). It should also be observed that the word for "Greek" in this excerpt is *rūmī*. As previously noted, this is a relatively plastic term that encompassed more peoples than

Greeks alone. However, the fact that this *rūmī* speaks Greek clears up the ambiguity in this case.

61. Rūmī, *Maṣnavī*, 2: 3688–92. The Arabic is a quotation from the Qur'an (7:204).

62. Rūmī, *Maṣnavī*, 2: 3699. Although Reynold Nicholson originally preferred the variant of "people of envy," *ahl-i ḥasad*, in this line, he later corrected his critical edition to read *ahl-i jasad*, "people of the body" (*Maṣnavī*, vol. 7, 366).

63. Rūmī, *Maṣnavī*, 2: 3710.

64. ʿĀşıḳ Paşa, *Garib-nâme*, vol. 1, pt. 1, 146–47, line 644.

65. ʿĀşıḳ Paşa, *Garib-nâme*, vol. 1, pt. 1, 146–47, line 646.

66. ʿĀşıḳ Paşa, *Garib-nâme*, vol. 1, pt. 1, 146–47, line 651.

67. ʿĀşıḳ Paşa, *Garib-nâme*, vol. 1, pt. 1, 148–49, lines 656–58.

68. ʿĀşıḳ Paşa, *Garib-nâme*, vol. 2, pt. 1, 204–5, lines 6698–99.

69. ʿĀşıḳ Paşa, *Garib-nâme*, vol. 2, pt. 1, 204–5, line 6700.

70. Peacock has similarly argued that the choice to compose in Turkish was not "merely" about the need to communicate with local audiences but also concerned "the author's means of testifying to his own unique relationship with God as a channel of his communication." Thus, as Peacock suggests, "the choice of a vernacular can serve a role in discourses of power—indeed, in asserting the most important form of power of all, religious power" (*Islam, Literature and Society in Mongol Anatolia*, 164–65).

71. On ʿĀşıḳ Paşa's death, see Elvān Çelebī, *Menâkıbu'l-Kudsiyye fî Menâsıbi'l-Ünsiyye*, 132–38.

Chapter 6: Cilician Riddles

1. Asatur Mnatsʿakanyan, *Hay mijnadaryan hanelukner*, 250. For other general collections and studies of riddles in Armenian, see S. B. Harutʿyunyan, *Hay zhoghovrdakan hanelukner*; Makʿsim Oskanyan, *Saghmosner, banasteghtsutʿyunner, zhoghovrdakan banarvesti mshakumner, aṛakner, hanelukner*; Yuri Sahakyan, *Hay zhoghovrdakan hanelukner*.

2. Hrachʿeay Achaṛean, in a short discussion of the word, notes that *tʿughtʿ* clearly meant "letter" or "epistle" long before it meant "paper"; Nersēs likely intended its epistolary sense here (*Hayeren armatakan baṛaran*, 630–31).

3. Nersēs Shnorhali, *Tʿughtʿ ĕndhanrakan*, 53.

4. Nersēs Shnorhali, *General Epistle*, 17; for the Armenian, see Nersēs Shnorhali, *Tʿughtʿ ĕndhanrakan*, 60–61.

5. For a general orientation to the Armenian settlements in Cilicia, see Sirarpie Der Nersessian, "The Kingdom of Cilician Armenia"; for broader historical background on Cilicia, with a focus on the Armenian kingdom there, see the detailed study by Claude Mutafian, *La Cilicie au carrefour des empires*. On the relationship between Armenians and Mongols in this period, see Bayarsaikhan Dashdondog, *The Mongols and the Armenians*.

6. Nersēs Shnorhali, *Oghb Edesioy*, 72, line 457.

7. Nersēs Shnorhali, *Oghb Edesioy*, 72, lines 459–60.

8. Nersēs Shnorhali, *Oghb Edesioy*, 88–89, lines 599–603. James R. Russell, in an important article on Nersēs's entwined literary production and communicative strategies, aptly notes that the term for "good news," *awetik'*, with its strong Christian connotations, would have struck medieval audiences as "grotesquely out of place" coming from the mouths of an invading Muslim army ("The Credal Poem *Hawatov Xostovanim*," 204—includes his translation of this passage). He also suggests that "worshipers of lifeless stone" perhaps refers to the Armenian *khach'k'ar*, an art form in which elaborate crosses were carved on stone monoliths (204–5). Theo Maarten van Lint alternatively proposes, in his annotated translation of the poem, that the line alludes to the altars of Christian churches (Nersēs Shnorhali, "*Lament on Edessa* by Nersēs Šnorhali," 81).

9. Nersēs Shnorhali, *Oghb Edesioy*, 89–90.

10. Kirakos Gandzakets'i, *Patmut'iwn hayots'*, 120.

11. On Nersēs's activity as a musician, see Nikoghos T'ahmizyan, *Nerses Shnorhalin.*

12. Kirakos Gandzakets'i, *Patmut'iwn hayots'*, 119.

13. Russell, "Credal Poem *Hawatov Xostovanim*," 215.

14. Kirakos Gandzakets'i, *Patmut'iwn hayots'*, 120.

15. *Zhamagirk' ateni*, 187.

16. Karla Mallette, "The Mediterranean Is Armenian," 319.

17. On Nersēs's use of his great-grandfather's literary innovation, see Theo Maarten van Lint, "Seeking Meaning in Catastrophe," 34.

18. Russell, "Credal Poem *Hawatov Xostovanim*," 208.

19. For instance, the late ninth- and early tenth-century historian and catholicos of the Armenian Church Hovhannēs Draskhanakertts'i reports that Shapuh Bagratuni wrote his (now lost) history in a "rustic" or "country" language (*geghjuk baniw*) (*Patmut'iwn hayots'*, 132).

20. Mkhit'ar Herats'i, *Mkhit'aray Bzhshkapeti Herats'woy jermants' mkhit'arut'iwn*, viii. Mkhit'ar also describes his writing as *ardzak*, usually understood as "prose." S. Peter Cowe, in conversation with me, offered a possible secondary reading: "free"—that is, "unbridled," no longer constricted by the rules of Classical Armenian. I am grateful for his observation.

21. On the development of "Middle" Armenian, see Ghewond V. Hovnanean, *Hetazōtut'iwnk' nakhneats' ṛamkōrēni vray*; Josef Karst, *Historische Grammatik des Kilikisch-Armenischen.* On Middle Armenian as a literary language, see Ēduard Bagrati Aghayan and Gevorg Beglari Jahukyan, *Aknarkner mijin grakan hayereni patmut'yan*; G. B. Jahukyan, *Hayots' lezvi zargats'umĕ ev kaṛuts'vatsk'ĕ.* Other scholars have pushed back on terming Middle Armenian a "literary" (*grakan*) language, however, in part by stressing that it remained internally heterogeneous both lexically and grammatically (see, e.g., Yuri Avetisyan, *Grakan hayereni zargats'man erku shrjap'ulerĕ*). Yet other early vernacular cultures were also internally heterogeneous, such as Middle English—in whose case to such a degree that the "southern" Parson in Chaucer's *Canterbury Tales* famously finds the English alliterative poetry of the north incomprehensible (330). Somewhat similarly, Middle Armenian's internal linguistic heterogeneity does not preclude the fact that the works composed in this language—particularly poems—generally derived their aesthetics, forms, genres, and conventions from the

"codes" *of* literary languages, especially Classical Armenian but also Persian and Turkish, although in unequal ways. It is therefore probably more accurate to say that different senses of "the literary" emerge, to different degrees, within the varied body of Middle Armenian poetic culture than to uniformly apply or reject the label of "the literary."

22. Kirakos Gandzakets'i, *Patmut'iwn hayots'*, 147.

23. Shahab Ahmed, *What Is Islam?*, 306-10.

24. Mnats'akanyan, *Hay mijnadaryan hanelukner*, 250.

25. On riddles and the riddling aspects of Sanāʾī's poetry, see A. A. Seyed-Gohrab, *Courtly Riddles*, 133–43.

26. Seyed-Gohrab, *Courtly Riddles*, 76–84.

27. About three hundred Byzantine riddles have been published. Čelica Milovanović-Barham has divided them into three categories: folk, literary, and subliterary. The last type are composed in a simple prose style but still "draw their inspiration from a literary text, namely from the Bible, not from popular imagination" ("Aldhelm's *Enigmata* and Byzantine Riddles," 54).

28. Mustafa Argunşah and Galip Güner, *Codex Cumanicus*, 339–49.

29. Russell, "Credal Poem *Hawatov Xostovanim*," 201–3n26.

30. Take, for instance, the following riddle about Elijah in Nersēs's collection: "The lad didn't eat, except for fire; / the raven fed that mighty one stew. / Riding a fiery steed, he came swiftly; / he poured us water from the clouds" (Mnats'akanyan, *Hay mijnadaryan hanelukner*, 232–33). Though the riddle is dense with biblical allusions (1 Kings 17:6; 2 Kings 2:11), the first line is extrabiblical, likely from the Armenian translation of the apocryphal *Lives of the Prophets* (21:2), which says that as a baby, Elijah was swaddled in flaming clothes and given fiery food.

31. Even pre-Christian mythical figures feature prominently in Nersēs's riddles. For instance, immediately following a riddle on the biblical Samson, whose locks are severed by a wily Delilah, the audience encounters a different kind of hero: "There was a warrior lauded among Armenians, / even more triumphant than Samson. / He plucked up a great, vexatious boulder, / hurled it into the sea, set up a statue" (Mnats'akanyan, *Hay mijnadaryan hanelukner*, 228). The answer is nowhere to be found in scripture: this is a riddle about Tork', an Armenian demigod and descendant of Hayk, the equally mythical progenitor of the Armenians. Movsēs Khorenats'i, a historian who claimed to be writing in the fifth century but was perhaps from a later time (see Nina Garsoïan, "Movsēs Xorenac'i"), was the first to compare his strength and Samson's. In Movsēs's eyes, not even the Persian hero Rustam equaled Tork'. After all, Tork' could easily heft boulders, tossing them like skipping stones at ships on the sea. He could carve indelible reliefs of eagles and other animals into rock with just his fingernail. He was the embodiment of a past, an era of mythos making, that the Armenians had seemingly left far behind, consigned to the Classical Armenian of an ancient history book. However, Nersēs's riddles resurrect Tork' as part of a vernacular history of Armenian Christianity. Other heroic figures from Armenian history join Tork''s ranks in Nersēs's collection, such as the late fourth-century King Varazdat, who leaped

over the entire Euphrates. It appears, then, that Nersēs aimed to supplant cultures of epic or mythic storytelling in part with something that was not always so different in character. Moreover, by placing these enigmas culled from Armenian history and legend within his series of biblical riddles, he arguably guided his audience to understand such narratives in the proper light: that is to say, in the light of Christ.

32. Mnatsʻakanyan, *Hay mijnadaryan hanelukner*, 8. For English definitions of the verb *hanel* in Classical Armenian, see Matthias Bedrossian, *New Dictionary Armenian-English*, 383–84. Bedrossian lists *haneluk*, "riddle," as a synonym of *aṛeghtsuats*, which he defines as "explication; enigma; proverb" (61).

33. Scribes usually wrote the solution to a riddle immediately above or below it. There are some exceptions, however. As Mnatsʻakanyan observes, one scribe provided a list of all the answers to his collection of riddles up front, so as not to divulge their solutions too easily (*Hay mijnadaryan hanelukner*, 10). The scribe asks the reader's forgiveness for any errors in his numbering. In another Armenian collection, the solutions appear in Georgian. Other times, to the apparent consternation of readers, the answers were simply omitted.

34. Mnatsʻakanyan, *Hay mijnadaryan hanelukner*, 11.

35. Rudolf, "Riddling and Reading," 499–500.

36. Rudolf, "Riddling and Reading," 501; Aldhelm, *Aldhelm, the Poetic Works*, 63.

37. Mnatsʻakanyan, *Hay mijnadaryan hanelukner*, 6–8.

38. Mnatsʻakanyan, *Hay mijnadaryan hanelukner*, 265. My translation follows the variant *bazum steghambk*ʻ, "with many shoots," which, in my view, reflects the most logical reading of the final line.

39. Mnatsʻakanyan, *Hay mijnadaryan hanelukner*, 274–75.

40. Mnatsʻakanyan, *Hay mijnadaryan hanelukner*, 298.

41. Mnatsʻakanyan, *Hay mijnadaryan hanelukner*, 269. Other animals embody more complex characteristics of the Islamicate world, as seen through Nersēs's eyes: "She wore red undergarments, / and she has a dappled shirt. / Rounded like a ball of thread, / she fights like a small Arab [*arabik*]" (*Hay mijnadaryan hanelukner*, 274). The answer is a partridge (*kakʻaw*), who for all her pugnacity still wears red drawers (*vartik*ʻ). Here, in satiric guise, Nersēs invites his readers to reflect not only upon the partridge but also upon the martial prowess of Arabs.

42. Mnatsʻakanyan, *Hay mijnadaryan hanelukner*, 259, 260, 258.

43. In this sense, although Grigor A. Hakobyan somewhat rigidly divided Nersēs's "religious" and "secular" riddles, both categories require their audiences to perform similar hermeneutic labor ("Nerses Shnorhalu antip haneluknerě"; this otherwise valuable article brought many of Nersēs's previously unpublished riddles to light).

44. Mnatsʻakanyan, *Hay mijnadaryan hanelukner*, 242.

45. Francis Joseph Steingass, *A Comprehensive Persian-English Dictionary*, 1062.

46. Nersēs Shnorhali, *Oghb Edesioy*, 70, line 440.

47. Mary Boyce, "The Parthian *Gōsān* and Iranian Minstrel Tradition."

48. Mnatsʻakanyan, *Hay mijnadaryan hanelukner*, 218.

49. As Adam T. Smith argues, "What is conspicuous about the Mashtots statue (as well as its contemporary, an equestrian monument to the Armenian hero David of Sasun) is that it commemorates the achievements of a specifically national hero—a hero of Armenia, not Soviet Armenia. Prior to the 1950s, the only monumental statues to be erected in the city [of Yerevan] were to Soviet leaders (like Merkurov's statue of Stalin) and local Bolsheviks (such as Stepan Shahumyan, the 'Caucasian Lenin'). The avowedly sectional valorization expressed in the Matenadaran [the Mesrop Mashtots' Institute of Ancient Manuscripts] and similar monuments foreshadowed a radical turn in the production of Yerevan's urban fabric and the construction of a formidable Soviet National material ensemble" ("'Yerevan, My Ancient Erebuni,'" 67–68).

50. For a concise overview of the debate surrounding the dating of Movsēs Khorenats'i, "the Father of Armenian History," see Garsoïan, "Movsēs Xorenac'i."

51. We might not even know his real name. Armenian manuscripts rarely attest "Frik" as a name, and the only premodern Armenian definition of the word comes from a fifteenth-century compendium of the remedial properties of plants and animals, which describes *frik* simply as "unripe wheat, that is burned in fire and eaten" (Amirdovlat' Amasiats'i, *Angitats' anpēt kam bararan bzhshkakan niwt'ots'*, 624). Hakob G. Zhamkoch'yan has proposed this definition as the meaning of the poet's name, which he believed to be a nom de plume ("Patma-banasirakan ditoghut'yunner," 228). Others have advanced different theories. Acharean, for instance, suggested that the name may be an Armenian corruption of "Frederick" (*Hayots' andznanunneri bararan*, 253–55); Manuk Abeghyan likewise thought it unlikely that "Frik" is a pen name (*Hayots' hin grakanut'yan patmut'yun*, vol. 2, 246). Finally, James Russell has suggested that "Frik" may have an Iranian origin: a third-century Sasanian inscription records the name, which in this context means "beloved" ("Frik," 261).

52. See Archbishop Tirayr's introduction to Frik, *Diwan*, 29–35. This hypothesis is partly based on Frik's allusion to having spent time in Hargay, another name for Hachn (*Diwan*, 362, line 9). However, Archbishop Tirayr's interpretation is contested. For instance, both Ashot Hovhannisyan and Zhamkoch'yan argue that "Hargay" is a reference to a province in Arran where the Mongols wintered. See Zhamkoch'yan's short overview of this debate, "Patma-banasirakan ditoghut'yunner," 229.

53. Zhamkoch'yan, "Patma-banasirakan ditoghut'yunner," 228–31. See also the discussion in Hovhannisyan, *Frikě patmak'nnakan luysi tak*, 111–18.

54. Frik, *Diwan*, 363, line 26. This possible itinerary, like much of our information about Frik, is highly speculative. For a brief overview and discussion of Frik's potential whereabouts, see Zhamkoch'yan, "Patma-banasirakan ditoghut'yunner," 228–31.

55. Pollock, "India in the Vernacular Millennium," 41.

56. Frik's dating is generally not based on codicological evidence. Instead, scholars of Armenian literary history have pored over his poetry, nearly line by line, in an attempt to correlate this body of work with known events from the late thirteenth century, sometimes productively and at other times to diminishing returns. For an early study in this vein, see A. Ghanalanyan, *Frik*. The pioneering work in this field is Hovhannisyan's *Frikě*

patmak'nnakan luysi tak, which describes, among other things, Frik's knowledge of the *ortaq* system of mercantile guilds that formed with the participation of Mongolian aristocrats (21–22, 30–40). Hovhannisyan places Frik's birth in the 1240s and his death sometime in the first quarter of the fourteenth century, making him a contemporary of the Armenian poet Kostandin Erznkats'i (118). This chapter does not attempt to wade into thorny questions of biography or dating, which would require a separate study in and of itself, but rather proposes a shift in how literary scholars read Frik, away from a method that seeks only to correlate his poetry with discrete historical events.

57. Frik, *Diwan*, 287. He does, however, seem to suggest that his father was a priest and the source of some part of his education (Abeghyan, *Hayots' hin grakanut'yan patmut'yun*, 247).

58. Frik, *Diwan*, 348, lines 4–10.

59. Frik, *Diwan*, 349, lines 14–15.

60. Frik, *Diwan*, 352, lines 52–53.

61. Frik, *Diwan*, 352–53, lines 60–63.

62. Transcription of Bodleian Library MS Arm. F. 16, fols. 121v–122r. Archbishop Tirayr transcribes this quatrain slightly differently (Frik, *Diwan*, 353, lines 64–67).

63. Tellingly, the scribe who copied this manuscript made several errors in transcribing the Persian text. Some words, such as գարաշիղ, are accidentally transcribed as one word in the Armenian; others, such as մուրդ, արպուաթ, incorrectly divide Persian words in two and combine them with other words; and still other transliterations, such as յարմուտ պախի, not only incorrectly break the Persian word in two but also employ the wrong letters (in this case, յ or *h* instead of what should be an initial դ or *d*). It stands to reason, then, that this manuscript's early modern scribe—or someone in the chain of transmission before him—did not understand this quatrain and would have needed Frik's accompanying translation to make any sense of it.

64. V. Avt'andilyan and H. P'ap'azyan, "Friki 'Divani' parskeren k'aṛyakě," 88–89. As Cowe has observed, Frik titled his body of work simply *Frik Girk'*, "Book of Frik," and not *Diwan* (the Armenian spelling of the Persian *dīvān*), an appellation applied by Archbishop Tirayr, who seems to have been (unnecessarily) reaching to find an "eastern orientation" for his poetry ("Models for the Interpretation of Medieval Armenian Poetry," 31–32).

65. Although Archbishop Tirayr observes that Bodleian Library MS Arm. F. 16 does not provide a separate title for the translation and gloss in Middle Armenian, his *Diwan* frames the third and fourth sections as a separate poem because their rhyme scheme differs from that of the first two sections (Frik, *Diwan*, 354). For my purposes, I treat all four "sections" as contributing to a single reading.

66. See B. L. Ch'ugaszyan's chapter on Frik, *Hay-iranakan grakan aṛnch'ut'yunner*, 112–28.

67. A. H. Shakhsuvaryan, "Frikě Khak'anu k'aṛyaki t'argmanich'." On this discovery, see Mihrdat T'ireak'yan, "Prof. Sa'id Nefisi khastate, or Khaghanin ē heghinakě Friki parskeren k'aṛyakin." Ch'ugaszyan remained skeptical that one can definitively cite Khāqānī as the source for Frik's adaptation, just as he maintained the impossibility of disproving the Khāqānī hypothesis ("Ardyok' Khakanin ē Frikyan k'aṛyaki heghinakě"). However,

it is worth noting that the debate in Armenian studies over the original authorship of this quatrain has not been informed by the critical edition of Khāqānī's *Dīvān*, edited by Żiyā' al-Dīn Sajjādī, which is based on four manuscripts, including the oldest copy of Khāqānī's poetry, and notably does not include our wandering quatrain. Nor does the more recent edition of Khāqānī's *Dīvān* edited by Mīr Jalāl al-Dīn Kazzāzī.

68. See Ch'ugaszyan's concise summary of the quatrain's many potential authors, "Ardyok' Khakanin ē Frikyan k'aṛyaki heghinakě," 85–86.

69. Jalāl al-Dīn Rūmī, *Maktab-i Shams*, 55.

70. The term "wandering quatrain" was first used to describe a large number of poems that were originally attributed to 'Umar Khayyām but also exist in the collections of other poets. See Valentin Alekseyevich Zhukovskiĭ's study, translated into English as "'Omar Khayyâm and the 'Wandering' Quatrains."

71. Khāqānī, *Dīvān-i Khāqānī Shirvānī* (ed. Manṣūr), 479. I have adjusted an error in this edition, *nashukand*, to *nakushand.*

72. Russell, "Frik," 261.

73. Frik, *Diwan*, 354, lines 3–6. Though Ṛ. A. Ghazaryan and H. M. Avetisyan read *ghěbělen* as an adjective ("they are acceptable"; *Mijin hayereni baṛaran*, 460), it is clear from the manuscript, which does not place a space between *ghěběl* and *en*, and, more important, from the usage of this word with the accusative *ězk'ez* in line 10 of the same poem, that Frik employs it as a verb.

74. Ch'ugaszyan, *Hay-iranakan grakan aṛnch'ut'yunner*, 122. Similarly, although Frik refers to a "kitchen of love" (*maṭbakh-i 'ishq*) in his Persian quatrain, his Armenian translation prefers the variant "holy altar"—again using imagery that is congruent with the Armenian Church. Thus, as Ch'ugaszyan notes, Frik's poem transforms the Islamic kitchen of love into the holy altar of the Christian church.

75. Russell, "Frik," 261.

76. Paul E. Losensky, *Welcoming Fighānī,* 108.

77. Shams al-Dīn Aḥmad Aflākī, *Manāqib al-'ārifīn*, vol. 1, 221.

78. Frik, *Diwan*, 354, lines 7–10.

79. Frik, *Diwan*, 354, line 12.

80. Pseudo-Callisthenes, *Patmut'iwn Aghek'sandri Makedonats'woy*, 195n1. For a discussion of Khach'atur Kech'aṛets'i's role in "correcting" the Armenian translation of the *Alexander Romance*, see Albert Mugrdich Wolohojian's introduction to Pseudo-Callisthenes, *The Romance of Alexander the Great*, 14–21.

81. This manuscript (V424) is housed in the Mekhitarist Library on San Lazzaro in Venice. On the Armenian Christianization of the *Alexander Romance*, see especially Alex MacFarlane's important works "Alexander Re-mapped" and "'This Shocking Lobster.'" For an analysis of the close relationships between these vernacular *kafa*s, the Classical Armenian text of the *Alexander Romance*, and the accompanying miniatures in the manuscript tradition, see Christina Maranci, "Word and Image in the Armenian *Alexander Romance.*"

82. In one memorable scene from Khach'atur's vernacular quatrains, Alexander counsels the servants of the Persian king Darius to heed the brevity of this life. "Let me give

instruction [*khrat*], mighty king," he implores, warning that everything built will eventually come to ruin. These *kafa*s even compare the world to a *dōlap* (Persian: *dūlāb*), or waterwheel, which "turns up and down," reversing the fortunes of all (*Khach'atur Kech'aṛets'i*, 185–87, stanzas 7, 19, 27).

83. Frik, *Diwan*, 375, line 39.

84. This assessment is repeated, for instance, by the editors of the popular anthology *The Heritage of Armenian Literature*, which serves as a primary reference work on medieval Armenian literature for the anglophone world. "One of the most outstanding examples of Frik's literary legacy is 'Enddem falakin' (Against fate)," they write, "a dialogue in which the poet attempts to account for inequalities and injustices by attributing them to destiny, never forgetting, though, that the ultimate origin of all things is God." The editors find this theme in others of Frik's poems as well, such as his equally famous "Gangat" (Complaint): "As the sufferings and humiliations of Armenians quickly piled up, Frik once again felt the weight of the evil that seemed to dominate the world, and the poem bristles with a bold (if temporary) defiance of God. . . . For the first time in medieval Armenian literature, a mortal is audacious enough to lay his doubts at the feet of the Almighty; unlike his predecessors, Frik demands an explanation for the injustice that is rampant in the world" (Agop J. Hacikyan et al., *The Heritage of Armenian Literature*, 525–26).

85. It is worth noting that some scholars have speculated—without a great deal of evidence—that Frik and Khach'atur were the same poet. This view was widespread in the late nineteenth and early twentieth centuries, supported by Arshak Ch'opanean and H. Poturyan, but has since been largely abandoned. It rested in part on the attribution of a single poem in Matenadaran MS 2939, copied in the eighteenth century, to both poets: "A spirit-nourishing counsel recited by Khach'atur Kech'aṛets'i or Frik," the heading reads. In the 1950s, Mayis T'. Avdalbegyan posited first that Frik and Khach'atur are concerned with different matters and (more problematically) have different temperaments as poets, and second, on somewhat firmer ground, that Frik employs a slightly different Middle Armenian lexicon than Khach'atur. For an overview of this debate, which is largely defunct today, see Avdalbegyan's introduction to Khach'atur Kech'aṛets'i, *Khach'atur Kech'aṛets'i*, 22–34.

86. Frik, *Diwan*, 371, line 7.

87. Frik, *Diwan*, 372–74, lines 11–26.

88. Frik, *Diwan*, 374, lines 31, 32.

89. Frik, *Diwan*, 374, line 28.

90. Frik, *Diwan*, 375, line 39.

91. See Hacikyan et al., *Heritage of Armenian Literature*, 528–29.

92. Frik, *Diwan*, 376, line 46.

93. Vienna Mekhitarist Library, MS 745 (old no. 797), fols. 124v–125v.

94. See Archbishop Tirayr's critical notes on line 47 in Frik, *Diwan*, 376.

95. Frik, *Diwan*, 376–77, lines 47–56.

96. Frik, *Diwan*, 377, lines 57–60.

97. Frik, *Diwan*, 377, line 61.

98. Frik, *Diwan*, 377–78, lines 63–66.

99. Varak Nersissian offers a representative summary of this view: "The words of blame and sorrow against Falaki are really directed against the Creator and it is through these imaginary arguments, this creative dialogue that Frig's own ideas come through and at the same time formulate man's eternal protest and Falaki's self-justification" ("Medieval Armenian Poetry and Its Relation to Other Literatures," 100). Nersissian's continual reference to fate as "Falaki," which is the dative form of the Armenian word, underscores his apparent lack of awareness of *falak*'s Arabo-Persian derivation. Other scholars have offered more nuanced interpretations of this poem even while not differing greatly in conclusion. Abeghyan, for instance, suggests that Frik, although he comes close to criticizing God indirectly, is mainly troubled by social and class inequality. "A spirit of doubt that God is not a 'righteous judge,' " Abeghyan posits, "shines in his mind for only a moment." However, Abeghyan concludes that Frik is ultimately a product of his time, and in the thirteenth century it was impossible for an Armenian poet to cast serious doubt on Christian doctrine (*Hayots' hin grakanut'yan patmut'yun*, 259–60). The underlying assumptions of these interpretations are similar: Frik either doubts his creator or perhaps would doubt his creator if he could but was constrained by the mores of his society. And beneath these assumptions is another, hearkening back to the notion of "lyric" poetry that long dominated twentieth-century literary criticism in the West: as a poet, Frik cannot help but reveal his turbulent inner state in an unmediated and truthful fashion. The notion that his poetry might aim to do something other than either impart a biographical account of his life and times or, similarly, offer a critique of his society has rarely informed scholarship on his body of work. The corrective question that needs to be asked is thus not merely what else Frik wrote about but rather how he wrote—that is, how his devotional and didactic poetry worked upon its audiences in particular ways.

100. There is at least one notable exception, which should be addressed here. This is, of course, Frik's famous poem "Gangat" ("Complaint"), which rhetorically positions the poet as both an accuser and a supplicant in God's court. Favoring a biographical reading, critics have widely speculated that Frik composed "Gangat" after "Ĕnddēm Falak'in," at the end of his increasingly bitter life. Consequently, the logic follows, "Gangat" adopts a harsher stance against God, detailing the shattered hopes and dreams of the historical Frik—and offering the earliest glimmers of a secular Armenian poetry. However, it should be noted that in "Gangat" the poet still emphasizes God's essential goodness. "Righteous and just God," the poem begins, "charitable to all, / I come to you [as] a witness in quarrel." What Frik then articulates is not exactly a withering critique of God the Father but rather his surprise and alarm that so many different peoples have sprung from the line of Adam and Eve. In fact, a principal thrust of his "complaint" is that many of these diverse peoples "do not know the Father and the Son, / nor [do they know] there is a God [who is] worthy of worship, / the Lord and the Inquisitor of all" (*Diwan*, 529–31, lines 5–7, 46–48). Why, he then wonders, did God deem it just to hand over the country to Muslims and heretics? As in "Ĕnddēm Falak'in," Frik does not have a compelling answer. He can only observe that

some people are rich and some are poor; some have many sons, some have none; some live many years, some die young. Hence, in a manner that does not deviate substantially from that of the Psalms, he simply asks God to remember that humans are but flesh and blood and need divine mercy and compassion, even though "You have become furious at the Armenian people, just as with the Jews of Israel" (533, lines 99–100). And the poem thus concludes, as it began, with an affirmation: God's judgments are righteous, although they are not always comprehensible (540).

So, does Frik offer a diatribe against God based on his own lived experience? There is good reason to unsettle this straightforward biographical interpretation of the poem, aside from the short reading I have sketched here. "Gangat" is best classified as another "wandering" poem: it has been attributed to the pens of other Armenian poets over the centuries. This has led some critics, such as Archbishop Tirayr (see Frik, *Diwan*, 529) and Khorēn Aramuni ("Chshmartut'iwnner Friki 'Gangat'-i masin"), to suggest that Frik may not be the poem's author. Aramuni, in drawing parallels with medieval Persian complaint poetry, has further suggested that "Gangat" may be a translation from another literary tradition. However, other scholars, such as Hovhannisyan (*Frikĕ patmak'nnakan luysi tak*, 94–110), have remained unconvinced by this hypothesis and have insisted that there is no serious reason to doubt the attribution to Frik, in part because the poem stylistically and thematically matches his body of work. My intention here is not to take up the question of attribution but rather to observe that at the least, medieval audiences do not seem to read this poem as commenting on Frik's life specifically—hence its multiple attributions to other poets. As Aramuni shows, the poem is part of a broad genre of complaint literature, common in medieval Persian and Arabic poetry and hardly unique to Frik. The fact that Frik uses Arabic and Persian terms culled from this genre only reinforces the point that he is part of a broader literary ecosystem that, unfortunately, biographical readings of his poetry tend to obscure. Hence, it would be productive to temper readings of Frik's poetry that attempt to recover his true feelings, such as his seeming wrath toward an unjust universe, with an awareness that he is participating in a larger discursive sphere.

101. Russell has briefly noted the correspondence between fatalism in Frik's poetry and in Islamicate literature more generally, aptly describing Frik's Christian conversion of this theme as a "harmonious innovation" ("Frik," 257).

102. Khāqānī, *Dīvān-i Khāqānī Shirvānī* (ed. Manṣūr), 23. For the definitive exegesis of this poem, see Vladimir Minorsky, "Khāqānī and Andronicus Comnenus." For a sophisticated analysis of how Khāqānī configures himself as a Christian in part to engage—as a Muslim—with Islamic law and the political imaginary, see Rebecca Gould, "The Political Cosmology of Prison Poetics"; "Wearing the Belt of Oppression."

103. Khāqānī, *Dīvān-i Khāqānī Shirvānī* (ed. Manṣūr), 27. Darius (Dārā in Persian) is killed by his own men in the *Shāh-nāma.*

104. Firdawsī, *Shāh-nāma*, vol. 2, lines 847, 849, 856–71. See also Cameron Cross's discussion of the tyranny of fate in the *Shāh-nāma*, including a short overview of its descriptors "hunchbacked" and wicked (" 'If Death Is Just, What Is Injustice?' ").

105. ʿUmar Khayyām, *Ṭarab-khāna*, 125.

106. Aḥmed Faḳīh, *Çarh-name*, 4–9.

107. Armenians, of course, were long aware of Iranian concepts of fate and destiny. The fifth-century writer Eznik Koghbatsʿi, in his polemic against "the sects," thus equates *bakht* with Zurvan, the Zoroastrian deity of Time (see D. Pingree and C. J. Brunner, "Astrology and Astronomy in Iran"). However, Koghbatsʿi's aim was to discredit notions of Zoroastrian cosmology, whereas Frik attempts not to debunk contemporary concepts of fate but rather to guide his audience to understand them in the proper way. On the legacy of pre-Islamic notions of fate and fatalism in New Persian poetry, see Helmer Ringgren, *Fatalism in Persian Epics*.

Chapter 7: An Education in Erznka

1. Shams al-Dīn Aḥmad Aflākī, *Manāqib al-ʿārifīn*, vol. 1, 24.

2. "Greater Armenia is a very large province," Marco Polo reported. "It begins at a city called Erzincan, where they make the best buckram in the world and practice countless other crafts. Here are found the most beautiful baths fed by the best spring water on earth. The people are Armenians and are vassals of the Tartars. There are many towns and cities. The noblest of all is Erzincan, which is the seat of an archbishop. Among the others are Erzurum and Ercis. And in a village called Bayburt, which lies on the road from Trebizond to Tabriz, there is a great silver mine" (*The Travels*, 18).

3. Kostandin Erznkatsʿi, *Tagher*, 209. James R. Russell notes that "*jayn* [*dzayn*] 'voice' probably refers not only to metre, but also to the chant traditionally employed by Persians in reciting their national epic" (*Yovhannēs Tʿlkurancʿi and the Mediaeval Armenian Lyric Tradition*, 7).

4. Manuk Abeghyan, perhaps the foremost Armenian literary historian of the twentieth century, observed that Armenians still performed poetry *i dzayn*, or "in a voice," in 1933 (*Hayotsʿ hin grakanutʿyan patmutʿyun*, 552–54). At least in the modern period, this mode of recitation required a performer to stress certain syllables while chanting in a melodic fashion. However, the erudite Armenologist Charles Dowsett later expressed skepticism that Kostandin was successful in performing the *mutaqārib* meter in a *dzayn*, maintaining that his verses merely reproduce "a mixture of anapests and iambs" and do not exhibit a true Persian quantitative meter ("A Metrical Experiment," 50). In his dissertation, Theo Maarten van Lint pushes back against Dowsett, arguing that performers could choose to stress syllables that otherwise would not be stressed according to the rules of Armenian versification, analogous to what Abeghyan described in his day. See Van Lint's overview of the scholarship on Kostandin's meter in his "Kostandin of Erznka," 260–62.

5. Kostandin Erznkatsʿi, *Tagher*, 209, lines 1–10.

6. Russell, *Yovhannēs Tʿlkurancʿi*, 6–7.

7. Firdawsī, *Shāh-nāma*, vol. 1, 3, line 1.

8. More specifically, as Van Lint explains, "the first syllable of the three-syllabic foot is unstressed, the second one stressed, while the third one receives a secondary, weaker stress,

which is sometimes replaced by a full stress. The last foot of a line consists of an unstressed followed by a stressed syllable, yielding the following result: -‘ʻ / -‘ʻ / -‘ʻ / -‘. This metrical pattern clears the way for a performance in the way of the *Šāh-nāma.*" Of course, as Van Lint also observes, this contradicts the principle of Armenian versification that the end of a foot corresponds with the end of a word, enabling one to approximate a quantitative metrical system with an "Armenian syllabic-accentual one" ("Kostandin of Erznka," 260, 261).

9. Van Lint, "Kostandin of Erznka," 262.

10. Hülya Küçük, "Sulṭān Walad's Role in the Foundation of the Mevlevi Sufi Order," 44–47.

11. Kostandin likely composed his poem sometime after the death in 1304 of the Ilkhanid ruler Ghāzān, an event to which it alludes.

12. For a review of the scholarship on Kostandin's dates of birth and death, see Van Lint, "Kostandin of Erznka," 8–12.

13. There were, in fact, several Armenian monasteries and churches in the region of Erznka. It is sometimes assumed that Kostandin studied at Tirashēn, in part because of its prominence and proximity to Erznka and in part because of the colophon record's allusion to both Tirashēn and a monk named Kostandin, though the latter name was not uncommon. See Armenuhi Srapyan's short overview of monasteries near Erznka in her introduction to Kostandin Erznkatsʻi, *Tagher*, 29–33. For a translation of the colophons that perhaps refer to Kostandin, see Van Lint, "Kostandin of Erznka," 390–92.

14. Kostandin Erznkatsʻi, *Tagher*, 188, line 13.

15. Kostandin Erznkatsʻi, *Tagher*, 188, line 15.

16. Kostandin Erznkatsʻi, *Tagher*, 189, lines 21–24. For a detailed discussion of this passage and its various interpretations, including the contested reading of "robe," see Kevork B. Bardakjian, "Kostandin Erznkacʻi's Vision-Poem," 97–99.

17. Kostandin Erznkatsʻi, *Tagher*, 187. This description is found in the poem's heading.

18. Bardakjian has argued that this corresponds to the Sufi practice of *dawsa*, prevalent in premodern Egypt, in which a shaykh trod upon his disciples in a ceremony of initiation ("Kostandin Erznkacʻi's Vision-Poem").

19. Kostandin Erznkatsʻi, *Tagher*, 189, line 33.

20. Kostandin Erznkatsʻi, *Tagher*, 190, lines 45–48.

21. Kostandin Erznkatsʻi, *Tagher*, 190, line 49.

22. See S. Peter Cowe, "The Politics of Poetics," 399; Seta B. Dadoyan, "A Case Study for Redefining Armenian-Christian Cultural Identity in the Framework of Near Eastern Urbanism," 263; Van Lint, "Kostandin of Erznka," 153. Bardakjian, conversely, argues that the youth must be the Holy Spirit ("Kostandin Erznkacʻi's Vision-Poem," 101–3).

23. Kostandin Erznkatsʻi, *Tagher*, 187.

24. Theo Maarten van Lint, "The Poet's Legitimization," 15–17.

25. Kostandin Erznkatsʻi, *Tagher*, 191, lines 59–60.

26. Kostandin Erznkatsʻi, *Tagher*, 187. This accusation appears in the poem's heading.

27. Kostandin Erznkatsʻi, *Tagher*, 191, lines 54–55.

28. Kostandin Erznkatsʻi, *Tagher*, 188, lines 9–10.

29. Kostandin Erznkats'i, *Tagher*, 187–88, lines 5–8.

30. On potential precedents for the vision in the Armenian context, see James R. Russell, "The Dream Vision of Anania Širakac'i." However, Russell has posited that the vision "probably should be traced back to the Zoroastrian past, to evocations of the Sun-eyed Ahura Mazdā, of sunlike Mithra, of the fiery Verethraghna" (introduction to Derenik Demirchyan, *The Book of Flowers*, 11). Others have similarly drawn associations between Kostandin's poetic imagery and the figure of Mithra more generally: see, e.g., Manuk Abeghyan, *Erker*, 368. But while Kostandin's poetics may reflect a Zoroastrian Armenian past, so too do they evoke an Islamicate present. In an important cross-cultural reading of the poem, Theo Maarten van Lint suggests that Kostandin's initiation rite mirrors the initiation-visions of other poets in Anatolia, the Caucasus, and the Middle East ("The Gift of Poetry"). In this tradition, which continued into the modern period, Elijah, John the Baptist, or Khiḍr appeared before would-be poets at night, offering them a drink or a blessing. Upon waking, those who experienced the vision claimed the ability to compose poetry. Finally, Bardakjian has likewise argued for an Islamicate orientation of the poem ("Kostandin Erznkac'i's Vision-Poem"). Although the debate regarding the vision's cultural origins continues today, it is clear that Kostandin certainly marshaled a poetic language with resonance beyond the Armenian context alone.

31. The most extensive work in this vein has been done by Van Lint in his illuminating article "The Gift of Poetry," which provides needed context for Kostandin's vision in relation to those of other medieval and early modern poets. Here I seek to open a complementary pathway of reading across languages to shed light on the epistemic role that poetry played in the societies of medieval Anatolia.

32. Aflākī, *Manāqib al-'ārifīn*, vol. 1, 291.

33. Sulṭān Valad, *Ibtidā-nāma*, 65.

34. Van Lint, "Kostandin of Erznka," 193–97.

35. I have used "earthen vessels" in place of the NRSV's "clay jars" for consistency.

36. Yūnus Emre, *Yûnus Emre Dîvânı*, vol. 2, 235.

37. Edward William Lane, *An Arabic-English Lexicon*, 735. On the large number of loanwords present in Kostandin's poetry, see "How Did New Persian and Arabic Words Penetrate the Middle Armenian Vocabulary?" by Andrzej Pisowicz, who suggests that several Arabic and Persian terms may have entered the Armenian lexicon in Erznka through the intermediary of Turkish.

38. A. J. Arberry, *The Koran Interpreted*, vol. 1, 282.

39. Jalāl al-Dīn Rūmī, *Kitāb-i fīhi mā fīh*, 62. As Rūmī continues, men and women are thus able to "conduct their business in this world in a manner suitable to Him: from scraps of hearing, and from scraps of speech, and from scraps of reason, and from scraps of kindness, and from scraps of learning."

40. Compare this assertion by Kostandin, which likewise emphasizes God as the source of all things: "From you is color, from you is beauty, / from you are flavor and sweet fragrance, / from you is the impression of radiance." This stanza does not appear in Srapyan's

critical edition but can be found in Van Lint's dissertation ("Kostandin of Erznka," 248), which uses an important early manuscript of Kostandin's poetry, copied in 1336 in Tabriz and catalogued as MS No. 103 at the Mekhitarist Library on San Lazzaro, Venice. The translation here is mine.

41. Rūmī, *Kitāb-i fīhi mā fīh*, 62.

42. Jalāl al-Dīn Rūmī, *Maṣnavī*, 4: 1960.

43. Rūmī, *Maṣnavī*, 4: 1964.

44. In fact, the notion that true knowledge descends from a higher realm had been common in Rūm for some time. For instance, Shihāb al-Dīn Yaḥyā al-Suhrawardī (d. 1191) posited that revelatory visions could transport people to a "world of likeness" (*ʿālam al-mithāl*), where radiant beings of light would bestow upon them "experiential knowledge" (*ʿilm al-ḥuḍūrī*), which cannot be earned through any amount of study, as opposed to "acquired knowledge" (*ʿilm al-ḥuṣūlī*). See the short discussion of these terms in Nile Green, *Sufism*, 75–76. For an introduction to al-Suhrawardī's "Illuminationist" philosophy, along with a critical edition and translation of the *Ḥikmat al-ishrāq*, his foundational treatise, see al-Suhrawardī, *The Philosophy of Illumination.*

45. Cowe makes a similar point about Kostandin's distinction between intellectual knowledge and spiritual insight in the context of another poem ("Patterns of Armeno-Muslim Interchange," 88–90).

46. For a valuable study on Hovhannēs's erudition and intellectual activity, see Armenuhi Srapyan, *Hovhannes Erznkatsʿi Pluz*. See also the work by Seda Parsumean-Tatoyean (Seta Dadoyan) on Hovhannēs's philosophical writings in relation to Arab and Muslim intellectual trends, *Hay-arabakan mshakutʿayin haraberutʿeantsʿ patmutʿenēn ZhG dar.*

47. Other early poets of Middle Armenian took up similar concerns in their poetry. Frik, in a poem on the danger of fratricide, attempts to instill feelings of fraternal love in his audience, in part by appealing to the better nature of one "brother," whom he praises in verse as "kind to strangers [Persian: *gharīb-dūst*] and exceedingly wise" (*Diwan*, 475, line 42).

48. Dadoyan, "Case Study for Redefining Armenian-Christian Cultural Identity"; Dadoyan, "The Constitution for the Brotherhood of Erznkay (1280) by Yovhannēs Erznkacʿi"; Rachel Goshgarian, "Beyond the Social and the Spiritual"; Goshgarian, "*Futuwwa* in Thirteenth-Century Rūm and Armenia."

49. Hovhannēs Erznkatsʿi, *Matenagrutʿiwn*, 397. Scholars were largely unaware of the Armenian brotherhood in Erznka before Levon Khachʿikyan's influential article "1280 tʿvakanin Erznkayum kazmakerpvatsʿ 'Eghbayrutʿiwně,' " which he followed by publishing Hovhannēs's constitution in 1962 ("Erznka kʿaghakʿi 'Eghbartsʿ miabanutʿean' kanonadrutʿyuně"). On Hovhannēs's constitution, see also Dadoyan, *The Armenians in the Medieval Islamic World*, vol. 3, 84–90.

50. Hovhannēs Erznkatsʿi, *Matenagrutʿiwn*, 406.

51. Goshgarian, "*Futuwwa* in Thirteenth-Century Rūm and Armenia," 228.

52. Hovhannēs Erznkatsʿi, *Hovhannes Erznkatsʿi*, 208, lines 2–4. *I grēn* can mean "from writing" more generally, but given the highly scriptural orientation of the poem, it seems

likely that Hovhannēs had the Bible in mind. Armenuhi Srapyan, who compiled the critical edition of his poetry, first posited this reading, suggesting that the poem was composed for the benefit of the Armenian confraternity in Erznka (73). Van Lint likewise agrees with this interpretation of the line ("Kostandin of Erznka," 25).

53. Hovhannēs Erznkats'i, *Hovhannes Erznkats'i*, 217, line 126.

54. Of course, this is highly speculative. But underlying this speculation is a demonstrable correspondence between Hovhannēs and Kostandin, both of whom produced poetry that thematizes the transmission of instruction (*khrat*) to a group of youths (*manuk*) through the composition of poetry. Had Kostandin read (or heard) Hovhannēs's poetry, which certainly seems likely, he would have found something deeply resonant in the elder poet's words. Indeed, one of Hovhannēs's poems addresses its audience in a manner similar to that of Kostandin's vision-poem: "Behold, brothers, my dear ones and spiritual sons, / this instruction [*khrat*], which I composed, is a spiritual discourse; / love God and the Lord, the Heavenly Father, / keep my command, the glorious light, / whether you are a boy [*tghay*] or a youth [*manuk*] and servant of Christ, / whether you are old and ripe in age or a man and a priest; / whether you are healthy, whether you are an infirm son of Adam, / whether righteous or a sinner, attend to yourself" (*Hovhannes Erznkats'i*, 215, lines 97–104). In short, both poets composed poems or spiritual discourses (*ban*) that subtly refract the Word of God (*ban*), for the explicit purpose of bestowing instruction (*khrat*) upon their audiences. Another correspondence is Kostandin's self-identification as a *manuk* (youth), also his word for his radiant physician, which is the Armenian equivalent of the Arabic *fatā*, from which the term *futuwwa* derives.

55. Van Lint, "Kostandin of Erznka," 3–5. On Hovhannēs's didactic and homiletic activity in general, see Ē. M. Baghdasaryan, *Hovhannes Erznkats'in ev nra khratakan ardzakě.*

56. Scholars have attributed five poems to Kostandin that do not appear in the manuscript copied in 1336. Van Lint suggests that there is no serious reason to doubt four of these attributions: only one of the poems does not tonally or thematically correspond to Kostandin's larger body of work ("Kostandin of Erznka," 28–36).

57. Kostandin Erznkats'i, *Tagher*, 163, lines 1–4.

58. Kostandin Erznkats'i, *Tagher*, 165, lines 41–44. Armenian does not distinguish between male and female in the third-person singular, so the dancer could also potentially be a young man, as nothing in the poem genders the dancer.

59. Dadoyan reads poems such as this as depicting a vital ethos of the brothers and thus not merely or simply reflecting a literary topos. As she writes, the "evening and garden parties of the *fityān*/*manuks* were perhaps the most important elements of their culture, for it was during these gatherings that poets recited their verses, musicians played and at least some of the dancing girls were *qayyāns*, who also recited poetry, sang and played instruments" ("Case Study for Redefining Armenian-Christian Cultural Identity," 250).

60. Kostandin Erznkats'i, *Tagher*, 165, lines 49–52. Obviously, today we cannot know what that "voice" sounded like. Still, Kostandin leaves some clues. He composed his "poem of love" in octosyllabic meter, employing a poetics common to both Turkish and Armenian

poetry. If the voice was well known, so was its imagery: the beloved's fragrance intoxicates the poet, just as in Persian and Turkish poetry from this period; her face (*ṣūrat*, an Arabo-Persian loanword) is luminous as the moon; her hair is wild and black (*siyāh*, another Arabo-Persian loanword). Most strikingly, like the heroes in romances such as *Digenēs Akritēs* and *Varḳa and Gülşāh*, Kostandin rises to woo his beloved with music and song—specifically, as he says, with a long-necked lute known as the *sāz*, common to Armenian, Persian, and Turkish musical cultures.

61. Kostandin Erznkats'i, *Tagher*, 155, line 33; 154, line 14.

62. Kostandin Erznkats'i, *Tagher*, 156, lines 37–38.

63. Kostandin Erznkats'i, *Tagher*, 156, lines 45, 47.

64. Kostandin Erznkats'i, *Tagher*, 157, lines 55–56.

65. Yūnus Emre, *Yûnus Emre Dîvânı*, vol. 2, 245.

66. Jalāl al-Dīn Rūmī, *Kullīyāt-i Shams yā Dīvān-i kabīr*, 271. Here I have preferred the variant of a "singing" nightingale.

67. Denison B. Hull, *Digenis Akritas*, 101.

68. Kostandin Erznkats'i, *Tagher*, 137.

69. Kostandin Erznkats'i, *Tagher*, 139, line 26.

70. Kostandin Erznkats'i, *Tagher*, 141, lines 37–38.

71. Kostandin Erznkats'i, *Tagher*, 141, line 44.

72. Cowe, "Politics of Poetics," 391–96 (provides a detailed overview of this trope's entrance into Middle Armenian poetry, along with some of its relevant analogues in Persian poetry). Conversely, V. S. Nersisyan has argued that Armenian poets need not have borrowed this trope directly from Persian poetics, especially given its broad diffusion throughout Middle Eastern literary cultures ("Vardi u sokhaki aylabanut'yan hay-parskakan mshakumneri aṙnch'ut'yan harts'i masin").

73. *Gul bā shakar* in a Persian transliteration. Here I have preferred the variant "and keep [me] as a remedy," which corresponds to the same line in Kostandin's exegesis of this poem, discussed later in this chapter.

74. Kostandin Erznkats'i, *Tagher*, 144, lines 65–72.

75. Kostandin Erznkats'i, *Tagher*, 145.

76. Kostandin Erznkats'i, *Tagher*, 145–46, lines 1–12.

77. Kostandin Erznkats'i, *Tagher*, 146, line 14.

78. Kostandin Erznkats'i, *Tagher*, 147, lines 18–19.

79. Kostandin Erznkats'i, *Tagher*, 145, 187, line 5. Kostandin regularly demonstrates a concern with and attempts to inform his audience's interpretive stance. For instance, in another poem featuring the rose and the nightingale, he instructs his audience that his words must be understood through "another kind" of sight (*Tagher*, 131).

80. Some critics have answered this question in reductive ways. Abeghyan, for instance, suggests that the exegesis on the rose and the nightingale does not correspond to the secular spirit of the original poem (*Erker*, 366–68, 377). B. L. Ch'ugaszyan even speculates that Kostandin's instruction to not read according to "the flesh" or "the world" might simply

be a cover to avoid religious persecution and thus need not be taken seriously (*Hay-iranakan grakan aṙnch'ut'yunner*, 137). Conversely, Russell ("Here Comes the Sun") and Van Lint ("Kostandin of Erznka," 38–47) have argued that the religious dimension of Kostandin's poetry cannot be expunged; Russell's article includes a short assessment of secular misreading of medieval Armenian poetry in general.

81. Christine van Ruymbeke, "The *Kalīla wa Dimna* and Rūmī," 87.

82. Rūmī, *Maṣnavī*, 4: 2203.

83. Rūmī, *Maṣnavī*, 2: 3617.

84. Rūmī, *Maṣnavī*, 2: 3641–80. The story featuring these verses is immediately followed by another on the perils of cleaving too rigidly to outward form: this is, of course, Rūmī's tale of the four travelers who each use a different word for "grape" although their hearts all desire the same thing.

85. Rūmī, *Maṣnavī*, 2: 3622–24.

86. The drive to instill "wisdom" in an audience, to teach them to do interpretive work, is also made clear in a second exegesis that Kostandin composed on this same poem. Here he explicitly correlates the rose conserve with "instruction [*khrat*] in the scriptures," which he likewise calls a "godly remedy for souls wounded by sin" (Van Lint, "Kostandin of Erznka," 243). Rūmī conceptualizes the rose in a highly similar manner in his poetry. "What is the rose's fragrance," he wonders, if not "the breath of reason and wisdom [*khirad*]?" (*Maṣnavī*, 5: 3350). In both cases, the heuristic of the rose guides the audience to attain wisdom (*khrat/khirad*). See also my article "The Rose of Muḥammad, the Fragrance of Christ" for a comparison of the uses of fragrance in Rūmī's and Kostandin's poetry.

87. Kostandin Erznkats'i, *Tagher*, 148, lines 25–36.

88. On this pun and the symbolism of the rose in New Persian poetry more generally, see the groundbreaking chapter by Maria E. Subtelny, "Visionary Rose."

89. On the ubiquity of rose products around the medieval Mediterranean, see Zohar Amar and Efraim Lev, "The Significance of the Genizah's Medical Documents for the Study of Medieval Mediterranean Trade." As James R. Russell notes, the Cairo Geniza also includes a manuscript with a list of twenty Judaeo-Arabic words and their Armenian equivalents in the Hebrew script ("On an Armenian Word List from the Cairo Geniza"). Tellingly, one of those words is *vard*, which is Armenian for "rose."

90. Van Lint has also suggested that Kostandin's convivial poetry may possess "a layer of meaning beyond the one that is immediately given," accounting for the overwhelming devotional and didactic thrust of his work ("Kostandin of Erznka," 340).

91. Kostandin Erznkats'i, *Tagher*, 209, lines 1–2.

92. Kostandin Erznkats'i, *Tagher*, 209, line 8.

93. Kostandin Erznkats'i, *Tagher*, 210, lines 19–28.

94. Kostandin Erznkats'i, *Tagher*, 209, line 10.

95. Kostandin Erznkats'i, *Tagher*, 165, line 52; Van Lint, "Kostandin of Erznka," 266.

96. Kostandin Erznkats'i, *Tagher*, 211, line 45.

97. Firdawsī, *Shāh-nāma*, vol. 1, 4, lines 16–18.

98. Firdawsī, *Shāh-nāma*, vol. 1, 4, line 22.

99. Firdawsī, *Shāh-nāma*, vol. 1, 4, line 24.

100. Firdawsī, *Shāh-nāma*, vol. 1, 5, line 25.

101. Kostandin Erznkatsʻi, *Tagher*, 210, line 27.

102. Nasrin Askari, *The Medieval Reception of the Shāhnāma as a Mirror for Princes*, 30. On the reception and adaptation of the *Shāh-nāma* in Anatolia after this period, see Lâle Uluç, "The *Shahnama* of Firdausi in the Lands of Rum."

103. Hovhannēs Erznkatsʻi, *Hovhannes Erznkatsʻi*, 208, lines 3–4.

Epilogue

Epigraphs: Mnatsʻakanyan, *Hay mijnadaryan hanelukner*, 211; Gülşehrī, *Gülşehri'nin Mantıku't-Tayr'ı*, vol. 2, 656, line 4428.

1. See the entry for *mit* in Matthias Bedrossian's *New Dictionary Armenian-English*, 478. Fr. Gabriēl Awetikʻean and Fr. Khachʻatur Siwrmēlean's *Nor baṙgirkʻ haykazean lezui* similarly lists *imast*, "sense" or "meaning," under *mitkʻ* (281).

2. Hovhannēs Erznkatsʻi, *Hovhannes Erznkatsʻi*, 165–66, lines 31–46.

3. Hovhannēs Erznkatsʻi, *Hovhannes Erznkatsʻi*, 166, lines 55–58.

4. Hovhannēs Erznkatsʻi, *Hovhannes Erznkatsʻi*, 167, lines 61–62. The somewhat ambiguous nature of the last line here has prompted different readings. Hence, whereas James R. Russell translates these lines as "I will bring you an Armenian girl, / And give you to a priest for blessing" (*Yovhannēs Tʻlkurancʻi and the Mediaeval Armenian Lyric Tradition*, 114), S. Peter Cowe renders them as "Let me get you an Armenian's young daughter / And have you ordained a married priest" ("The Politics of Poetics," 402). The point remains that in either case, this relationship must be mediated through the church.

5. Hovhannēs Erznkatsʻi, *Hovhannes Erznkatsʻi*, 167, lines 69–70.

6. Hovhannēs Erznkatsʻi, *Hovhannes Erznkatsʻi*, 169, lines 95–100.

7. Hovhannēs Erznkatsʻi, *Hovhannes Erznkatsʻi*, 167–68, lines 71–76.

8. Cemal Kafadar, *Between Two Worlds*, 27.

9. Charlton T. Lewis, *An Elementary Latin Dictionary*, 865.

10. Hovhannēs Erznkatsʻi, *Hovhannes Erznkatsʻi*, 168, lines 77–84. See also Srapyan's discussion of this reference to Erznka and the poem's attribution in her introduction to this edition, 87–90.

11. See the introduction to this book for a brief survey of scholarship on these practices in later periods.

WORKS CITED

Sources

Aflākī, Shams al-Dīn Aḥmad. *The Feats of the Knowers of God: Manāqeb al-ʿārefīn.* Translated by John O'Kane. Leiden: Brill, 2002.

———. *Manāqib al-ʿārifīn.* Edited by Tahsin Yazıcı. 2 vols. Ankara: Türk Tarih Kurumu Basımevi, 1959–61.

Aḥmed Faḳīh. *Çarhname.* Edited by Mecdut Mansuroğlu. Istanbul: Pulhan Matbaası, 1956.

Aldhelm. *Aldhelm, the Poetic Works.* Translated by Michael Lapidge and James L. Rosier. Cambridge: D. S. Brewer, 1984.

Alfonsi, Petrus. *The Disciplina Clericalis of Petrus Alfonsi.* Translated by Eberhard Hermes and P. R. Quarrie. London: Routledge and K. Paul, 1977.

Amirdovlatʿ Amasiatsʿi. *Angitatsʿ anpēt kam baṙaran bzhshkakan niwtʿotsʿ.* Vienna: Mekhitarist Press, 1926.

Arberry, A. J., trans. *The Koran Interpreted: A Translation.* 2 vols. in 1. New York: Simon and Schuster, 1996.

Argunşah, Mustafa, and Galip Güner, eds. *Codex Cumanicus.* Istanbul: Kesit Yayınları, 2015.

ʿĀşıḳ Paşa [Âşık Paşa]. *Garib-nâme: Tıpkıbasım, Karşılaştırmalı Metin ve Aktarma.* Edited by Kemal Yavuz. 2 vols., in 2 pts. each. Ankara: Türk Dil Kurumu, 2000.

Betts, Gavin, trans. *Three Medieval Greek Romances: Velthandros and Chrysandza, Kallimachos and Chrysorroi, Livistros and Rodamni.* New York: Garland Publishing, 1995.

Chaucer, Geoffrey. *The Canterbury Tales: Seventeen Tales and the General Prologue.* Edited by V. A. Kolve and Glending Olson. 3rd ed. New York: W. W. Norton, 2018.

Dawkins, R. M., ed. *More Greek Folktales.* London: Oxford University Press, 1955.

Dedes, Yorgos, ed. *Battalname: Introduction, English Translation, Turkish Transcription, Commentary and Facsimile.* 2 vols. Cambridge, MA: Harvard University Press, 1996.

Elvān Çelebī [Elvan Çelebi]. *Menâkıbu'l-Kudsiyye fî Menâsıbi'l-Ünsiyye: Baba İlyas-ı Horasânî ve Sülâlesinin Menkabevî Tarihi.* Edited by İsmail E. Erünsal and Ahmet Yaşar Ocak. Istanbul: Edebiyat Fakültesi Matbaası, 1984.

Epiphanios. *The Lamentations of Matins of Holy and Great Saturday.* Translated by Holy Transfiguration Monastery. Boston: Holy Transfiguration Monastery, 1981.

Firdawsī. *Shāh-nāma.* Edited by Djalal Khaleghi-Motlagh as *The Shahnameh (Book of Kings).* 8 vols. New York: Bibliotheca Persica, 1987–2008.

Frik. *Diwan.* Edited by Archbishop Tirayr [Melik Mushkambarian]. New York: Publication of the Armenian General Benevolent Union Melkonian Fund, 1952.

Gölpınarlı, Abdülbâki, ed. *Manakıb-ı Hacı Bektâş-ı Velî: "Vilâyet-nâme."* Istanbul: İnkılâp, 1990.

Grigor Magistros. *Magnalia Dei: Biblical History in Epic Verse by Grigor Magistros.* Translated and edited by Abraham Terian. Leuven: Peeters, 2012.

Gülşehrī [Gülşehri]. "'Arūż-ı Gülşehrī." In Ali Emîrî, *Farsça yazmalar,* no. 517, fols. 46v–61v. İstanbul Millet Kütüphanesi.

———. *Gülşehri'nin Mantıku't-Tayr'ı (Gülşen-nâme): Metin ve Günümüz Türkçesine Aktarma.* Edited by Kemal Yavuz. 2 vols. Ankara: Kırşehir Valiliği Kültür Yayınları, 2007.

———. *Gülşehri ve Felek-nâme: Inceleme ve Metin.* Edited by Saadettin Kocatürk. Ankara: Ankara Üniversitesi Dil ve Tarih-Coğrafya Fakültesi Yayınları, 1984.

Hovhannēs Draskhanakertts'i. *Patmut'iwn hayots' (History of Armenia).* Delmar, NY: Caravan Books, 1980. Reprint of 1912 Tbilisi ed., edited by M. Emin.

Hovhannēs Erznkats'i [Hovhannes Erznkats'i]. *Hovhannes Erznkats'i: Usumnasirut'yun ev bnagrer.* Edited by Armenuhi Srapyan. Yerevan: Haykakan SSR GA Hratarakch'ut'yun, 1958.

———. *Matenagrut'iwn,* vol. 1, *Chaṛer ew k'arozner.* Edited by Armenuhi Erznkats'i-Tēr-Srapyan and Ēdvard Baghdasaryan. Yerevan: "Nairi" Hratarakch'ut'yun, 2013.

Hujvīrī, ʿAlī ibn ʿUṣmān. *Kashf al-maḥjūb*. Edited by Valentin Alekseevich Zhukovskiĭ. Tehran: Kitābkhāna-yi Ṭahūrī, 1979.

Hull, Denison B., trans. *Digenis Akritas: The Two-Blood Border Lord*. Athens: Ohio University Press, 1972.

Ibn al-Dawādārī. *Durar al-tījān wa-ghurar tawārīkh al-azmān*. Edited version in *Die Epitome der Universalchronik Ibn ad-Dawādārīs im Verhältnis zur Langfassung: Eine quellenkritische Studie zur Geschichte der ägyptischen Mamluken*, by Gunhild Graf. Berlin: K. Schwarz, 1990.

Ibn Baṭṭūṭa. *Riḥlat Ibn Baṭṭūṭa*. Edited by Karam al-Bustānī. Beirut: Dār Ṣādir, 1964.

———. *The Travels of Ibn Baṭṭūṭa, A.D. 1325–1354*. Translated by H. A. R. Gibb. Vol. 2. Cambridge: Published for the Hakluyt Society by Cambridge University Press, 1962.

Ibn Bībī. *Al-Awāmir al-ʿalāʾiyya fīʾl-umūr al-ʿalāʾiyya*. Edited by Zhāla Muttaḥidīn. Tehran: Pizhūhishgāh-i ʿUlūm-i Insānī va Muṭālaʿāt-i Farhangī, 2011.

Jeffreys, Elizabeth, ed. and trans. *Digenis Akritis: The Grottaferrata and Escorial Versions*. Cambridge: Cambridge University Press, 1998.

Kāshgharī, Maḥmūd al- [Maḥmūd al-Kāšγarī]. *Compendium of the Turkic Dialects*. Edited and translated by Robert Dankoff, in collaboration with James Kelly. 3 vols. Duxbury, MA: Harvard University Press, 1982–85.

Khachʿatur Kechʿaṛetsʿi. *Khachʿatur Kechʿaṛetsʿi: XIII–XIV d.d.* Edited by Mayis Tʿ. Avdalbegyan. Yerevan: Haykakan SSṘ GA Hratarakchʿutʿyun, 1958.

Khāqānī Shirvānī. *Dīvān-i Afẓal al-Dīn Badīl b. ʿAlī Najjār Khāqānī Shirvānī.* Edited by Żiyāʾ al-Dīn Sajjādī. Tehran: Kitābfurūshī-yi Zavvār, 1959.

———. *Dīvān-i Khāqānī Shirvānī.* Edited by Mīr Jalāl al-Dīn Kazzāzī. 2 vols. Tehran: Nashr-i Markaz, 1996.

———. *Dīvān-i Khāqānī Shirvānī.* Edited by Jahāngir Manṣūr. Tehran: Nigāh, 1996.

Kirakos Gandzaketsʿi. *Patmutʿiwn hayotsʿ*. Edited by Karapet Aghabeki Melikʿ-Ōhanjanyan. Yerevan: Haykakan SSṘ Gitutʿyunneri Akademiayi Hratarakchʿutʿyun, 1961.

Kostandin Erznkatsʿi. *Tagher*. Edited by Armenuhi Srapyan. Yerevan: Haykakan SSṘ GA Hratarakchʿutʿyun, 1962.

Laṭīfī. *Tezkiretü'ş-Şu'arâ ve Tabsıratü'n-Nuzamâ*. Edited by Rıdvan Canım. Ankara: Atatürk Kültür Merkezi Başkanlığı, 2000.

Lewis, Geoffrey, trans. *The Book of Dede Korkut*. Harmondsworth: Penguin, 1974.

Mansuroğlu, Mecdut, ed. *Sultan Veled'in Türkçe Manzumeleri*. Istanbul: Pulhan Matbaası, 1958.

Matt'eos Uṛhayets'i [Matthew of Edessa]. *Armenia and the Crusades: Tenth to Twelfth Centuries.* Translated by Ara Edmond Dostourian. Belmont, MA: National Association for Armenian Studies and Research, 1993.

Mélikoff-Sayar, Irène, ed. and trans. *La geste de Melik Dānişmend: Étude critique du Dānişmendnāme.* 2 vols. Paris: A. Maisonneuve, 1960.

Mkhit'ar Gosh. *The Lawcode (Datastanagirk') of Mxit'ar Gosh.* Translated by Robert W. Thomson. Amsterdam: Rodopi, 2000.

Mkhit'ar Herats'i. *Mkhit'aray bzhshkapeti Herats'woy jermants' mkhit'arut'iwn.* Venice: Mekhitarist Press, 1832.

Mnats'akanyan, Asatur, ed. *Hay mijnadaryan hanelukner: V–XVIII dd.* Yerevan: Haykakan SSH GA Hratarakch'ut'yun, 1980.

Nazaryan, Shushanik, ed. *Patmut'iwn Farman Mankann: (Mijnadaryan Poem).* Yerevan: Haykakan SSṚ GA Hratarakch'ut'yun, 1957.

Nersēs Shnorhali. *General Epistle.* Translated by Arakel Aljalian. New Rochelle, NY: St. Nersess Armenian Seminary, 1996.

———. "*Lament on Edessa* by Nersēs Šnorhali." Translated by Theo Maarten van Lint. In *East and West in the Crusader States: Context, Contacts, Confrontations—Acta of the Congress Held at Hernen Castle in May 1997*, vol. 2, edited by Krijnie Ciggaar and Herman Teule, 49–106. Leuven: Peeters, 1999.

———. *Oghb Edesioy.* Edited by Manik Mkrtch'yan. Yerevan: Haykakan SAH GA Hratarakch'ut'yun, 1973.

———. *T'ught' ĕndhanrakan.* Edited by Ē. M. Baghdasaryan. Yerevan: Gitut'yun, 1995.

Niẓāmī 'Arūżī. *Chahār maqāla.* Edited by Muḥammad Qazvīnī and Muḥammad Mu'in. Tehran: Kitābfurūshī-yi Zavvār, 1954.

Polo, Marco. *The Travels.* Translated by Nigel Cliff. London: Penguin Books, 2015.

Pseudo-Callisthenes. *Patmut'iwn Aghek'sandri Makedonats'woy.* Edited by R. T'reants'. Venice: Mekhitarist Press, 1842.

———. *The Romance of Alexander the Great.* Translated by Albert Mugrdich Wolohojian. New York: Columbia University Press, 1969.

Rūmī, Jalāl al-Dīn. *Kitāb-i fīhi mā fīh, az guftār-i Mawlānā Jalāl al-Dīn Muḥammad, mashhūr bi Mawlavī.* Edited by Badī' al-Zamān Furūzānfar. Fifth printing. Tehran: Amīr Kabīr, 1983.

———. *Kullīyāt-i Shams yā Dīvān-i kabīr.* Edited by Badī' al-Zamān Furūzānfar. Vol. 1. Tehran: Amīr Kabīr, 1977.

———. *Maktab-i Shams: Muntakhabī az bihtarīn ghazalīyāt-i Mawlānā.* Edited by Abū al-Qāsim Injavī Shīrāzī. Tehran: Kitābkhāna-yi Ibn Sīnā, 1958.

———. *Maṣnavī-yi maʿnavī.* Edited by Reynold Alleyne Nicholson with commentary and translation as *The Mathnawí of Jalálu'ddín Rúmí.* 8 vols. London: Luzac, 1925–40.

Russell, James R., trans. "The History of the Youth Farman (*Patmutʿiwn Farman Mankann*): A Mediaeval Armenian Romance." *Acta Orientalia* 50, nos. 1–3 (1997): 203–44.

Shotʿa Rustʿaveli. *The Man in the Panther's Skin: A Romantic Epic.* Translated by Marjory Scott Wardrop. London: Royal Asiatic Society, 1912.

Sipahsālār, Farīdūn ibn Aḥmad. *Risāla-yi Farīdūn ibn Aḥmad Sipahsālār dar aḥwāl-i Mawlānā Jalāl al-Dīn Mawlavī.* Edited by Saʿīd Nafīsī. Tehran: Iqbāl, 1947.

Suhrawardī, Shihāb al-Dīn Yaḥyā al-. *The Philosophy of Illumination (Ḥikmat al-ishrāq).* Translated and edited by John Walbridge and Hossein Ziai. Utah: Brigham Young University Press, 1999.

Sulṭān Valad. *Dīvān-i Sulṭān Valad, Bahāʾ al-Dīn Muḥammad Balkhī.* Edited by Aṣghar Rabbānī. Forward by Saʿīd Nafīsī. Tehran: Kitābfurūshī-yi Rūdakī, 1959.

———. *Ibtidā-nāma.* Edited by Muḥammad-ʿAlī Muvaḥḥid and ʿAlī-Riżā Ḥaydarī. Tehran: Shirikat-i Sahāmī, Intishārāt-i Khwārazmī, 2010.

———. *Rabāb-nāma.* Edited by ʿAlī Sulṭānī Gird-Farāmarzī. Tehran: McGill University and the University of Tehran, 1980.

Tezcan, Semih, and Hendrik Boeschoten, eds. *Dede Korkut Oğuznameleri.* Istanbul: Yapı Kredi Yayınları, 2001.

ʿUmar Khayyām. *Ṭarab-khāna: Rubāʿiyāt-i Ḥakīm Khayyām Nīshābūrī.* Edited by Yār Aḥmad ibn Ḥusayn Rashīdī Tabrīzī and Jalāl al-Dīn Humāʾī. Tehran: Anjuman-i Āṣār-i Millī, 1963.

Vardan Areweltsʿi, *Ashkharhatsʿoytsʿ Vardanay Vardapeti.* Edited by Haig Berberian. Paris: Arakʿs, 1960.

Yūnus Emre [Yunus Emre]. *Yûnus Emre Dîvânı.* Edited by Mustafa Tatçı. 4 vols. Istanbul: Millî Eğitim Bakanlığı Yayınları, 1997.

Yūsuf-i Meddāḥ. *Varqa ve Gülşāh: A Fourteenth Century Anatolian Turkish Meṣnevi.* Edited and translated by Grace Martin Smith. Leiden: Brill, 1976.

Yūsuf Khāṣṣ Ḥājib. *Wisdom of Royal Glory: A Turko-Islamic Mirror for Princes.* Translated by Robert Dankoff. Chicago: University of Chicago Press, 1983.

Zhamagirkʿ ateni. New York: St. Vartan Press, 1986.

Studies

Abeghyan, Manuk. *Erker.* Vol. 4. Yerevan: Haykakan SSH GA Hratarakchʿutʿyun, 1966.

———. *Hayots' hin grakanut'yan patmut'yun.* Vol. 2. Yerevan: Haykakan SSṚ Gitut'yunneri Akademiayi Hratarakch'ut'yun, 1946.

Achaṛean, Hrach'eay. *Hayeren armatakan baṛaran.* Vol. 4. Yerevan: Erevani Hamalsarani Hratarakch'ut'yun, 1926.

———. *Hayots' andznanunneri baṛaran.* Vol. 5. Yerevan: Petakan Hamalsarani Hratarakch'ut'yun, 1962.

Agapitos, Panagiotis A. "Contesting Conceptual Boundaries: Byzantine Literature and Its History." *Interfaces: A Journal of Medieval European Literatures* 1 (2015): 62–91.

Aghayan, Ēduard Bagrati, and Gevorg Beglari Jahukyan. *Aknarkner mijin grakan hayereni patmut'yan.* 2 vols. Yerevan: Haykakan SSH GA Hratarakch'ut'yun, 1972–75.

Ahmed, Shahab. *What Is Islam? The Importance of Being Islamic.* Princeton: Princeton University Press, 2016.

Akalın, Berrin Uyar. "The Poets Who Wrote and Translated Mantiku't Tayr in Turkish Literature." *International Journal of Central Asian Studies* 10, no. 1 (2005): 167–79.

Amar, Zohar, and Efraim Lev. "The Significance of the Genizah's Medical Documents for the Study of Medieval Mediterranean Trade." *Journal of the Economic and Social History of the Orient* 50, no. 4 (2007): 524–41.

Ambros, Edith Gülçin. "*Naẓīre*, The Will-o'-the-Wisp of Ottoman *Dīvān* Poetry." *Wiener Zeitschrift für die Kunde des Morgenlandes* 79 (1989): 57–83.

Andrews, Walter G. "Other Selves, Other Poets, and the Other Literary History: An Essay in Three Movements." In *Intersections in Turkish Literature: Essays in Honor of James Stewart-Robinson,* edited by Walter G. Andrews, 49–91. Ann Arbor: University of Michigan Press, 2001.

———. "The *Tezkere-i Şu'arā* of Latifi as a Source for the Critical Evaluation of Ottoman Poetry." PhD diss., University of Michigan, 1970.

Aramuni, Khorēn. "Chshmartut'iwnner Friki 'Gangat'-i masin." *Nawasard Amsagir* 1, no. 10 (1983): 57–60.

Arberry, A. J., trans. *Discourses of Rūmī.* London: John Murray, 1961.

Arslan, C. Ceyhun. "Canons as Reservoirs: The Ottoman Ocean in Ziya Pasha's *Harabat* and Reframing the History of Comparative Literature." *Comparative Literature Studies* 54, no. 4 (2017): 731–48.

Askari, Nasrin. *The Medieval Reception of the Shāhnāma as a Mirror for Princes.* Leiden: Brill, 2016.

Aslanian, Sebouh David. "From 'Autonomous' to 'Interactive' Histories: World History's Challenge to Armenian Studies." In *An Armenian Mediterranean: Words and Worlds in Motion,* edited by Kathryn Babayan and Michael Pifer, 81–125. Cham, Switzerland: Palgrave Macmillan, 2018.

Austin, J. L. *How to Do Things with Words.* Cambridge, MA: Harvard University Press, 1962.

Avetisyan, Yuri. *Grakan hayereni zargatsʻman erku shrjapʻulerě: Grabar ev ashkharhabar.* Yerevan: EPH Hratarakchʻutʻyun, 2016.

Avtʻandilyan, V., and H. Pʻapʻazyan. "Friki 'Divani' parskeren kʻaṛyakě." *Teghekagir* 3 (1956): 88–89.

Awetikʻean, Fr. Gabriēl, Fr. Khachʻatur Siwrmēlean, and Fr. Mkrtichʻ Awgerean. *Nor baṛgirkʻ haykazean lezui.* Vol. 2. Reprint, Yerevan: Erevani Hamalsarani Hratarakchʻutʻyun, 1979.

Baghdasaryan, Ē. M. *Hovhannes Erznkatsʻin ev nra khratakan ardzakě.* Yerevan: Haykakan SSH GA Hratarakchʻutʻyun, 1977.

Bakhtin, M. M. "The Problem of Speech Genres." In *Speech Genres and Other Late Essays,* translated by Vern W. McGee, edited by Caryl Emerson and Michael Holquist, 60–102. Austin: University of Texas Press, 1986.

Bardakjian, Kevork B. "Kostandin Erznkacʻi's Vision-Poem: Who Bestows Poetic Grace and How." In *Mélanges Jean-Pierre Mahé,* edited by Agnès Ouzounian, Aram Mardirossian, and Constantin Zuckerman, 95–104. Paris: Association des amis du Centre d'histoire et civilisation de Byzance, 2014.

Başgöz, İlhan. *Turkish Folklore and Oral Literature: Selected Essays of İlhan Başgöz.* Edited by Kemal Sılay. Bloomington: Indiana University Press, 1998.

Başkal, Zekeriya. "Claiming Yunus Emre: Historical Contexts and the Politics of Reception." PhD diss., University of Wisconsin–Madison, 2004.

———. *Yunus Emre: The Sufi Poet in Love.* İzmir: Blue Dome Press, 2010.

Bauer, Thomas. *Die Kultur der Ambiguität: Eine andere Geschichte des Islams.* Berlin: Verlag der Weltreligionen, 2011.

Bauer, Thomas, Angelika Neuwirth, Judith Pfeiffer, Michael Hess, and Börte Sagaster, eds. *Ghazal as World Literature,* vol. 2, *From a Literary Genre to a Great Tradition: The Ottoman Gazel in Context.* Würzburg: Ergon Verlag, 2005.

Baumstark, Anton. *Geschichte der syrischen Literatur, mit Ausschluss der christlich-palästinensischen Texte.* Bonn: A. Marcus and E. Weber, 1922.

Beaton, Roderick. *The Medieval Greek Romance.* 2nd ed. London: Routledge, 1996.

Bedrossian, Matthias. *New Dictionary Armenian-English.* Venice: S. Lazarus Armenian Academy, 1875.

Beihammer, Alexander Daniel. *Byzantium and the Emergence of Muslim-Turkish Anatolia, ca. 1040–1130.* London: Routledge, 2017.

Blair, Sheila S. "The Coins of the Later Ilkhanids: A Typological Analysis." *Journal of the Economic and Social History of the Orient* 26, no. 3 (1983): 295–317.

Blessing, Patricia, and Rachel Goshgarian, eds. *Architecture and Landscape in Medieval Anatolia, 1100–1500*. Edinburgh: Edinburgh University Press, 2017.

Bloom, Harold. *The Anxiety of Influence: A Theory of Poetry*. 2nd ed. New York: Oxford University Press, 1997.

———. *A Map of Misreading*. Oxford: Oxford University Press, 1975.

Boratav, P. N. "Maddāḥ." In *Encyclopaedia of Islam*. 2nd ed. Edited by Th. Bianquis, P. Bearman, C. E. Bosworth, E. van Donzel, and W. P. Heinrichs, 2012. http://dx.doi.org/10.1163/1573-3912_islam_SIM_4728.

Boyadjian, Tamar M. *The City Lament: Jerusalem across the Medieval Mediterranean*. Ithaca, NY: Cornell University Press, 2018.

Boyce, Mary. "The Parthian *Gōsān* and Iranian Minstrel Tradition." *Journal of the Royal Asiatic Society of Great Britain and Ireland* 89, nos. 1–2 (1957): 10–45.

Braun, Joachim. "Musical Instruments in Byzantine Illuminated Manuscripts." *Early Music* 8, no. 3 (1980): 312–27.

Browne, Edward G. *A Literary History of Persia: From the Earliest Times until Firdawsí*. Vol. 1. New York: Charles Scribner's Sons, 1902.

Cahen, Claude. *The Formation of Turkey—The Seljukid Sultanate of Rūm: Eleventh to Fourteenth Century*. Translated and edited by P. M. Holt. Harlow, UK: Longman, 2001.

———. *Pre-Ottoman Turkey: A General Survey of the Material and Spiritual Culture and History, c. 1071–1330*. Translated by J. Jones-Williams. London: Sidgwick and Jackson, 1968.

Canby, Sheila R., Deniz Beyazit, Martina Rugiadi, and A. C. S. Peacock, eds. *Court and Cosmos: The Great Age of the Seljuqs*. New York: Metropolitan Museum of Art, 2016.

Carruthers, Mary J. *The Book of Memory: A Study of Memory in Medieval Culture*. 2nd ed. Cambridge: Cambridge University Press, 2008.

Chittick, William C. "The Real Shams-i Tabrizi." In *In Search of the Lost Heart: Explorations in Islamic Thought*, by William C. Chittick, edited by Mohammed Rustom, Atif Khalil, and Kazuyo Murata, 49–55. Albany: State University of New York Press, 2012.

Chʻugaszyan, B. L. "Ardyokʻ Khakanin ē Frikyan kʻaṛyaki heghinakě." *Teghekagir* 10 (1965): 79–86.

———. *Hay-iranakan grakan aṛnchʻutʻyunner (V–XVIII dd.): Hetakhuzumner*. Yerevan: Haykakan SSR GA Hratarakchutʻyun, 1963.

Conrad, Jo Ann. "Polyphemus and Tepegöz Revisited: A Comparison of the Tales of the Blinding of the One-Eyed Ogre in Western and Turkish Traditions." *Fabula* 40, nos. 3–4 (1999): 278–97.

Copeland, Rita. *Rhetoric, Hermeneutics, and Translation in the Middle Ages: Academic Traditions and Vernacular Texts.* Cambridge: Cambridge University Press, 1991.

Cornish, Alison. *Vernacular Translation in Dante's Italy: Illiterate Literature.* Cambridge: Cambridge University Press, 2011.

Cowe, S. Peter. "Models for the Interpretation of Medieval Armenian Poetry." In *New Approaches to Medieval Armenian Language and Literature,* edited by Joseph Johannes Sicco Weitenberg, 29–45. Amsterdam: Rodopi, 1995.

———. "Patterns of Armeno-Muslim Interchange on the Armenian Plateau in the Interstice between Byzantine and Ottoman Hegemony." In *Islam and Christianity in Medieval Anatolia,* edited by A. C. S. Peacock, Bruno De Nicola and Sara Nur Yıldız, 77–106. Burlington, VT: Ashgate, 2015.

———. "The Politics of Poetics: Islamic Influence on Armenian Verse." In *Redefining Christian Identity: Cultural Interaction in the Middle East since the Rise of Islam,* edited by J. J. van Ginkel, H. L. Murre-van den Berg, and Theo Maarten van Lint, 379–403. Leuven: Peeters, 2005.

Cross, Cameron. " 'If Death Is Just, What Is Injustice?' Illicit Rage in *Rostam and Sohrab* and *The Knight's Tale.*" *Iranian Studies* 48, no. 3 (2015): 395–422.

———. "The Lives and Afterlives of *Vis and Rāmin.*" *Iranian Studies* 51, no. 4 (2018): 517–56.

Dadoyan, Seta B. *The Armenians in the Medieval Islamic World: Paradigms of Interaction, Seventh to Fourteenth Centuries.* 3 vols. New Brunswick, NJ: Transaction Publishers, 2011–14.

———. "A Case Study for Redefining Armenian-Christian Cultural Identity in the Framework of Near Eastern Urbanism—13th Century: The Nāṣirī *Futuwwa* Literature and the Brotherhood Poetry of Yovhannēs and Kostandin Erzěnkac'i, Texts and Contexts." In *Redefining Christian Identity: Cultural Interaction in the Middle East since the Rise of Islam,* edited by J. J. van Ginkel, H. L. Murre-van den Berg, and T. M. van Lint, 237–64. Leuven: Peeters, 2005.

———. "The Constitution for the Brotherhood of Erznkay (1280) by Yovhannēs Erznkac'i (d. 1293): An Armenization of the *Futuwwa* Reform Project and Literature of Abbasid Caliph al-Nāṣir li-Din Allāh (d. 1225)." *Revue des Études Arméniennes* 29 (2005): 117–65.

———. *See also* Parsumean-Tatoyean, Seda.

Dashdondog, Bayarsaikhan. *The Mongols and the Armenians (1220–1335).* Leiden: Brill, 2011.

Dedes, Dimitris. "Τά ἐλληνικά ποιήματα τοῦ Μαυλανᾶ Ρουμῆ καί τοῦ γυιοῦ του Βαλέντ κατά τόν 13ον αἰώνα." *Ta Istorika* 10, nos. 18–19 (1993): 3–22.

Demirchyan, Derenik. *The Book of Flowers.* Translated by James R. Russell. Belmont, MA: Armenian Heritage Press, 2003.

Der Nersessian, Sirarpie. "The Kingdom of Cilician Armenia." In *The Later Crusades, 1189–1311*, edited by Robert Lee Wolff and Harry W. Hazard, 630–59. Vol. 2 of *A History of the Crusades*, edited by Kenneth M. Setton. Philadelphia: University of Pennsylvania Press, 1962.

DeWeese, Devin. Foreword to *Early Mystics in Turkish Literature,* by Mehmet Fuat Köprülü, viii–xxix. Translated by Gary Leiser and Robert Dankoff. London: Routledge, 2006.

Diez, Heinrich Friedrich von. *Der neuentdeckte oghuzische Cyklop verglichen mit dem Homerischen.* Berlin: Buchhandlung des Hallischen Waisenhauses, 1815.

Dihkhudā, ʿAlī Akbar. *Lughat-nāma.* Edited by Muḥammad Muʿīn and Jaʿfar Shahīdī. 14 vols., with appendix. Tehran: Dānishgāh-i Tihrān, 1993–94.

Dowsett, Charles. "A Metrical Experiment." *Raft* 3 (1989): 37–56.

Eastmond, Antony. *Tamta's World: The Life and Encounters of a Medieval Noblewoman from the Middle East to Mongolia.* Cambridge: Cambridge University Press, 2018.

Elias, Jamal J. "Ṣūfī Tafsīr Reconsidered: Exploring the Development of a Genre." *Journal of Qur'anic Studies* 12, nos. 1–2 (2010): 41–55.

Erkoç, Ethem. *Âşık Paşa ve Oğlu Elvan Çelebi.* Çorum: Pegasus Görsel İletişim Hizmetleri, 2005.

Esteʿlami, Muhammad. "Understanding Rumi's *Mathnawi.*" *Mawlana Rumi Review* 3 (2012): 7–19.

Feldman, Walter. "Imitatio in Ottoman Poetry: Three Ghazals of the Mid-Seventeenth Century." *Turkish Studies Association Bulletin* 21, no. 2 (Fall 1997): 41–58.

Flemming, Barbara. "Faḫrī's *Ḫusrev u Şīrīn* from the Year 1367: A Turkish Meṣnevī from the Emirate period." Translated by John O'Kane. In *Essays on Turkish Literature and History*, 1–35. Leiden: Brill, 2018.

———. "Faḫrī's *Ḫusrev u Šīrīn* vom Jahre 1367: Eine vergessene türkische Dichtung aus der Emiratszeit." *Zeitschrift der Deutschen Morgenländischen Gesellschaft* 115 (1965): 36–64.

———. "Languages of Turkish Poets." Translated by John O'Kane. In *Essays on Turkish Literature and History*, 117–30. Leiden: Brill, 2018.

———. "Old Anatolian Turkish Poetry in Its Relationship to the Persian Tradition." Translated by Vanessa Karam. In *Turkic-Iranian Contact Areas: Historical and Linguistic Aspects,* edited by Lars Johanson and Christiane Bulut, with the editorial assistance of Sevgi Ağcagül and Vanessa Karam, 49–68. Wiesbaden: Harrassowitz Verlag, 2006.

Fletcher, Joseph F. "Integrative History: Parallels and Interconnections in the Early Modern Period, 1500–1800." In Joseph F. Fletcher, *Studies on Chinese and*

Islamic Inner Asia, edited by Beatrice Forbes Manz, 1–35. Aldershot, UK: Variorum, 1995.

Fomkin, M. S. "On the Literary Fate of Works by Sultan Veled." *Manuscripta Orientalia* 7 (2001): 27–32.

———. *Sultan Veled ī ego tiurkskaia poeziia.* Moscow: Akademia Nauk, 1994.

Frishkopf, Michael. "Music." In *The Islamic World,* edited by Andrew Rippin, 510–26. London: Routledge, 2008.

Furūzānfar, Badīʿ al-Zamān. *Aḥadīs-i Masnavī.* Tehran: Dānishgāh-i Tihrān, 1955.

———. *Ma'ākhiz-i qiṣaṣ va tamsīlāt-i Masnavī.* Tehran: Majlis, 1954.

Garsoïan, Nina. "Movsēs Xorenacʿi." In *Encyclopædia Iranica,* online ed. Last modified October 2, 2012. http://www.iranicaonline.org/articles/movses-xorenaci.

Ghanalanyan, A. *Frik.* Yerevan: Haykakan SSṚ Gitutʿyunneri Akademiayi Hratarakchʿutʿyun, 1944.

Ghazaryan, Ṛ. A., and H. M. Avetisyan. *Mijin hayereni baṙaran.* Yerevan: EPH Hratarakchʿutʿyun, 2009.

Gibb, E. J. W. *A History of Ottoman Poetry.* Vol. 1. London: Luzac, 1900.

Gölpınarlı, Abdülbâki. *Mevlânâ'dan sonra Mevlevîlik.* Istanbul: İnkılâp ve Aka Kitabevleri, 1983.

Goshgarian, Rachel. "Beyond the Social and the Spiritual: Redefining the Urban Confraternities of Late Medieval Anatolia." PhD diss., Harvard University, 2007.

———. "*Futuwwa* in Thirteenth-Century Rūm and Armenia: Reform Movements and the Managing of Multiple Allegiances on the Seljuk Periphery." In *The Seljuks of Anatolia: Court and Society in the Medieval Middle East,* edited by A. C. S. Peacock and Sara Nur Yıldız, 227–63. London: I. B. Tauris, 2013.

Gould, Rebecca. "The Political Cosmology of Prison Poetics: Khāqānī of Shirwān on Muslim-Christian Difference." *Literature Compass* 11, no. 7 (2014): 496–515.

———. "Wearing the Belt of Oppression: Khāqānī's Christian Qasida and the Prison Poetry of Medieval Shirvān." *Journal of Persianate Studies* 9, no. 1 (2016): 19–44.

Green, Nile. "Introduction: The Frontiers of the Persianate World (ca. 800–1900)." In *The Persianate World: The Frontiers of a Eurasian Lingua Franca,* edited by Nile Green, 1–71. Oakland: University of California Press, 2019.

———. *Sufism: A Global History.* Chichester, UK: Wiley-Blackwell, 2012.

Grégoire, Henri, and Roger Goossens. "Byzantinisches Epos und arabischer Ritterroman." *Zeitschrift der Deutschen Morgenländischen Gesellschaft* 88, nos. 3–4 (1934): 213–32.

Grimm, Wilhelm. "Die Sage von Polyphem." *Abhandlungen der Königlichen Akademie der Wissenschaften zu Berlin, philologische-historische Klasse* (1857): 1–30.

Haarmann, Ulrich. "Alṭun Ḫān und Čingiz Ḫān bei den ägyptischen Mamluken." *Der Islam* 51 (1974): 1–36.

———. "Turkish Legends in the Popular Historiography of Medieval Egypt." In *Proceedings of the Sixth Congress of Arabic and Islamic Studies,* edited by Frithiof Rundgren, 97–107. Leiden: Brill, 1975.

Hacikyan, Agop J., Gabriel Basmajian, Edward S. Franchuk, and Nourhan Ouzounian, eds. *The Heritage of Armenian Literature,* vol. 2, *From the Sixth to the Eighteenth Century.* Detroit: Wayne State University Press, 2002.

Hagen, Gottfried. "Heroes and Saints in Anatolian Turkish Literature." *Oriente Moderno* 89, no. 2 (2009): 349–61.

———. "Updated Prolegomena to a Social Prehistory of the Ottoman Language." Workshop paper presented at the fourteenth Great Lakes Ottomanist Workshop, University of Michigan, Ann Arbor, April 2017.

Hakobyan, G. A. "Nerses Shnorhalu antip haneluknerě." *Patma-banasirakan handes* 4 (1962): 105–14.

Halman, Talât Sait. "The Turk in Rumi / Rumi in Turkey." In *Rapture and Revolution: Essays on Turkish Literature,* by Talât Sait Halman, edited by Jayne L. Warner, 262–96. Syracuse, NY: Syracuse University Press, 2007.

Halman, Talât Sait, and Metin And. *Mevlana Celaleddin Rumi and the Whirling Dervishes: Sufi Philosophy, Whirling Rituals, Poems of Ecstasy, Miniature Paintings.* Istanbul: Dost, 1983.

Hammer-Purgstall, Joseph von. *Geschichte der osmanischen Dichtkunst bis auf unsere Zeit.* 4 vols. Pesth [Pest, Hungary]: C. A. Hartleben, 1836–38.

Hanaoka, Mimi. "The View from Anatolia." In *Authority and Identity in Medieval Islamic Historiography: Persian Histories from the Peripheries,* 220–50. Cambridge: Cambridge University Press, 2016.

Harutʿyunyan, S. B. *Hay zhoghovrdakan haneluknеr.* Yerevan: Haykakan SSṚ GA Hratarakchʿutʿyun, 1965.

Hasluck, Frederick William. *Christianity and Islam under the Sultans.* Edited by Margaret M. Hasluck. 2 vols. London: Oxford University Press, 1929.

Hodgson, Marshall G. S. *The Venture of Islam: Conscience and History in a World Civilization.* Vol. 1. Chicago: University of Chicago Press, 1974.

Holbrook, Victoria Rowe. "Originality and Ottoman Poetics: In the Wilderness of the New." *Journal of the American Oriental Society* 112, no. 3 (1992): 440–54.

Hovhannisyan, Ashot. *Frikě patmakʿnnakan luysi tak.* Yerevan: Haykakan SSṚ GA Hratarakchʿutʿyun, 1955.

Hovnanean, Ghewond V. *Hetazōtut'iwnk' nakhneats' ṛamkōrēni vray: Usumnasirut'iwnk' ew k'aghuatsk'ner.* 2 vols. Vienna: Mekhitarist Press, 1897.

Hunger, Herbert. "On the Imitation (*Mimesis*) of Antiquity in Byzantine Literature." *Dumbarton Oaks Papers* 23–24 (1969–70): 15–38.

Hurşid, Sait. *La langue de Yunus Emre: Contribution à l'histoire du turc pré-ottoman.* Vol. 1. Ankara: Ministry of Culture, 1991.

İnalcık, Halil. "The Origins of Classical Ottoman Literature: Persian Tradition, Court Entertainments, and Court Poets." Translated by Michael D. Sheridan. *Journal of Turkish Literature* 5 (2008): 5–75.

Inan, Murat Umut. "Rethinking the Ottoman Imitation of Persian Poetry." *Iranian Studies* 50, no. 5 (2017): 671–89.

Ingenito, Domenico. " 'Tabrizis in Shiraz Are Worth Less than a Dog': Sa'dī and Humām, a Lyrical Encounter." In *Politics, Patronage, and the Transmission of Knowledge in 13th–15th Century Tabriz,* edited by Judith Pfeiffer, 77–128. Leiden: Brill, 2014.

Iqbal, Afzal. *The Life and Work of Jalal-ud-din Rumi.* 6th ed. Islamabad: Pakistan National Council of the Arts, 1991.

Jackson, Virginia. *Dickinson's Misery: A Theory of Lyric Reading.* Princeton: Princeton University Press, 2005.

Jahukyan, G. B. *Hayots' lezvi zargats'umĕ ev kaṛuts'vatsk'ĕ.* Yerevan: "Mitk'" Hratarakch'ut'yun, 1969.

Janowitz, Anne F. *Lyric and Labour in the Romantic Tradition.* Cambridge: Cambridge University Press, 1998.

Johanson, Lars. "Rūmī and the Birth of Turkish Poetry." *Journal of Turkology* 1, no. 1 (1993): 23–37.

Kafadar, Cemal. *Between Two Worlds: The Construction of the Ottoman State.* Berkeley: University of California Press, 1995.

———. "A Rome of One's Own: Reflections on Cultural Geography and Identity in the Lands of Rum." *Muqarnas* 24 (2007): 7–25.

Kaladze, Inga. "The Georgian Translation of *Vis and Rāmin*: An Old Specimen of Hermeneutics." *Journal of Persianate Studies* 2 (2009): 137–42.

Kappler, Matthias. "Graphic Adaptation in Sultân Veled's Greek and Turkish Verses." *Turkic Languages* 6, no. 2 (2002): 215–28.

Karamustafa, Ahmet T. *God's Unruly Friends: Dervish Groups in the Islamic Later Middle Period, 1200–1550.* Oxford: Oneworld, 2006.

———. *Sufism: The Formative Period.* Berkeley: University of California Press, 2007.

Karst, Josef. *Historische Grammatik des Kilikisch-Armenischen.* Strasbourg: Karl J. Trübner, 1901.

Keshavarz, Fatemeh. *Reading Mystical Lyric: The Case of Jalal al-Din Rumi.* Columbia: University of South Carolina Press, 1998.

Khach'ikyan, Levon. "Erznka k'aghak'i 'Eghbarts' miabanut'ean' kanonadrut'yunĕ (1280)." *Banber Matenadarani* 6 (1962): 365–76.

———. "1280 T'vakanin Erznkayum kazmakerpvats' 'Eghbayrut'iwnĕ.' " *Teghekagir Haykakan SSṚ Gitut'yunneri Akademiayi* 12 (1951): 73–84.

Khayrābādī, 'Abbās. *Sirr-i dilbarān: Sharḥ va tafsīr-i qiṣṣa-yi shāh va kanīzak az Masnavī-yi ma'navī.* Tehran: Kalhur, 2001.

Koç, Mustafa. "Anadolu'da İlk Türkçe Telif Eser." *Bilig* 57 (2011): 159–72.

Köksal, M. Fatih. *Sana Benzer Güzel Olmaz: Divan Şiirinde Nazire.* Ankara: Akçağ Yayınları, 2006.

Köprülü, Mehmet Fuat [Mehmed Fuad Köprülü]. "Arûz." In *İslâm Ansiklopedisi: İslâm Âlemi Tarih, Coğrafya, Etnografya ve Biyografya Lugatii,* vol. 1, 625–53. Istanbul: Millî Eğitim Basımevi, 1945.

———. *Early Mystics in Turkish Literature.* Translated and edited by Gary Leiser and Robert Dankoff. London: Routledge, 2006.

———. "Method in Turkish Literary History." *Middle Eastern Literatures* 11, no. 1 (2008): 53–84.

———. "Ozan." In *Edebiyat Araştırmaları,* 131–44. Ankara: Türk Tarih Kurumu Basımevi, 1966.

———. "Ozan." Translated by Gary Leiser. In *Turkish Language, Literature, and History: Traveler's Tales, Sultans, and Scholars since the Eighth Century,* edited by Bill Hickman and Gary Leiser, 208–22. London: Routledge, 2016.

———. *The Seljuks of Anatolia: Their History and Culture according to Local Muslim Sources.* Translated by Gary Leiser. Salt Lake City: University of Utah Press, 1992.

———. *Türk Edebiyatı'nda İlk Mutasavvıflar.* 3rd ed. Ankara: Türk Tarih Kurumu Basımevi, 1976. First published 1918 by Maṭba'a-yı 'Āmire (Istanbul).

———. *Türk Edebiyatı Tarihi.* Edited by Orhan F. Köprülü and Nermin Pekin. Istanbul: Ötüken, 1986.

Korkmaz, Zeynep. "Selçuklular Çağı Türkçesinin Genel Yapısı." *Türk Dili Araştırmaları Yıllığı* 20 (1972): 17–34.

Korobeinikov, Dimitri. *Byzantium and the Turks in the Thirteenth Century.* Oxford: Oxford University Press, 2014.

Kozmoyan, Armanush. *Hayots' ev parsits' mijnadaryan k'narergut'yan hamematakan poetikan (10–16 dd).* Yerevan: HH GAA "Gitut'yun" Hratarakch'ut'yun, 1997.

Krstić, Tijana. "The Ambiguous Politics of 'Ambiguous Sanctuaries': F. Hasluck and Historiography on Syncretism and Conversion to Islam in 15th and 16th Century Ottoman Rumeli." In *Archaeology, Anthropology and Heritage in the Balkans and Anatolia: The Life and Times of F. W. Hasluck, 1878–1920*, edited by David Shankland, vol. 3, 247–62. Istanbul: Isis Press, 2013.

———. *Contested Conversions to Islam: Narratives of Religious Change in the Early Modern Ottoman Empire.* Stanford, CA: Stanford University Press, 2011.

Krumbacher, Karl. *Geschichte der byzantinischen Litteratur von Justinian bis zum Ende des Oströmischen Reiches (527–1453).* Handbuch der Klassischen Altertumswissenschaft 9.1. Munich: C. H. Beck, 1891.

———. *Geschichte der byzantinischen Litteratur von Justinian bis zum Ende des Oströmischen Reiches (527–1453).* 2nd ed. Handbuch der Klassischen Altertumswissenschaft 9.1. Revised in collaboration with Albert Ehrhard and Heinrich Gelzer. Munich: C. H. Beck, 1897.

Küçük, Hülya. "Sulṭān Walad's Role in the Foundation of the Mevlevi Sufi Order." *Mawlana Rumi Review* 3 (2012): 22–50.

Küçükhüseyin, Şevket. "Some Reflections on Hagiography with Reference to the Early Mawlawī-Christian Relations in the Light of the *Manāqib al-ʿārifīn.*" *Al-Masāq* 25, no. 2 (2013): 240–51.

Kuru, Selim S. "Destânı Mesnevîde Anlatmak: Gülşehrî, Âşık Paşa ve Mes'ûd'un Eserleri Hakkında Gözlemler." In *Mesnevî: Hikâyenin Şiiri*, edited by Hatice Aynur, Müjgân Çakır, Hanife Koncu, Selim S. Kuru, and Ali Emre Özyıldırım, 195–216. Istanbul: Turkuaz, 2011.

———. "Fuat Köprülü ve Eski Edebiyat I: Sürekli bir Gelecek Adına Mazinin İnkarı." In *Eski Türk Edebiyatı Çalışmaları*, vol. 2, *Eski Türk Edebiyatına Modern Yaklaşımlar I, 24 Nisan 2006, Bildiriler*, edited by Hatice Aynur, Müjgân Çakır, Hanife Koncu, and Selim S. Kuru, 220–42. Istanbul: Turkuaz, 2007.

———. "Gülşehrî the Seventh Sheikh of the Universe: Authorly Passions in Fourteenth-Century Anatolia." *Journal of Turkish Studies* 40 (2013): 281–89.

———. "Portrait of a Shaykh as Author in Fourteenth-Century Anatolia: Gülşehri and His *Falaknāma.*" In *Islamic Literature and Intellectual Life in Fourteenth- and Fifteenth-Century Anatolia*, edited by A. C. S. Peacock and Sara Nur Yıldız, 173–96. Würzburg: Ergon Verlag in Kommission, 2016.

Lane, Edward William. *An Arabic-English Lexicon.* Vol. 1. Cambridge: Islamic Texts Society, 1984. First published 1863–69 by Williams and Norgate (London).

La Porta, Sergio. "Conflicted Coexistence: Christian-Muslim Interaction and Its Representation in Medieval Armenia." In *Contextualizing the Muslim Other in Medieval Christian Discourse,* edited by Jerold C. Frakes, 103–23. New York: Palgrave Macmillan, 2011.

———. "A Fish out of Water? Armenia(ns) and the Mediterranean." In *An Armenian Mediterranean: Words and Worlds in Motion,* edited by Kathryn Babayan and Michael Pifer, 59–77. Cham, Switzerland: Palgrave Macmillan, 2018.

Latour, Bruno. *Reassembling the Social: An Introduction to Actor-Network-Theory*. Oxford: Oxford University Press, 2005.

Lewis, Charlton T. *An Elementary Latin Dictionary*. New York: Harper and Brothers, 1895.

Lewis, Franklin Dean. "The Rise and Fall of a Persian Refrain: The *Radīf 'Ātash u Āb*.'" In *Reorientations: Arabic and Persian Poetry*, edited by Suzanne Pinckney Stetkevych, 199–226. Bloomington: Indiana University Press, 1994.

———. *Rumi: Past and Present, East and West—The Life, Teaching and Poetry of Jalâl al-Din Rumi*. Rev. pbk. ed. Oxford: Oneworld, 2008.

———. "Solṭân Valad and the Poetical Order: Framing the Ethos and Praxis of Poetry in the Mevlevi Tradition after Rumi." In *Persian Language, Literature and Culture: New Leaves, Fresh Looks*, edited by Kamran Talattof, 23–47. New York: Routledge, 2015.

———. "Towards a Chronology of the Poems in the *Dīvān-i Shams*: A Prolegomenon for a Periodization of Rumi's Literary Oeuvre." In *The Philosophy of Ecstasy: Rumi and the Sufi Tradition*, edited by Leonard Lewisohn, 145–76. Bloomington, IN: World Wisdom, 2014.

Lewisohn, Leonard. "The Esoteric Christianity of Islam: Interiorisation of Christian Imagery in Medieval Persian Sufi Poetry." In *Islamic Interpretations of Christianity*, edited by Lloyd Ridgeon, 127–56. Richmond, UK: Curzon, 2001.

———. "Mawlānā Jalāl al-Dīn Rūmī." In *Christian-Muslim Relations: A Bibliographical History*, vol. 4, *1200–1350*, edited by David Thomas and Alex Mallett, 491–508. Leiden: Brill, 2012.

———. "The Sacred Music of Islam: *Samā'* in the Persian Sufi Tradition." *British Journal of Ethnomusicology* 6 (1997): 1–33.

Lindner, Rudi Paul. *Explorations in Ottoman Prehistory*. Ann Arbor: University of Michigan Press, 2007.

Losensky, Paul E. "To Revere, Revise and Renew: Ṣā'ib of Tabriz Reads the *Ghazals* of Rūmī." *Mawlana Rumi Review* 4 (2013): 10–49.

———. *Welcoming Fighānī: Imitation and Poetic Individuality in the Safavid-Mughal Ghazal*. Costa Mesa, CA: Mazda Publishers, 1998.

MacFarlane, Alex. "Alexander Re-mapped: Geography and Identity in the *Alexander Romance* in Armenia." PhD diss., University of Oxford, 2020.

———. " 'This Shocking Lobster': Understanding the Fantastic Creatures of the Armenian *Alexander Romance*." In *Transmitting and Circulating the Late Antique and Byzantine Worlds*, edited by Mirela Ivanova and Hugh Jeffery, 125–48. Leiden: Brill, 2019.

Mallette, Karla. "The Mediterranean Is Armenian." In *An Armenian Mediterranean: Words and Worlds in Motion,* edited by Kathryn Babayan and Michael Pifer, 309–21. Cham, Switzerland: Palgrave Macmillan, 2018.

Mansuroğlu, Mecdut. "Anadolu'da Türk Dili ve Edebiyatının İlk Mahsulleri." *Türk Dili ve Edebiyati Dergisi* 1, no. 1 (1946): 9–25.

———. "Calāladdīn Rūmī's türkische Verse." *Ural-altaische Jahrbücher* 24 (1952): 106–15.

———. "Mevlâna Celâleddin Rumî'de Türkçe Beyit ve İbareler." *Türk Dili Araştırmaları Yıllığı Belleten* (1954): 207–20.

———. "The Rise and Development of Written Turkish in Anatolia." *Oriens* 7, no. 2 (1954): 250–64.

———. "Turkish Literature through the Ages (with Bibliography)." *Central Asiatic Journal* 9, no. 2 (1964): 81–112.

Maranci, Christina. "Word and Image in the Armenian *Alexander Romance.*" *Journal of the Society for Armenian Studies* 13 (2003–4): 19–28.

Meeker, Michael E. "The Dede Korkut Ethic." *International Journal of Middle East Studies* 24, no. 3 (1992): 395–417.

Meier, Friedrich Max. *Bahā'-i Walad: Grundzüge seines Lebens und seiner Mystik.* Leiden: Brill, 1989.

Mill, John Stuart. "Thoughts on Poetry and Its Varieties." In *Autobiography and Literary Essays,* edited by John M. Robson and Jack Stillinger, 341–65. Vol. 1 of *The Collected Works of John Stuart Mill.* Toronto: University of Toronto Press, 1981.

Miller, Lloyd. *Music and Song in Persia: The Art of Āvāz.* Salt Lake City: University of Utah Press, 1999.

Milovanović-Barham, Čelica. "Aldhelm's *Enigmata* and Byzantine Riddles." *Anglo-Saxon England* 22 (1993): 51–64.

Minorsky, Vladimir. "Khāqānī and Andronicus Comnenus." *Bulletin of the School of Oriental and African Studies* 11, no. 3 (1945): 550–78.

Mojaddedi, Jawid. "Rūmī." In *The Blackwell Companion to the Qur'ān,* edited by Andrew Rippin, 362–72. Malden, MA: Blackwell Publishing, 2008.

Moretti, Franco. "Conjectures on World Literature." *New Left Review* 68, no. 1 (2000): 54–68.

Mundy, C. S. "Polyphemus and Tepegöz." *Bulletin of the School of Oriental and African Studies* 18, no. 2 (1956): 279–302.

Musawi, Muhsin J. al-. *The Medieval Islamic Republic of Letters: Arabic Knowledge Construction.* Notre Dame, IN: University of Notre Dame Press, 2015.

Mutafian, Claude. *La Cilicie au carrefour des empires.* 2 vols. Paris: Les Belles Lettres, 1988.

Nersissian, Varak. "Medieval Armenian Poetry and Its Relation to Other Literatures." In *Review of National Literatures: Armenia,* edited by Vahe Oshagan, 93–120. New York: Griffon House Publications, 1984.

Nersisyan, V. S. "Vardi u sokhaki aylabanut'yan hay-parskakan mshakumneri aṛnch'ut'yan harts'i masin." *Banber Erevani Hamalsarani* 3, no. 9 (1969): 226–32.

Ocak, Ahmet Yaşar. *Babaîler İsyanı: Alevîliğin Tarihsel Altyapısı yahut Anadolu'da İslam-Türk Heterodoksisinin Teşekkülü.* Istanbul: Dergâh Yayınları, 2009.

———. *La révolte de Baba Resul, ou La formation de l'hétérodoxie musulmane en Anatolie au XIIIe siècle.* Ankara: Türk Tarih Kurumu, 1989.

———. "Social, Cultural and Intellectual Life, 1071–1453." In *The Cambridge History of Turkey,* edited by Kate Fleet, 353–422. Cambridge: Cambridge University Press, 2009.

Ohlander, Erik S. *Sufism in an Age of Transition: 'Umar al-Suhrawardī and the Rise of the Islamic Mystical Brotherhoods.* Leiden: Brill, 2008.

Oktay Uslu, Zeynep. "The *Şaṭḥiyye* of Yūnus Emre and Ḳayġusuz Abdāl: The Creation of a Vernacular Islamic Tradition in Turkish." *Turcica* 50 (2019): 9–52.

Oskanyan, Mak'sim. *Saghmosner, banasteghtsut'yunner, zhoghovrdakan banarvesti mshakumner, aṛakner, haneluknér.* Yerevan: "Munetik" Hratarakch'ut'yun, 2012.

Otto-Dorn, Katharina. "Figural Stone Reliefs on Seljuk Sacred Architecture in Anatolia." *Kunst des Orients* 12, nos. 1–2 (1978): 103–49.

Öztürkmen, Arzu. "Orality and Performance in Late Medieval Turkish Texts: Epic Tales, Hagiographies, and Chronicles." *Text and Performance Quarterly* 29, no. 4 (2009): 327–45.

Paker, Saliha. "On the Poetic Practices of 'A Singularly Uninventive People' and the Anxiety of Imitation: A Critical Re-appraisal in Terms of Translation, Creative Mediation and 'Originality.' " In *Tradition, Tension and Translation in Turkey,* edited by Şehnaz Tahir Gürçağlar, Saliha Paker, and John Milton, 27–52. Amsterdam: John Benjamins, 2015.

———. "Terceme, Te'lîf ve Özgünlük Meselesi." In *Eski Türk Edebiyatı Çalışmaları,* vol. 9, *Metnin Hâlleri: Osmanlı'da Telif, Tercüme ve Şerh,* edited by Hatice Aynur, Müjgân Çakır, Hanife Koncu, Selim S. Kuru, and Ali Emre Özyıldırım, 36–71. Istanbul: Klasik Yayınları, 2014.

———. "Translation as *Terceme* and *Nazire*: Culture-Bound Concepts and Their Implications for a Conceptual Framework for Research on Ottoman Translation History." In *Crosscultural Transgressions: Research Models in Translation Studies,* vol. 2, *Historical and Ideological Issues,* edited by Theo Hermans, 120–43. Manchester: St. Jerome Publishing, 2002.

Pancaroğlu, Oya. "Devotion, Hospitality and Architecture in Medieval Anatolia." *Studia Islamica* 108, no. 1 (2013): 48–81.

P'ap'azean, Vrt'anēs. *Patmut'iwn hayots' grakanut'ean (banahiwsut'ean patmut'iwn): Skzbits' minch'ew mer ōrerĕ.* Tbilisi: Ēlektrasharzh Tparan, 1910.

Parsumean-Tatoyean, Seda. *Hay-arabakan mshakut'ayin haraberut'eants' patmut'enēn ZhG dar: Hovhannēs Pluz Erznkatsii "I tachkats' imastasirats'"ĕ ew imastasirakan ardzakĕ islamakan aghbiwrnerun loysin tak.* Beirut: 1991.

———. *See also* Dadoyan, Seta B.

Peacock, A. C. S. *Islam, Literature and Society in Mongol Anatolia.* Cambridge: Cambridge University Press, 2019.

———. "Islamisation in the Golden Horde and Anatolia: Some Remarks on Travelling Scholars and Texts." *Revue des mondes musulmans et de la Méditerranée* 143 (2018): 151–64.

Peacock, A. C. S., Bruno De Nicola, and Sara Nur Yıldız, eds. *Islam and Christianity in Medieval Anatolia.* Farnham, UK: Ashgate, 2015.

Peacock, A. C. S., and Sara Nur Yıldız, eds. *Islamic Literature and Intellectual Life in Fourteenth- and Fifteenth-Century Anatolia.* Würzburg: Ergon Verlag in Kommission, 2016.

———. *The Seljuks of Anatolia: Court and Society in the Medieval Middle East.* London: I. B. Tauris, 2013.

Perry, John. "Tajik I. The Ethnonym: Origins and Application." In *Encyclopædia Iranica,* online ed. Last modified July 20, 2009. http://www.iranicaonline.org/articles/tajik-i-the-ethnonym-origins-and-application.

Perry, Thomas Sergeant. *A History of Greek Literature.* New York: H. Holt, 1890.

Pfeiffer, Judith. "Mevlevi-Bektashi Rivalries and the Islamisation of the Public Space in Late Seljuq Anatolia." In *Islam and Christianity in Medieval Anatolia,* edited by A. C. S. Peacock, Bruno De Nicola, and Sara Nur Yıldız, 309–27. Farnham, UK: Ashgate, 2015.

Pifer, Michael. "The Age of the *Gharīb*: Strangers in the Medieval Mediterranean." In *An Armenian Mediterranean: Words and Worlds in Motion,* edited by Kathryn Babayan and Michael Pifer, 13–38. Cham, Switzerland: Palgrave Macmillan, 2018.

———. "Introduction: A Movable Armenia." In *An Armenian Mediterranean: Words and Worlds in Motion,* edited by Kathryn Babayan and Michael Pifer, 1–10. Cham, Switzerland: Palgrave Macmillan, 2018.

———. "The Rose of Muḥammad, the Fragrance of Christ: Liminal Poetics in Medieval Anatolia." *Medieval Encounters* 26, no. 3 (2020): 285–320.

Pingree, D., and C. J. Brunner. "Astrology and Astronomy in Iran." In *Encyclopædia Iranica,* vol. 2, fasc. 8, 858–71. London: Routledge and Kegan Paul, 1989. Available at http://www.iranicaonline.org/articles/astrology-and-astronomy-in-iran-. Last modified August 17, 2011.

Pisowicz, Andrzej. "How Did New Persian and Arabic Words Penetrate the Middle Armenian Vocabulary? Remarks on the Material of Kostandin Erznkacʿi's Poetry." In *New Approaches to Medieval Armenian Language and Literature,* edited by Joseph Johannes Sicco Weitenberg, 96–109. Amsterdam: Rodopi, 1995.

Pollock, Sheldon. "India in the Vernacular Millennium: Literary Culture and Polity, 1000–1500." *Daedalus* 127, no. 3 (1998): 41–74.

———. *The Language of the Gods in the World of Men: Sanskrit, Culture, and Power in Premodern India.* Berkeley: University of California Press, 2006.

———. "Sanskrit Literary Culture from the Inside Out." In *Literary Cultures in History: Reconstructions from South Asia,* edited by Sheldon Pollock, 39–130. Berkeley: University of California Press, 2003.

Rassi, Salam. "Justifying Christianity in the Islamic Middle Ages: The Apologetic Theology of ʿAbdīshōʿ bar Brīkhā (d. 1318)." PhD diss., University of Oxford, 2015.

Redford, Scott. "Anatolian Seljuk Palaces and Gardens." In *The Emperor's House: Palaces from Augustus to the Age of Absolutism,* edited by Michael Featherstone, Jean-Michel Spieser, Gülru Tanman, and Ulrike Wulf, 231–42. Berlin: De Gruyter, 2015.

Reichl, Karl. "Medieval Turkish Epic and Popular Narrative." In *Medieval Oral Literature,* edited by Karl Reichl, 681–700. Berlin: De Gruyter, 2012.

———. *Singing the Past: Turkic and Medieval Heroic Poetry.* Ithaca, NY: Cornell University Press, 2000.

———. *Turkic Oral Epic Poetry: Tradition, Forms, Poetic Structure.* New York: Garland, 1992.

Renard, John. *All the King's Falcons: Rumi on Prophets and Revelation.* Albany: State University of New York Press, 1994.

Rhoby, Andreas, and Elisabeth Schiffer, eds. *Imitatio—Aemulatio—Variatio: Akten des internationalen wissenschaftlichen Symposions zur byzantinischen Sprache und Literatur (Wien, 22.–25. Oktober 2008).* Vienna: Verlag der Österreichischen Akademie der Wissenschaften, 2010.

Rifai, Kenan. *Listen: Commentary on the Spiritual Couplets of Mevlana Rumi.* Translated by Victoria Holbrook. Louisville, KY: Fons Vitae, 2011.

Ringgren, Helmer. *Fatalism in Persian Epics.* Uppsala: Uppsala University Årsskrift, 1952.

Rosenthal, Franz. "The Stranger in Medieval Islam." *Arabica* 44, no. 1 (1997): 35–75.

Rudolf, Winfried. "Riddling and Reading: Iconicity and Logogriphs in Exeter Book Riddles 23 and 45." *Anglia* 130, no. 4 (2012): 499–525.

Russell, James R. "An Armeno-Persian Love Poem of Grigoris Aght'amarts'i." *Journal of the Society for Armenian Studies* 6 (1992–93): 99–105.

———. "The Credal Poem *Hawatov Xostovanim* ('I Confess in Faith') of St. Nersēs the Graceful." In *Redefining Christian Identity: Cultural Interaction in the Middle East since the Rise of Islam,* edited by J. J. van Ginkel, H. L. Murre-van den Berg, and T. M. van Lint, 185–236. Leuven: Peeters, 2005.

———. "The Dream Vision of Anania Širakac'i." *Revue des Études Arméniennes* 21 (1988–89): 159–70.

———. "Frik: The Bridge of Poetry." In *Anathēmata Heortika: Studies in Honor of Thomas F. Mathews,* edited by Thomas F. Mathews, Joseph D. Alchermes, Helen C. Evans, and Thelma K. Thomas, 256–64. Mainz: Philipp von Zabern, 2009.

———. "Here Comes the Sun: A Poem of Kostandin Erznkats'i." *Journal for the Society of Armenian Studies* 3 (1987): 119–27.

———. "On an Armenian Word List from the Cairo Geniza." *Iran and the Caucasus* 17, no. 2 (2013): 189–214.

———. "Polyphemos Armenios." *Revue des Études Arméniennes* 26 (1996–97): 25–38.

———. "The Šāh-nāme in Armenian Oral Epic." In *Armenian and Iranian Studies,* 1063–70. Cambridge, MA: Harvard University Press, 2004.

———. *Yovhannēs T'lkuranc'i and the Mediaeval Armenian Lyric Tradition.* Atlanta: Scholars Press, 1987.

Ruymbeke, Christine van. "The *Kalīla wa Dimna* and Rūmī: 'That Was the Husk and This Is the Kernel.' " *Mawlana Rumi Review* 4 (2013): 85–105.

Sadr, Amin Azad. "Love, Death, and Submission: The Role of the Reader in Rumi's *Masnavi.*" PhD diss., University of Chicago, 2014.

Sahakyan, Yuri. *Hay zhoghovrdakan hanelukner.* Yerevan: Zangak-97, 1998.

Salemann, Carl Germanovich. "Noch einmal die seldschukischen Verse." *Mélanges asiatiques, tirés du Bulletin de l'Académie impériale des sciences de St.-Pétersbourg* 10 (1894): 173–245.

Sanjian, Avedis K. "Gregory Magistros: An Armenian Hellenist." In *To Hellenikon: Studies in Honor of Speros Vryonis, Jr.,* edited by Jelisaveta Stanojevich Allen, Christos P. Ioannides, John S. Langdon, and Stephen W. Reinert, 111–30. New Rochelle, NY: Artistide D. Caratzas, 1993.

Sanni, Amidu. "Again on *Taḍmīn* in Arabic Theoretical Discourse." *Bulletin of the School of Oriental and African Studies, University of London* 61, no. 1 (1998): 1–19.

Scheindlin, Raymond P. *The Song of the Distant Dove: Judah Halevi's Pilgrimage.* Oxford: Oxford University Press, 2008.

Schimmel, Annemarie. "Christianity VII. Christian Influences in Persian Poetry." In *Encyclopædia Iranica*, vol. 5, fasc. 5, 542–44. Costa Mesa: Mazda Publishers, 1991. Available at http://www.iranicaonline.org/articles/christianity-vii. Last modified October 18, 2011.

———. "Jesus and Mary as Poetical Images in Rumi's Verse." In *Christian-Muslim Encounters,* edited by Yvonne Yazbeck Haddad and Wadi Z. Haddad, 143–57. Gainesville: University Press of Florida, 1995.

———. *The Triumphal Sun: A Study of the Works of Jalaloddin Rumi.* Albany: State University of New York Press, 1993.

Şerefeddin [Yaltkaya], Mehmed. "Mevlânâ'da Türkçe Kelimeler ve Türkçe Şiirler." *Türkiyat Mecmuası* 4 (1934): 111–67.

Seyed-Gohrab, A. A. *Courtly Riddles: Enigmatic Embellishments in Early Persian Poetry.* Leiden: Leiden University Press, 2010.

Shackle, Christopher. "Representations of ʿAṭṭār in the West and in the East: Translations of the *Manṭiq al-ṭayr* and the Tale of Shaykh Ṣanʿān." In *ʿAṭṭār and the Persian Sufi Tradition: The Art of Spiritual Flight,* edited by Leonard Lewisohn and Christopher Shackle, 165–93. London: I. B. Tauris, 2006.

Shakhsuvaryan, A. H. "Frikě Khakʿanu kʿaṛyaki tʿargmanichʿ." *Teghekagir* 11 (1962): 85–87.

Shankland, David, ed. *Archaeology, Anthropology and Heritage in the Balkans and Anatolia: The Life and Times of F. W. Hasluck, 1878–1920.* 3 vols. Istanbul: Isis Press, 2004–13.

Shepherd, Vanessa Margaret. "The Turkish Mystical Poet Gülşehrī with Particular Reference to His Manṭiq al-Ṭayr." PhD diss., University of Cambridge, 1979.

Shiloah, Amnon. "Music and Religion in Islam." *Acta Musicologica* 69, no. 2 (1997): 143–55.

———. *Music in the World of Islam: A Socio-cultural Study.* Aldershot, UK: Scolar Press, 1995.

Shukurov, Rustam. *The Byzantine Turks, 1204–1461.* Leiden: Brill, 2016.

Simms, Rob, and Amir Koushkani. *The Art of Avaz and Mohammad Reza Shajarian: Foundations and Contexts.* Lanham, MD: Lexington Books, 2012.

Simonyan, Hasmik A. *Hay mijnadaryan kafaner (X–XVI dd.).* Yerevan: Haykakan SSH GA Hratarakchʿutʿyun, 1975.

Smith, Adam T. " 'Yerevan, My Ancient Erebuni': Archaeological Repertoires, Public Assemblages, and the Manufacture of a (Post-) Soviet Nation." In *The Archaeology of Power and Politics in Eurasia: Regimes and Revolutions,* edited by Charles W. Hartley, G. Bike Yazicioğlu, and Adam T. Smith, 57–77. Cambridge: Cambridge University Press, 2012.

Srapyan, Armenuhi. *Hovhannes Erznkats'i Pluz: Kyankě u gortsě.* Yerevan: "Nairi," 1993.

Steingass, Francis Joseph. *A Comprehensive Persian-English Dictionary, Including the Arabic Words and Phrases to Be Met With in Persian Literature.* London: Routledge and K. Paul, 1892.

Subtelny, Maria E. "Visionary Rose: Metaphorical Interpretation of Horticultural Practice in Medieval Persian Mysticism." In *Botanical Progress, Horticultural Innovation and Cultural Changes,* edited by Michel Conan and W. John Kress, 13–34. Washington, DC: Dumbarton Oaks Research Library and Collection, 2007.

Taeschner, Franz. *Gülschehrîs Mesnevi auf Achi Evran, den Heiligen von Kırschehir und Patron der türkischen Zünfte.* Wiesbaden: Steiner, 1955.

T'ahmizyan, Nikoghos. *Nerses Shnorhalin: Ergahan ev erazhisht.* Yerevan: Haykakan SSH GA Hratarakch'ut'yun, 1973.

Takahashi, Hidemi. "The Reception of Ibn Sīnā in Syriac: The Case of Gregory Barhebraeus." In *Before and after Avicenna: Proceedings of the First Conference of the Avicenna Study Group,* edited by David C. Reisman and Ahmed H. al-Rahim, 249–81. Leiden: Brill, 2003.

Taylor, David G. K. " 'Your Sweet Saliva Is the Living Wine': Drink, Desire, and Devotion in the Syriac Wine Songs of Khāmīs Bar Qardāḥē." In *The Syriac Renaissance,* edited by Herman Teule, Carmen Fotescu Tauwinkl, Bas ter Haar Romeny, and Jan van Ginkel, 31–52. Leuven: Peeters, 2010.

Tekin, Talat. "Determination of Middle-Turkic Long Vowels through *'Arūḍ*." *Acta Orientalia Hungarica* 20 (1967): 151–70.

Teule, Herman. "The Interaction of Syriac Christianity and the Muslim World in the Period of the Syriac Renaissance." In *Syriac Churches Encountering Islam: Past Experiences and Future Perspectives,* edited by Dietmar W. Winkler, 110–28. Piscataway, NJ: Gorgias Press, 2010.

———. "The Syriac Renaissance." In *The Syriac Renaissance,* edited by Herman Teule, Carmen Fotescu Tauwinkl, Bas ter Haar Romeny, and Jan van Ginkel, 1–30. Leuven: Peeters, 2010.

Tezcan, Semih. "Anadolu Türk Yazınının Başlangıç Döneminde bir Yazar ve *Çarḫ-nāme*'nin Tarihlendirilmesi Üzerine." *Türk Dilleri Araştırmaları* 4 (1994): 75–88.

Theodoridis, Dimitri. "Versuch einer Neuausgabe von drei griechischen Doppelversen aus dem *Dīwān* von Sulṭān Walad." *Byzantion* 74, no. 2 (2004): 433–51.

Thomson, Robert W. "The Influence of Their Environment on the Armenians in Exile in the Eleventh Century." In *Proceedings of the XIIIth International Congress of Byzantine Studies,* edited by J. M. Hussey, D. Obolensky, and S. Runciman, 432–38. London: Oxford University Press, 1967.

T'ireak'yan, Mihrdat. "Prof. Sa'id Nefisi khastate, or Khaghanin ē heghinakě Friki parskeren k'aṛyakin." *Teghekagir* 6 (1964): 91–93.

Tolan, John Victor. *Petrus Alfonsi and His Medieval Readers.* Gainesville: University Press of Florida, 1993.

Tourage, Mahdi. *Rūmī and the Hermeneutics of Eroticism.* Leiden: Brill, 2007.

Trépanier, Nicolas. *Foodways and Daily Life in Medieval Anatolia: A New Social History.* Austin: University of Texas Press, 2014.

Tsuge, Gen'ichi. "Āvāz." In *Encyclopædia Iranica,* vol. 3, fasc. 1, 32–35. London: Routledge and Kegan Paul, 1989. Available at http://www.iranicaonline.org/articles/avaz. Last updated August 17, 2011.

———. "Rhythmic Aspects of the *Âvâz* in Persian Music." *Ethnomusicology* 14, no. 2 (1970): 205–27.

Uluç, Lâle. "The *Shahnama* of Firdausi in the Lands of Rum." In *Shahnama Studies,* vol. 2, *The Reception of Firdausi's Shahnama,* edited by C. P. Melville and Gabrielle van den Berg, 159–80. Leiden: Brill, 2012.

Utas, Bo. " 'Genres' in Persian Literature 900–1900." In *Literary History: Towards a Global Perspective,* vol. 2, *Literary Genres: An Intercultural Approach,* edited by Gunilla Lindberg-Wada, 199–241. Berlin: De Gruyter, 2006.

Uzunçarşılı, İsmail Hakkı. *Anadolu Beylikleri ve Akkoyunlu, Karakoyunlu Devletleri.* Ankara: Türk Tarih Kurumu Basımevi, 1984.

Vacca, Alison. "The Fires of Naxčawan: In Search of Intercultural Transmission in Arabic, Armenian, Greek, and Syriac." *Le Muséon* 129, nos. 3–4 (2016): 323–62.

van Lint, Theo Maarten. "The Gift of Poetry: Khidr and John the Baptist as Patron Saints of Muslim and Armenian *'Āšiqs-Ašułs.*" In *Redefining Christian Identity: Cultural Interaction in the Middle East since the Rise of Islam,* edited by J. J. van Ginkel, H. L. Murre-van den Berg and T. M. van Lint, 335–78. Leuven: Peeters, 2005.

———. "Kostandin of Erznka: An Armenian Religious Poet of the XIIIth–XIVth Century." PhD diss., University of Leiden, 1996.

———. "The Poet's Legitimization: The Case of Kostandin Erznkac'i." In *New Approaches to Medieval Armenian Language and Literature,* edited by Joseph Johannes Sicco Weitenberg, 11–28. Amsterdam: Rodopi, 1995.

———. "Seeking Meaning in Catastrophe: Nersēs Šnorhali's *Lament on Edessa.*" In *East and West in the Crusader States: Context, Contacts, Confrontations—Acta of the Congress Held at Hernen Castle in May 1997,* vol. 2, edited by Krijnie Ciggaar and Herman Teule, 29–47. Leuven: Peeters, 1999.

Vásáry, István. "The Beginnings of Western Turkic Literacy in Anatolia and Iran (13th–14th Centuries)." In *Irano-Turkic Cultural Contacts in the 11th–17th Centuries,* edited by Éva M. Jeremiás, 245–53. Piliscsaba, Hungary: Avicenna Institute of Middle Eastern Studies, 2003.

Virani, Nargis. " 'I Am the Nightingale of the Merciful': Rumi's Use of the Qur'an and Hadith." *Comparative Studies of South Asia, Africa and the Middle East* 22, nos. 1–2 (2002): 100–111.

Vryonis, Speros. *The Decline of Medieval Hellenism in Asia Minor and the Process of Islamization from the Eleventh through the Fifteenth Century.* Berkeley: University of California Press, 1971.

Wacks, David A. *Framing Iberia: Maqamat and Frametale Narratives in Medieval Spain.* Leiden: Brill, 2007.

Wellek, René, and Austin Warren. *Theory of Literature.* 3rd ed. New York: Harcourt, Brace, and World, 1956.

Wolper, Ethel Sara. *Cities and Saints: Sufism and the Transformation of Urban Space in Medieval Anatolia.* University Park: Pennsylvania State University Press, 2003.

Wright, William. *A Short History of Syriac Literature.* London: Adam and Charles Black, 1894.

Yaghoobi, Claudia. "Subjectivity in ʿAttār's Shaykh Sanʿān Story in *The Conference of the Birds.*" *CLCWeb: Comparative Literature and Culture* 16, no. 1 (2014): https://doi.org/10.7771/1481-4374.2425.

Yar-Shater, Ehsan. "Affinities between Persian Poetry and Music." In *Studies in Art and Literature of the Near East: In Honor of Richard Ettinghausen,* edited by Peter J. Chelkowski, 59–78. New York: University of Utah and New York University Press, 1974.

Yavuz, Kemal. "Çeşitli Yönleri ile Mantıku't-Tayr ve Garib-nâme Mesnevileri." *Türk Dili ve Edebiyatı Dergisi* 31 (2004): 345–56.

Yıldız, Sara Nur. "Aydınid Court Literature in the Formation of an Islamic Identity in Fourteenth-Century Western Anatolia." In *Islamic Literature and Intellectual Life in Fourteenth- and Fifteenth-Century Anatolia,* edited by Sara Nur Yıldız and A. C. S. Peacock, 197–241. Würzburg: Ergon Verlag in Kommission, 2016.

———. "Battling *Kufr* (Unbelief) in the Land of Infidels: Gülşehri's Turkish Adaptation of ʿAṭṭār's *Manṭiq al-Ṭayr.*" In *Islam and Christianity in Medieval Anatolia,* edited by A. C. S. Peacock, Bruno De Nicola, and Sara Nur Yıldız, 329–47. Farnham, UK: Ashgate, 2015.

———. "Karamanoğlu Mehmed Bey: Medieval Anatolian Warlord or Kemalist Language Reformer? History, Language Politics and the Celebration of the Language Festival in Karaman, Turkey, 1961–2008." In *Religion, Ethnicity and Contested Nationhood in the Former Ottoman Space,* edited by Jørgen S. Nielsen, 147–70. Leiden: Brill, 2012.

———. "Mongol Rule in Thirteenth-Century Seljuk Anatolia: The Politics of Conquest and History Writing, 1243–1282." PhD diss., University of Chicago, 2006.

Zhamkoch'yan, Hakob G. "Patma-banasirakan ditoghut'yunner Friki ew nra tagheri masin." *Patma-banasirakan handes* 1 (1958): 194–244.

Zhukovskiĭ, Valentin Alekseyevich. "'Omar Khayyâm and the 'Wandering' Quatrains." Translated by E. D. Ross in "*Al-Muzaffariyé*: Containing a Recent Contribution to the Study of 'Omar Khayyâm." *Journal of the Royal Asiatic Society* 30 (1898): 349–66.

Zipoli, Riccardo. *The Technique of the Ǧawāb: Replies by Nawāʾī to Ḥāfiẓ and Ǧāmī.* Venice: Cafoscarina, 1993.

Zumthor, Paul. *Oral Poetry: An Introduction.* Translated by Kathryn Murphy-Judy. Minneapolis: University of Minnesota Press, 1990.

INDEX

Page numbers in italic type indicate illustrations.